PSYCHOPATHOLOGY
AND
BRAIN DYSFUNCTION

Psychopathology
and
Brain Dysfunction

Edited by

Charles Shagass, M.S., M.D.
Professor of Psychiatry
Temple University
Director of Temple Clinical Services
Eastern Pennsylvania Psychiatric Institute
Philadelphia, Pennsylvania

Samuel Gershon, M.D.
Professor of Psychiatry
Director, Neuropsychopharmacology Research Unit
New York University Medical Center
New York, New York

Arnold J. Friedhoff, M.D.
Professor of Psychiatry
Director of Millhauser Laboratories
New York University Medical Center
New York, New York

Raven Press ■ New York

Raven Press, 1140 Avenue of the Americas, New York, New York 10036

Made in the United States of America

International Standard Book Number 0–89004–120–2
Library of Congress Catalog Card Number 76–55487

Preface

This volume results from the 66th Annual Meeting of the American Psychopathological Association in March, 1976. In deciding to center the conference on the topic of Psychopathology and Brain Dysfunction, the Association expresses its continuing interest in a traditional area of psychopathological study. Since earliest times, psychiatric thought has been concerned with the problems of relating abnormal psychological phenomena to altered structure and function of the brain. Recent developments in several disciplines, including psychology, biochemistry, and neurophysiology, have renewed optimism that clinically relevant answers are on the way. Many of the chapters provide comprehensive up-to-date reviews of particular areas of investigation, while others concentrate on specific research findings. Although not all of the chapters deal directly with clinical problems, relevance to psychopathology was the unifying theme in selecting contributors from the large domain of research in brain and behavior.

Concepts dealing with functional specialization of the brain hemispheres have come to the fore in recent years following the pioneer work of Sperry with split-brain preparations. Current emphasis is on methods which reveal hemispheric functional lateralization in the intact organism. The chapters by Drs. Alpert and Witelson review studies in which such methods have been applied to clinical problems of schizophrenia and developmental dyslexia, and report new data.

Dr. Heath's chapter deals with the brain organization for emotional expression and seizure activity in experimental animals and in patients in whom electrodes have been implanted. Heath's findings, based upon more than a quarter century of investigation, suggest that the current limbic system concept may be insufficiently comprehensive to account for emotional phenomena. Dr. Locke's chapter provides an overview of conceptual issues in the investigation of relations between mind, brain, and behavior. The section on brain organization is rounded out by Dr. Pribram's Hoch Award Lecture. It reviews many years of research on brain-behavior relationships and presents a novel hypothesis concerning the functions of the basal ganglia, in which their role in processing sensory input is emphasized in addition to their well known motor functions.

Neurochemistry may be the most flourishing area of current research in biological psychiatry. Dr. Fuxe and his collaborators have pioneered some of the more important recent work relating neurotransmitters to brain pathways. Their chapter exemplifies high level investigation in this area. Although conjectural with respect to possible relations to schizophrenia, the speculation is exciting in its implications. Dr. Smythies, an early theorist on the role of deviant catecholamine metabolism in schizophrenia, reviews recent findings in this field. Dr. Schildkraut and his co-workers present recent studies on norepinephrine metabolism in depressive disorders, with particular emphasis on the possibility that clinically meaningful subtypes may result from biochemical classification. Finally, in his Presidential Address, Dr. Friedhoff deals with the concept of receptor sensitivity modification and offers preliminary evidence that this concept may be used with profit in the treatment of tardive dyskinesia.

A section was devoted to seizure phenomena because seizures offer a paradigm of brain dysfunction, and associations between seizure phenomena and mental illness continue to be proposed. Also, induced seizures still provide a powerful psychiatric therapy. This section begins with Drs. Woodbury and Kemp's comprehensive review of the basic mechanisms of seizures from both neurophysiological and biochemical points of view; this chapter should provide a point of departure for anyone wishing to undertake serious study of the area. Dr. Stevens' chapter documents the validity of distinguishing between recorded electrical discharge activity and clinical seizure phenomena. This concept is pertinent to Dr. Stevens' observations in psychotic patients, and also to the findings reported by Dr. Struve and his colleagues on the relationship between paroxysmal EEG events and suicide behavior in psychiatric patients.

Dr. Fink's chapter provides a scholarly discussion of the effects of electroconvulsive therapy, with special emphasis on risks and their avoidance. His contribution is particularly important in the light of recent controversies centering around psychiatric electrotherapy.

Two chapters deal with physiological studies of the sociopath syndrome. Dr. Monroe and his group describe the results of a comprehensive neurological and sociological study of recidivist aggressors. Dr. Ziskind and his collaborators present evidence concerning the hypothesis that sociopaths are deviant in conditioning behavior.

Dr. Whittier's chapter on Huntington's chorea places special emphasis on the lessons for psychopathology to be gleaned from study of this syndrome. It represents the distillation of thinking of a long time investigator of this hereditary disorder.

The electrophysiology section contains four chapters which deal with clinical correlates of scalp-recorded brain potentials processed by computer methods. Drs. Gershon and Buchsbaum's chapter presents the findings obtained by applying a specific averaged evoked potential method to studies of genetic factors in affective disorders. The chapter by Dr. John and his group is a detailed report of the results obtained in learning disorders with a new comprehensive approach to the quantification of electrophysiological (EEG and evoked potential) data. The impressive ability of their quantitative indicators to discriminate between clinical groups seems to augur a bright future for "neurometrics." Dr. Dongier and his group review information bearing on the relevance of the slow event-related potentials to psychiatry. In contrast to the sensory evoked potentials, the slow potentials of interest appear to be more related to motor activity or the intention to move. They seem clearly deviant in several serious psychiatric disorders.

In the final chapter, Dr. Shagass discusses some basic issues concerning electrophysiological research in psychiatry and reviews EEG and evoked potential findings in the major psychoses.

Although the reader may wish that we now had more definitive answers to the question "Exactly what is wrong with the brain in mental illness?," he could hardly leave this volume without being convinced that some answers are on the way.

Charles Shagass, M.D.
Samuel Gershon, M.D.
Arnold J. Friedhoff, M.D.

Contents

IV. STUDIES OF SOCIOPATHY

V. HUNTINGTON'S DISEASE

VI. ELECTROPHYSIOLOGY

Contributors

L. Agnati
Department of Histology
Karolinska Institute
S-104 01 Stockholm 60, Sweden

H. Ahn
Brain Research Laboratories and
* Neurophysiology Clinic*
Departments of Psychiatry and
* Physiology*
New York Medical College
New York, New York 10029

M. Alpert
Millhauser Laboratories of the
* Department of Psychiatry*
New York University School of
* Medicine*
550 First Avenue
New York, New York 10016

R. S. Arko
Child Development Center
Coney Island Hospital
2601 Ocean Parkway
Brooklyn, New York 11235

G. Balis
Department of Psychiatry
University of Maryland School of
* Medicine*
645 West Redwood Street
Baltimore, Maryland 21201

J. D. Barcik
Department of Psychiatry
University of Maryland School of
* Medicine*
645 West Redwood Street
Baltimore, Maryland 21201

D. R. Becka
451 Repton Road
Riverside, Illinois 60546

M. S. Buchsbaum
National Institute of Mental Health
Building 10, Room 3N 218
Bethesda, Maryland 20014

J. F. Cahill
19 Parsons Street
Brighton, Massachusetts 02135

J. O. Cole
McLean Hospital
Belmont, Massachusetts 02178

M. Dongier
Department of Psychiatry
Allan Memorial Institute
1025 Pine Avenue West
Montreal, Quebec, Canada

B. Dubrovsky
Department of Psychiatry
Allan Memorial Institute
1025 Pine Avenue West
Montreal, Quebec, Canada

F. Engelsmann
Department of Psychiatry
Allan Memorial Institute
1025 Pine Avenue West
Montreal, Quebec, Canada

M. Fink
Department of Psychiatry
Health Sciences Center
S.U.N.Y. at
Stony Brook, New York 11790

S. H. Frazier
McLean Hospital
Belmont, Massachusetts 02178

A. J. Friedhoff
Department of Psychiatry
New York University School of
*   Medicine*
550 First Avenue
New York, New York 10016

K. Fuxe
Department of Histology
Karolinska Institute
S-104 01 Stockholm 60, Sweden

E. S. Gershon
Department of Research
Jerusalem Mental Health Center
Ezrath Nashim
Jerusalem, Israel

J. E. Gudeman
Neuropsychopharmacology
*   Laboratory*
Massachusetts Mental Health Center
Boston, Massachusetts 02115

R. G. Heath
Department of Psychiatry and
*   Neurology*
Tulane University School of Medicine
1430 Tulane Avenue
New Orleans, Louisiana 70112

T. Hökfelt
Department of Histology
Karolinska Institute
S-104 01 Stockholm 60, Sweden

B. Hulfish
Department of Psychiatry
University of Maryland School of
*   Medicine*
645 West Redwood Street
Baltimore, Maryland 21201

O. Johansson
Department of Histology
Karolinska Institute
S-104 01 Stockholm 60, Sweden

E. R. John
Brain Research Laboratories and
*   Neurophysiology Clinic*
Departments of Psychiatry and
*   Physiology*
New York Medical College
New York, New York 10029

M. John
Brain Research Laboratories and
*   Neurophysiology Clinic*
Departments of Psychiatry and
*   Physiology*
New York Medical College
New York, New York 10029

B. Z. Karmel
Brain Research Laboratories and
*   Neurophysiology Clinic*
Departments of Psychiatry and
*   Physiology*
New York Medical College
New York, New York 10029

J. W. Kemp
Department of Pharmacology
University of Utah College of
*   Medicine*
Salt Lake City, Utah 84132

D. F. Klein
N.Y.S. Psychiatric Institute
College of Physicians and Surgeons
Columbia University
New York, New York 10032

R. A. LaBrie
12 Arrow Street
Cambridge, Massachusetts 02138

J. Lion
Department of Psychiatry
University of Maryland School of
*   Medicine*
645 West Redwood Street
Baltimore, Maryland 21201

Å. Ljungdahl
Department of Histology
Karolinska Institute
S-104 01 Stockholm 60, Sweden

S. Locke
Neurological Unit
Boston State Hospital
591 Morton Street
Boston, Massachusetts 02124

I. Maltzman
Department of Psychology
UCLA
Los Angeles, California 90026

M. J. Martz, Jr.
Millhauser Laboratories of the
    Department of Psychiatry
New York University School of
    Medicine
550 First Avenue
New York, New York 10016

M. McDonald
Department of Psychiatry
University of Maryland School of
    Medicine
645 West Redwood Street
Baltimore, Maryland 21201

R. R. Monroe
Department of Psychiatry
University of Maryland School of
    Medicine
645 West Redwood Street
Baltimore, Maryland 21201

P. J. Orsulak
Neuropsychopharmacology
    Laboratory
Massachusetts Mental Health Center
Boston, Massachusetts 02115

M. Perez de la Mora
Department of Histology
Karolinska Institute
S-104 01 Stockholm 60, Sweden

K. H. Pribram
Department of Psychology
Stanford University
Stanford, California 94305

L. S. Prichep
Brain Research Laboratories and
    Neurophysiology Clinic
Departments of Psychiatry and
    Physiology
New York Medical College
New York, New York 10029

W. A. Rohde
McLean Hospital
Belmont, Massachusetts 02178

J. Rubin
Department of Psychiatry
University of Maryland School of
    Medicine
645 West Redwood Street
Baltimore, Maryland 21201

K. R. Saraf
Research Department
Long Island Jewish-Hillside Medical
    Center
Glen Oaks, New York 11004

A. F. Schatzberg
McLean Hospital
Belmont, Massachusetts 02178

J. J. Schildkraut
Neuropsychopharmacology
    Laboratory
Massachusetts Mental Health Center
Boston, Massachusetts 02115

C. Shagass
Eastern Pennsylvania Psychiatric
    Institute
Henry Avenue and Abbottsford Road
Philadelphia, Pennsylvania 19129

J. R. Smythies
Department of Psychiatry and the
    Neurosciences Program
University of Alabama Medical Center
Birmingham, Alabama 35294

J. R. Stevens
Division of Neurology
University of Oregon Medical School
3181 S.W. Sam Jackson Park Road
Portland, Oregon 97201

F. A. Struve
Department of
 Electroencephalography
Hillside Division Clinical-Research
 Electroencephalographic
 Laboratory
Long Island Jewish-Hillside Medical
 Center
Glen Oaks, New York 11004

K. Syndulko
Gateways Hospital
1891 Effie Street
Los Angeles, California 90026

J. R. Whittier
State of New York Department of
 Mental Hygiene
Long Island Research Institute
Central Islip, New York 11722

S. F. Witelson
Department of Psychiatry
Chedoke Hospitals
McMaster University
Hamilton, Ontario, Canada L8N 3L6

D. M. Woodbury
Department of Pharmacology
University of Utah College of
 Medicine
Salt Lake City, Utah 84132

E. Ziskind
Gateways Hospital
1891 Effie Street
Los Angeles, California 90026

Psychopathology and Brain Dysfunction, edited by C. Shagass, S. Gershon, and A. J. Friedhoff. Raven Press, New York © 1977.

Cognitive Views of Schizophrenia in Light of Recent Studies of Brain Asymmetry

Murray Alpert and Merrill J. Martz, Jr.

Millhauser Laboratories of the Department of Psychiatry, New York University School of Medicine, New York, New York 10016

INTRODUCTION

Over the past quarter of a century there has been a remarkable increase in our understanding of mechanisms relating brain function, cognitive processes, and performance. Perhaps it is inevitable that insights developed in an exciting and very active "breakthrough" area come to be applied to a whole range of other issues, and there have been a number of suggestions that the asymmetry of the cerebral hemispheres is germane to an understanding of schizophrenia. Our purpose here is to examine this notion.

The point of contrast around which the hemispheres are thought to be specialized differs in the emphasis of different authors. Traditionally, the contrast has developed around language function, whereas more recently there has been a focus on cognitive or information processing contrasts. Since we don't know which brain mechanisms underlie the asymmetry, we should recognize the tentative nature of contrasts, such as lexical versus imaginal; logical versus intuitive; analytic versus holistic; sequential versus parallel; or Apollonian versus Dionysian. One further caution is to note that the specialization of the hemispheres is not complete and the functioning of both sides is to some extent overlapping.

In our review we will first consider evidence from patients with brain lesions, in whom it has been suggested that schizophreniform sequelae are more likely after left-sided lesions. Although the evidence from this work is weak (but persistent), it carries an intuitive appeal since the cardinal symptoms of schizophrenia — thinking disorders, verbal hallucinations, and even flat affect — are language-laden behaviors. The relations between symptoms and asymmetry will be considered after discussion of a number of studies contrasting schizophrenics and controls on measures in which the hemispheres have differential participation. We have been impressed, in the course of our review, with the powerful range of technology that has become available to experimental psychopathologists as a consequence of the hypothesis connecting asymmetry and schizophrenia. It strikes us that whatever the salience of this hypothesis, the field will be enriched with a broad range of neuropsychological methods.

PSYCHOSIS IN PATIENTS WITH BRAIN LESIONS

Temporal Lobe Epilepsy

Flor-Henry (8) has explored the hypothesis that schizophrenic-like behaviors are associated with damage to the left hemisphere, and we will examine his evidence for this view in some detail. He compared 50 cases of temporal lobe epilepsy who showed psychotic symptoms with a sample of 49 cases of temporal lobe epilepsy without psychotic symptoms. The data in Table 1 are from Flor-Henry (8), and he interprets the table as indicating that the group with psychotic symptoms are more likely to have left-sided foci.

However, as Flor-Henry notes, patients in the control group with unilateral foci are twice as likely to have right-sided foci. Actually, these cells contribute most to the magnitude of the χ^2. Flor-Henry cites Falconer and Serafetinides (10) and Hughes and Schlagenhauff (14), each of whom examined series of 100 cases and reported an equal incidence of left and right foci in their samples. Thus, some measure of Flor-Henry's ability to associate psychosis with left-sided foci derives from an atypical characteristic of his controls. If we test the distribution of Flor-Henry's psychotic temporal lobe epileptics (19 left, 9 right) against an expectation of equal left-right incidence (14, 14), the deviation from expectation is only marginally credible ($0.05 < p < 10$).

A second problem that might be noted with Table 1 is concerned with the number of bilateral foci in Flor-Henry's psychotic group (22 of 50) when compared with his controls (11 of 49). Although the deviation of this distribution was not tested by Flor-Henry, we computed that this difference is reliable ($\chi^2 = 5.17$; df $= 1$; $p < 0.05$). The issue of an increased frequency of bilateral foci associated with psychosis is less relevant for Flor-Henry since a bilateral focus would include the required left side. However, we will consider below an alternate hypothesis, suggested by Beaumont and Dimond (4), that schizophrenia may be associated with a disturbance in integration of transcallosal mechanisms. A significant increase in the incidence of bilateral lesions may be seen as supportive of this alternate hypothesis.

TABLE 1. *Laterality of epileptic focus in psychotic and not psychotic patients with temporal lobe epilepsy*

	Left hemisphere	Bilateral	Right hemisphere	Total
Psychotic	19	22	9	50
Not psychotic	13	11	25	49
Total	32	33	34	99

$\chi^2 = 12.31$; df $= 2$; $p < 0.01$. Data from ref. 8.

Flor-Henry further subdivides his psychotic group into four subgroups of schizophrenics, confusionals, schizoaffectives, and manic-depressives. He interprets the resulting breakdown of subgroup by focus as evidence for a left-hemisphere focus in schizophrenia and a right-hemisphere focus in affective psychoses. However, with only 50 cases unequally sorted among 12 cells ($\chi^2 = 6.07$; df $= 6$; $0.3 < p < 0.5$), we find this evidence unconvincing.

Flor-Henry also reviewed a considerable body of literature in developing his hypothesis of left-hemisphere damage in schizophrenia. He cited Bingley (5) who studied temporal lobe epileptics in terms of their personality changes and intellectual capacities. Bingley sorted his 90 cases into dominant ($N = 33$), non-dominant ($N = 24$), and shifting ($N = 33$) focus; and into tumor side (dominant $= 9$; nondominant $= 7$). He found that the predominant personality type in all groups except dominant-side tumor was toward the epileptic personality (ixophrenia), which he described as involving perseveration in thought, mood, and will, circumstantiality, quarrelsomeness, hypochondriasis, and mild paranoia. Of those cases with a dominant-lobe tumor, however, none manifested ixophrenia and eight out of the nine exhibited flat affect (which is infrequent among the other groups: 5 of 81). [An association between a space-occupying tumor accompanied by an increase in ventricular pressure and shallow affect is not uncommon (17), but Bingley reports that his patients showed normal pressure.]

Bingley also reported on the performance of his cases on a number of tests of intellectual functioning. The dominant-lobe tumor group did the worst, followed by the dominant-lobe focus group and the shifting focus groups, when compared with the nondominant lobe groups. The disadvantage of the first group could be seen in lexical, arithmetic, memory, and spatial tasks. The findings appear quite robust and are not easy to explain. However, these results cannot be seen as consistent with those of other work, including some discussed below, indicating that individuals with nondominant lesions would be expected to do less well on spatial tasks. Perhaps the general deficit of the group with dominant-hemisphere lesions reflects some artifact of the testing situation, whereby all tasks whether lexical or spatial required verbal skills in understanding or in responding to the questions.

Penetrating Brain Wounds

Looking for a variety of medical and psychiatric disturbances, Hillbom (13) studied a sample of 451 Finnish soldiers who sustained brain injuries during World War II. He reported finding 160 cases (35% of his sample) of mental disturbance beyond the amnesia and confusion common in the first few weeks after injury. Among his study group there were 288 whose injury was confined to one hemisphere (69% of the disturbed and 61% of those not mentally disturbed were among these). Table 2 summarizes the distribution of lateralized injuries, and it can be seen that there is an excess of mentally disturbed cases among those injured in the left hemisphere. However, only in the case of the psychoses does this association remain statistically significant when comparing each category separately against those with no disturbance ($\chi^2 = 4.58$; df $= 1$; $p < 0.05$). Nevertheless, the trend of all of the disturbed groups is in the same direction, and one is hard put to defend the argument for a specific laterality for psychosis. Further, 7 of the 138 with right-hemisphere lesions (5%) were psychotic, suggesting that such an outcome can occur at a significant frequency in association with right-sided lesions.

For our purposes the designation "psychosis" may be too broad. However, Hillbom conveniently supplies an appendix giving the details of many of the noteworthy cases, including all of the 33 experiencing psychoses. Hillbom states that there were no cases of manic-depressive psychosis in his material. It appears from his case summaries that many do not fit the category schizophrenia (e.g., those afflicted with hallucinations in connection with epileptic fits). Brief summaries of the 33 psychotic cases were presented to several of our clinical colleagues who were asked to judge whether the person seemed schizophrenic. Information about the location of the head injury was withheld. With this informal selection procedure we came up with 17 cases of schizophrenia-like psychoses. Roughly speaking, the selected cases exhibited some mixture of auditory hallucinations not associated with epileptic fits, paranoia, queer behavior and language, or social withdrawal. Among these 17 cases 7 were injured on the left side, 6 were injured on the right, and 4 had either bilateral or diffuse contusional injuries. Our distillation hardly purified the data.

In the United States Walker and Jablon (22) studied a large group of soldiers who had received head injuries in World War II. They administered the MMPI and reported the scores separately for those showing aphasia ($N = 45$) and those without language deficit ($N = 289$). This permits us to examine the association between psychopathology and disturbance of

TABLE 2. *Psychiatric disturbances from head wounds by site of lesion*

	Left	Right	Total
Psychosis	17	7	24
Neurosis	17	11	28
Personality change	32	22	54
Dementia/amnesia	4	1	5
No disturbance	80	97	177
Total	150	138	288

$\chi^2 = 10.25$; df $= 4$; $p < 0.05$. Data from ref. 13.

language functions rather than anatomical location, a more direct approach than assuming that language resides in the left hemisphere, at least for those with aphasia. They report an increased frequency of high scores in the aphasic group on the schizophrenia scale. We found this increase to be statistically significant ($\chi^2 = 5.59$; df $= 1$; $p < 0.02$). This finding supports the idea of an association between language center disturbance and schizophrenia.

Thus we have seen that Flor-Henry and Bingley studying epileptics and Hillbom and Walker and Jablon studying patients with penetrating war wounds have all developed evidence that weakly but fairly persistently suggests an association between dominant-hemisphere lesions and schizophrenic-like behavioral disturbances. Several other methods of study permit us to converge on this question.

STUDIES WITH SCHIZOPHRENIC PATIENTS

EEG

In our own laboratory we have recently replicated observations reported by Doyle, Ornstein, and Galin (6). They studied EEG recorded from electrodes over the left and right hemispheres while their subjects were engaged in a series of tasks selected because they require primarily verbal (e.g., writing a letter) or spatial (e.g., the block design subtest of the Wechsler Adult Intelligence Scale) cognitive mediators. They found that the left/right ratio of alpha band activity (8 to 13 Hz) of the EEG was sensitive to the type of task performed. Alpha tended to be greater from the hemisphere presumed not to be involved in a particular task. They suggested that alpha be viewed as an idling rhythm. As the hemisphere becomes engaged in cognitive activity the alpha disappears. This suggestion, if generalizable, makes available a nonintrusive method for study of asymmetry applicable to intact subjects. We have explored this possibility with schizophrenics.

Using methods similar to those of Doyle, Ornstein, and Galin (6), we have been able to replicate their observations with a group of normal subjects, mainly medical students, and then found the same effect in a somewhat attenuated form in a group of recently hospitalized schizophrenic patients from the adult services of Bellevue Psychiatric Hospital. The results will be reported in full separately, with some additional controls for drugs, age, and motivation. In brief, EEG was recorded from temporal areas referred to a common vertex lead. Band-pass filtering eliminated non-alpha activity. Figure 1 presents samples from two subjects on two tasks.

Among those tasks performed by all 12 controls and 10 schizophrenics, five were selected for quantitative analysis: concentration on breathing (deemed a neutral task), reading and writing (both considered verbal), and block design, and yarn sorting (both considered nonverbal). For this purpose the alpha activity from each hemisphere was integrated over the 2-min

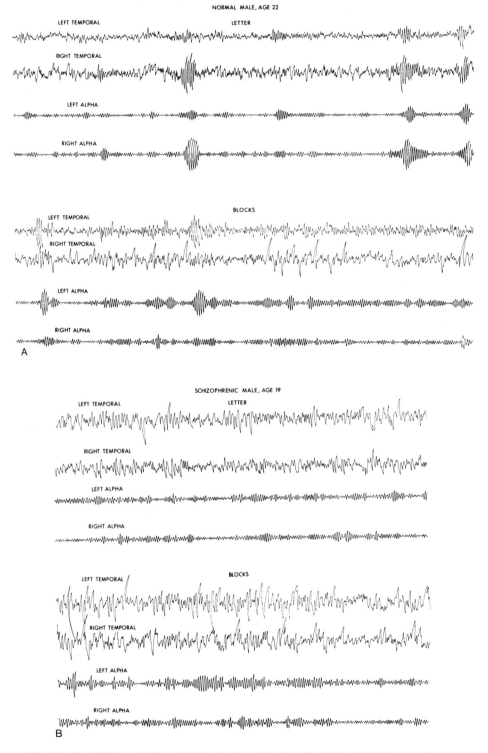

FIG. 1.A: Raw EEGs and filtered alpha-band activity from the left and right temporal areas in a normal male while writing a letter and while working on the WAIS block design subtest. **B:** Same data as in **A** except from a male schizophrenic patient.

duration of each task and converted into the proportion of the total alpha activity from that hemisphere.

Figure 2 depicts the mean alpha activity from the two hemispheres in each group for the five tasks. Statistical significance for the various effects was assessed with a three-factor split-plot analysis of variance, with repeated measures on hemisphere and task. Transformation of the data to proportions precluded finding group or hemisphere effects, but the possibilities for interactions involving either or both of them with tasks were still permitted. Task proved to be significant ($p < 0.001$), as did the task-by-hemisphere interaction ($p < 0.05$). Inspection of Fig. 2 suggests that the groups might differ in alpha asymmetry at least between the letter writing and block design tasks. When an analysis of variance was repeated on just these two tasks, task and task-by-hemisphere again both emerged as significant ($p < 0.01$), but the three-way group-by-task-by-hemisphere interaction fell short of significance ($F = 3.23$; $df = 1: 20$; $p < 0.10$). Thus it appears that both normals and schizophrenics evince similar shifts in alpha patterns as they go from language-laden activities to those relatively free of language, although there is a weak suggestion that schizophrenics are less polarized than normals in their alpha-shifting patterns.

An Integrative Defect in Schizophrenia

Beaumont and Dimond (4) have proposed a different hypothesis concerning the role of brain asymmetry in schizophrenia. They cited a neuropathological study reported by Rosenthal and Bigelow (20), who had found at

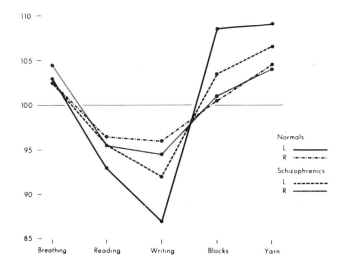

FIG. 2. Relative amounts of alpha activity in each task from the two hemispheres for the normal and schizophrenic groups. The mean for each of the four curves is 100.

post-mortem examination that chronic schizophrenics showed a significant increase in the size of the corpus callosum. Beaumont and Dimond speculated that the increase in size reflected a compensatory attempt to overcome a basic defect in interhemispheric communication, and proposed that the behaviors encountered in schizophrenics could be understood as a relative disconnection of the two hemispheres. To test the hypothesis they presented stimuli tachistosopically to their subjects so placed in the visual fields that they would be directed to one or the other of the hemispheres. The stimuli were letters, digits, and abstract shapes. When the task was to identify the stimuli the schizophrenic subjects ($N = 12$) performed as well as a psychiatric control group and a group of nonpsychiatric medical patients. When two stimuli were presented simultaneously and the task was to judge "same" or "different," schizophrenics showed some deficit within the left hemisphere when matching letters and within the right hemisphere when matching digits and shapes. However, they showed much greater deficit when the members of the pairs of stimuli to be matched were presented to different hemispheres, and the authors feel that the cross-hemisphere difficulty is greater than can be explained by the within-hemisphere deficits. The small number of subjects studied limits the generalizability of the results, but the data may be interpreted as suggesting that a unilateral lesion would be insufficient to explain the impaired performance of schizophrenics on this task.

However, Beaumont and Dimond's results are also consistent with an alternate view of the situation, namely, that some schizophrenics are dysfunctional for right-sided processing whereas others show a defect in response to left-sided demands. Unilateral dysfunctions would lower group averages for all bilateral tasks but only for unilateral tasks involving their specific disability. We can't choose between the alternate hypotheses with our present information. It is interesting that Beaumont and Dimond found a left-sided defect for letters but not shapes and a right-sided defect for shapes but not letters. Although we are addressing complicated possibilities with scanty information, it seems worth noting that cognitive as well as cerebral asymmetry appears to be implicated; the sides appear nonoptimally specialized.

Performance Measures

Gruzelier and Venables (12) found asymmetries in the skin conductance orienting response in schizophrenics. Among their 20 schizophrenics who manifested orienting responses, they found 6 who had no response on the left side and the remaining 14 had a diminished left-side orienting response compared to that on the right. They argue that, unlike other output pathways, the electrodermal response is under control of the ipsilateral rather than the contralateral hemisphere. Hence, they continue, their findings are evidence for a left-hemisphere dysfunction among their subjects. On the other hand (literally), they also ran a group of depressed patients in whom they found the opposite asymmetry—their right-side orienting response was considerably smaller than that on the left. This, they note, fits nicely with Flor-Henry's suggestion that affective disorders are associated with right-hemisphere anomalies whereas schizophrenia is linked with problems on the left side.

Subsequently, Gruzelier and Hammond (11) explored for further asymmetries among schizophrenics and in selected instances examined the interaction of antipsychotic medication with these phenomena. Inconclusive evidence for asymmetrical auditory sensitivity among schizophrenics is reported, but the authors do note a complex difference in the threshold frequency function between schizophrenics and controls. In an auditory detection task schizophrenics did poorer when the targets were delivered to the right ear. Further, their right ear (but not left ear) sensitivity to targets improved with chlorpromazine compared to performance during a placebo period.

Also included among the dependent measures in this study were Wechsler Adult Intelligence Scale IQ scores. Here they found that schizophrenics did less well on the language-laden subtests (comprehension, similarities, vocabulary) than they did on the relatively language-free ones (block design, object assembly). However, they failed to replicate the orienting-response GSR asymmetry in these subjects.

Flor-Henry (9) also studied performance measures in groups of schizophrenics and found that they did well on spatial tasks but poorly on tests requiring lexical mediators, although manic-depressives showed the opposite pattern of abilities. Some of Flor-Henry's tasks are similar to those in the Wechsler series of tests used by Gruzelier and Hammond. Since these tests have been extensively studied in schizophrenia, it would seem desirable to compare these observations with the contrary impression put forth by Matarazzo in his revision of Wechsler's textbook: "Put simply, no robust, or modestly robust Wechsler subtest pattern or profile, or subtest scatter or deviation index has been reported which reliably differentiates 'schizophrenic' patients from either normal individuals, or from patients described clinically as falling into other psychiatric diagnostic categories" (9, p. 432). Thus the findings in these two studies are in striking contrast to those reported in an extensive literature.

Asymmetrical Mechanisms in Symptom Formation

Another approach to the study of schizophrenia and hemispheric specialization is to consider the relations among brain and cognitive asymmetries and psychotic symptoms. Many authors have bemoaned the heterogeneity of the schizophrenic syndrome, and one strategy for the study of brain-behavior mechanisms underlying schizophrenia might be to group schizophrenics according to whether they possess one or another of the cardinal symptoms, and then to examine cognitive mechanisms in these subgroups. In a series of such studies, we have found that patients with some symptoms differ from those lacking them in some aspect relevant to asymmetry. For example, schizophrenics with flat affect do less well than those without flat affect on measures of visual imagery, schizophrenics with auditory hallucinations prefer and have greater facility on measures of auditory imagery (15,18), and differences in imagery style and stimulus imagery are associated with abstract or concrete and autistic responses to proverbs (2). Before we review some of this work, we will consider some of the different ways that imagery can affect performance of a cognitive task.

Paivio (19) and his co-workers have reported on an extensive program of investigation into the functional significance of postulated verbal and imagery processes mediating cognitive behaviors. Imagery, as a mediating system, has many characteristics that appear isomorphic with the specialized abilities of the nondominant hemisphere. Paivio points out the importance of distinguishing among the different defining operations for imagery, which include: (a) the type of stimulus—stimuli, including words, can be high or low in imagery; (b) task characteristics, e.g., the sorts of differences between tasks that we described in the EEG study; and (c) individual differences in imaginal and verbal associative abilities or preferences. We have attempted to exploit some of these operations to study the contribution of brain and cognitive asymmetries to the genesis of psychotic symptoms.

Initially, our studies of flat affect were attempts to improve the reliability of measurement of affects, moods, and emotions. As we studied the communication of feelings in voice we noted that the range of vocal emphasis patterns was more constricted in patients with flat affect (1). It seemed that normal talkers generally use their vocal dynamics to help the listener locate and "tune into" the significant words in a phrase or sentence. We hypothesized that talkers who fail to do this would give the listener the impression of not attaching differential feelings to the different symbols. As we pursued this issue we identified word imagery as one of the predictors of word loudness. In a direct study we found that, in contrast with schizophrenics not deemed flat, schizophrenics with flat affect failed to say high-imagery words louder than low-imagery words.

The mechanisms contributing to vocal emphasis patterns are not well enough understood to make our explanation compelling. In order to converge on our hypothesis experimentally, we studied a well-known effect of word imagery on learning and found that schizophrenics with flat affect show less of a differential in learning rate for high- compared with low-imagery words than do schizophrenics without flat affect; that is, flat schizophrenics do not readily use imagery. Thus, in a series of studies we were able to demonstrate differences in response to stimulus and task characteristics as well as individual stylistic differences in schizophrenics with this cardinal sign. Whether these studies should be interpreted as implicating flat affect as a right-hemisphere defect is not clear. Results from study of the information processing characteristics of each hemisphere in appropriate subjects would be of considerable interest.

Similar pivotal symptom analysis may be applied with respect to hallucinations. We have found that hallucinators tend to report more vivid auditory imagery but perform less well than nonhallucinators in auditory detection situations (18). We suggested that enhanced auditory imagery together with defective testing were factors "permissive" of hallucination formation. Recently, Slade (21) has come to a similar conclusion. We have since been able to show that hallucinators are superior to nonhallucinators on subjective and psychometric measures of imagery and spatial ability (16).

In two direct studies of brain asymmetry we compared hallucinating and nonhallucinating schizophrenics and controls in auditory tasks in which the auditory information was delivered to one ear at a marginal signal-to-noise ratio while the contralateral ear received masking noise. The experimental procedures were designed to capitalize on the preferential crossing of auditory fibers. We attempted to reduce the signal-to-noise ratio in one hemisphere below intelligibility and thus experimentally force information processing, at least in initial stages, into the contralateral hemisphere. In one study we found differences between the schizophrenic groups in the side better able to manage semantic information, with some evidence suggesting that the nonhallucinators were defective in left-hemisphere language function (3).

In another study using similar groups and methods, we asked our subjects to interpret proverbs rather than report back sentences. In blind scoring of the responses we found that the hallucinators gave more abstract responses than the nonhallucinators. The hallucinators also provided more autistic responses than did the other groups, but not differentially according to ear of input or imagery value of the stimulus proverb. We had selected the hallucinator-nonhallucinator separation as representing individual differences in facility with and preference for auditory imagery, and we interpreted our results as being consistent with Paivio's (19) prediction of an association between imagery and autistic thinking. In addition to the above findings and perhaps consistent with the model, the nonhallucinators had a higher frequency of autistic responses for left-ear inputs and also for low-imagery proverbs.

CONCLUSIONS

To summarize these last several studies, we have exploited a research design that compares, among schizophrenics, those with and those without a specific sign or symptom. This research strategy is aimed at the identification of pathoplastic (disease shaping) rather than pathogenic factors since all subjects were schizophrenic and pathogenic factors were presumably represented in both groups. From our review it appears that schizophreniform consequences may be correlated with localized brain lesions. The increased heterogeneity within the schizophrenic syndrome may result from the behavioral final common pathway being dominated by pathoplastic influences.

Alternatively, much of the evidence is also consistent with the view that the basis of schizophrenia is nonoptimal information processing that appears to be associated with many symptoms. In this view symptoms are not *de novo* phenomena discontinuous with normal behaviors. Rather, flattening of affect, for instance, is the endpoint of a parameter reflecting a tendency to invest symbols with feelings. A thinking disorder would reflect a relative excess (above some cutting score defined by the social context) of disruptions of communication. Even hallucinations may be seen as a misapplication of normal perceptual mechanisms. This view represents a real shift to a conception of a continuity of normal and psychopathic behaviors, which perhaps can be portrayed most clearly by contrasting Esquirol's (7) definition of a hallucination as a perception without an object with Kluver's (16) suggestion that every perception is part hallucination. Although these suggestions could be (and were) derived independently of concern with asymmetry, they become especially apt because asymmetry has emphasized cognitive mediating processes and because of the powerful experimental methodology implicit in the approach.

Considering our clinical familiarity with schizophrenic patients, we all can recall some who appear lacking in ability with lexical, sequential, and analytic processing, and some who appear locked in this mode. Some schizophrenic patients appear to be lacking in ability with spatial, holistic, and intuitive operations and others appear to approach the world entirely in this mode. Certainly the idea of integrative difficulties is intrinsic to Bleuler's conceptualization of schizophrenia. In the main, the cardinal symptoms by which we recognize the disorder—including thinking disorders, flat affect, and hallucinations—all involve language (dys)function, and the dominant hemisphere is most implicated both from the clinical and the brain lesion evidence. However, the evidence that process schizophrenics can show changing patterns of symptoms in the course of their disease, and the fact that humans with disconnected hemispheres do not resemble schizophrenics, suggests that other factors must be operating. Schizophrenics appear to rely on nonoptimal or inappropriate modes of information processing. The experiments to test such suggestions have not been done, and, to date, the main contribution of the work in brain and cognitive asymmetry to our understanding of psychopathology is in the experimental methods and questions newly available.

ACKNOWLEDGMENTS

Supported in part by USPHS Grants MH 08618 and MH 08636. We thank Martin Kesselman for his helpful comments on an earlier draft of this chapter.

REFERENCES

1. Alpert, M., and Anderson, L. T. (1976): Imagery mediation of vocal emphasis in flat affect. *Arch. Gen. Psychiatry (in press).*
2. Alpert, M., Kesselman, M., and Anderson, L. T. (1977): Cerebral and cognitive asymmetry and autistic thinking. Presented at the 5th Annual Meeting of the International Neuropsychological Society, Santa Fe, New Mexico.
3. Alpert, M., Rubinstein, H., and Kesselman, M. (1976): Asymmetry of information processing in hallucinators and non-hallucinators. *J. Nerv. Ment. Dis.,* 162:258–265.
4. Beaumont, J. G., and Dimond, S. J. (1973): Brain disconnection and schizophrenia. *Br. J. Psychiatry,* 123:661–662.
5. Bingley, T. (1958): Mental symptoms in temporal lobe epilepsy and temporal lobe gliomas. *Acta Psychiatr. Neurol. Scand. [Suppl.],* 33:120.
6. Doyle, J. C., Ornstein, R., and Galin, D. (1974): Lateral specialization of cognitive mode. II: EEG frequency analysis. *Psychophysiology,* 11:567–578.
7. Esquirol, J. E. D. (1845): *Mental Maladies: A Treatise on Insanity,* translated by E. K. Hunt. Lea and Blanchard, Philadelphia.
8. Flor-Henry, P. (1969): Psychosis and temporal lobe epilepsy: A controlled investigation. *Epilepsia,* 10:363–395.
9. Flor-Henry, P. (1977): Lateralized temporal-limbic dysfunction and psychopathology. In: *Origins and Evolution of Language and Speech,* edited by H. Steklis, S. Harnad, and J. Lancaster. *Ann. N.Y. Acad. Sci.* 280 *(in press).*
10. Falconer, M. A., and Serafetinides, E. A. (1963): A follow-up study of surgery in temporal lobe epilepsy. *J. Neurol. Neurosurg. Psychiatry,* 26:154–165.
11. Gruzelier, J., and Hammond, N. (1976): Schizophrenia: A dominant hemisphere temporal-limbic disorder? *Res. Commun. Psychol. Psychiatry Behav.,* 1:33–72.
12. Gruzelier, J., and Venables, P. (1974): Bimodality and laterality of skin conductance orienting activity in schizophrenics: Replication and evidence of lateral asymmetry in patients with depression and disorders of personality. *Biol. Psychiatry,* 8:55–73.
13. Hillbom, E. (1960): After-effects of brain injuries. *Acta Psychiatr. Neurol. Scand. [Suppl.],* 35:142.
14. Hughes, J. R., and Schlagenhauff, R. E. (1961): Electroclinical correlation in temporal lobe epilepsy with emphasis on interareal analysis of the temporal lobe. *Electroencephalogr. Clin. Neurophysiol.,* 13:333–339.
15. Kesselman, M., and Alpert, M. (1976): Measures of imagery in a schizophrenic population. *(In preparation).*
16. Kluver, H. (1965): Neurobiology of perception. In: *Psychopathology of Perception,* edited by P. Hoch and J. Zubin, pp. 1–40. Grune & Stratton, New York.
17. Merritt, H. H. (1973): *A Textbook of Neurology, 5th Ed.* Lea & Febiger, Philadelphia.
18. Mintz, S., and Alpert, M. (1972): Imagery vividness, reality testing and schizophrenic hallucinations. *J. Abnorm. Psychol.,* 79:310–316.
19. Paivio, A. (1971): *Imagery and Verbal Processes.* Holt, Rinehart and Winston, New York.
20. Rosenthal, R., and Bigelow, L. B. (1972): Quantitative brain measurements in chronic schizophrenia. *Br. J. Psychiatry,* 121:259–264.
21. Slade, P. D. (1976): An investigation of psychological factors involved in the predisposition to auditory hallucinations. *Psychol. Med.,* 6:123–132.
22. Walker, A. E., and Jablon, S. (1961): *A Follow-up Study of Head Wounds in World War II.* Government Printing Office, Washington.

Psychopathology and Brain Dysfunction, edited
by C. Shagass, S. Gershon, and A. J. Friedhoff.
Raven Press, New York © 1977.

Neural and Cognitive Correlates of Developmental Dyslexia: Age and Sex Differences

Sandra F. Witelson

*Department of Psychiatry, Chedoke Hospitals, McMaster University,
Hamilton, Ontario, Canada, L8N 3L6*

This chapter concerns the syndrome of developmental dyslexia. I shall attempt to define it objectively and place it within the context of the wide spectrum of the heterogeneous group of children who exhibit learning difficulties. A brief survey of the various neural postulates suggested as etiological or correlated factors of the disorder will be presented, including Orton's (54) hypothesis that atypical cerebral dominance underlies this disorder. Orton's theorizing served as the original impetus for the several recent studies of hemisphere specialization in dyslexia, which will be reviewed here briefly. I then will describe the specific hypotheses related to hemisphere specialization underlying my own research, the methods and results of these studies, and the implications they may have for the etiology, nature, and remediation of developmental dyslexia.

CHILDREN WITH LEARNING DIFFICULTIES

Recent epidemiological studies indicate that as many as 30% of school-age children may have some type of learning problem (4). Such figures, however, are likely based on samples that include heterogeneous groups of children. Although the "phenotype," as manifested by the presenting symptom of poor school performance, may be similar among such children, the "genotype," that is, the underlying deficit and cause of the symptoms, may be quite different. In some cases the children may be of limited general intelligence; in others, their difficulties may be the sequelae of definite brain damage; in some, social or cognitive deprivation may be important factors; some children may be handicapped by severe and uncorrected auditory or visual acuity defects; in others, emotional disturbance may be the primary cause; and in others, attentional characteristics, often associated with hyperactivity, may be the basic deficit (14). There is at least one other subgroup, that of children with specific reading disability or developmental dyslexia. This last group is combined by some authors (e.g., 70) with the "attentional-hyperactivity" subgroup, and the combined group is often referred to as children with specific learning disabilities or "minimal brain dysfunction." Figure 1 presents schematically a possible classification of the different types of children with learning difficulties.

SYNDROME OF DEVELOPMENTAL DYSLEXIA

The subgroup of developmental dyslexia is discussed in this chapter. This subgroup accounts for only a small proportion of the total group of children with learning difficulties. Its estimated incidence is approximately 3 to 4% of the total school-age population (4). I will subsequently suggest that a more precise label for this disorder may be "specific cognitive deficit," even though this area already has more than enough interchangeable labels as Fry (19) so effectively indicates with his "Do-it-yourself terminology Generator." The main presenting symptom of this syndrome as the term dyslexia or reading disability indicates is difficulty in reading in individuals who are otherwise normal intellectually, emotionally, and medically. The etiology of the disorder is not known. There are no delineated pathognomonic types of reading errors or other symptoms that definitively identify the disorder. Accordingly, the diagnosis of developmental dyslexia is mainly a negative diagnosis, dependent on exclusion of the other possible causes of poor reading as listed above, which in itself is not always an unequivocal task. This makes the diagnosis of dyslexia a difficult task that has repercussions both for clinical management and for the precision with which research cases are selected.

NEUROLOGICAL THEORIES OF DYSLEXIA

Although the etiology of developmental dyslexia remains unknown, a constitutional basis is assumed by many students of this disorder. This assumption is reflected in the definition of developmental dyslexia formulated by the World Federation of Neurology in 1968: "A disorder manifested by difficulty in learning to read despite conventional instruction, adequate intelligence and socio-cultural opportunity. It is dependent upon fundamental cognitive disabilities which are frequently of constitutional origin" (12, p. 11).

Two consistent findings have contributed to the notion of a biological basis of the disorder: (a) there is a sex difference in the incidence of the disorder (the male-female ratio is reported to be as high as 10:1) (4,74); and (b) there appears to be a genetic factor in dyslexia (16).

The first neurological theory proposed was probably that of Fisher (17) who suggested that there is an agenesis of the angular gyrus of the left hemisphere. This concept developed in the context of adult neurology in which the importance of the angular gyrus was already documented for acquired dyslexia subsequent to brain damage (2). However, there is con-

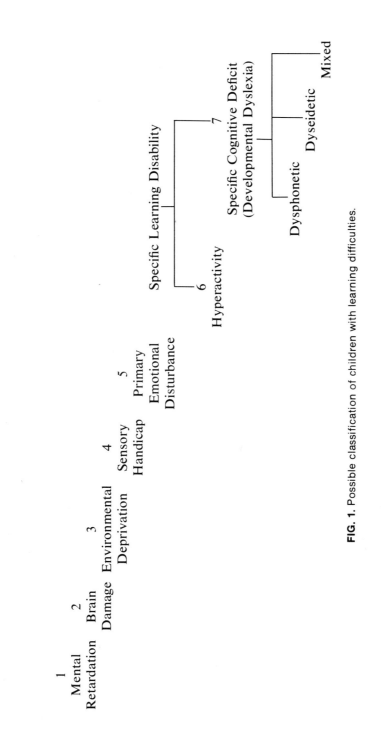

FIG. 1. Possible classification of children with learning difficulties.

siderable evidence to indicate that the immature brain is more plastic than the mature brain, that is, has a greater ability for functional reorganization (67). Accordingly, it was soon realized that agenesis of the angular gyri of both hemispheres, that is, bilateral agenesis, would have to be postulated for congenital dyslexia. Because this is a highly improbable situation, this hypothesis fell out of favor. To my knowledge, however, there have been no post-mortem anatomical studies of the brains of dyslexic individuals to confirm or disprove this hypothesis.

More recently, Kinsbourne and Warrington (35) postulated left-hemisphere dysfunction in two types of dyslexics, separated on the basis of different cognitive (WISC) patterns. Satz and Sparrow (61) and also Kinsbourne (33) have suggested that the neural substrate of developmental dyslexia may be a lag in the maturation of left hemisphere development rather than an actual qualitative deficit. Another hypothesis implicates cerebellar-vestibular dysfunction as the neural correlate of dyslexia (18).

However, as Benton (4) pointed out in his recent review, there is no strong evidence to date to support any neurological theory of dyslexia. In fact, the opposite viewpoint is represented in many theories that offer educational and environmental factors as the cause of the reading difficulties (see 12), but these have received even less supporting and more contraindicative evidence.

CEREBRAL DOMINANCE AS THE NEURAL DEFICIT

One other neurological theory of dyslexia, proposed several decades ago, is Orton's (54) theory of faulty cerebral dominance. It is well established now that the two cerebral hemispheres are asymmetrical in their role in mediating the various intellectual functions. The left hemisphere has the major role in sequential, analytic, linguistic processing of information, and the right hemisphere in parallel, holistic, spatial processing (e.g., 13,51). The term cerebral dominance has been generally replaced by more specific terms, such as hemisphere functional asymmetry and hemisphere specialization, which reflect the fact that each hemisphere is dominant for different functions and that cerebral dominance involves relative, not absolute, lateralization of function. Each hemisphere is the major hemisphere for one type of cognitive processing, but the other hemisphere also may have some capacity for this cognitive mode.

Considerably less was known at the time of Orton's work, particularly in reference to the right hemisphere and to lateralization of function in children. It is therefore understandable that Orton's theory was not specific in terms of which hemisphere was not dominant for what cognitive functions. Because of a lack of methods which allowed investigation of this speculation, the hypothesis remained untested until the last decade. It was maintained, however, on the basis of the frequent reports of the greater incidence of left-handed and ambidextrous individuals among dyslexics than among normal children (80), in view of the accepted correlation between hand preference and speech lateralization.

The development within the last decade of noninvasive techniques with which to study hemisphere specialization in non-brain-injured individuals (see 75) has resulted in considerable knowledge concerning normal children and some data concerning various clinic groups, including developmental dyslexics. The basic technique used in most of these studies involves perceptual tests of verbal or nonverbal stimulation in the lateral sensory fields. With the use of such techniques, there is now evidence that hemisphere specialization likely exists in children as young as 3 years and possibly even in neonates (for review, see 75). Such data provide the necessary basis with which to interpret the performance of dyslexics on such tests considered to reflect neural organization.

Evidence Concerning Hemisphere Specialization in Dyslexia

Several studies using perceptual tests involving lateral stimulation such as dichotic listening and lateral tachistoscopic stimulation have been reported for variously defined groups of children with learning problems. Although the samples studied are not strictly comparable and some of the tasks employed have methodological difficulties (see 75), the results of the various reports are quite consistent. A few studies have reported nonsignificant trends suggestive of an abnormality in cerebral dominance (e.g., 8,82). The strongest evidence indicative of abnormal hemisphere specialization comes from studies of children whose cognitive deficits include language or dysphasic problems that are more pervasive than just reading (65,77). In general, however, the results of most of the studies report right ear superiority on verbal dichotic tasks (41,50,60,62,66,79) and right visual field superiority in tachistoscopic presentation of linguistic stimuli (46,49,53,79) in the learning-impaired children as in normal children. By inference, these results indicate that the left hemisphere is the major hemisphere for speech and language in children with reading problems, as in the case of normal children. This conclusion, however, is contrary to much discussion in the literature and to the widely held belief that there is abnormal left hemisphere specialization in dyslexia.

All these studies used tests that presented only linguistic stimuli and therefore they are relevant only to the issue of left-hemisphere specialization. This bias may exist because reading traditionally has been conceptualized as a linguistic skill and the implicit assumption of the researchers was that specialization of the left hemisphere must be the deficient aspect of neural organization. None of the work investigated right hemisphere specialization for nonlinguistic, spatial, gestalt information processing. There are, however, several theoretical reasons why right hemisphere specialization may be a relevant factor in dyslexia. First, within the framework of the current knowledge of hemisphere specialization, Orton's nonspecific hypothesis "that engrams exist in the non-dominant [*right*] hemisphere which may, if not completely elided, cause confusion in recognition and recall" (54, p. 153) may be interpreted as too weak a left hemisphere, as has been the general interpretation, but it may also mean too strong a right hemisphere, which has not been considered to date. Second, the process of reading (as far as alphabetic languages such as English are concerned) involves left hemisphere functions of sound analysis and linguistic processing (11). But reading may also involve right hemisphere functions of nonlinguistic form perception, as in the visual discrimination of letters and gestalt perception and memory of the total word as a picture (63). That this is the case is supported by reports from clinical neurology which indicate that although acquired dyslexia is usually associated with left hemisphere damage, lesions in the right hemisphere may also lead to loss of reading skills. In these cases there is particular difficulty in the visual perceptual aspects of reading (34). To the extent, then, that learning to read does involve gestalt perception and right hemisphere processing, specialization of the right hemisphere may be a possible factor in developmental dyslexia (74).

The series of studies that I shall report here concerns specialization of the right hemisphere for nonlinguistic spatial processing in dyslexic children, as well as specialization of the left hemisphere for linguistic processing in the same individuals. Specific reference will be made to how the factors of age and sex may be related to this aspect of brain organization in dyslexia. I shall suggest that the results of these studies support the notion of abnormal cerebral dominance as a neural substrate of dyslexia, but only in regard to the right hemisphere. As far as the left hemisphere is concerned, the results support the conclusion of typical lateralization of speech and language functions to the left hemisphere but also the hypothesis of left hemisphere dysfunction. These neural correlates appear to have meaning for the cognitive correlates of dyslexia and also implications for remedial education.

PRESENT RESEARCH: METHOD

Subjects

A group of 113 children were stringently selected as cases of developmental dyslexia from a total pool of 200 referrals of possible cases that were made to the research study over a period of 5 years. Each child was seen in the Child and Family Unit of the Chedoke-McMaster Centre in which departments of both psychiatry and pediatrics are involved. The following clinical assessments and tests were administered to each case in order to ascertain whether the child met the criteria of the objective definition of dyslexia as used in this study:

Neuropediatric assessment

Psychiatric family assessment

Clinical psychological testing, including:

  Wechsler Intelligence Scale for Children (WISC) (69)

  Wide Range Achievement Test (WRAT) (26)

  Harris Tests of Lateral Dominance (22)

  Puretone audiological testing (0.25, 0.5, 1, and 2 kHz)

  Visual acuity (Snellen Chart) and stereopsis testing (WIRT Stereopsis Test) (71)

  Detailed developmental and medical history, including birth records

  Detailed school record

Each child included in the sample had to achieve an IQ score of at least 85 on the Wechsler Performance Scale. Many children with reading problems have lower verbal than nonverbal spatial abilities. For this reason the Stanford-Binet Intelligence Scale (68), which yields one composite IQ score that is heavily dependent on language skills, and the Full Scale WISC IQ, which may mask a large difference between verbal and nonverbal (Performance) abilities, were not used as selection criteria. Each child also had to have a difference of at least 1.5 grade levels between his actual reading grade level on the WRAT Reading subtest and that expected on the basis of his chronological age at the time of testing. In the case of younger children whose expected reading level was below grade 3, the criterion was that they were virtually nonreaders on the test. Each child also had to have at least the usual academic opportunities to learn to read, and to have shown reading difficulty from the start of his academic career. This latter criterion is considered important because any child who is able to progress in reading appropriately within the first few grades but who subsequently shows a reading problem likely does not have a basic difficulty in the cognitive skills required to learn to read, but some emotional difficulty which thwarts the use of the abilities he does have, making the reading problem a secondary disturbance. Each child also had no detectable brain damage or history of definite neural insult, had no diagnosed primary emotional disturbance, and was receiving no medication for behavioral difficulties. Each child did have the social and cognitive experiences of the middle socioeconomic class and had English as his first language. All children included in the sample also had adequate visual and auditory sensory acuity so that the experimental perceptual tasks could be validly administered.

Of the 113 such children found, 100 were strongly right handed: defined as right-hand preference for handwriting at the time of testing with no history of previous left-hand preference, and right-hand preference on at least 7 of the 10 unimanual tasks of the Harris Test. Only 13 were either left handed or ambidextrous. Since hand preference has been consistently found to be correlated to some degree with patterns of hemisphere specialization (e.g., 24), the right- and non-right-handed children were studied separately. Only the right-handed children are discussed in this report as the remaining group of 13 non-right-handed children is too small for analysis, particularly because of the likely heterogeneous nature of neural organization in sinistrals (e.g., 43,81).

This was not an epidemiological study and therefore no definitive statement may be made about the relative incidence of left and right hand preference among dyslexic children. However, no selection procedures were involved that discriminated against left-handed individuals. The results clearly indicate that many, if not most, cases of developmental dyslexia may have well-established right-hand preference. This is contrary to the widely held belief that a lack of right hand preference may be indicative of dyslexia, a notion that has no empirical foundation.

The subjects ranged in age from 6 to 14 years. Age has for some time been considered an important variable in respect to hemisphere specialization in normal children (36,40). However, in a recent theoretical review (75), I suggested that hemisphere specialization is present and functional at birth, and that what changes with age is not the development of lateralization of function, but the extent of the repertoire of cognitive skills available for lateralization and the degree of interhemisphere equipotentiality. Age has also been suggested as a relevant variable in dyslexia by theorists such as

TABLE 1. *Descriptive data for dyslexic and normal groups of children*

	Boys		Girls	
	Dyslexics $\bar{X}$	Controls $\bar{X}$	Dyslexics $\bar{X}$	Controls $\bar{X}$
N	85	156	15	76
Age (yr): range	6–14	6–14	8–14	8–14
mean	10.6	10.5	10.4	11.2
WISC FS IQ	102.1	112.2[a]	101	104.6[a]
V IQ	97.4		94.1	
P IQ	106.9		108.6	
Vocab SS	10.2	11.4	9.7	10.9
Block Design				
SS	11.3	11.9	10.6	10.4
WRAT Standard Scores				
Reading	80.7	113.3	83.7	110.3
Reading lag				
(grades)	2.6		1.9	
Spelling	79.3	105.9	81.7	108.2
Arithmetic	87.9	104.3	87.9	⁻ 99.4

[a] A short form of the WISC was used with the normal children which included Arithmetic, Vocabulary and Block Design subtests.

Benton (3) and Satz and Sparrow (61) who suggest that the deficits manifested in dyslexia may vary at different ages. Accordingly, the total group of dyslexics was subdivided into four age subgroups (6 to 7, 8 to 9, 10 to 11, and 12 to 14 years) for analyses of their performance on the experimental tests.

Of the 100 right-handed dyslexic children, there were 85 boys and 15 girls, giving a ratio of approximately 6:1, which is consistent with many other reports of a much higher incidence of dyslexia among males than females as indicated previously. Sex has also been recently shown to have some relationship to patterns of hemisphere specialization. It appears that females may have less lateralization of function than males, both for language functions at maturity (37) and for spatial functions, in this case both at maturity (31,38,48) and during childhood (73). Since the dependent variable in the present studies is the pattern of hemisphere specialization, the two sexes were treated separately.

Table 1 gives the descriptive information such as age, IQ, and reading level for each sex group of dyslexics and the control groups of normal children matched for sex, age, and socioeconomic status, but who had no medical, behavioral, or academic difficulties.

Perceptual Tests of Hemisphere Specialization

Five tests of perception were used which involved verbal or nonverbal spatial stimuli presented in the lateral sensory fields. Tests were used involving each of the three sensory modalities: audition, vision, and touch. The basic rationale of these tests depends on the fact that there is a predominance of the crossed anatomical connections between sensory field and the brain. Therefore stimulation presented in the lateral fields is initially transmitted, either predominantly as in the auditory and somesthetic systems, or completely as in the visual system, to the contralateral hemisphere. Consequently, any asymmetry in hemisphere processing of particular stimuli may be reflected in right-left asymmetry in accuracy or in reaction time of response to right versus left stimulation. On this basis these tests are considered to be indices of different aspects of hemisphere specialization.

Neural organization is not observed directly in this study but is inferred on the basis of test performance. Such theorizing should proceed with caution. For this reason the present research employed several experimental tests as indices of the same hypothetical neural process to allow for the possible convergence of different sets of data. Inferences of neural organization may be more definite when based on several different but consistent sets of data.

Each of the five tests was administered to each child individually. However, no results are reported for the female dyslexics on the tachistoscopic tests as no female control groups have yet been tested.

(a) A typical verbal dichotic (auditory) stimulation task (e.g., 27) was used as an index of left hemisphere specialization for speech and language. (b) Dichhaptic (touch or haptic) stimulation with nonsense shapes (72) and (c) lateral tachistoscopic (visual) presentation of pictures of human figures (e.g., 29) were tasks used as indices of right hemisphere specialization for form and spatial perception. (d) Dichhaptic stimulation with letters (72) was used as a task requiring both spatial and verbal processing and thus the participation of both hemispheres, and (e) lateral tachistoscopic presentation of letters was used, which may be a task that also involves either or both types of cognitive processing.

Dichotic Listening: Digits

The specific task used involved the simultaneous presentation of pairs of different digits (1 to 10, excluding the two-syllable digit, 7), one to each ear, via Sharpe HA-10 Mark II headphones and a two-channel Tandberg tape recorder (Model 1200X). The intensity of the stimuli at the earphones was 70 dB SPL, which is a subjectively comfortable loudness level. The audiological pretesting ensured that the only children used as subjects on this test were those whose pure tone thresholds for each ear were within the normal range and did not differ by more than 5 dB in favor of one ear on two or more of the four tested frequencies. The stimuli were presented at the rate of two pairs per second, in ten sets each of two and of three pairs, making a maximum possible score of 50 per ear. A free recall method of response was used in which the subject was asked to report as many numbers as he could. The scores obtained were the number of right and of left ear digits correctly reported, regardless of order of report. With this rate of presentation, the typical order of response is the Ear Order of Report in which numbers from one ear are reported first, followed by those from the other ear (7,76).

On such dichotic tasks, most individuals show greater accuracy in the recall of information presented to the right than left ear. This right ear advantage is considered to reflect left hemisphere superiority for the processing of verbal information (27,30).

Dichhaptic Stimulation: Shapes

In this test the subject was required to feel, out of view, two different two-dimensional nonsense shapes (3.8 cm^2) simultaneously for 10 sec, one to each hand using the index and middle fingers. Many pretest trials were given to provide practice in continuous and simultaneous palpation of the two stimuli. The subject responded by choosing the two test stimuli from a visual recognition display of six shapes. A total of 10 test trials was given and the scores obtained were the number of left and of right hand objects correctly recognized. The maximum possible score per hand is 10.

Because each hand transmits information predominantly to the contralateral hemisphere, greater accuracy for left hand objects is considered to reflect right hemisphere superiority for shape discrimination. This is a less familiar task than is dichotic listening. It was recently devised by the author in order to study right hemisphere specialization in children. Its theoretical rationale is more fully described in previous papers (72,73).

Lateral Tachistoscopic Presentation: Human Figures

The particular visual task used involved a set of stimuli of unfamiliar pictures of human figures 6 mm^2 in size. Each stimulus card presented either two identical or two different pictures in a vertical array in either the left or right visual field. Binocular viewing in a two-channel Scientific Prototype tachistoscope (Model 800-F) was used and the subject fixated on a central dot before each stimulus presentation. The distance from the fixation point to the near edge of the stimulus was 3.2 cm, which subtends a visual angle of 2 degrees, 12 min at a viewing distance of 82.6 cm, thus placing the stimulus outside the field of possible bilateral cortical representation. For each stimulus card the subject had to indicate orally whether the two stimuli were the same or different. Twenty such stimulus cards were presented and the scores obtained were the number of left and of right stimulus pairs correctly discriminated. The maximum possible score per field is 10.

Stimulus exposure time was determined individually for each subject by the psychophysical method of limits to yield approximately 75% accuracy. However, exposure time was never allowed to exceed 150 msec, as exposure beyond this duration may allow eye movements that could bring the peripheral stimulus into central vision and thus allow bihemispheric stimulation.

The only children used as subjects for this test were those who indicated on ophthalmological screening that their visual acuity for each eye on a Snellen chart, with glasses if necessary, was at least 20/40, and that they had fine stereopsis (WIRT Stereopsis Test) and therefore fusion which ensured that they were viewing the tachistoscopic stimuli with homologous peripheral areas of the retina of both eyes.

On such tachistoscopic tasks, individuals typically show greater accuracy for stimuli presented in the left visual field, which is considered to reflect right hemisphere superiority for spatial form perception (32).

Dichhaptic Stimulation: Letters

In this test of dichhaptic perception, the stimuli were two-dimensional letters (approximately 2 × 2.5 cm^2), which were presented to the subject in pairs of simultaneously presented different letters. There were ten sets of two pairs, each pair presented for 2 sec with a 1-sec interpair interval. The subject's task was to report orally the names of the four letters he had just felt. The maximum possible score for each hand was 20.

On the basis of the results of previous work with normal children (72), this task is considered to require both spatial processing in order to recognize the stimuli initially and linguistic processing in order to translate the perceived shape into a verbal code for naming. Such cognitive processing would engage the specialized functions of both hemispheres. Any observed hand asymmetry may thus indicate the predominant hemisphere and, by further inference, the predominant cognitive strategy used for the task.

Lateral Tachistoscopic Presentation: Letters

This tachistoscopic test was identical in all aspects to the visual test described above involving pictures of human figures, except that in the present test the stimuli were pairs of same or different upper-case letters. The task was originally designed as a linguistic task in the visual system in order to study left hemisphere specialization, in addition to the use of the dichotic listening task in the auditory modality. However, this study was started before I was aware of the work of Posner and Mitchell (57) and before the further studies were reported which adapted this work to the study of hemisphere specialization (10,20). The results of these studies indicate the possibility of making a "physical match" or shape discrimination of letters that are physically identical without making a "verbal match" or using any linguistic processing. Thus, although the task was designed to be a linguistic task, the task must be considered as one in which either spatial or verbal processing, or possibly both, may be used. The results support such a reinterpretation of the task.

RESULTS

Left Hemisphere Specialization

Boys

The performance of the group of dyslexic boys ($N = 85$) was compared to that of a normal group of boys ($N = 156$) on the dichotic digits test. The results are presented in Fig. 2. A three-way mixed-design analysis of variance was done with Group and Age as between factors and Ear as the within factor. Age was a significant main factor (F = 33.95, df = $^3/_{233}$, $p <$ 0.01) indicating that overall (right plus left ear) accuracy increased with age for both groups. Group was also a significant main effect (F = 105.76, df = $^1/_{233}$, $p < 0.01$) indicating that the overall performance of the dyslexic

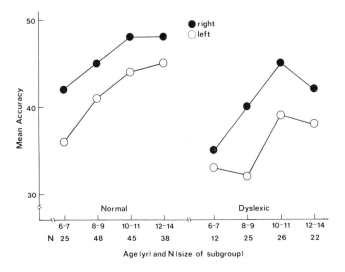

FIG. 2. Mean accuracy scores on verbal dichotic listening for normal and dyslexic boys.

boys was significantly lower than that of the normal boys. The Group by Age interaction was not significant, indicating that the dyslexic boys differed from normal boys to the same extent at all age levels.

Ear was also a significant main factor, indicating that right ear accuracy was significantly greater than left ear accuracy. There was no Ear by Age, Ear by Group, or Ear by Age by Group interaction. This result indicates that the right ear advantage was present in both the dyslexic and normal groups at all age levels.

Although the Group by Ear interaction term was not significant, one of the main purposes of the study was to determine whether dyslexics do in fact show a right ear superiority on a verbal dichotic stimulation task. Accordingly two Duncan Multiple Range Tests (15) were done to test right versus left ear accuracy for the dyslexic and normal groups separately. For each group the right ear score was significantly greater than the left ear score (df = 233, $p < 0.001$).

Right ear superiority was observed in both groups not only in terms of accuracy scores but also in terms of the number of individuals who showed greater right ear scores. Approximately 70% of each group showed a right ear superiority. There was no difference between the dyslexic and normal groups ($\chi^2 = 0.02$).

Girls

The group of dyslexic girls ($N = 15$) was not divided into age subgroups because of its small size. Table 2 presents the results on the dichotic listen-

TABLE 2. *Mean accuracy scores on the dichotic digits test*

| | | Normal | | | | | Dyslexic | | | |
| | | Ear | | | | | Ear | | | |
	N	Right	Left	p	Total	N	Right	Left	p	Total
Girls	68	46.7	44.5	0.001	91.2	15	43.3	37.3	0.05	80.5
Boys	156	46.0	42.1	0.001	88.2	85	41.1	35.6	0.001	76.7

Maximum score per ear is 50.

ing task for the total group of dyslexic girls in comparison to a matched group of normal girls ($N = 68$). The results for the total groups of boys are also presented for easy comparison.

The dyslexic girls showed a right ear superiority, as did normal girls. The total accuracy of the dyslexic girls was significantly lower than that of the normal girls ($t = 2.79$, df $= 81$, $p < 0.01$). These results are similar to those reported above in the case of boys. It is noted that the overall accuracy for dyslexic girls and dyslexic boys is comparable (80.5 and 76.7, $t = 0.96$, df $= 98$). Moreover, the overall accuracy of the dyslexic girls is 88.3% of that of the normal girls, and the overall accuracy of the dyslexic boys is 87% of that of the normal boys, indicating comparable deficits in both dyslexic groups.

Right Hemisphere Specialization

Boys

The performance of the dyslexic boys ($N = 49$) was compared to that of a normal group of boys ($N = 100$) on the dichhaptic shapes test. Only 49 dyslexic boys were tested as this test was not yet devised at the start of this study. The results are presented in Fig. 3. Again, a three-way mixed-design analysis of variance was done with Group and Age as between factors and Hand as the within factor. Age was a significant factor ($F = 14.22$, df $= 3/141$, $p < 0.001$) indicating that accuracy increased with age. The Group factor was not significant, which indicates that the dyslexics did not differ from the normals in overall accuracy (left plus right hand scores). The Group by Age interaction was not significant indicating that the groups performed similarly at the different age levels.

Hand was a significant factor ($F = 7.27$, df $= 1/141$, $p < 0.01$) indicating greater left than right hand accuracy. Hand by Age was not a significant factor indicating that the left hand superiority was present at all ages. However, Group by Hand was a significant interaction ($F = 6.99$, df $= 1/141$, $p < 0.01$), which indicates that the normal and dyslexic groups differed in

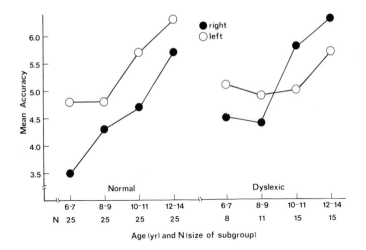

FIG. 3. Mean accuracy scores on dichhaptic stimulation with nonsense shapes for normal and dyslexic boys.

left versus right hand accuracy. Individual comparisons were made using the Duncan Multiple Range Test. For the normal group the left hand score was significantly greater than the right hand score (df = 141, $p < 0.01$). For the dyslexic group, there was no difference between left and right hand scores. Moreover, the right hand score of the dyslexics was significantly greater than the right hand score of the normal children (df = 141, $p < 0.01$). Left hand scores did not differ significantly between groups. The Group by Hand by Age interaction was not significant indicating that the group difference in hand asymmetry was present at the different age levels.

An analysis was done to determine if the groups also differed in terms of the number of individuals who showed greater left hand accuracy. A χ^2 test indicated that more normal than dyslexic boys had a left-hand superiority ($\chi^2 = 6.29$, $p < 0.02$).

Performance on this task was also analyzed in terms of whether the first shape selected in each of the 10 test trials was a left- or right-hand object. Such a score would reflect any asymmetry in order of report of left and right hand objects. Only trials in which the first choice was a correct choice were used for this analysis. Accordingly, the total number of responses starting with either a left or right hand object is usually less than 10, since both groups make some errors on this task. Figure 4 presents these data for both the normal and dyslexic groups. A simple *t*-test for correlated means was done for each total group. For the normal group, left hand shapes were reported first more frequently than right hand shapes (3.1 versus 2.6, $t = 2.34$, df = 99, $p < 0.05$). In contrast, for the dyslexic group, there was no hand difference in object of first report (3.0 versus 3.0, $t = 0.12$, df = 48).

Specialization of the right hemisphere for spatial form perception was also

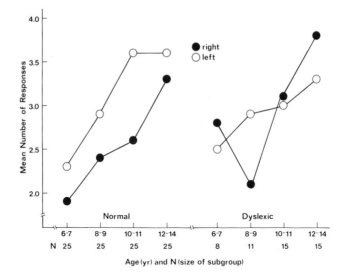

FIG. 4. Mean number of responses starting with left and right hand stimuli on dichhaptic shapes for normal and dyslexic boys.

studied with the use of the visual test of lateral tachistoscopic presentation of pictures of human figures. The performance of the dyslexic boys ($N = 82$) was compared to that of a normal group of boys ($N = 85$) on this task. Figure 5 presents the results. Simple t-tests for correlated data were done for each total group. The normal group obtained a greater mean accuracy score for left than right visual field stimuli (6.0 and 5.5, $t = 2.28$, df = 84,

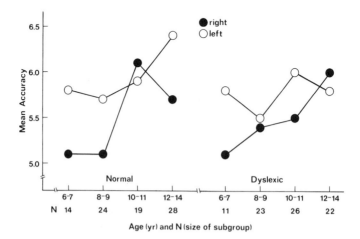

FIG. 5. Mean accuracy scores on tachistoscopic stimulation of human figures in lateral half-fields for normal and dyslexic boys.

$p < 0.05$). In contrast, the dyslexic group showed no accuracy difference for left and right stimuli (5.8 and 5.6, $t = 0.96$, df $= 81$). Although the groups differed in terms of asymmetry in perception, their overall accuracy was not different (11.5 versus 11.4).

Girls

The group of dyslexic girls ($N = 12$) were compared to a matched group of normal girls ($N = 75$) on the dichhaptic shapes test. I have found previously that on this test normal girls show no hand asymmetry, in contrast to normal boys who show significant left hand superiority. This difference in performance has been interpreted as a sex difference in the neural organization underlying spatial form perception. Boys as young as 6 years of age show right hemisphere dominance for spatial perception, but girls as old as 14 years show bilateral representation for spatial perception (73). In this context, then, it is important to compare the performance not of dyslexic girls to dyslexic boys, but of dyslexic girls to normal girls, and to determine if this comparison is similar to that for dyslexic boys and normal boys. The results for the dyslexic and normal girls on the dichhaptic shapes test are presented in Table 3 with the results for the boys as well.

The dyslexic girls showed no difference in the accuracy scores for each hand. This performance is similar to that of the group of normal girls who also showed no hand asymmetry. An analysis of the side of the first reported shape was done for the girls as it was for the boys. For the normal girls, the mean numbers of responses starting with a left or right hand shape were 3.1 and 3.0, respectively, which are not different. For the dyslexic girls, there also was no significant difference in side of first report, although there was a tendency to a right bias, in contrast to the left bias in normal boys (left and right mean scores were 2.6 and 3.4, respectively, $t = 1.70$, df $= 11$, $0.20 > p > 0.10$).

The results in Table 3 also indicate that overall accuracy on the dichhaptic shapes test was the same for the dyslexic and normal girls (10.3 versus 10.6). In fact, overall accuracy is comparable for all four groups. However,

TABLE 3. *Mean accuracy scores on the dichhaptic shapes test*

		Normal					Dyslexic			
		Hand					Hand			
	N	Right	Left	p	Total	N	Right	Left	p	Total
Girls	75	5.3	5.3	ns	10.6	12	5.3	5.0	ns	10.3
Boys	100	4.6	5.4	0.001	10.0	49	5.4	5.2	ns	10.6

Maximum score per hand is 10.

dyslexic girls did not differ from normal girls in their pattern of hand asymmetry, whereas dyslexic boys did differ from normal boys in pattern of hand asymmetry.

Dual Hemisphere Participation

Boys

The group of dyslexic boys ($N = 46$) was compared to a matched group of normal boys ($N = 28$) on the dichhaptic letters test. The results are presented in Fig. 6. A three-way mixed-design analysis of variance (Group × Age × Hand) was carried out for accuracy scores. Once again, Age was a significant factor ($F = 6.11$, df $= 2/68$, $p < 0.005$) indicating that accuracy scores increased with age. Group was not a significant factor, which indicates that the dyslexic boys did not differ from the normal boys in overall accuracy (right plus left hand scores). Group by Age was not a significant interaction indicating that there was no difference between groups in overall accuracy at any age.

Hand was not a significant factor, nor was the Hand by Age interaction. However Group by Hand was a significant interaction ($F = 9.97$, df $= 1/68$, $p < 0.005$), which was further analyzed by individual comparisons using Duncan Multiple Range Tests. For the normal group, the right-hand score

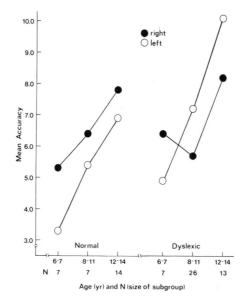

FIG. 6. Mean accuracy scores on dichhaptic stimulation with letters for normal and dyslexic boys.

was significantly greater than the left hand score (df $= 68, p < 0.05$). For the dyslexic group, a significant hand difference was found in the opposite direction: their left hand score was greater than their right hand score (df $= 68$, $p < 0.05$). Moreover, the left hand score of the dyslexics was significantly greater than the left-hand score of the normal group (df $= 68$, $p < 0.001$). However, right hand scores did not differ significantly between groups. The Group by Age by Hand interaction was not significant, indicating that the hand difference between groups was similar at all ages.

A χ^2 analysis of the number of children with greater left or right hand scores in each group indicated that the groups differed in terms of this measure as well ($\chi^2 = 7.62$, $p < 0.01$). More normal boys showed a right hand superiority and more dyslexic boys showed a left hand superiority.

Performance on this dichhaptic letters test was also analyzed for the side of the first letter named. This analysis of order of report was done in identical fashion to that described for the dichhaptic shapes test. Figure 7 presents these data for both groups of boys. A simple t-test for correlated means was done for each group. For the normal group, there was no difference between side of the first letter named (right and left scores were 2.7 and 2.2, respectively, $t = 0.84$). In contrast, for the dyslexic group, letters presented to the left hand were reported first more frequently than letters presented to the right hand (means scores were 3.7 versus 1.7, $t = 4.04$, df $= 45$, $p < 0.001$).

The group of dyslexic boys ($N = 83$) were compared to a matched group of normal boys ($N = 86$) on the tachistoscopic letters test, which may

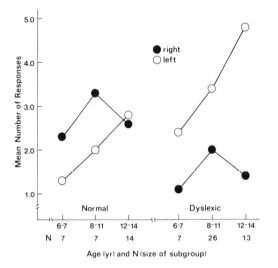

FIG. 7. Mean number of responses starting with left and right hand stimuli on dichhaptic letters for normal and dyslexic boys.

involve participation of both hemispheres. The results are presented in Fig. 8. A three-way mixed-design analysis of variance (Group by Age by Visual Field) indicated no significant main factors or interactions. However, visual inspection of the graphs suggests some field asymmetry differences between groups as a function of age. Young normal boys appear to show perceptual asymmetry in one direction and older dyslexic boys in the other direction. A simple t-test for correlated means indicated that for the youngest group of normal boys, accuracy for letters presented in the right field was significantly greater than for letters in the left field ($t = 3.16$, df $= 13$, $p < 0.01$). Thereafter, up until age 14, there was no significant field difference. For the dyslexics, no right field superiority was observed for the youngest group as it was for normal boys. The oldest dyslexic group showed a tendency for greater accuracy for letters in the left than right visual field ($t = 1.71$, df $= 21$, $p \doteq 0.10$).

Girls

The group of dyslexic girls ($N = 12$) was compared to a matched group of normal girls ($N = 27$) on the dichhaptic letters test. This task is considered to require some participation of each hemisphere for its specialized functions. However, as indicated previously, normal girls may have bilateral representation for spatial processing, whereas in normal boys the right hemisphere appears to have the major role in spatial processing. For these reasons, hand asymmetry on this task may be different for normal boys and girls. Therefore, again, it is most meaningful to compare the performance of the dyslexic girls to that of normal girls, and to determine if this com-

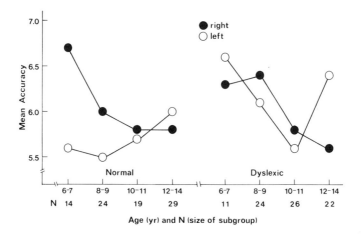

FIG. 8. Mean accuracy scores on tachistoscopic stimulation of letters in lateral half-fields for normal and dyslexic boys.

TABLE 4. *Mean accuracy scores on the dichhaptic letters test*

		Normal					Dyslexic			
		Hand					Hand			
	N	Right	Left	p	Total	N	Right	Left	p	Total
Girls	27	8.0	8.3	ns	16.2	12	7.2	8.6	>0.10	15.7
Boys	28	6.8	5.6	>0.10	12.5	46	6.5	7.7	0.01	14.2

Maximum score per hand is 20.

parison is similar to that for dyslexic boys and normal boys. The results for the girls on the dichhaptic letters test are presented in Table 4 along with the results for the total groups of boys for easy reference.

The normal girls showed no difference in accuracy between right and left hand letters. In contrast, the dyslexic girls showed a tendency toward greater left than right hand scores ($t = 1.41$, df = 11, $0.20 > p > 0.10$). Asymmetry in perception was further studied by analyzing performance on this task in respect to side of first response. This analysis is identical to that described above for boys on this test. For the normal girls, there was no difference in frequency of side of first named letter (right and left hand scores were 3.1 and 3.3, respectively). For the dyslexic girls, some bias in favor of the left hand was again noted (3.5 versus 2.4, $t = 1.31$, df = 11). This suggestion of a difference in favor of the left hand for dyslexic girls, but not for normal girls, is similar to the clearer difference observed between normal and dyslexic boys on this test.

The results in Table 4 also indicate that the dyslexic girls did not differ in total accuracy from normal girls (15.7 versus 16.2). The dyslexic girls' overall accuracy was also comparable to that of the dyslexic boys (15.7 versus 14.2; $t = 0.70$). However, overall accuracy for the normal girls was significantly greater than that for the normal boys ($t = 2.5$, df = 53, $p < 0.02$). This result may have implications for neural and cognitive differences between normal girls and normal boys. To the extent that the dichhaptic letters test may require cognitive processes similar to those required in reading, the results may have relevance for sex differences in reading ability.

DISCUSSION

Some general comments follow first. There has been considerable controversy as to whether the syndrome variously referred to as development dyslexia (e.g., 3,12,61), primary reading retardation (58), strephosymbolia (54), and congenital word-blindness (25), among other labels, exists as a disorder that is distinct from the many other more well-established childhood disorders associated with poor reading. It has been suggested also that the alleged syndrome is merely a result of "teaching disability," and that this subgroup is composed of children who are at the lower end of a normally distributed continuum of verbal ability (1). The position of this chapter is that the present sample of children with deficient reading ability, in whom other possible disorders were carefully excluded and who were subjected to the same educational programs as other children, the vast majority of whom do learn to read, does constitute a distinct group of children with some disorder of constitutional etiology.

The large majority of this group appears to be boys, as has been observed in many other reports (4,12). Most do have right-hand preference in contrast to the popular but unfounded notion that left handedness may itself indicate the presence of some learning problem. Finally, most of these children have a profile on the Wechsler Intelligence Scale for Children of considerably higher Performance than Verbal IQ, as has been frequently reported in other studies (4).

Neural Correlates

LEFT HEMISPHERE SPECIALIZATION

The dichotic stimulation task involving digits is well established as an index of lateralization of speech (30). Right ear superiority is considered to indicate left hemisphere specialization for speech and language functions. In the present study, a clear right ear superiority was observed for normal and dyslexic boys at all ages studied, from 6 to 14 years. Right ear superiority was also observed for the normal and dyslexic girls. On the basis of these data, it is suggested that the left hemisphere is the major hemisphere for speech and language in both male and female dyslexic children, as is the case in normal children. This conclusion of left lateralization of speech is consistent with the data of the previous studies reviewed earlier concerning cerebral dominance in children with reading difficulty.

This hypothesis must be restricted, however, to left hemisphere representation of language for only those aspects of linguistic processing that are required in the dichotic task used in the present research. The possibility remains that a different situation may exist for linguistic functions that require other levels of information processing (see 56), either simpler or earlier stages of linguistic processing, as for example with meaningless consonant-vowel syllables, or more difficult semantic and mnemonic processing, as with more complex words. To date, some evidence indicates left hemisphere specialization in dyslexics for simple linguistic functions as well (64). Moreover, it also remains to be determined whether other aspects of cognition that appear to be dependent on left hemisphere functioning, such as analytic processing (5) and temporal processing (9), have similar neural representation in normal and dyslexic children.

LEFT HEMISPHERE DYSFUNCTION

The conclusion of the normal pattern of specialization of the left hemisphere for language in dyslexia does not rule out the possibility that although it is mediating the typical cognitive process, its functioning *per se* may be deficient. Overall performance of the dyslexic group on the dichotic test, a task considered to be mediated predominantly by the left hemisphere, was markedly impaired compared to that of normal children. This was the case for both male and female dyslexics within the entire age range studied. This finding is consistent with the data of the previous studies of dichotic listening in learning-impaired children (although usually only boys were studied) in which total recall was also found to be impaired (41, 77,79,82).

Such depressed total recall of dichotic verbal stimulation is similar to that observed for preoperative as well as postoperative brain-damaged patients, but only for those with left (speech dominant) hemisphere lesions (27,28). On the basis of this similarity in performance, it is suggested that there may be some dysfunction in left hemisphere processing in dyslexics.

RIGHT HEMISPHERE SPECIALIZATION

The normal boys, even though right handed, showed a left hand superiority for accuracy and order of report on the dichhaptic shapes test, which is considered to reflect dominance of the right hemisphere for spatial form perception (72). The dyslexic boys, in contrast, showed no significant hand asymmetry on either response measure. It is suggested that the lack of performance asymmetry in the dyslexic boys indicates bilateral representation of spatial form perception.

This hypothesis is supported by a similar difference in performance between dyslexic and normal boys on the spatial task in the visual modality (tachistoscopic presentation of human figures). Again, the lack of a left visual field superiority in the dyslexic boys, in contrast to the left field superiority in the normal boys, suggests that in dyslexics the right hemisphere is not dominant for spatial perception but that there is bilateral representation of spatial processing.

What about this aspect of neural organization in dyslexic girls? This question is complicated by the fact that there appears to be a sexual dimorphism in the neural organization underlying spatial perception during a major period of childhood and perhaps also to some degree at maturity (73). In the present study, the dyslexic girls showed no hand asymmetry on the dichhaptic shapes in accuracy or in order of report. This is similar to the performance observed for normal girls. On the basis of these data it is suggested that dyslexic girls have bilateral hemisphere representation of spatial perception, as do normal girls. This suggestion must be considered tentative, however, since it is based on only a small sample of dyslexic girls and on only one set of data to date.

NEURAL SUBSTRATE OF DYSLEXIA: POSSIBLE SEX DIFFERENCE

In summary, the neural substrate of dyslexia in boys may be bilateral representation of spatial perception and dysfunction in the left-hemisphere processing of language functions. The question may be raised whether both neural correlates are necessary factors for dyslexia or whether either factor alone is sufficient. The results of the present study cannot clearly answer this question.

In the case that both factors are involved, the further question arises whether they are relatively independent factors, both manifestations of another but more antecedent factor; or, alternately, whether they are inter-dependent factors. It may be that the deficient functioning of the left hemisphere does not provide the necessary impetus or conditions for the occurrence of right hemisphere specialization for nonlinguistic spatial functions. Or a reverse situation may hold in which the bilateral representa-tion of spatial processing interferes with the left hemisphere's processing of linguistic functions. The idea here is that the left hemisphere is handicapped or overloaded by having to mediate both its native linguistic functions plus nonlinguistic spatial functions; by having to do double duty, as it were. The general idea that neural localization of function may exist because it is the most efficient manner for the brain to subserve different cognitive func-tions was suggested several decades ago by Lashley (39, p. 384): "cerebral localization is determined by the separation of such incompatible mecha-nisms." Levy (42) used this general idea to offer an explanation for the finding that left-handed individuals, in whom bilateral representation of speech is more frequent than in right-handed individuals, have lower spatial than verbal abilities. Specifically, the hypothesis is that spatial processing suffers because the right hemisphere is involved in two different types of cognitive processing, and the cognitive function inherent to the over-loaded hemisphere is the one that suffers.

In the case of dyslexia in girls, it appears that the neural substrate may involve only one factor, deficient left hemisphere functioning. Embryo-logical evidence indicates that early in fetal life male and female brains are similar, but subsequently hormonal factors come into effect and the male brain becomes differentiated from the previous more general form (e.g., 23). In this context there may be fewer events in the course of female neural development which can occur incorrectly. Specialization of the right hemisphere for the spatial, holistic mode of cognitive processing may be one such event.

Thus we may have a situation in which either left hemisphere dysfunction, or a lack of functional specialization of the right hemisphere, or possibly either neural factor and its effects on the other hemisphere may be a sufficient substrate for the manifestation of dyslexia in boys. In contrast, in girls, it may be that only the factor of left hemisphere dysfunction is sufficient for dyslexia. Such a situation could underlie the well-established fact that dyslexia occurs much more frequently in males than females. It also has been suggested elsewhere (73) that the lack of right hemisphere specialization for spatial perception in girls may be associated with greater functional plasticity of the right hemisphere in girls than in boys. This may be another factor related to the lower incidence of dyslexia in females.

The question may be raised as to why bilateral representation of spatial processing may be associated with dyslexia in boys, as suggested here, but is also hypothesized to be the typical neural organization in normal girls who have no reading problems. This situation may appear paradoxical at first. If one considers, however, that there may be a sexual dimorphism in the neural organization between normal boys and girls—in other words, that the brain may be a sex organ—then it follows that what may be satisfactory for one sex may not be for the other, as is the case with other sex organs. From a different viewpoint, it may be that dyslexia in boys is associated not only with bilateral spatial representation, but also with deficient left hemisphere functioning. Normal females have no deficient left hemisphere.

The neural factors proposed as a substrate of developmental dyslexia appear to be present in dyslexics as late as adolescence. However, specialization of the right hemisphere for spatial perception has been demonstrated as early as 6 years and may exist by birth in normal boys (73,75). In this context, it is difficult to conceive of the suggested lack of right hemisphere specialization in dyslexic boys as a lag in neural maturation, a neural model postulated by several authors (e.g., 33,61). A difference in neural organization between normal and dyslexic children for at least 15 years hardly seems a lag, but rather a qualitative difference. Moreover, a dysfunctioning left hemisphere suggested as another possible neural correlate of dyslexia also does not readily fit a model of neural maturational lag but rather one of a neural deficit.

However, a neural deficit hypothesis does not preclude the manifestation of a lag in the development of cognitive skills. In fact, most disorders result in test performance that is at least superficially comparable to that of normal children at some earlier chronological age. It is this general observation that seems to have led to the maturational lag postulate. But such a model implies that individuals, such as dyslexics, eventually catch up and become normal, a situation for which there is no empirical support. The logical difficulty of such a model may be noted by taking the example of intellectually retarded children, whose mental age can be equated to that of children of some earlier chronological age, but who certainly do not eventually become normal. The logical fallacy of inferring a neural lag from an observed lag in cognitive development may be seen more clearly if one considers the reverse situation. Within this framework, one would be led to conclude that the 3-year-old normal child whose language is at the same developmental level as that of a 12-year-old autistic child has a developmental lag, and by age 12 the normal child will become autistic.

Dyslexia was defined in the present study as reading disability in individuals with no known neurological damage. Children with birth histories that could be considered at high risk for neural trauma were not excluded as there is no perfect correlation between high-risk births and demonstrable neural effects. Considerable evidence indicates that many children with such births subsequently show no signs of neural damage (e.g., 21). Of the total group of 100 dyslexic children, birth records were obtainable for 87. Many had no reported birth complications at all. However, a large majority of the group did. Factors that were noted very frequently were subclinical (physiological) jaundice as well as clinical jaundice, and also a high incidence of mothers with Rh negative blood. The birth records of a group of normal children known to have adequate academic and intellectual ability, and matched to the dyslexic group for age, socioeconomic status, and geographic area of birth were available for study. Only a small proportion of these cases showed any high-risk birth factors. Given the imprecise nature of such retrospective records, the results must be considered cautiously. It is possible, however, that what is currently considered medically to be a subclinical level of hyperbilirubinemia is not without subsequent effects.

The results of the analysis of the birth histories also suggest that the hypothesized neural deficit in dyslexia may have a heterogeneous etiology. Zangwill (80) made a similar suggestion. In some cases of dyslexia there may be an acquired constitutional factor that has been suggested by many authors for some time now (55), but in other cases there may be a built-in genetic factor. The notion of a hereditary component in dyslexia is also not a new concept. Most recently the studies of Finucci and colleagues (16) have found evidence to support a hereditary factor in dyslexia. However, to date, the mode of genetic transmission of dyslexia has not been delineated. This may be because diagnosis of cases of developmental dyslexia in children, and perhaps even more so in the adult family members, is without precision, and therefore the identification of affected individuals carries considerable errors of inclusion and omission. Moreover, there may be more than one genotype of developmental dyslexia, both within and between sexes, but without clear phenotypic separation.

AGE FACTORS

The group of dyslexic boys was sufficiently large that age could be studied as a possibly relevant factor in patterns of hemisphere specialization in dyslexia. The statistical analyses indicated that age was not a significant factor in differentiating dyslexic from normal children on any of the perceptual tasks, either on overall performance or on left-right perceptual asymmetry. However, visual inspection of the graphs suggests a consistency concerning right-left asymmetry that warrants some comment. Unfortunately, the youngest dyslexic subgroup was smaller than the other age subgroups, and this may have led to the lack of statistical significance or to unreliable findings.

On most tests the youngest group of dyslexics tended to differ from their matched control groups in a different direction than did the older dyslexics from their control groups. On the dichotic digits test, in which the total groups both showed right ear superiority, the young dyslexics tended to show less ear asymmetry compared to normals. In contrast, on the dichhaptic shapes, tachistoscopic figures, and dichhaptic letters tests, in which the total groups of dyslexic boys differed in perceptual asymmetry from the normal boys, the young dyslexics tended to show a behavioral asymmetry in the same direction as the young normal children which was opposite in direction compared to the difference between older dyslexics and normals. These results suggest that the young dyslexics may be a different type or subgroup of dyslexics. Because of their early age at the time of referral, their deficits may well be different from those of the children referred at a later age. In this regard, Benton (3) also has suggested that young dyslexics (up to about 8 years) may exhibit symptoms different from those of older dyslexics, with the former showing visuospatial perceptual difficulties and the latter verbal difficulties. Satz and Sparrow (61) made a similar suggestion. Such speculations are not inconsistent with the data of the present study.

Alternately, it is possible that the performance differences between the younger and older dyslexics merely reflect a different manifestation of the same dysfunction at different stages of development. Changes in neural organization, particularly in interhemispheric communication, occur during this period of childhood and these may lead to the different patterns of right-left asymmetry observed in the different dyslexic subgroups. Yakovlev and Lecours (78) have suggested that myelination of the corpus callosum is complete by about age 10 years, and this is the age at which the differences between the dyslexic and normal groups appear to reverse. Study is presently in progress concerning the possibility that the group of young dyslexics is a different subgroup. This group is being retested now that they are comparable in age to the other dyslexics.

HEMISPHERE AND COGNITIVE BIAS

Two of the experimental tests of perception involved the possibility of either or both types of cognitive processing (linguistic and spatial) and therefore the contribution of either or both hemispheres. On the dichhaptic letters test the normal boys showed greater right hand accuracy. These results are suggested to indicate that although some spatial processing was necessarily involved, the major cognitive mode used, perhaps the strategy of choice, was the linguistic cognitive mode mediated by the left hemisphere. In contrast, the dyslexic boys showed a clear left-hand superiority, both in accuracy and in order of report of response. In the case of the dyslexics, although some linguistic processing was obviously necessary in order to name the letters, the left hand superiority suggests that the predominant hemisphere involved was the right hemisphere. What this could indicate may not be immediately discernible. One hypothesis considered was that the right hemisphere in dyslexics is doing what the left hemisphere does in normals, that is, predominantly linguistic processing on this task. This is untenable, however, in view of the findings from the dichotic listening task, which indicate that the left hemisphere is the language hemisphere in both normal and dyslexic children. Another suggestion considered was that the right hemisphere does both types of processing in dyslexics and this accounts for the marked left hand superiority of dyslexics on this task. But this too is unlikely in view of the results from the dichotic digits test.

One possible interpretation, and the only one I can think of at this point, is as follows. The right hemisphere is not the language hemisphere in dyslexics, nor is it the major hemisphere for spatial perception, but it is involved in spatial processing as indicated in the dichhaptic shapes and tachistoscopic figures tests. Therefore the right hemisphere predominance on the dichhaptic letters test may indicate that the major cognitive mode used by dyslexics on this task involved spatial processing. Furthermore, perhaps in general there is a cognitive strategy bias in dyslexics to focus on spatial processing wherever possible. The question then arises, why should the right hemisphere be the major spatial processor on this task when this was not the case for the other "purer" spatial tasks (dichhaptic shapes and tachistoscopic figures)? A possible explanation of this situation follows. Language functions may be lateralized to the left hemisphere in dyslexia, but they appear to be processed very poorly. The dichhaptic letters test differs from the other spatial tasks in that in the former some linguistic processing is necessary. Given that left hemisphere functioning is deficient in dyslexics, the linguistic processing required on the dichhaptic letters test may be sufficient to tax the left hemisphere's functioning and prevent it from engaging in spatial processing, thus leaving the spatial processing to be done by the right hemisphere in this case. And if dyslexic boys are deficient in left-hemisphere linguistic processing, this may lead them to the cognitive bias of using spatial processing as much as possible.

The results of the dyslexic and normal boys on the tachistoscopic letters test support these speculations, although the results are less clear. The young normal boys show a right field superiority and, by inference, a left hemisphere linguistic analysis of this task, but this disappears with age. This may reflect a bias, given the opportunity, for children to process letters linguistically at an age when they are in the primary school grades and are first learning to use letters as linguistic symbols. With age and further experience, the letters may become so overlearned and unrelated to total word recognition that visual pictorial processing of letters is preferred. The dyslexic children never show a right field superiority for visual letters but with age tend to show a left field effect. Perhaps dyslexic children never readily process letters phonetically as do normals and thus do not show a left hemisphere predominance. With continued exposure over the years, they may become familiar with letters, but as pictures rather than sound symbols. This may result in the tendency of the older dyslexics to show a left field superiority for visual letters, reflecting a right hemisphere spatial strategy approach. Dyslexic children have less marked left field superiority for tachistoscopic letters as compared to dichhaptic letters perhaps because the visual letters test may allow scope for linguistic processing but does not require it in each trial, but the dichhaptic letters test does require linguistic processing.

Is there evidence that this hemisphere and associated cognitive bias is present in female dyslexics as well? Normal girls show no hand asymmetry on the dichhaptic letters test. Given that girls show an earlier and more accelerated language development in childhood than boys (44), one might have expected a right-hand superiority and, by inference, a left hemisphere linguistic predominance at least as great as in boys. Perhaps because of their greater linguistic development this task is a simpler linguistic task for them and thus requires less participation of the left hemisphere. That this task is a simpler task for girls is supported by the finding that the overall accuracy for the girls on this task was significantly greater than that for the boys. And this was the only task for which there was a sex difference in overall accuracy between normal groups. However, it is noted that this is only one possible *post hoc* explanation.

The dyslexic girls tended to perform differently from the normal girls, in a manner consistent to that of the dyslexic boys. They tended to show greater accuracy for left hand stimuli and more frequent first reports of left hand letters. This performance may be owing to factors similar to those suggested for dyslexic boys. Spatial processing appears bilaterally represented in dyslexic girls, although this is suggested to be the typical neural organization for normal girls. On a task involving both types of cognitive processing, as in the dichhaptic letters test, the linguistic processing may completely engage the capacities of the deficient left hemisphere, leaving spatial processing to be mediated by the right hemisphere. The poor linguistic processing may lead to a bias to use the spatial cognitive strategy wherever possible. Thus in terms of hemisphere and cognitive strategy bias, male and female dyslexics may be similar.

Neural Organization and Cognitive Ability

The question arises as to what relationship the hypothesized neural correlates of dyslexia could have to the level of cognitive ability and to reading in particular. For example, is bilateral representation of spatial processing associated with difficulties in cognition, such as spatial perception? The present study provides some data relevant to such questions. A rather consistent profile of cognitive skills was observed for dyslexic children. On those tasks in which the normal pattern of hemisphere specialization was observed, overall level of performance of the dyslexic children was impaired relative to that of normal children, but, in contrast, on those tasks in which an atypical pattern of lateralization of function was observed, overall level of performance was definitely as good as that of the normal children. This pattern of deficits in cognitive skills which show normal lateralization and no deficits in those skills which do not show typical lateralization may seem surprising, even illogical. However, this is not necessarily so. There is no evidence, even for normal individuals, that atypical patterns of neural representation of cognitive functions are associated with impaired ability of those functions.

On the tasks involving spatial perception (dichhaptic shapes, tachistoscopic figures, and dichhaptic letters), the dyslexic boys showed atypical lateralization of function, but their overall accuracy was at least equal to that of the normal boys. Good spatial ability in the dyslexic boys is corroborated by their mean WISC Performance IQ of 106.9, which is well within the normal range, and by their performance on the WISC Block Design subtest, which is at least average and comparable to that of the matched control group (mean scores were 11.3 and 11.9, respectively, $t = 1.30$, df $= 239$). The dyslexic girls also showed adequate spatial ability on both the dichhaptic shapes and dichhaptic letters tests, and on the WISC Performance IQ ($\bar{X} = 108.6$) and Block Design subtest ($\bar{X} = 10.6$), which is comparable to that of the normal girls ($\bar{X} = 10.4$). However, the dyslexic girls did not differ from normal girls in neural organization for spatial perception.

On the one experimental test involving only linguistic processing (dichotic digits), both dyslexic boys and dyslexic girls showed the typical pattern of left hemisphere specialization for language functions. However, both groups were significantly impaired in level of overall performance on this task. Poor linguistic ability in dyslexics is also corroborated by their lower Verbal than Performance WISC IQ scores (boys: 97.4 versus 106.9, $t = 5.49$, df $= 84$, $p < 0.001$; girls: 94.1 versus 108.6, $t = 5.06$, df $= 14$, $p < 0.001$). Moreover, WISC Vocabulary scores were lower in both dyslexic groups compared to the normal children (boys: 10.2 versus 11.4, $t = 3.44$, df $= 239$, $p < 0.001$; girls: 9.7 versus 10.9, $t = 1.78$, df $= 86$, $0.10 > p > 0.05$).

Impaired linguistic ability may be a result of left hemisphere dysfunction *per se* postulated for both male and female dyslexics. Or, in the case of boys, it may also be owing to overload or interference in left hemisphere functioning resulting from bilateral representation of spatial perception. Thus deficient left hemisphere functioning and associated impaired linguistic processing may result from two different factors in dyslexic boys, but from only one factor in dyslexic girls. This situation may be one reason for the more frequent occurrence of the disorder in boys than in girls.

If linguistic processing is impaired, the preference for a spatial cognitive strategy wherever possible, as suggested previously, becomes quite reasonable. This preference for spatial processing, however, may be the most immediate factor in causing reading difficulty in these children. Reading, particularly learning to read, likely involves both types of cognitive processes: linguistic processing to decode letters phonetically and spatial processing to recognize whole words visually. Dyslexics may focus on the latter, the visuospatial approach to reading. But perhaps one cannot read (English) by spatial processing alone.

If these speculations are valid, one might predict that dyslexics would have less difficulty with those written languages (orthographies) which involve little or no phonetic coding of the visual symbols but mainly spatial processing, no matter how complex. Consequently, cultures with such languages may have a lower incidence of dyslexia. There is some support for these predictions. Rozin and colleagues (59) have shown that a group of children who were very poor English readers (specific diagnosis is not clear) were readily able to learn to read Chinese logographs, individually and in paragraphs, within several hours of instruction. Makita (45) has reported that the incidence of dyslexia in Japanese children is very low, less than 1%. Japanese orthographies involve more spatial and less phonetic processing than does English.

It is suggested that to the extent that reading a language requires a cognitive process deficient in dyslexic children, reading will be deficient and will manifest as part of the clinical syndrome. But if the orthography involved does not require the deficient cognitive process, there will be no reading difficulty although the cognitive disability will still be present. For this reason the disorder referred to as developmental dyslexia may be more precisely described as "specific cognitive deficit."

Finally, it is noted that linguistic deficits may be the cognitive profile in the majority of dyslexics. However, there may be other subgroups of dyslexia, with different cognitive profiles. For example, it was tentatively suggested that those dyslexics diagnosed at a young age may be a different subgroup, and in some dyslexics the main deficit has been described as visuospatial, as in Myklebust's (52) visual dyslexics, Boder's (6) dyseidetic dyslexics, and Mattis and colleagues' (47) dyslexics with visuo-perceptual disorder.

Practical Implication

Reading may be somewhat analogous to the dichhaptic letters test in that both tasks may require the two types of cognitive processing. It was observed that although dyslexics may use a different cognitive approach to the task than do normals, the overall level of accuracy was comparable for both groups. The linguistic processing required for the dichhaptic letters test is clearly less demanding than that required in reading. However, to the extent that an analogy between the two tasks may be drawn, it may be a worthwhile endeavor to try to design an approach to reading which has that balance between linguistic processing (the phonetic approach) and spatial processing (the "look-say" method of teaching reading) that would allow dyslexics to master reading as well as they do the dichhaptic letters test. Such a balance would have to take into consideration (a) the level of each cognitive mode of which dyslexics are capable and (b) what minimal requirements in each cognitive mode are essential to read English effectively.

ACKNOWLEDGMENTS

The research reported in this chapter has been supported by the Ontario Mental Health Foundation Research Grant No. 322. I also acknowledge support from the U.S. National Institute of Mental Health Research Training Grant in Biological Psychiatry at New York University School of Medicine (No. MH 08638) for the Postdoctoral Research Fellowship during which many of the issues of this research were formulated. I would like to thank the members of the Wentworth County Roman Catholic Separate School Board, particularly Principal R. Peet, for generous cooperation in allowing such extensive testing of their students; the clinicians who referred their patients to the research project; and of course the dyslexic children and their families who gave so willingly of their time and effort. I am also indebted to Hope Evenden, Marilyn Irvine, and Janice Swallow who did most of the testing and some of the data analyses; to Robert MacFarlane for the birth records of his normal subjects; and to Elaine Laxton for her help in typing the many drafts of this paper, and to Diane Clews for her skill and devotion in finalizing this manuscript.

REFERENCES

1. Bannatyne, A. D. (1966): The aetiology of dyslexia. *The Slow Learning Child,* 13:20–34.
2. Benson, D. F., and Geschwind, N. (1969): The alexias. In: *Handbook of Clinical Neurology, Vol. 4: Disorders of Speech Perception, and Symbolic Behaviour,* edited by P. J. Vinken and G. W. Bruyn, pp. 112–140. North-Holland Publishing Co., New York.
3. Benton, A. L. (1962): Dyslexia in relation to form perception and directional sense. In: *Reading Disability. Progress and Research Needs in Dyslexia,* edited by J. Money, pp. 81–102. Johns Hopkins Press, Baltimore.
4. Benton, A. L. (1975): Developmental dyslexia: Neurological aspects. In: *Advances in Neurology, Vol. 7,* edited by J. Friedlander, pp. 1–47. Raven Press, New York.
5. Bever, T. G. (1975): Cerebral asymmetries in humans are due to the differentiation of two incompatible processes: holistic and analytic. Developmental psycholinguistics and communication disorders. *Ann. N.Y. Acad. Sci.,* 263:251–262.

6. Boder, E. (1973): Developmental dyslexia: A diagnostic approach based on three atypical reading-spelling patterns. *Dev. Med. Child Neurol.,* 15:663–687.
7. Bryden, M. P. (1962): Order of report in dichotic listening. *Can. J. Psychol.,* 16:291–299.
8. Bryden, M. P. (1970): Laterality effects in dichotic listening: Relations with handedness and reading ability in children. *Neuropsychologia,* 8:443–450.
9. Carmon, A., and Nachshon, I. (1971): Effect of unilateral brain damage on perception of temporal order. *Cortex,* 7:410–418.
10. Cohen, G. (1972): Hemisphere differences in a letter classification task. *Percept. Psychophysiol.,* 11:139–142.
11. Conrad, R. (1972): Speech and reading. In: *Language by Ear and by Eye,* edited by J. F. Kavanagh and I. G. Mattingly, pp. 205–240. MIT Press, Cambridge.
12. Critchley, M. (1970): *The Dyslexic Child.* Heinemann, London.
13. Dimond, S. J., and Beaumont, J. G. (Eds.) (1974): *Hemisphere Function in the Human Brain.* Elek Science, London.
14. Douglas, V. I. (1972): Stop, look and listen: The problem of sustained attention and impulse control in hyperactive and normal children. *Can. J. Behav. Sci.,* 4:259–282.
15. Duncan, D. G. (1955): Multiple range and multiple F tests. *Biometrics,* 11:1–42.
16. Finucci, J. M., Guthrie, J. T., Childs, A. L., Abbey, H., and Childs, B. (1976): The genetics of specific reading disability. *Ann. Hum. Genet.,* 40:1–23.
17. Fisher, J. H. (1910): Congenital word blindness. Inability to learn to read. *Trans. Ophthalmol. Soc. U.K.,* 30:216–225.
18. Frank, J., and Levinson, H. (1973): Dysmetric dyslexia and dyspraxia. Hypothesis and study. *J. Child Psychiatry,* 12:690–701.
19. Fry, E. (1968): Do-it-yourself terminology generator. *J. Reading,* 12:428.
20. Geffen, G., Bradshaw, J. L., and Nettleton, N. C. (1972): Hemispheric asymmetry: Verbal and spatial encoding of visual stimuli. *J. Exp. Psychol.,* 95:25–31.
21. Graham, F. K., Ernhart, C. B., Thurston, D., and Craft, M. (1962): Development three years after perinatal anoxia and other potentially damaging newborn experiences. *Psychol. Monogr,* 76:(3, Whole No. 522).
22. Harris, A. J. (1958): *Harris Tests of Lateral Dominance, 3rd Ed.* Psychological Corporation, New York.
23. Harris, G. W., and Levine, S. (1965): Sexual differentiation of the brain and its experimental control. *J. Physiol.,* 181:379–400.
24. Hécaen, H., and Sauguet, J. (1971): Cerebral dominance in left-handed subjects. *Cortex,* 7:19–48.
25. Hinshelwood, J. (1917): *Congenital Word-blindness.* Lewis, London.
26. Jastak, J. F., and Jastak, S. R. (1965): *The Wide Range Achievement Test.* Guidance Associates, Wilmington, Delaware.
27. Kimura, D. (1961*a*): Some effects of temporal-lobe damage on auditory perception. *Can. J. Psychol.,* 15:156–165.
28. Kimura, D. (1961*b*): Cerebral dominance and the perception of verbal stimuli. *Can J. Psychol.,* 15:166–171.
29. Kimura, D. (1966): Dual functional asymmetry of the brain in visual perception. *Neuropsychologia,* 4:275–285.
30. Kimura, D. (1967): Functional asymmetry of the brain in dichotic listening. *Cortex,* 3:163–178.
31. Kimura, D. (1969): Spatial localization in left and right visual fields. *Can. J. Psychol.,* 23:445–457.
32. Kimura, D., and Durnford, M. (1974): Normal studies on the function of the right hemisphere in vision. In: *Hemisphere Function in the Human Brain,* edited by S. J. Dimond and J. G. Beaumont, pp. 25–47. Elek Science, London.
33. Kinsbourne, M. (1973): Minimal brain dysfunction as a neurodevelopmental lag. In: *Minimal Brain Dysfunction,* edited by F. Fode la Cruz, B. H. Fox, and R. H. Roberts. *Ann. N.Y. Acad. Sci.,* 205:268–273.
34. Kinsbourne, M., and Warrington, E. K. (1962): A variety of reading disability associated with right hemisphere lesions. *J. Neurol. Neurosurg. Psychiatry,* 25:339–344.
35. Kinsbourne, M., and Warrington, E. K. (1963): Developmental factors in reading and writing backwardness. *Br. J. Psychol.,* 54:145–156.

36. Krashen, S. D. (1975): The critical period for language acquisition and its possible bases. Developmental psycholinguistics and communication disorders. *Ann. N.Y. Acad. Sci.,* 263:211–224.
37. Lake, D. A., and Bryden, M. P. (1976): Handedness and sex differences in hemispheric asymmetry. *Brain Lang.,* 3:266–282.
38. Lansdell, H. (1962): A sex difference in effect of temporal-lobe neurosurgery on design preference. *Nature,* 194:852–854.
39. Lashley, K. S. (1937): Functional determinants of cerebral localization. *Arch. Neurol. Psychiatry,* 38:371–387.
40. Lenneberg, E. (1967): *Biological Foundations of Language.* John Wiley & Sons, New York.
41. Leong, C. K. (1976): Lateralization in severely disabled readers in relation to functional cerebral development and synthesis of information. In: *The Neuropsychology of Learning Disorders: Theoretical Approaches,* edited by R. Knights and D. Bakker, pp. 221–231. University Park Press, Baltimore.
42. Levy, J. (1969): Possible basis for the evolution of lateral specialization of the human brain. *Nature,* 224:614–615.
43. Levy, J. (1976): Variations in writing posture and cerebral organization (*submitted for publication*).
44. Maccoby, E. E. (1966): *The Development of Sex Differences.* Stanford University Press, Stanford, California.
45. Makita, K. (1968): The rarity of reading disability in Japanese children. *Am. J. Orthopsychiatry,* 38:599–614.
46. Marcel, T., Katz, L., and Smith, M. (1974): Laterality and reading proficiency. *Neuropsychologia,* 12:131–139.
47. Mattis, S., Franch, J. H., and Rapin, I. (1975): Dyslexia in children and young adults: Three independent neuropsychological syndromes. *Dev. Med. Child Neurol.,* 17:150–163.
48. McGlone, J., and Davidson, W. (1973): The relation between cerebral speech laterality and spatial ability with special reference to sex and hand preference. *Neuropsychologia,* 11:105–113.
49. McKeever, W. F., and Huling, M. D. (1970): Lateral dominance in tachistoscopic word recognitions of children at two levels of ability. *Q. J. Exp. Psychol.,* 22:600–604.
50. McKeever, W. F., and VanDeventer, A. D. (1975): Dyslexic adolescents: Evidence of impaired visual and auditory language processing associated with normal lateralization and visual responsivity. *Cortex,* 11:361–378.
51. Mountcastle, V. B. (Ed.) (1962): *Interhemispheric Relations and Cerebral Dominance.* Johns Hopkins Press, Baltimore.
52. Myklebust, H. (1965): *Development and Disorders of Written Language, Vol. 1: Picture Story Language Test.* Grune & Stratton, New York.
53. Olson, M. E. (1973): Laterality differences in tachistoscopic word recognition in normal and delayed readers in elementary school. *Neuropsychologia,* 11:343–350.
54. Orton, S. T. (1937): *Reading, Writing and Speech Problems in Children.* W. W. Norton, New York.
55. Pasamanick, B., and Knobloch, H. (1966): Retrospective studies on the epidemiology of reproductive casuality: Old and new. *Merrill-Palmer Q. Behav. Devel.,* 12:7–26.
56. Porter, R. J., Jr., and Berlin, C. I. (1975): On interpreting developmental changes in the dichotic right-ear advantage. *Brain Lang.,* 2:186–200.
57. Posner, M. I., and Mitchell, R. F. (1967): Chronometric analysis of classification. *Psychol. Rev.,* 74:392–409.
58. Rabinovitch, R. D., Drew, A. L., de Jong, R. N., Ingram, W., and Withey, L. (1956): A research approach to reading retardation. In: *Neurology and Psychiatry in Childhood, Vol. 34.* Research publications of the Association for Research in Nervous and Mental Disease. Williams & Wilkins, Baltimore.
59. Rozin, P., Poritsky, S., and Sotsky, R. (1971): American children with reading problems can easily learn to read English represented by Chinese characters. *Science,* 171:1264–1267.
60. Satz, P. (1976): Cerebral dominance and reading disability: An old problem revisited. In: *The Neuropsychology of Learning Disorders: Theoretical Approaches,* edited by R. Knights and D. J. Bakker, pp. 273–294. University Park Press, Baltimore.

61. Satz, P., and Sparrow, S. S. (1970): Specific developmental dyslexia: A theoretical formulation. In: *Specific Reading Disability. Advances in Theory and Method,* edited by D. J. Bakker and P. Satz, pp. 17–40. Rotterdam University Press, Rotterdam.
62. Satz, P., Rardin, D., and Ross, J. (1971): An evaluation of a theory of specific developmental dyslexia. *Child Dev.,* 42:2009–2021.
63. Smith, F. (1971): *Understanding Reading.* Holt, Rinehart and Winston, New York.
64. Sobotka, K. R. (1974): Neuropsychological and neurophysiological correlates of developmental dyslexia. Master's thesis, University of New Orleans.
65. Sommers, R. K., and Taylor, M. L. (1972): Cerebral speech dominance in language-disordered and normal children. *Cortex,* 8:224–232.
66. Sparrow, S., and Satz, P. (1970): Dyslexia, laterality and neuropsychological development. In: *Specific Reading Disability: Advances in Theory and Method,* edited by D. J. Bakker and P. Satz, pp. 41–60. Rotterdam University Press, Rotterdam.
67. Sperry, R. W. (1971): How a developing brain gets itself properly wired for adaptive function. In: *The Biopsychology of Development,* edited by E. Tobach, L. R. Aronson, and E. Shaw, pp. 27–42. Academic Press, New York.
68. Terman, L. M., and Merrill, M. A. (1960): *Stanford-Binet Intelligence Scale: Manual for the 3rd Revision, Form L-M.* Houghton Mifflin Co., Boston.
69. Wechsler, D. (1949): *Wechsler Intelligence Scale for Children. Manual.* Psychological Corporation, New York.
70. Wender, P. H. (1971): *Minimal Brain Dysfunction in Children.* Wiley-Interscience, New York.
71. WIRT Stereopsis Test (1960): Titmus Optical Co., Petersburg, Virginia.
72. Witelson, S. F. (1974): Hemisphere specialization for linguistic and nonlinguistic tactual perception using a dichotomous stimulation technique. *Cortex,* 11:3–17.
73. Witelson, S. F. (1976a): Sex and the single hemisphere: right hemisphere specialization for spatial processing. *Science,* 193:425–427.
74. Witelson, S. F. (1976b): Abnormal right hemisphere specialization in developmental dyslexia. In: *The Neuropsychology of Learning Disorders: Theoretical Approaches,* edited by R. Knights and D. Bakker, pp. 232–256. University Park Press, Baltimore.
75. Witelson, S. F. (1976c): Early hemisphere specialization and interhemisphere plasticity: An empirical and theoretical review. In: *Language Development and Neurological Theory,* edited by S. Segalowitz and F. Gruber. Academic Press, New York.
76. Witelson, S. F., and Rabinovitch, M. S. (1971): Children's recall strategies in dichotic listening. *J. Exp. Child Psychol.,* 12:106–113.
77. Witelson, S. F., and Rabinovitch, M. S. (1972): Hemispheric speech lateralization in children with auditory-linguistic deficits. *Cortex,* 8:412–426.
78. Yakovlev, P. I., and Lecours, A. R. (1967): The myelogenetic cycles of regional maturation in the brain. In: *Regional Development of the Brain in Early Life,* edited by A. Minowski, pp. 3–70. Blackwell, Oxford.
79. Yeni-Komshian, G. H., Isenberg, S., and Goldberg, H. (1975): Cerebral dominance and reading disability: Left visual field deficit in poor readers. *Neuropsychologia,* 13:83–94.
80. Zangwill, O. L. (1962): Dyslexia in relation to cerebral dominance. In: *Reading Disability,* edited by J. Money, pp. 103–113. Johns Hopkins Press, Baltimore.
81. Zurif, E. B., and Bryden, M. P. (1969): Familial handedness and left-right differences in auditory and visual perception. *Neuropsychologia,* 7:179–188.
82. Zurif, E. B., and Carson, G. (1970): Dyslexia in relation to cerebral dominance and temporal analysis. *Neuropsychologia,* 8:351–362.

Psychopathology and Brain Dysfunction, edited by C. Shagass, S. Gershon, and A. J. Friedhoff. Raven Press, New York © 1977.

Subcortical Brain Function Correlates of Psychopathology and Epilepsy

Robert G. Heath

Department of Psychiatry and Neurology, Tulane University School of Medicine, New Orleans, Louisiana 70112

By relating data from studies in experimental animals to signs and symptoms of patients, we evolved a therapeutic rationale that was fundamental in developing methods for implantation of brain electrodes into specific subcortical nuclear sites of human subjects (3). These therapeutic methods, which we have used in patients since 1950, permit recordings from deep and surface brain sites, as well as repeated treatment by electrical or chemical stimulation, or both, for as long as 3 years. Over the past 26 years, a wealth of recording data have been obtained from patients while their mental activity, as reflected in verbal reports of thoughts and feelings, was simultaneously monitored during vacillating behavioral states.

Our patients have had a variety of psychiatric and neurologic disorders that have been resistant to commonly used therapy. Many of the patients were intermittently psychotic, and a few were continuously psychotic. In some, the psychosis was a consequence of schizophrenia. In other patients, psychosis was a result of other disorders affecting the brain. Within the patient series, all clinical subcategories of epilepsy were represented. The group also included patients with intractable pain, who were free of conventional behavioral pathology, as well as patients with other disorders. The data from the nonpsychotic and nonepileptic patients are important to this chapter only in providing additional control for the findings we obtained in psychotic and epileptic patients.

A review of the aggregate of our data yielded certain significant correlations between brain function and emotional state, the most consistent having been obtained during (a) the psychotic state, (b) pleasurable or painful emotional states, and (c) epileptic seizures. Moreover, the brain sites where activity correlated with specific emotional states proved to be the same as those involved in epileptic seizures.

Obviously, investigations of the *mind* can be carried out only in human subjects capable of reporting thoughts and feelings (reported introspection). Only in human subjects, therefore, in whom brain activity and behavior (subjective as well as objective components) can be explored simultaneously, can meaningful correlations be made between brain function and behavior (which must include activity of the mind).

In our patients, findings suggested that brain mechanisms involved in emotion and in epileptic seizures do not coincide with those conventionally presented in scientific publications (10–12). In our laboratories for the past several years, studies designed to delineate those brain mechanisms significant in emotion have led to demonstration of previously undescribed anatomic connections, and to identification of brain sites not previously thought to be implicated in emotional expression (10–12).

This chapter reviews some of the significant data we have collected from patients and describes how they have been extended to "animal models" in which functional interrelations have been shown among certain brain sites that are proving important in both emotional expression and epilepsy.

STUDIES IN PATIENTS

The brain sites at which activity correlates with altered emotion, as well as with epileptic seizures, are the septal region, hippocampus, and amygdala, all of which have been shown by a variety of studies to be interconnected (4,6,11,16–20). Further, the septal region, whose activation is associated with pleasure, has been shown to be the most critical. On the other hand, when the septal region functions abnormally, the emotional correlate is the antithesis of pleasure—that is, pain. Activation of the interrelated hippocampus is likewise associated with painful emotion. The third key site revealed by our studies, the amygdala, functions partly in congruity with the septal region (during pleasurable emotion) and partly with the hippocampus (during painful emotion). Although these same three brain sites (septal region, hippocampus, and amygdala) have been shown to be involved in the propagation of epileptic seizures, their activity during seizures is unlike that recorded during fluctuating emotional states.

Deep and Surface Recordings During Psychotic Behavior

The psychotic state is a syndrome that can be generated by a variety of causes, of which schizophrenia is probably the most common. Whereas some of its features are constant, others may differ with the underlying cause. The psychotic state is characterized by gross impairment of feelings and emotional expression, a fluctuating level of (sometimes profound reduction in) psychologic awareness, and disturbances in sensory perception. When the cause is schizophrenia, the altered emotionality is manifested by defective integration of pleasurable feelings, often associated with excessively painful (emergency) behavior. In our series of patients prepared with deep and surface electrodes, the psychotic state has invariably been associated with abnormal recordings (spikes and slow waves) from the septal region (6,11,16,18). Particularly when the etiology of the psychosis was other than schizophrenia, other brain regions (usually connected directly with the septal region) were sometimes also involved.

A number of epileptic patients in our series have displayed interictal psychotic behavior. Characteristically, their electroencephalograms (EEGs) were dominated by aberrant activity in deep temporal nuclei (hippocampus and amygdala). Most patients in this group have had virtually continuous bursts of abnormal activity. Whereas spiking has been predominant at times, slow activity has prevailed at other times. When the aberrant activity was confined to other brain sites—that is, when the septal region was *not* implicated—the patient did not display psychotic behavior. For example, the deep and surface recordings shown in Fig. 1 were obtained from an epileptic patient while he was displaying psychotic signs and symptoms. In addition to ongoing bursts of epileptiform activity in the hippocampus and amygdala, sharp waves intermingled with slow activity appeared in recordings from the septal region. The recordings in Fig. 2, on the other hand, were obtained from another epileptic patient when she was agitated but *not* psychotic. Whereas hippocampal spindling was recorded in association with her agitation, septal recordings were normal.

These findings in patients provide a neurologic localization for signs and symptoms of altered emotion, manifested by an integrative defect in ability to experience pleasure.

Deep and Surface Recordings During Pleasurable and Painful Emotional States

In our patients, the EEG correlate of pleasure, whether spontaneous or induced, has been altered recordings from the septal region. Activation of the septal region by electrical (or chemical) stimulation induced intense pleasure. Feelings of pleasure have always correlated with activity of the septal region and occasionally of other directly connected sites, as evidenced by EEGs. When the pleasurable state was one of relaxation, such as the behavior induced by recall of pleasant memories during free association, septal recordings were characterized predominantly by bursts of slow, high-amplitude activity (17). Administration of certain drugs induced more intense pleasure. Marihuana, for example, activated the septal region, as reflected in more frequent, high-amplitude rhythmical bursts of slow activity concomitant with bursts (rushes) of pleasure (8). When pleasure was intense and explosive during sexual orgasm, EEGs from septal leads were characterized by faster frequencies of high-amplitude and sharp spiking, often coupled with a slow wave, resembling activity we have recorded throughout the brain during an epileptic seizure (9). Whereas this activity was most distinct

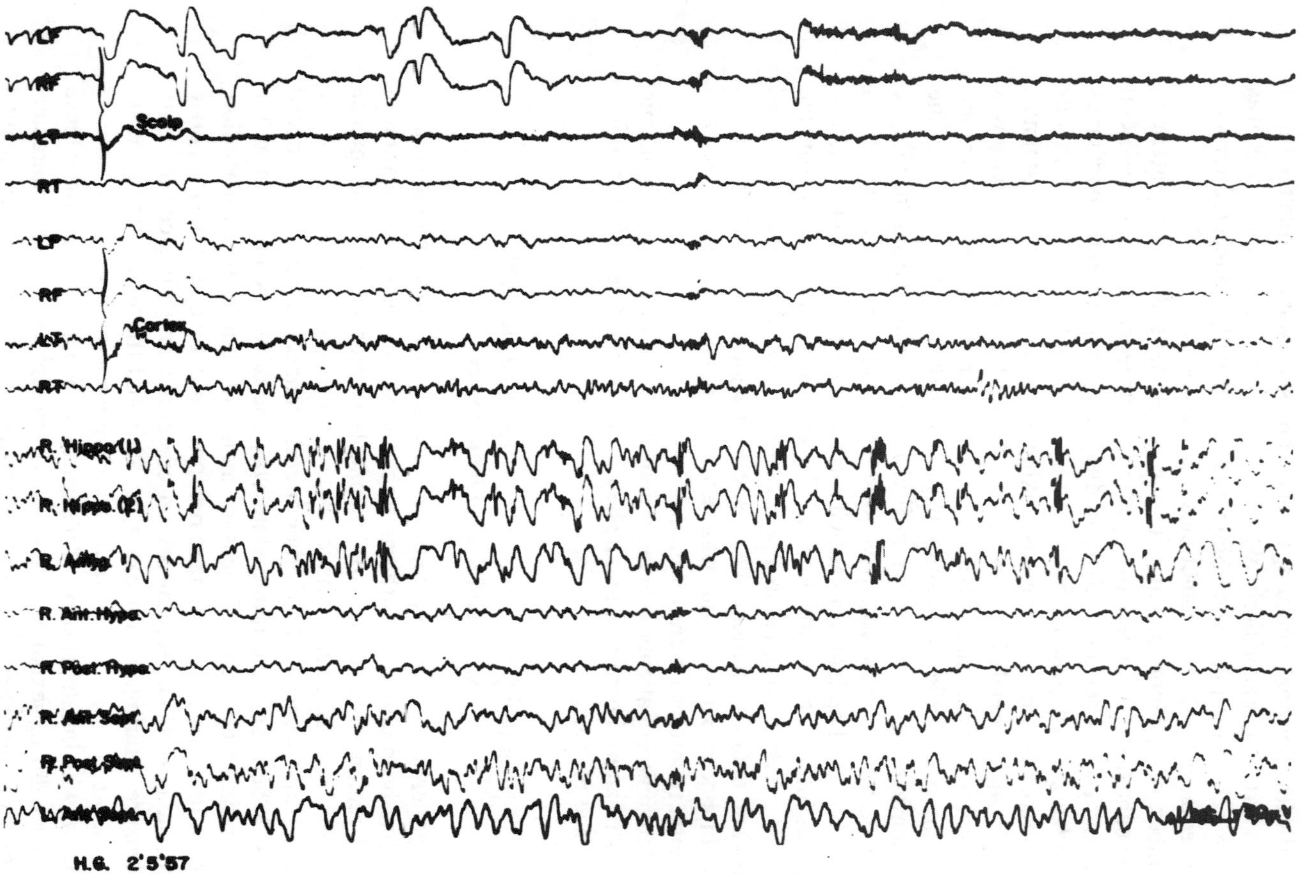

FIG. 1. Deep and surface recordings from an epileptic patient when he was displaying psychotic signs and symptoms. Intermittent bursts of epileptiform activity in hippocampal leads are accompanied by sharp waves intermixed with slow activity in septal leads. No unusual activity is evident in surface leads (cortical and scalp).

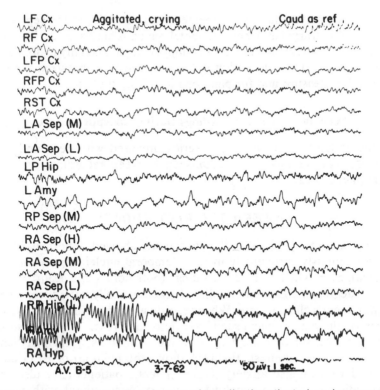

FIG. 2. Deep and surface recordings from another epileptic patient when she was agitated but not psychotic. Whereas ongoing bursts of abnormal epileptiform activity are occurring in the hippocampus and amygdala, activity in the septal region is normal. No unusual activity is evident in cortical leads.

in the septal region, it was also observed, in less-intense form, in directly connected brain sites, particularly in part of the amygdala and in somatosensory relay nuclei.

During painful emotional states (rage and fear), whether spontaneous or activated by psychiatric interview, high-amplitude, fast spindling (12 to 14/sec) focal in the hippocampus or amygdala appeared spontaneously (11,13,16–18). A similar EEG pattern occurred during a state of anticipatory arousal, not necessarily painful or pleasurable, but one of expectation.

These EEG changes were also reflected at other sites shown in studies in animals to have monosynaptic connections to the hippocampus and amygdala. Data from treatment of recent patients in our series also demonstrate these recording changes in deep cerebellar nuclei, somatosensory thalamus, and the cingulate gyrus. (Other sites, shown in animal studies to be directly connected, have not been implanted with electrodes in human subjects.)

When painful emotion prevails—associated with EEG changes in the hippocampus, amygdala, and connected sites—activity of the septal region decreases. Contrariwise, when the septal region is activated during pleasurable emotion, as evidenced by EEGs, hippocampal and amygdaloid activity diminishes. A reciprocal relation is thereby suggested between systems of the brain for pleasure and for pain, one inhibiting the other.

Deep and Surface Recordings During Epileptic Seizures

In the epileptic patients in our series prepared with deep and surface electrodes, correlations were established between recordings and certain clinical phenomena.

INTERICTAL RECORDINGS

During interictal periods, epileptic patients showed abnormal EEG activity continuously, principally in deep temporal nuclei (hippocampus and amygdala), even when surface recordings (both cortex and scalp) were normal. The degree of EEG abnormality characteristically varied, concomitant with the patient's clinical state. When recordings showed infrequent seizural-like bursts, the patient was usually asymptomatic (Fig. 3). As the seizural-like bursts intensified, epileptic signs and symptoms, principally altered emotions, became manifest. Figure 4 shows the build-up of EEG activity associated with intense anxiety. Other epileptic patients have also shown intensification of the abnormal EEG pattern concomitant with rage and profound agitation. With development of characteristic aura (usually altered emotion, sometimes visceral symptoms), the abnormality of the recording pattern further intensified.

GRAND MAL RECORDINGS

Electroencephalographic seizural activity during grand mal followed a consistent migratory pattern. Build-up was first observed in the deep temporal nuclei (hippocampus, amygdala, or both), bursts at these sites occurring close together. The bursts then became continuous, soon implicating the septal region and finally involving the entire brain as the grand mal seizure began (Fig. 5). Postictally, slow waves persisted longer at the septal region than at other sites, EEG activity correlating with the patient's postictal reduced awareness.

RECORDINGS DURING PSYCHOMOTOR SEIZURES

With onset of a psychomotor seizure, build-up of epileptiform activity at deep sites was similar to that observed during development of a grand mal. Involvement of the cortex, however, was usually negligible except in

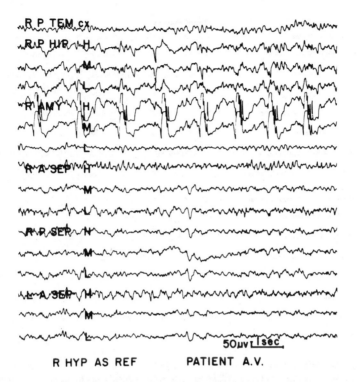

R HYP AS REF   PATIENT A.V.

FIG. 3. Deep recordings and recordings from one surface lead of an epileptic patient when she was asymptomatic. Note the kind of ongoing epileptiform activity that prevails in the hippocampus and amygdala, varying and migrating between these two sites.

patients who had lapses of consciousness when the cortex became involved (5).

In summary, in our patients we have consistently found that there are specific brain sites where activity occurs concomitantly with altered emotion (that is, the subjective components of emotion from extremes of pleasure to pain to the psychotic state). Further, these same sites are also involved in the clinical seizure, as well as in altered emotion associated with the aura of epilepsy. Interictal EEGs from the epileptic patient are characteristically different, however, and when a seizure occurs, seizural activity encompasses the cortex.

ANIMAL MODELS

Clinical and animal behavioral data indicated consistent interrelations of subjective aspects of emotion with other behavioral phenomena. These findings were the basis for designing anatomic and physiologic experiments in animals aimed at a more complete delineation of anatomic and physiologic correlates of emotion. Several behavioral manifestations, consistently re-

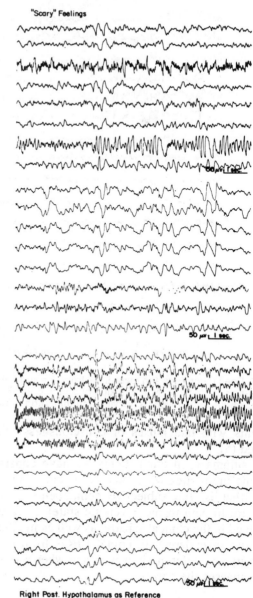

FIG. 4. Recordings from the same epileptic patient as in Fig. 3 when she had profound anxiety. Epileptiform activity is more intense and widespread than it was when she was asymptomatic.

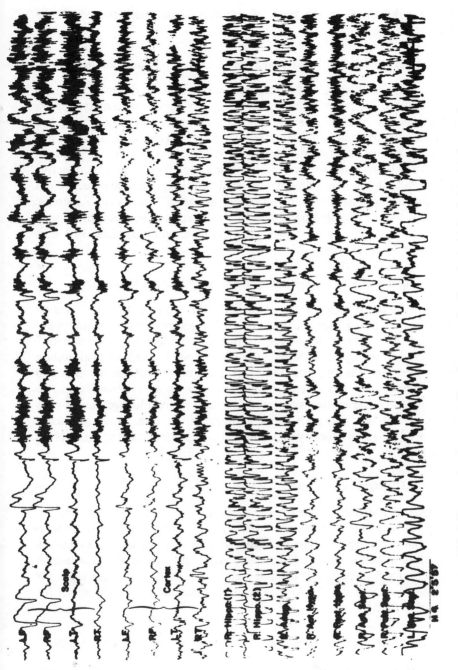

FIG. 5. Deep and surface recordings from an epileptic patient obtained at onset of a grand mal seizure. Note seizural activity prevailing in the hippocampus and septal region before it spreads to implicate other deep brain sites and the temporal cortex, and then other surface sites.

lated to subjective components of emotion, suggested the anatomic-physiologic relations.

Sensory Perception and Emotional State: Clinical and Anatomic Relation

One's emotional state influences his perception, and sensory stimuli affect emotion. Extreme isolation from sensory input profoundly impairs mechanisms for emotional expression (sensory isolation psychosis), and perceptual disturbance is a characteristic of the psychotic state. In animal models of sensory isolation developed by Harlow and Mason, we obtained EEGs from brain sites where activity correlated with human subjective emotion and, at the same time, from sensory relay nuclei, and recordings at both these functional sites showed grossly abnormal activity (7). Anatomic studies have since revealed back-and-forth connections between all sensory relay nuclei and the septal region, hippocampus, and amygdala, key sites for emotional expression (1,2,14,15).

Emotion and Facial Expression: Clinical and Anatomic Relation

Changes in facial expression, particularly the "look in the eye," are an outward reflection of feelings. Extremes of emotion, from love and well-being to anxious expectation to rage or terror to the look of the "madman," are reflected in the eyes. A classic sign of the epileptic seizure is alteration of eye movement, ranging from the blank stare of a psychomotor attack to various stereotyped movements associated with other types of seizures. These clinical observations suggested a structural relation of neural sites subserving eye function with those subserving emotion. Anatomic techniques have revealed monosynaptic neural connections among these brain sites (12,15).

Changes in Transmitter Release at the Synaptic Cleft

Changes in transmitter release are basic to recording variations and associated behavioral phenomena. Monosynaptic connections have been demonstrated among sites for emotional expression, sensory relay nuclei, neural sites affecting expression of the eyes, and neural sites containing cell reservoirs for specific transmitter chemicals (the substantia nigra for dopamine, the locus ceruleus for norepinephrine, and the raphe nuclei for serotonin) (12,15).

Proprioception-Coordination and Emotion: Clinical and Anatomic Relation

One's emotional state influences proprioception and coordination. Neural connections to and from the sites for emotional expression have been traced into the inferior olive, as well as into deep cerebellar nuclei and vestibular nuclei, sites subserving proprioception and coordination. A diagram of these principal connections is shown in Fig. 6. Brain sites and pathways shown in our studies to be significant are superimposed on a diagram of conventionally accepted limbic connections.

Activity Induced with Psychotomimetics and Epileptogenic Methods

To demonstrate the functional significance of anatomically connected brain sites, we induced model psychosis and model epilepsy in rhesus

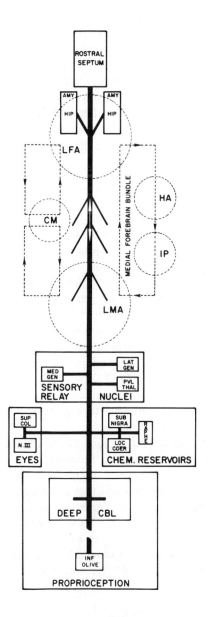

FIG. 6. Schematic diagram of brain sites and pathways demonstrated in Tulane studies to be functionally significant in emotional expression (*solid lines*) superimposed on a diagram of conventional limbic forebrain and midbrain sites and pathways (*broken lines*). ROSTRAL SEPTUM, rostral septal region; AMY, amygdala; HIP, hippocampus; LFA, limbic forebrain area; CM, corpus mammillare; HA, habenula; IP, nucleus interpeduncularis; LMA, limbic midbrain area; MED GEN, medial geniculate; LAT GEN, lateral geniculate; PVL THAL, ventroposterior lateral thalamus; SUP COL, superior colliculus; SUB NIGRA, substantia nigra; N III, oculomotor nuclei; LOC COER, locus ceruleus; RAPHE, raphe nuclei; DEEP CBL, fastigial nucleus cerebellum and dentate nucleus cerebellum; INF OLIVE, inferior olive.

monkeys prepared with deep and surface electrodes. In the monkeys, electrodes were implanted into brain sites where activity has been shown to correlate with psychotic behavior and with epilepsy in human subjects, as well as into monosynaptically connected sites considered important in emotional expression.

MODEL PSYCHOSIS

While deep and surface recordings were obtained, LSD or phencyclidine was used to induce model psychosis in the monkey. Effects of the two chemical psychotomimetics were similar. With the display of gross behavioral changes, characterized by reduced awareness with catatonic features, recording changes occurred in rostral forebrain structures where aberrant brain activity correlated with psychotic behavior in patients (Fig. 7). The EEG abnormalities also involved other brain regions considered to be significant functionally in the neural substrate for emotional expression, that is, the sensory relay nuclei, chemical transmitter sites, and sites for proprioception and coordination.

MODEL EPILEPSY

Induction of epileptiform activity by implantation of minute cobalt crystals into subcortical sites served as a model for both psychosis and epilepsy. By this method, spiking induced by irritation at the implantation site characteristically migrated to reveal functional connections. When spiking involved the septal region, the animal was catatonic. Contrariwise, when the septal region was *not* implicated, as reflected in EEGs, profound behavioral changes were not evident. Figure 8, EEGs from a monkey with cobalt implanted into the right hippocampus, illustrates the migration of activity. The epileptiform activity resulting from perturbation of the hippocampus by cobalt clearly implicates the other anatomically connected sites, particularly the midbrain and hindbrain. Similar EEG patterns were obtained in monkeys with cobalt implanted at several other functional brain sites (fastigial nucleus of the cerebellum, ventroposterior lateral thalamus).

In animal models for epilepsy in which grand mal seizure occurred, the final pattern of seizural spread was the same as that we recorded in our epileptic patients. In animals in which recordings were obtained from sites not implanted in human subjects, however, EEGs showed that preliminary epileptiform activity implicated other functional sites, including sensory relay nuclei, chemical transmitter sites, and the olivovestibular cerebellar system.

Figure 9 shows migration of activity during a seizure induced by electrical stimulation to the hippocampus. The pattern of spread after administration

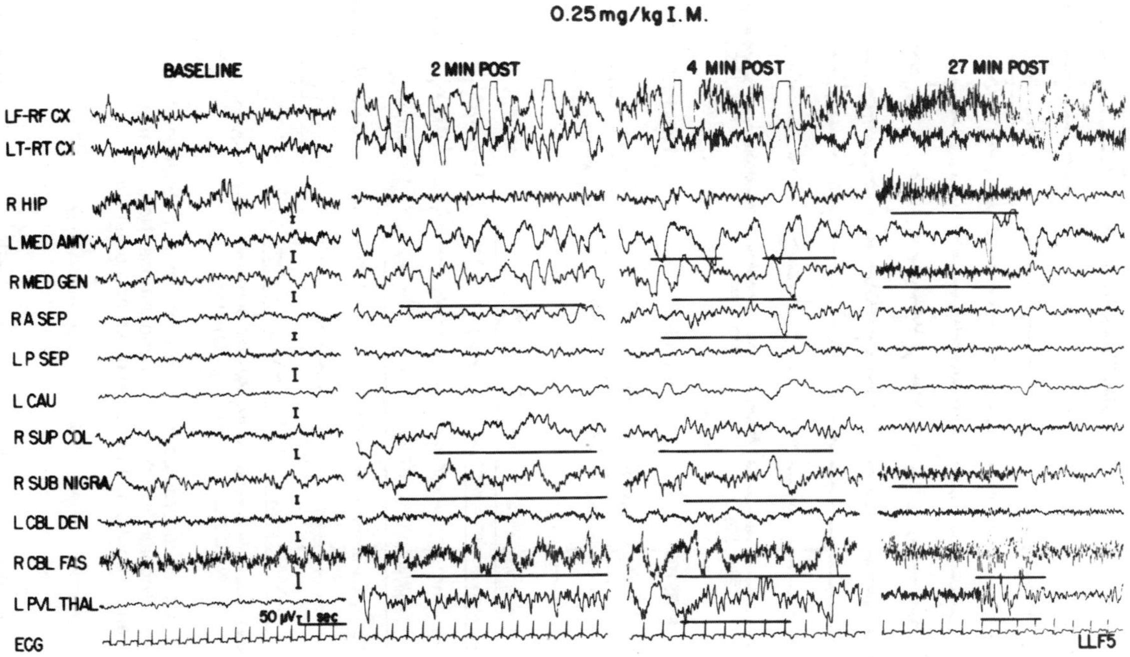

FIG. 7. Deep and surface recordings from a rhesus monkey showing EEG effects of intramuscular administration of phencyclidine.

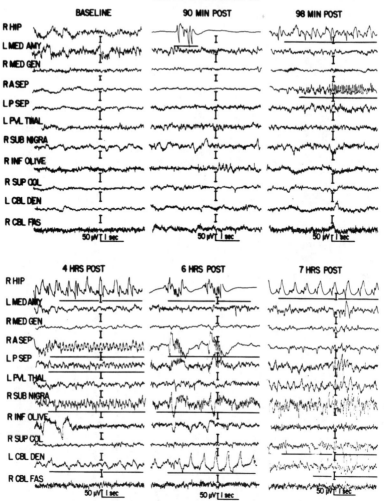

FIG. 8. Deep and surface recordings from a rhesus monkey obtained at various intervals after implantation of cobalt into the right hippocampus. Note the migration of seizural activity demonstrating functional relationships among brain sites.

of pentylenetetrazol (Metrazol®) was very similar. In these animal models, the final stages of the migration of the seizural discharge were similar to those recorded in patients. The recordings from the animals, however, demonstrate the additional brain sites involved in the seizure. By this method, the full extent of the brain organization for emotion and epilepsy is revealed.

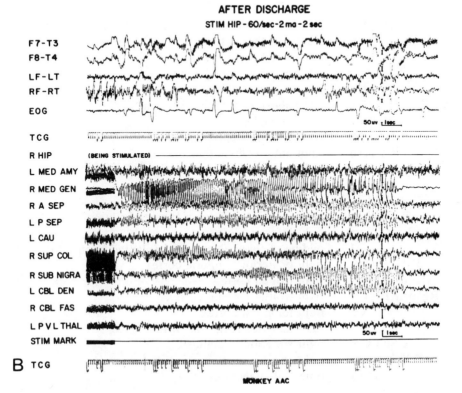

FIG. 9. Deep and surface recordings from a rhesus monkey before (base line; *top*) and after (*bottom*) electrical stimulation of the hippocampus (0.5 msec biphasic pulse, 60 Hz, at 2 mA for 2 sec). Note the spread of seizural activity.

SUMMARY

Studies in patients and in experimental animals have demonstrated the subcortical organization of the brain for emotional expression, including changes reflected in EEGs during psychosis and epileptic seizures. Whereas the same brain structures are implicated in both clinical phenomena, associated EEG activity is different. These observations provided direction for studies that led to identification of numerous heretofore undescribed brain pathways. Our findings indicate that brain organization for emotional expression and seizural activity is much more extensive than the current limbic system concept implies.

Abbreviations on EEGs

ECG, EKG	electrocardiogram
EOG	extra oculogram
H	highest of three electrodes implanted in structure
L Amy	left amygdala
L Med Amy	left medial amygdala
LF or LF Cx	left frontal cortex
LA Sep	left anterior septal region
L Cau	left caudate nucleus
L Cbl Den	left dentate nucleus of the cerebellum
L	lowest of three electrodes implanted in structure
LF or LFP Cx	left frontal parietal cortex
LP Hip	left posterior hippocampus
LT	left temporal cortex
L Pvl Thal	ventroposterior lateral thalamus
R Amy	right amygdala
RA Sep	right anterior septal region
RA Hyp	right anterior hypothalamus
R Med Gen	right medial geniculate
RP Sep	right posterior septal region
RP Hip	right posterior hippocampus
R Cbl Fas	right fastigial nucleus of the cerebellum
R Inf Olive	right inferior olive
M	middle of three electrodes implanted in structure
RP Tem Cx	right posterior temporal cortex
RF or RF Cx	right frontal cortex
RF or RFP Cx	right frontal parietal cortex
RT	right temporal cortex
RST Cx	right superior temporal cortex
R Sup Col	right superior colliculus
R Sub Nigra	right substantia nigra
TCG	time code generator

REFERENCES

1. Harper, J. W., and Heath, R. G. (1973): Anatomic connections of the fastigial nucleus to the rostral forebrain in the cat. *Exp. Neurol.,* 39:285–292.
2. Harper, J. W., and Heath, R. G. (1974): Ascending projections of the cerebellar fastigial nuclei: Connections to the ectosylvian gyrus. *Exp. Neurol.,* 42:241–247.
3. Heath, R. G. (1954): The theoretical framework for a multidisciplinary approach to human behavior. In: *Studies in Schizophrenia,* edited by R. G. Heath and the Tulane University Department of Psychiatry and Neurology, pp. 9–55. Harvard University Press, Cambridge.
4. Heath, R. G. (1962): Common characteristics of epilepsy and schizophrenia: Clinical observation and depth electrode studies. *Am. J. Psychiatry,* 118:1013–1026.
5. Heath, R. G. (1963): Closing remarks with commentary on depth electroencephalography in epilepsy and schizophrenia. In: *EEG and Behavior,* edited by G. H. Glaser, pp. 377–393. Basic Books, New York.
6. Heath, R. G. (1966): Schizophrenia: Biochemical and physiologic aberrations. *Int. J. Neuropsychiatry,* 2:597–610.
7. Heath, R. G. (1972a): Electroencephalographic studies in isolation-raised monkeys with behavioral impairment. *Dis. Nerv. Syst.,* 33:157–163.
8. Heath, R. G. (1972b): Marihuana: Effects on deep and surface electroencephalograms of man. *Arch. Gen. Psychiatry,* 26:577–584.
9. Heath, R. G. (1972c): Pleasure and brain activity in man: Deep and surface electro-encephalograms during orgasm. *J. Nerv. Ment. Dis.,* 154:3–18.
10. Heath, R. G. (1972d): Physiologic basis of emotional expression: Evoked potential and mirror focus studies in rhesus monkeys. *Biol. Psychiatry,* 5:15–31.
11. Heath, R. G. (1975): Brain function and behavior: I. Emotion and sensory phenomena in psychotic patients and in experimental animals. *J. Nerv. Ment. Dis.,* 160:159–175.
12. Heath, R. G. (1976): Correlation of brain function with emotional behavior. *Biol. Psychiatry,* 11:463–480.
13. Heath, R. G., and Gallant, D. M. (1964): Activity of the human brain during emotional thought. In: *The Role of Pleasure in Behavior,* edited by R. G. Heath, pp. 83–106. Hoeber Medical Division, Harper & Row, New York.
14. Heath, R. G., and Harper, J. W. (1974): Ascending projections of the cerebellar fastigial nucleus to the hippocampus, amygdala, and other temporal lobe sites: Evoked potential and histological studies in monkeys and cats. *Exp. Neurol.,* 45:268–287.
15. Heath, R. G., and Harper, J. W. (1976): Descending projections of the rostral septal region: An electrophysiological-histological study in the cat. *Exp. Neurol.,* 50:536–560.
16. Heath, R. G., and the Tulane University Department of Psychiatry and Neurology (1954): *Studies in Schizophrenia.* Harvard University Press, Cambridge.
17. Heath, R. G., Cox, A. W., and Lustick, L. S. (1974): Brain activity during emotional states. *Am. J. Psychiatry,* 131:858–862.
18. Heath, R. G., John, S. B., and Fontana, C. J. (1968): The pleasure response: Studies by stereotaxic technics in patients. In: *Computers and Electronic Devices in Psychiatry,* edited by N. Kline and E. Laska, pp. 178–189. Grune & Stratton, New York.
19. Heath, R. G., Peacock, S. M., and Miller, W. H. (1953): Induced paroxysmal electrical activity in man recorded simultaneously through subcortical and scalp electrodes. *Trans. Am. Neurol. Assoc.,* 78:247.
20. Mickle, W. A., and Heath, R. G. (1957): Electrical activity from subcortical, cortical, and scalp electrodes before and during clinical epileptic seizures. *Trans. Am. Neurol. Assoc.,* 82:63.

Psychopathology and Brain Dysfunction, edited
by C. Shagass, S. Gershon, and A. J. Friedhoff.
Raven Press, New York © 1977.

Brain and Behavior

Simeon Locke

Neurological Unit, Boston State Hospital, Boston, Massachusetts 02124

Man's continuing effort to understand himself and his place in the universe returns again and again to the question of mind. Indeed, this self-conscious concern constitutes one of mind's defining characteristics. Yet, despite long-standing interest, persistent attempts at analysis, and usage of the techniques of philosophy, psychology, neurology, neurophysiology, and psychiatry, the intimate understanding of the organization of mind, in anything more than a descriptive sense, remains incomplete. Investigators as distinguished as Sherrington (28), Eccles (8), and Penfield (27) ultimately accepted an attitude of dualism. Lashley (18), in contrast, held to the notion that "the phenomena of behavior and of mind are ultimately describable in the concepts of the mathematical and physical sciences." His commitment was perhaps a consequence of his emphasis on organization, the factor that distinguishes a system from its anatomical substrate and from its component constituents. Bertalanffy (2) quotes Eddington (9) to underscore this separation. "We often think that when we have completed our study of *one* we know all about *two,* because 'two' is 'one and one.' We forget we still have to make a study of 'and.' Secondary physics is the study of 'and'—that is to say, of organization." Neurological systems, which presumably cannot operate in the absence of a spatially distributed morphological base with its constituent contributions, may be hierarchically ordered without the "levels" of organization necessarily referable to spatial distribution (33). "Mind," said Lashley (19) "is a complex organization, held together by interaction of processes. . . . it has no distinguishing features other than its organization."

An obvious access route for exploration of the problem of the organization of mind is a study of behavior. Behavior has the advantage of being overt. It underlies communication, which implies mind because intent is a requisite of communication. Behavior means movement, which has no implication at all, except perhaps that a study of movement might constitute a suitable beginning for a study of the defiant problem of mind, even though analysis of the organization of movement can hardly be expected to generate a theory of mind. The formulations that result can be considered, at best, pretheoretical, serving to point a direction for further study; they are neither explanatory nor predictive. The distinction between mind and behavior is fundamental: behavior requires movement, is purposeful, but may be mindless; mind requires no overt manifestation but implies intent, volition, decision, or choice. "Most life is, I imagine, mindless, although the behavior is purposeful. Mind is always an inference from behavior" (29).

Customarily, movement is thought to be "represented" at various places in the nervous system and "rerepresented" or modulated at other places in the nervous system. Two ambiguities are inherent in this view: the what and the where of representation. What is represented need not be an aspect of the movement in the sense of muscle contraction. Where it is represented may be meaningful only in terms of the organization of the entire system. The argument might be more forcefully expressed by conceiving the fundamental behavioral output of the nervous system to be one of posture and of tone — a static state and a bias, set, or readiness to change. Movement then becomes transition between postures and requires sequencing; behavior is conceived as goal-directed movement that operates on the environment. Isolation of parts of the neuraxis reveals predominance of one or another posture at various levels. Flexion, for example, is prepotent after spinal section and is released in part by tactual stimuli. Flexor reflex afferents include a cutaneous contribution which, in the intact preparation, interacts with descending fibers to activate interneurons. The flexor reflex afferents "are viewed as a segmental activating system subserving descending activation of a variety of interneuronal pathways to motoneurons" (21). Extension, which can be elicited from isolated spinal cord, receives additional bias from neck and labyrinthine input (7).

Modification of function occurs with neurological accession, and some anatomical pathways which underlie it are known. Brainstem contributions (in monkey) consist of a lateral and a ventromedial group. The lateral pathway originates in the contralateral magnocellular red nucleus and terminates in the dorsolateral part of the spinal intermediate zone unilaterally. The ventromedial fibers originate in the vestibular nuclei, the interstitial nucleus of Cajal, and the medial pontine and medullary reticular formation; they terminate preferentially in the ventral and medial parts of the internuncial zone of the spinal gray bilaterally. Interruption of the ventromedial pathways produces a flexion bias of trunk and limbs, with severe impairment of axial and proximal extremity movements. Interruption of the lateral brainstem pathways disrupts independent distal movements and impairs ability to flex the extended limb. The function of the lateral system is superimposed on the more basic activity of the ventromedial pathways, which are concerned with maintenance of erect posture, integrated body and limb movements, and the course of progression. Fibers of cortical origin terminate in the internuncial spinal zone, overlapping those of both brainstem projections. In addition, they terminate directly on spinal motor neurons — particularly those for limb musculature — further fractionating distal extremity movements (20).

Spinal postures are thus modulated by the ventromedial brainstem pathway, which "is especially concerned with steering body and integrated body-limb movements and movements of the whole limb. The lateral brain stem pathways add further resolution, and provide the capacity for individual movements of the extremities, in particular of their distal parts. The cortico-spinal fibers further amplify this control and, probably by way of their direct connexions to motoneurons, provide the capacity for a high degree of frac-tionation of movements, for example in relatively independent finger movements" (3). This need not imply the "representation" of finger movements in motor cortex. Rather, it may signify "spatial adjustments that accurately adapt the movement to the spatial attributes of the stimulus" (7). These spatial adjustments may be "conceptualized" by the nervous system in terms of force and pattern of contraction (11), rather than as an isomorphic spatial representation.

In cortex, efferent zones controlling movement at a given joint are close together (1). These zones, organized in columns, have sharp boundaries and low threshold to microstimulation, most particularly in layer V. They receive afferents from skin, joints, and muscles involved in the movements produced on microstimulation (14). This input, often a reafference secondary to output, allows movement generated by the organism to be distinguished from movement of the organism generated from without (4). Pavlov (26) recognized the importance of such a distinction as long ago as 1911.

> Undoubtedly, not only an analysis of the external world is of importance to the organism; it also needs a signalling upwards and an analysis of everything taking place inside the organism itself. In a word, in addition to the external analyzers already mentioned, there must be internal analyzers, the most important of which is the motor analyzer, the analyzer of movement. We know that from all parts of the motor apparatus—from the joints, tendons, etc., there stretch centripetal nerves which signalize every movement the slightest detail of the act of movement. All these nerves unite at the supreme points—in the cerebral cells. The various peripheral endings of these nerves, the nerves themselves, as well as the nerve cells, in which they end, in the cerebral hemispheres, constitute a special analyzer which decomposes the motor act with its enormous complexity into a large number of the most delicate elements; this ensures the enormous variety and the precision of our skeletal movements.

This feedback, which is so essential in high-level performance, is clearly not necessary for the realization of the fundamental motor program. The spinal scratch reflex, for example, is not affected by complete section of the dorsal roots of the scratching limb. This shows "that the organization . . . and the primary spatial orientation of the response is inherent in the pattern of reflex activation, and not in any 'feed-back mechanism' " (7). Rather, it seems that the "effector mechanism can be present or primed to discharge at a given intensity, or for a given duration, in independence of any sensory controls" (18).

If, then, the motor program is independent of feedback, what is the role of the reafferent input? This input apparently constitutes a regulating system that compares the results achieved with an antecedent "plan," evaluating and readjusting the effects of a given action (24). Motor cortex constitutes only a trigger apparatus of voluntary movement, and is itself under the control of systems responsible for direction and coordination of movement. Basal ganglia (5,32,34) and cerebellum receive widespread input from cerebral cortex, bringing information from visual, somatosensory, and "association" areas. They in turn project to nucleus ventralis lateralis of the thalamus, which sends fibers to motor cortex. Cerebellum and basal ganglia discharges appear in advance of voluntary movement (6,13), with which nucleus ventralis lateralis is concerned, as passive movement evokes but little response in this nucleus (13).

The triggering by cortex results in the selection of an appropriate motor program to meet the requirements of an objective situation. The afferent input that determines the motor program differs in accordance with the goal. The more complex the structure of the movement required, the richer the afferent input, and the more conscious its character (24). The representation of the goal in the program determines the subsequent course of movements. These programs constitute the "preliminary excitation giving the movement its required direction" (24) and must precede the movement. Feedback allows comparison with the original plan and necessary correction if the two do not correspond.

The central regulation by cerebral cortex accounts for the "resolution and fractionation" of movement patterns; they result not so much from suppression of subcortical function as from the including of "elementary synergies into new functional systems organized at the cortical level" (24). Some of this organization occurs in prefrontal cortex, for "this region is absolutely essential for the maintenance of the programs of an action and for comparison between the actual result of the action and the motor pattern to which it must conform" (24). Not only does sensory input occur in reflex and spontaneous movements, but it also exists in association with learned movements.

Some cortical cells that demonstrate sensory input have small, unimodal, contralateral receptive fields; others respond to multimodal input from wide receptive fields ipsilaterally as well as contralaterally. Vision, as well as kinesthetic input, has an effect at motor cortex (12,31). Delegation from a proprioceptive origin to an exteroceptive surrogate permits increased conscious regulation of behavior (22). Just as there is afferent input to central systems, so there is central control of the afferent systems—output control of input, which constitutes a feedback loop for most sensory inputs. This control accounts for active tuning of sensory receptors and is responsible for the initiation of selective reactions that extract the essential components of input information and control the perception of the objective world (23). The active tuning of the receptors underlies reafferentation and helps distinguish the operation of the organism on the environment from the opera-tion of the environment on the organism.

In addition to feedback operating on peripheral input, a feedforward system exists. With action, a corollary discharge (30) links motor cortex to appropriate "sensory" cortical areas. The corollary discharge constitutes an analogy of the predicted results; the reafferent signal displays the achieved end. Mismatch between the two allows for generation of an error signal and for compensation.

The hierarchical organization of the nervous system, in this formulation, should not be construed as one of anatomical levels. A functional system is distributed throughout its morphological substrate from periphery to most central representation. As Luria (23) pointed out, "it is obvious that the higher mental processes are functions of the brain as a whole and that the activity of the cerebral cortex can be examined only in conjunction with that of nervous structures at lower levels. . . . The structural basis of voluntary movement is a whole system of afferent and efferent links, situated in differ-ent parts and at different levels of the central nervous system. Each link of this system plays its own differential role (providing the motor task, the spatial or kinetic scheme of the movement, the tone and coordination of the muscle groups, the feedback of signals from the effect of the completed action, etc.). It is only by the close interaction of the elements of this func-tional system that its essential plasticity and self-regulation can be assured."

Voluntary movement reflects a spatiotemporal pattern, production of which requires a function generator. The cerebellum is thought to generate a step function, and the basal ganglia to operate as a ramp generator. Cerebral cortex serves as a feature detector, a data reduction device, and a memory store (17). The serial order of performance is determined by the volitional aspect of memory or by the intent. According to Lashley (18), "the intention to act or the ideas to be expressed determine the sequence." Intention is signaled by pyramidal tract neurons (PTNs), which serve as a signal analyzer as well as a trigger for central motor programs. PTNs in monkey (35) can signal the intention to move in the absence of overt move-ment. Response of these neurons to sensory stimuli can be gated by previ-ous instructions that control the response the animal intends to make. "This gating of PTN responsiveness to sensory inputs allows selectivity of motor behavior depending upon decisions made by the subject" (35). Cells of this sort – not always activated by sensory stimuli, not active during all move-ments of a given muscle group, and in which discharge is conditional – have been suggested as responsible for holistic commands for action (25). The commands are not detailed instructions for muscular contraction; they can be influenced *en route* by ongoing extroceptive activity, and they can be construed as a manifestation of volition.

In humans, too, such command potentials occur. A "readiness potential," widespread over precentral and parietal regions, occurs well in advance of a voluntary movement. A second event – premotor positivity – appears at a shorter interval (80 to 90 msec) before movement; it is also bilateral and widespread. Finally, a third potential, limited to the contralateral motor area, appears shortly before a voluntary movement (17). Similar command potentials may appear before speech, perhaps the most voluntary of human endeavors (10).

These high-level signals do not have to specify in detail what is to be done. They must merely initiate previously specified programs that are contained in subunits, commanded from above, and appear in strategic order guided by feedback and feedforward mechanisms related to the environmental input. The centrally patterned subprograms provide constraints on the output, "but these constraints do not exhaust the system's degrees of freedom; they leave room for more or less flexible strategies, guided by contingencies in the . . . local environment" (16). Hierarchical organization of the subprograms exists and determines the meaning of behavior in relation to environmental stimuli. The closer to the periphery the input or output component of a subprogram, the more stereotyped, inflexible, and particularized; the farther central in the system, the more abstract. "In motor hierarchies, an implicit intention or generalized command is particularized . . . in perceptual hierarchies . . . the peripheral input is more and more departicularized . . . during its ascent to the center. The output hierarchy concretizes, the input hierarchy abstracts" (16).

The demonstration of cortical command potentials is perhaps a partial fulfillment of Sherrington's prediction made in 1912 during his study on the instability of a cortical point. This instability of experimentally induced movement caused him to suggest that "such observations, besides tending to throw light on the reflex working of the neural machinery, have the further interest that they tend — although perhaps remotely — to make some approach towards study of the physiological conditions which underlie 'will,' if so bold a use of the term may be allowed" (15). Will, intention, and choice can be studied as they appear in the motor system, not as components of mind — an independent psychological entity — but rather as constituents and necessary outgrowths of a behavioral system. They cannot be examined in isolation because they are integral to the system and disappear with disruption of the organization. As Weiss (33) stated, "the system and its parts are coextensive and congruous, . . . nothing need be presumed to have been disrupted or lost in the dissection process except the pattern or orderly relation among the parts." We cannot examine the fundamental organization of mind in isolation, for the act of isolating disrupts the processes. Wordsworth knew that when he wrote:

> "Our meddling intellect
> Mis-shapes the beauteous form of things:
> We murder to dissect"

SUMMARY

Efforts to study the relation between mind and brain have been unsatisfactory because of the difficulty of objectifying the phenomena of mind. Behavior, in contrast, can be analyzed effectively because it is overt. Movement, the vehicle that underlies all behavior, may be conceived as the transition between postures. Postures constitute one of the fundamental "representations" in the nervous system, the basic patterns undergoing modification with accession of neurological structure and function. Representation is not isomorphic with that which is represented at any level of a functional system. Rather, the "representation" is dependent on the interaction of the subunits in the system. Movement results from interaction of motor cortex, cerebellum, basal ganglia, and spinal cord. Motor cortex functions as a "sensory analyzer" of input to the motor system. Some of these signals are reafferent input, indicating the effects of movement and allowing comparison with an antecedent plan. The plan, goal directed, is apparently dependent on cortical areas such as the prefrontal region and may relate to the existence of command neurons, which generate potentials contingent on factors such as intention, choice, and decision. These entities, related to volition, and physiologically based, may provide an access route by way of the study of behavior for an understanding of the phenomenon of mind.

REFERENCES

1. Asanuma, H., and Rosen, I. (1972): Topographical organization of cortical afferent zones projecting to distal forelimb muscles in monkey. *Exp. Brain Res.*, 14:243–256.
2. Bertalanffy, L. V. (1969): Chance or law. In: *Beyond Reductionism,* edited by A. Koestler and J. R. Smythies, pp. 56–84. Macmillan, New York.
3. Brinkman, J., and Kuypers, H. G. J. M. (1973): Cerebral control of contralateral and ipsilateral arm, hand and finger movements in the split brain Rhesus monkey. *Brain,* 96:653–674.
4. Bruner, J. S. (1969): On voluntary action and its hierarchical structure. In: *Beyond Reductionism,* edited by A. Koestler and J. R. Smythies, pp. 161–191. Macmillan, New York.
5. Carmen, J. B., Cowan, W. M., Powell, T. P. S., and Webster, K. E. (1965): A bilateral cortico-striatal projection. *J. Neurol. Neurosurg. Psychiatry,* 28:71–77.
6. De Long, M. R. (1974): Motor functions of the basal ganglia: single unit activity during movement. In: *The Neurosciences Third Study Program,* edited by F. O. Schmitt and F. G. Worden, pp. 319–325. MIT Press, Cambridge.
7. Denny-Brown, D. (1966): *The Cerebral Control of Movement.* Liverpool University Press, Liverpool.
8. Eccles, J. C. (1953): *The Neurophysiological Basis of Mind.* Clarendon Press, Oxford.
9. Eddington, A. (1958): *The Nature of Physics.* University of Michigan Press, Ann Arbor.
10. Ertl, J., and Schafer, E. W. (1967): Cortical activity preceding speech. *Life Sci.,* 6:473–479, 8:559.
11. Evarts, E. V. (1973): Brain mechanisms in movement. *Sci. Am.,* 229:96–103.
12. Evarts, E. V. (1974): Sensorimotor cortex activity associated with movements triggered by visual as compared to somesthetic inputs. In: *The Neurosciences Third Study Program,* edited by F. O. Schmitt and F. G. Worden, pp. 327–337. MIT Press, Cambridge.
13. Evarts, E. V. (1975): Activity of cerebral neurons in relation to movement. In: *The Nervous System: Vol. I. The Basic Neurosciences,* edited by D. Tower, pp. 221–233. Raven Press, New York.

14. Goldring, S., and Ratcheson, R. (1972): Human motor cortex: sensory input data from single neuron recordings. *Science,* 175:1493–1495.
15. Graham Brown, T., and Sherrington, C. S. (1912): On the instability of a cortical point. *Proc. R. Soc. Lond. [Biol.],* 85B:250–277.
16. Koestler, A. (1969): Beyond atomism and holism—the concept of the holon. In: *Beyond Reductionism,* edited by A. Koestler and J. R. Smythies, pp. 192–232. Macmillan, New York.
17. Kornhuber, H. H. (1974): Cerebral cortex, cerebellum and basal ganglia. An introduction to their motor functions. In: *The Neurosciences Third Study Program,* edited by F. O. Schmitt and F. G. Worden, pp. 267–280. MIT Press, Cambridge.
18. Lashley, K. S. (1951): The problem of serial order in behavior. In: *Cerebral Mechanisms in Behavior,* edited by L. A. Jeffress, pp. 112–146. John Wiley & Sons, New York.
19. Lashley, K. S. (1958): Cerebral organization and behavior. *Proc. Assoc. Res. Nerv. Ment. Dis.,* 36:1–18.
20. Lawrence, D. G., and Kuypers, H. G. J. M. (1968): The functional organization of the motor system in the monkey: II. The effects of lesions of the descending brain-stem pathways. *Brain,* 91:15–36.
21. Lundberg, A. (1975): Control of spinal mechanisms from the brain. In: *The Nervous System: Vol. I. The Basic Neurosciences,* edited by D. Tower, pp. 253–265. Raven Press, New York.
22. Luria, A. R. (1961): *The Role of Speech in the Regulation of Normal and Abnormal Behavior.* Liveright Publishing Co., New York.
23. Luria, A. R. (1966a): *Higher Cortical Functions in Man.* Basic Books, New York.
24. Luria, A. R. (1966b): *Human Brain and Psychological Processes.* Harper & Row, New York.
25. Mountcastle, V. B., Lynch, J. C., Georgopoulos, A., Sakata, H., and Acuna, C. (1975): Posterior parietal association cortex of the monkey: command functions for operations within extrapersonal space. *J. Neurophysiol.,* 38:871–909.
26. Pavlov, I. P. (1955): *Selected Works,* pp. 292–293. Foreign Languages Publishing House, Moscow.
27. Penfield, W. (1975): *The Mystery of the Mind.* Princeton University Press, Princeton.
28. Sherrington, C. S. (1947): *The Integrative Action of the Nervous System.* Cambridge University Press, Cambridge.
29. Sherrington, C. S. (1952): Introductory. In: *The Physical Basis of Mind,* edited by P. Laslett, pp. 1–4. Basil Blackwell, Oxford.
30. Teuber, H.-L. (1960): Perception. In: *Handbook of Physiology. Section I. Neurophysiology,* edited by J. Field and H. W. Magoun, pp. 1595–1668. American Physiological Society, Washington, D.C.
31. Teyler, T. J., Shaw, C., and Thompson, R. F. (1972): Unit responses to moving visual stimuli in the motor cortex of the cat. *Science,* 176:811–813.
32. Webster, K. E. (1965): The cortico-striatal projection in the cat. *J. Anat.,* 99:329–337.
33. Weiss, P. (1969): The living system: determinism stratified. In: *Beyond Reductionism,* edited by A. Koestler and J. R. Smythies, pp. 3–55. Macmillan, New York.
34. Yakovlev, P. I., and Locke, S. (1961): Limbic nuclei of the thalamus and connections of the limbic cortex. III. Corticocortical connections of the anterior cingulate gyrus: the cingulum and the subcallosal bundle in monkey. *Arch. Neurol.,* 5:364–400.
35. Yingling, C. (1975): Motor programs and feedback in control of movement. *BIS Conference Report,* 38:65–73.

Psychopathology and Brain Dysfunction, edited by C. Shagass, S. Gershon, and A. J. Friedhoff. Raven Press, New York © 1977.

New Dimensions in the Functions of the Basal Ganglia*

Karl H. Pribram

Department of Psychology, Stanford University, Stanford, California 94305

INTRODUCTION

Research in psychopathology is distinguished by the fact that it partakes in three basic areas of observation and experimentation: clinical, behavioral, and biological. As a rule two avenues of investigation of psychopathological problems are open to us, each addressing the three basic elements. These avenues are the direct, which uses clinical material, and the indirect, which employs models. The nature of the distinction between direct clinical observation and model building in the biochemical aspects of psychopathological research is familiar, as attested by such phrases as *"in vivo"* and *"in vitro."* Less well understood is the distinction in the neurobehavioral and neurophysiological approaches to psychopathology. Especially lacking has been the detailing of the development of neurobehavioral and neurophysiological models of clinical problems. I want therefore to describe one program of research in which such models were developed and to issue a brief "progress report" on the state of that program.

Thirty years ago I began research aimed at studying the role of cerebral cortex in human clinical disorders. Along with Bucy (4), I had published observations of a case of localized facial sweating because of an oligodendroglioma situated in the precentral motor cortex. These observations led to the belief, contrary to ones then current, that the cortex, not the hypothalamus, might be the "head ganglion" of the autonomic nervous system. I was in neurosurgical practice with J. G. Lyerly and helped devise a "superior" approach to the frontal cortex in order to assure a more restricted procedure when lobotomy was performed for obsessions, compulsions, and depressions. The "standard" Freeman and Watts procedure was proving to have unwanted cognitive side effects, was shown to invade "Broca's area" (19), and was much in need of careful quantitative evaluation. But perhaps of more lasting significance, I was able to work with Karl Lashley at the Yerkes Laboratories for Primate Biology in an attempt to make animal *models* of the clinical disorders presumably produced by cerebral dysfunction. Such models would allow precise specification of lesions and quantitative testing of behavior over prolonged periods.

---

* Paul H. Hoch Award Lecture.

A large surface of primate cortex was at the time "silent" to experimental manipulation. Lashley was making restricted resections of frontal, parietal, and temporal cortex with little apparent effect. I therefore took the opposite approach and made very large lesions of the frontal lobes, of the temporal lobes, and of the entire extent of the "association cortex" lying between the primary sensory projection areas. Because medial and basal forebrain structures such as cingulate cortex, precuneus, and hippocampus might be responsible for effects such as the Klüver-Bucy syndrome or the apraxias, the limbic portions of the cerebral mantle were excised in many of the experiments.

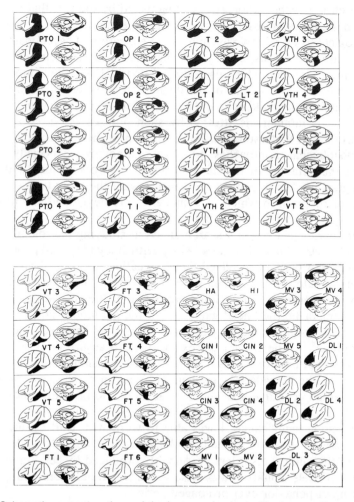

FIG. 1. Schematic reconstructions of the locus and extent of brain resections performed on 40 monkeys used for the multiple dissociation of brain lesion effects on behavior.

In order to assess the effects of this variety of large resections, investigators devised a battery of some 30 behavioral tests to study the monkeys. These tests ranged from the recording of general locomotor activity and performance of latch box manipulations, through a variety of sensory preference and discrimination tasks, to higher order delay and matching from sample procedures (Fig. 1).

A method was then devised (24) to relate the effects of the lesions to one or another of the tests. An arbitrary criterion was established for "failure" in a task: when postoperatively a monkey took more trials to master the task than he had needed preoperatively, a deficit was declared. Then all of the cortical resections that had produced such a "deficit" were spatially summed — as was the spatial extent of all of the resections that had produced "no deficit." The intercept of the two sums was then diagrammed by overlay and this intercept considered the "locus" responsible for the deficit. The conclusion was tested by restricting the next set of lesions to such loci and showing by multiple "double dissociations" that, in fact, the localization held up. By now approximately 1,500 monkeys have been studied in this fashion in my laboratory alone, and I feel we know a great deal about cerebral function in behavior as a result (Table 1, and Figs. 2, 3).

These initial studies that provided brain-behavior correlations were, of course, only the first steps in the program of research. What did a specific correlation mean? Two types of questions need to be answered. First, what is the *behavioral* significance of the sign that has become pathognomonic of the cerebral pathology? This is much like asking what the Babinski sign tells us about the behavioral development of a child. The second type of question deals with the *neural* mechanism responsible for the production of the sign. Thus we take the Babinski reflex to be an indicator of myelinization of the pyramidal motor system. What neural pathways are involved in the ability or disability to perform a visual discrimination?

As a final stage in the research, of course, the fruits of all of these studies

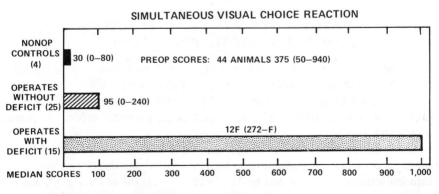

SIMULTANEOUS VISUAL CHOICE REACTION

NONOP CONTROLS (4) — 30 (0–80)   PREOP SCORES: 44 ANIMALS 375 (50–940)

OPERATES WITHOUT DEFICIT (25) — 95 (0–240)

OPERATES WITH DEFICIT (15) — 12F (272–F)

MEDIAN SCORES   100   200   300   400   500   600   700   800   900   1,000

FIG. 2. Summary graph of Table 1.

TABLE 1. *Simultaneous visual choice reaction*

Operates Without Deficit			Operates With Deficit		
	Pre	Post		Pre	Post
OP_1	200	0	PTO_1	120	272
OP_2	220	0	PTO_2	325	F
OP_3	380	0	PTO_3	180	F
LT_1	390	190	PTO_4	120	450
LT_2	300	150	T_1	940	F
H_1	210	220	T_2	330	F
HA	350	240	VTH_1	320	F
FT_1	580	50	VTH_2	370	F
FT_3	50	0	VTH_3	280	F
FT_4	205	0	VTH_4	440	F
FT_5	300	200	VT_1	240	F
FT_6	250	100	VT_2	200	F
DL_1	160	140	VT_3	200	890
DL_2	540	150	VT_4	410	F
DL_3	300	240	VT_5	210	F
DL_4	120	100			
MV_1	110	0			
MV_2	150	10	Nonoperate Controls		
MV_3	290	130			
MV_4	230	10	C_1	790	80
MV_5	280	120	C_2	230	20
CIN_1	120	80	C_3	750	20
CIN_2	400	60	C_4	440	0
CIN_3	115	74			
CIN_4	240	140			

Table of "deficit" and "no-deficit" performances on the visual choice reaction, which is shown to be selectively impaired by inferotemporal cortical resections on the basis of these data (see Fig. 3).

performed on nonhuman primates must be reflected back to the clinic and the human condition.

DISCOVERY OF THE VISUAL FUNCTIONS OF THE INFEROTEMPORAL CORTEX

To illustrate this program of investigation, I will focus on one cortical area, that lying on the inferior surface of the temporal lobe. I will present some of the highlights that changed the course of research when they occurred and end in what might be considered a progress report on current endeavors.

The inferior convolution of the temporal lobe was discovered by the multiple dissociation technique to be responsible for deficits in visual discrimination performance (see review in ref. 24). At the animal level, this was a welcome discovery because it parcelled out one part of the Klüver-Bucy

TABLE 2. *Baboons: Postoperative visual discrimination scores. Scores are no. trials preceding 90 correct in 100*

Pre-op Median	350	100	20	0
Subjects	▽ △	■ ●	D L	R G
T 1	F	760	F	750
T 2	F	F	F	540
VTH 1	F	F	F	790
VTH 2	F	F	F	100
VTH 3	F	F	F	990
VTH 4	F	F	0	10
LT 1	190	20	0	0
LT 2	150	450	0	0

F = Failure in 1,000 trials   (Underlined)＿ = initial acquisition

Table showing deficits in a variety of visual choice procedures in monkeys with resections of inferotemporal cortex.

syndrome from the rest. Klüver had shown that monkeys with temporal lobectomies were, aside from hyperoral and hypersexual, also "psychically blind"—i.e., they suffered from a visual agnosia. In our early experiments we were able to establish not only that the visual portion of the syndrome could be separated from the rest [which was attributable to amygdala resections

VISUAL CHOICE REACTION

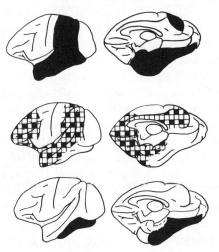

FIG. 3. Summary schematic reconstruction of the sums of the locus and extent of brain resections that produce the deficit (*top*) and those that do not (*middle*) in the visual choice procedure. Bottom diagrams show the intercept of these two sums and "localize" the effective lesion to the inferotemporal cortex.

TABLE 3. *Double dissociation between the effects of resections of parietal and of infero-temporal cortex*

		Preop. Learning	Preop. Retention	Postop. Retention	Postop. Learning
		SOMESTHETIC DISCRIMINATION			
P	Group A	408	5	687	—
	Group B	—	—	—	821
IT	Group A	410	54	19	—
	Group B	—	—	—	439
		VISUAL DISCRIMINATION			
P	Group A	—	—	—	331
	Group B	320	0	194	—
IT	Group A	—	—	—	1000f
	Group B	518	0	1000f	—

Parietal resections produce a somatosensory deficit but visual performance remains intact. Inferotemporal resection, conversely, leave somatosensory functions intact while impairing visual performances. The lesions producing these deficits did not invade the primary thalamocortical sensory systems.

(29)] but also that the visual agnosia was, in fact, visual and not global — e.g., not somatosensory, gustatory, or auditory (3), as shown in Tables 2 and 3.

On the clinical level, the finding that the inferotemporal cortex of monkeys is critical to visual discrimination performance was also important. First, visual symptoms associated with temporal lobe lesions had always been attributed at least in part to invasion of the optic radiations — even anteriorly placed lesions were assumed to produce their effect by interrupting Meyer's loop, a portion of the radiations assumed to sweep anterior to the temporal horn of the lateral ventricle in order to account for temporal lobe visual deficits. The existence of Meyer's loop was brought into question by the animal studies, and clinical neuropsychologists began to look seriously at the effects of temporal lobe lesions *per se* on visual performance and not as reflections of damage to the geniculostriate system. Thus Milner (20) was led to conclude that human temporal lobe cortex was in fact involved in making visual discriminations much as was monkey temporal cortex, but that in man the nonverbal visual functions were served by the right hemisphere. This was the first demonstration of hemispheric specialization rather than dominance.

WHAT IS A VISUAL AGNOSIA?

The question that immediately arose was how to distinguish the visual functions of the temporal cortex from those of the occipital geniculostriate system. Initially, a series of studies argued the issue in terms of changes in visual field. Battersby (1) claimed that changes in the visual field did occur, although Mishkin and Pribram (22) failed to note any such changes. The argument was reminiscent of classic ones based on clinical observations [e.g., by von Monakov (40)] and more currently pursued by Bay (2). Battersby did not mean to suggest that spatial scotoma resulted from the temporal lobe lesions. Rather, his point was that some as yet unspecifiable change in the total visual field accounted for the discrimination difficulty. As we shall see, subsequent research has borne out this early intuition.

Meanwhile our research suggested that the discrimination deficit produced by inferotemporal cortex resections was more akin to a motor than to a sensory difficulty. For instance, we trained monkeys to discriminate between a tobacco tin and an ashtray. Although deficient, animals with inferotemporal cortex resections could learn this very easy visual discrimination. We then changed the situation from one in which the cues (tobacco tin and ashtray) were presented simultaneously for choice between them to a situation in which they appeared successively. Thus the tobacco tin signaled that one behavioral response—e.g., reaching toward it or going to a cup on the right—needed to be made, whereas the ashtray signaled that a different response—e.g., withholding reach or going to the left—would be rewarded. Monkeys with inferotemporal cortex resections were markedly

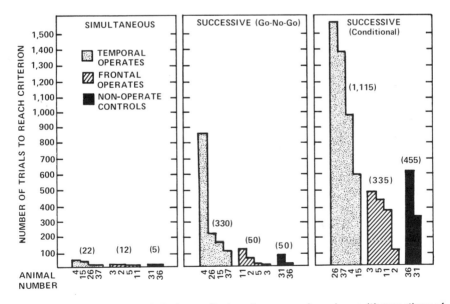

FIG. 4. Graph showing the relatively excellent performance of monkeys with resections of inferotemporal cortex on a simultaneous visual discrimination and markedly deficient performance on two forms of the successive version of the *same* task. These results suggest that the difficulty experienced by the lesioned monkeys is not so much an inability to distinguish cues as it is their inability to use the distinction.

deficient in performing the successive versions of the discriminations, and it could readily be shown that this was not because of any disability in distinguishing the cues, since the monkeys repeatedly performed well—even on the same day—in the simultaneous version of the task (28) (Fig. 4).

In another study (25) the monkeys were asked to choose among many objects. In this experiment the deficit of the animals with inferotemporal cortex lesions was shown to be dependent on a deficiency in the number of such objects they sampled. This finding was extended by Butter (6) to show that in the two-choice discrimination, the monkeys with the inferotemporal cortex lesions failed to sample as many features of the cues presented as the control monkeys. He showed this by eliminating first one and then additional features of cues that were being discriminated, and he demonstrated that the behavior of the monkeys with the lesions broke down much before that of their controls.

This result suggested that the sampling deficit shown by monkeys with inferotemporal cortex lesions need not be expressed by a motor response but could be "attentional." Evidence was therefore at hand to suggest a rapprochement between the view that inferotemporal cortex resections interfered either with visuomotor or visuosensory performance. Perhaps the difficulty was better characterized as "attentional." "Attention" is a central cognitive process that, if we could better understand it, might account for the agnosias produced by cortical lesions.

AN APPROACH TO THE NEUROPHYSIOLOGY
OF SELECTIVE ATTENTION

Unfortunately, the term "attention" is used to cover a variety of psychophysiological processes such as a phasic response to input, a tonic level of readiness, or a more selective process involving choice [see, e.g., reviews by Kahneman (15) and by Pribram and McGuinness (27)]. When we assign the effects of inferotemporal cortex resections (on the number of features of cues sampled) to problems in attention, we need, therefore, to distinguish clearly which form of attention we mean. Sampling is dependent on selection and choice. Thus, selective attention involves the inferotemporal cortex.

We set out to investigate the relationship between inferotemporal cortex and selective attention by using a situation that would necessitate different central processes even though identical cues were presented to the eyes of the monkeys. This was made possible by using colored patterns—i.e., cues with several obvious features—and reinforcing one feature (e.g., the color) at one time and another feature (e.g., the pattern) at another. Thus the feature attended depends on the reinforcing contingencies operating at the time of testing (Fig. 5).

Rather than making lesions in the temporal lobe, we implanted electrodes

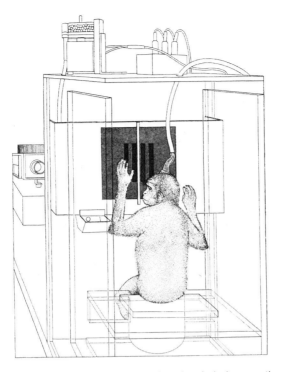

FIG. 5. View of a monkey performing a successive visual choice reaction while his brain electrical activity is being recorded.

and made records of the brain electrical activity evoked by the cue presentation (a brief flash of the colored pattern on a screen) and by the response (depression of either of two panels) of the monkey. A series of experiments using this technique (8,23,26,33) showed that the electrical activity of the inferior temporal cortex is distinctly different when the monkey attends the color and when he attends the pattern features of the cue. This difference becomes manifest approximately 50 to 100 msec before the monkey makes any overt behavioral response and is often, although not always, absent at the time of or shortly after the cue presentation. Overtraining predisposes to an early, cue-dependent difference in the brain electrical record, which then can become manifest in the occipital cortex as well (Fig. 6).

Another set of electrophysiological experiments related the activity of the inferotemporal cortex to attention. For reasons discussed below, we were investigating the effects of chronic electrical stimulation of inferotemporal cortex on recovery cycles within the geniculostriate visual system. After publishing our initial interesting results (36), we went through a 2-yr series of disappointing attempts at replication. Finally, we found that the electrical

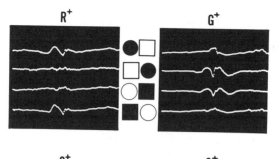

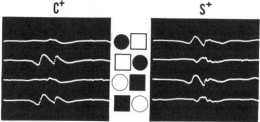

FIG. 6. Computerized averages of the electrical activity recorded from the inferotemporal cortex of a monkey solving a visual choice problem in a situation similar to that shown in Fig. 6. In this experiment, however, a simultaneous choice between colored circles (●) and stripes (□) is offered, and the monkey's response is shaped by reward contingencies; 500 msec of record is shown and the monkey's response occurs midway (at 250 msec) of the recording. Note that when colors (red R+; green G+) are rewarded the temporal lobe electrical activity reflects the position of the colors irrespective of the shape of the cues (i.e., records 1 and 4 and records 2 and 3 look alike). When the shape of the cues is rewarded (circles C+; stripes S+), the temporal lobe electrical activity reflects the position of these shapes irrespective of their colors (i.e., records 1 and 3 and records 2 and 4 now look alike).

stimulation of inferotemporal cortex interacted with the attention being paid spontaneously by the monkeys to one or another visual or auditory cue to produce a ceiling effect. When we brought the monkeys' attentional processes under strict control by eliminating distractors, the original finding was readily replicated (10).

When the results of the experiments described so far are summarized, a common thread can be discerned. Resections of the inferotemporal cortex produce visual discrimination deficits. These deficits are modality-specific and other modality-specific deficits are obtained from other restricted resections of posterior "association" cortex (e.g., audition from superior temporal cortex; taste from anterior temporal cortex; somatosensory signals from parietal cortex). The discrimination deficit is not due, however, to any disturbance in distinguishing cues. Rather, the deficit reflects a disordered selection process. Thus cognitive difficulties (e.g., tobacco tin signifies go to the right cup or key signifies lock) and attentional disturbances (color has been paying off) are produced.

THE PARADOX OF MODALITY-SPECIFIC OUTPUTS

Recall that this program of research can be analyzed in several stages. The first of these was correlational: a unique relationship between a cerebral locus and a behavioral sign was established. Next, the behavioral significance of that sign was explored. Thus the deficit in visual discrimination produced by inferotemporal cortex lesions was found to be owing to a disordered selection process limited to the visual mode and manifested in cognition and attention. We are now, therefore, ready to ask the third question: By what neural mechanism is the selection process organized?

The classic answer to this question, an answer still commonly held to be true, is that a hierarchy of abstractive steps characterizes the processing of "information" from the primary geniculostriate (or other sensory) system. These steps are thought to take place in progressively remote locations of the perisensory cortex until high-order abstractions are achieved in the association cortex [see, e.g., Luria (17) and Jones (14)]. For the most part these abstractive steps are assumed to rely exclusively on corticocortical connections with at best only minimal involvement of corticosubcortical pathways.

Unfortunately for these classic views, our laboratory experiments with animal models have time and time again produced data that are difficult to encompass in this fashion. Most critical has been the finding that extensive resections of the peristriate cortex fail to interfere, except temporarily, with visual discrimination performance (30) (Fig. 8).

This does not mean that such perisensory cortex resections have no effect.

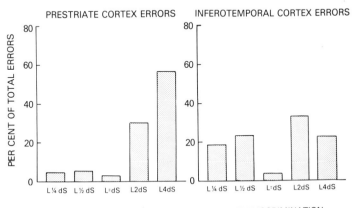

FIG. 7. Graph showing that after resections of prestriate cortex, monkeys rely on the retinal image size projected by a cue and ignore distances. (L$\frac{1}{4}$dS, L$\frac{1}{2}$dS, etc. are specific cue combinations.) Monkeys with resections of inferotemporal cortex do not adopt this "retinal-image-size" strategy—their failure is owing to a relatively random selection of cues.

On the contrary, peristriate lesions produce, for example, a monkey that is unable to display perceptual size constancy and instead responds to retinal image size (38). However, disordered size constancy is not necessarily a "step" involved in the selection process necessary to make visual discriminations. Rather, the deficit is distinct and can be clearly dissociated from that which characterizes lesions of the inferotemporal cortex (Fig. 7).

Recent anatomical studies have delineated three separate "visual systems." In addition to the geniculostriate, there is a collicular-peristriate and a pretectile-inferotemporal system (11,14). The thalamic connection of these extrageniculate systems is the pulvinar. One possibility for explaining the visual specificity of the functions of the inferotemporal cortex, therefore, is its pulvinar input. This possibility has been tested (7,21) and found wanting. Even extensive lesions of pulvinar fail to impair visual discrimination performance [unless cues are presented with a brief tachistoscopic flash (18)]. Thus the pulvinar input to the inferotemporal cortex is even less important than the peristriate input in explaining visual specificity.

The suggestion was therefore made (13) that perhaps the conjunction of inputs from peristriate and pulvinar becomes essential. In a study just completed, Ungerleider and I (39) have tested this alternative and found that even such drastic surgery does not produce a deficit comparable to that which follows inferotemporal cortex lesions.

In sharp contrast to these largely negative results, when pathways under-

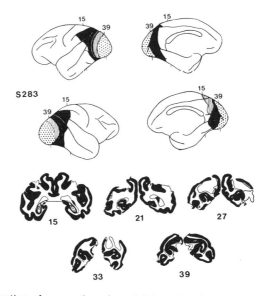

FIG. 8. Reconstruction of a resection of prestriate cortex that gives rise to a deficit in size constancy but does not severely and permanently impair other visual choices as does resection of inferotemporal cortex.

lying inferotemporal cortex are sectioned the full-blown deficit in visual discrimination behavior results. Further, the same result is obtained when lesions are made in the tail of the caudate nucleus and ventral putamen, the basal ganglia nearest the inferotemporal cortex (5,32).

Destructions were attempted in these nuclei of the basal ganglia because fiber tracts were traced to there from the inferotemporal cortex both neurohistologically (41) and electrophysiologically (31). The weight of this evidence thus suggests an important role for the basal ganglia in the selection process ascribed to the inferotemporal cortex (Fig. 9).

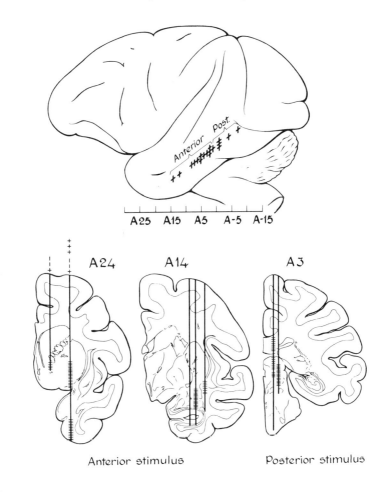

FIG. 9. a: Location of electrode placements used to stimulate inferotemporal cortex in order to trace subcortical efferent pathways. **b:** Location of responses evoked from electrical stimulations of inferotemporal cortex. Note heavy involvement of basal ganglia (especially putamen).

CELL: 05—01—75—4

VS

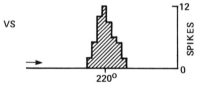

220°

LP

C

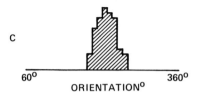

60°   360°

ORIENTATION°

FIG. 10. a: Poststimulus histogram showing a tuning curve of a receptive field
sensitivity to a line orientation at 220°.
Recording is from a single unit in the
visual cortex (of a cat). VS is the initial
response of the unit, LP shows the effects
of electrical stimulation of the putamen,
and C shows the control histogram obtained after cessation of the electrical
stimulation. **b:** Same as **a** except that
electrical stimulation is now of the caudate nucleus. Note that the effect is opposite that obtained when putamen is stimulated.

CELL: 05—01—74—4

C

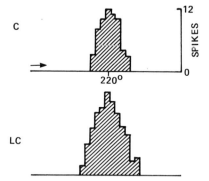

220°

LC

C

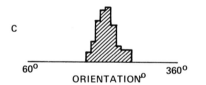

60°   360°

ORIENTATION°

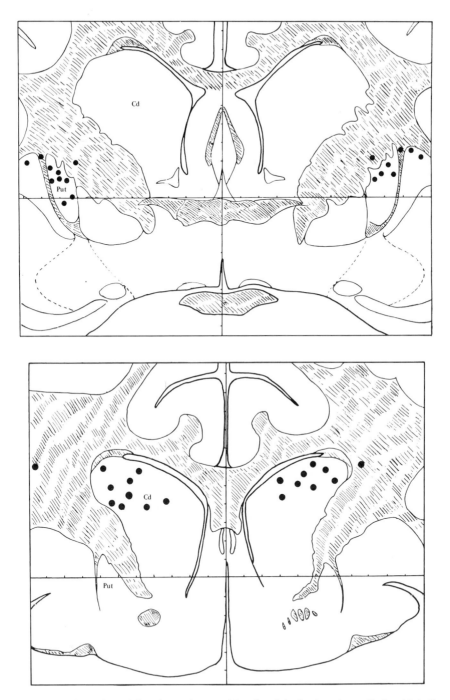

FIG. 11. a,b: Location of the electrodes used to stimulate the basal ganglia to obtain the changes in the visual receptive fields shown in Fig. 12. Cd, caudate; Put, putamen.

To complete the circuit, there must be connections from the basal ganglia to the geniculostriate visual system. (Connections to extrageniculate visual pathways would not help since these have already been ruled out as critical.) We have considerable indirect evidence that the basal ganglia are capable of influencing visual processing. Most recently we have electrically stimulated basal ganglia to elicit changes in visual receptive fields recorded from cells in the lateral geniculate nucleus (35) and the striate cortex (16). These changes are similar to those produced by changes in the inferotemporal cortex (37). (See Figs. 10 and 11.)

By what neuroanatomical pathways can the basal ganglia influence visual processes? We do not yet know but are actively searching, using the new autoradiographic techniques. Two hypotheses are of special interest. One concerns a thalamic "gate," the other involves the substantia nigra.

The thalamic gating of sensory input can readily occur through excitation of the thalamic reticular nucleus. Skinner and Yingling (34,42,43) have shown that such excitation modifies unit activity in primary sensory thalamic nuclei. Further, activity in the thalamic reticular nucleus is itself under the control of at least two systems. One reaches it through the median forebrain bundle from the mesencephalic reticular core. The other pathway constitutes a major portion of the thalamic peduncle. What is unknown is whether there are major basal ganglia contributions to this peduncle. Electrophysiological evidence has suggested that there are (9). Now anatomical verification is being sought.

Another major alternative is a route through the substantia nigra. When I recently attempted to trace the connections from inferotemporal cortex by means of autoradiography, my preparations revealed an odd artifact. Radioactive granules appeared on the surface of most of the cells of the substantia nigra bilaterally. This was true for both short time course (24 to 72 hr) proline-injected brains and long time course (20 days) leucine material. Such radioactive granules were absent from the nigra when frontal or motor cortex was injected. The granules looked much more like those obtained in retrograde preparations, such as when horseradish peroxidase is used, than the usual antegrade slides.

Thus I end this chapter with a puzzle, perhaps even an artifactious one. Nonetheless, the finding, if it proves to be real, may be important because Graybiel (12) has just established (using autoradiography) a point-to-point connectivity between substantia nigra and the superior colliculus. We cannot therefore as yet ignore a possible connection between inferotemporal cortex and the nigra.

CONCLUSION

By whatever route, the importance of the basal ganglia in processing sensory input (as well as motor function) is becoming evident. An intimate functional relationship between association cortex and basal ganglia is established and has been traced here with respect to the inferotemporal cortex, the tail of the caudate nucleus, and the ventral portion of the putamen. These structures in turn have been shown to influence receptive field properties in the primary sensory system. We now need to trace the pathways by which these influences are mediated and to clarify the precise nature of the changes.

When answers to these questions are available, perhaps we can begin to understand why patients with lesions in homologous regions of cortex suffer agnosias and pay such a high attentional price in making even the simplest selective discriminations.

REFERENCES

1. Battersby, W. S. (1956): Neuropsychology of higher processes: cerebral damage and visual perception. *Progress In Clinical Psychology, Vol. 2*, pp. 303–325. Grune & Stratton, New York.
2. Bay, Eberhard (1953): Disturbances of visual perception and their examination, Part 4. *Brain*, 76:515–550.
3. Blum, J. S., Chow, K. L., and Pribram, K. H. (1950): A behavioral analysis of the organization of the parieto-temporo-preoccipital cortex. *J. Comp. Neurol.*, 93:53–100.
4. Bucy, P. C., and Pribram, K. H. (1943): Localized sweating as part of a localized convulsive seizure. *Arch. Neurol. Psychiatry*, 50:456–461.
5. Buerger, A. A., Gross, C. G., and Rocha-Miranda, C. E. (1974): Effects of ventral putamen lesions on discrimination learning by monkeys. *J. Comp. Physiol. Psychol.*, 86(3):440–446.
6. Butter, C. M. (1968): The effect of discrimination training on pattern equivalence in monkeys with inferotemporal and lateral striate lesions. *Neuropsychologia*, 6:27–40.
7. Chow, K. L. (1954): Lack of behavioral effects following destruction of some thalamic association nuclei. *Arch. Neurol. Psychiatry*, 71:762–771.
8. Dawson, B. M., Ganz, L., and Pribram, K. H. (1976): The analysis of electrocortical activity evoked during tasks demanding match from sampling (*in preparation*).
9. Frigyesi, T. L. (1971): Organization of synaptic pathways linking the head of caudate nucleus to the dorsal thalamus. *Int. J. Neurol.*, 8:11–138.
10. Gerbrandt, L. K., Spinelli, D. N., and Pribram, K. H. (1970): The interaction of visual attention and temporal cortex stimulation on electrical activity evoked in the striate cortex. *Electroencephalogr. Clin. Neurophysiol.*, 29:146–155.
11. Graybiel, A. M. (1973): Studies on the anatomical organization of posterior association cortex. *Neurosciences*, 3:205–214.
12. Graybiel, A. M., and Sciascia, T. R. (1975): Origin and distribution of nigrotectal fibers in the cat. In: *Neuroscience Abstracts, Vol. 1.* Society for Neuroscience, Bethesda, Maryland.
13. Gross, C. G. (1976): Inferotemporal cortex and vision. In: *Progress in Physiological Psychology, Vol. 5*, edited by E. Stellar and J. M. Sprague. Academic Press, New York.
14. Jones, E. G. (1973): The anatomy of extrageniculostriate visual mechanisms. In: *The Neurosciences Third Study Program*, edited by Francis O. Schmitt and Frederic G. Worden, pp. 215–227. MIT Press, Cambridge.
15. Kahneman, D. (1973): *Attention and Effort.* Prentice-Hall, Englewood Cliffs, New Jersey.
16. Lassonde, M. C., Ptito, M., and Pribram, K. H. (1975): Are the basal ganglia only motor structures? In: *Programs and Abstracts*, American Physiological Society, Washington, D.C.
17. Luria, A. R. (1973): *The Working Brain: An Introduction to Neuropsychology.* The Penguin Press, London.
18. Macadar, A. W., Chalupa, L. M., and Lindsley, D. B. (1974): Differentiation of brain

stem loci with affect hippocampal and neocortical electrical activity. *Exp. Neurol.,* 43:499–514.

19. Mettler, F. A., and Rowland, L. P. (1948): Relation of the trephine opening (Freeman-Watts lobotomy point) to the underlying cerebrum. *Trans. Am. Neurol. Assoc.,* 73:156–158.

20. Milner, B. (1958): Psychological defects produced by temporal lobe excision. *The brain and human behavior. Proc. Assoc. Res. Nerv. Ment. Dis.,* XXXVI:244–257.

21. Mishkin, M. (1972): Cortical visual areas and their interaction. In: *The Brain and Human Behavior,* edited by A. G. Karczmar and J. C. Eccles, pp. 187–200. Springer-Verlag, Berlin.

22. Mishkin, M., and Pribram, K. H. (1954): Visual discrimination performance following partial ablations of the temporal lobe: I. Ventral vs. lateral. *J. Comp. Physiol. Psychol.,* 47:14–20, 1954.

23. Nuwer, M., and Pribram, K. H. (1976): The analysis of electrocortical activity evoked during tasks demanding selective attention in rhesus monkeys *(in preparation).*

24. Pribram, K. H. (1954): Toward a science of neuropsychology: (method and data). In: *Current Trends in Psychology and the Behavioral Sciences,* edited by R. A. Patton, pp. 115–142. University of Pittsburgh Press, Pittsburgh.

25. Pribram, K. H. (1959): On the neurology of thinking. *Behav. Sci.,* 4:265–284.

26. Pribram, K. H., Day, R. U., and Johnston, V. S. (1976): Selective attention: distinctive brain electrical patterns produced by differential reinforcement in monkey and man. In: *Behavior Control and Modification of Physiological Activity,* edited by D. I. Mostofsky. MIT Press, Cambridge. In press.

27. Pribram, K. H., and McGuinness, D. (1975): Arousal, activation, and effort in the control of attention. *Psychol. Rev.,* 82(2):116–149.

28. Pribram, K. H., and Mishkin, M. (1955): Simultaneous and successive visual discrimination by monkeys with inferotemporal lesions. *J Comp. Physiol. Psychol.,* 48:198–202.

29. Pribram, K. H., and Bagshaw, M. (1953): Further analysis of the temporal lobe syndrome utilizing fronto-temporal ablations. *J. Comp. Neurol.,* 99:347–375.

30. Pribram, K. H., Spinelli, D. N., and Reitz, S. L. (1969): Effects of radical disconnexion of occipital and temporal cortex on visual behaviour of monkeys. *Brain,* 92:301–312.

31. Reitz, S. L., and Pribram, K. H. (1969): Some subcortical connections of the inferotemporal gyrus of monkey. *Exp. Neurol.,* 25:632–645.

32. Rosvold, H. E., and Szwarcbart, M. K. (1964): Neural structures involved in delayed-response performance. In: *The Frontal Granular Cortex & Behavior,* edited by J. M. Warren and K. Akert, pp. 1–15. McGraw-Hill, New York.

33. Rothblat, L., and Pribram, K. H. (1972): Selective attention: input filter or response selection? *Brain Res.,* 39:427–436.

34. Skinner, J. E., and Yingling, C. D. (1977): Regulation of slow potential shifts in nucleus reticularis thalami by the mesencephalic reticular formation and the frontal granular cortex. *Electroencephalogr. Clin. Neurophysiol. (in press).*

35. Smerin, S., and Pribram, K. S. (1976): Effects of basal ganglia stimulation on visual receptive field properties of the lateral geniculate nucleus of the cat *(in preparation).*

36. Spinelli, D. N., and Pribram, K. H. (1966): Changes in visual recovery functions produced by temporal lobe stimulation in monkeys. *Electroencephalogr. Clin. Neurophysiol.,* 20:44–49.

37. Spinelli, D. N., and Pribram, K. H. (1967): Changes in visual recovery function and unit activity produced by frontal and temporal cortex stimulation. *Electroencephalogr. Clin. Neurophysiol.,* 22:143–149.

38. Ungerleider, L., and Pribram, K. H. (1976): Effects of pulvinar and prestriate lesions on visual discrimination behavior in monkeys *(in preparation).*

39. Ungerleider, L., Ganz, L., and Pribram, K. H. (1976): Deficits in size constancy discrimination: further evidence for dissociation between monkeys with inferotemporal and prestriate lesions *(in preparation).*

40. Von Monakov, C. (1889): Experimentalle und pathologische untersuchungen über optischen centren und bahden. *Arch. Psychiatr. Nervenker.,* 20:714–787.

41. Whitlock, D. G., and Nauta, W. J. (1956): Subcortical projections from the temporal neocortex in macaca mulatta. *J. Comp. Neurol.,* 106:183–212.

42. Yingling, C. D., and Skinner, J. E. (1975): Regulation of unit activity in nucleus reticularis thalami by the mesencephalic reticular formation and the frontal granular cortex. *Electroencephalogr. Clin. Neurophysiol.*, 39:1–9.
43. Yingling, C. D., and Skinner, J. E. (1976): Selective regulation of thalamic sensory relay nuclei by nucleus reticularis thalami. *Electroencephalogr. Clin. Neurophysiol.* (*submitted for publication*).

Psychopathology and Brain Dysfunction, edited by C. Shagass, S. Gershon, and A. J. Friedhoff. Raven Press, New York © 1977.

GABA-DA Interactions and Their Possible Relation to Schizophrenia*

K. Fuxe, M. Perez de la Mora, T. Hökfelt, L. Agnati, Å. Ljungdahl, and O. Johansson

Department of Histology, Karolinska Institute, S-104 01 Stockholm 60, Sweden

A number of ascending dopamine (DA) pathways from the midbrain are known to innervate the forebrain: neostriatum, subcortical limbic regions (e.g., nucleus accumbens and tuberculum olfactorium), limbic cortex, and frontal cortex (7,8,18,33,34). The neostriatal and accumbens DA innervations are important for sensorimotor integration and thus for posture and motor performance (see ref. 22). The DA innervation of other limbic regions and of frontal cortex may instead be involved in the control of mental activity, and it has been suggested that antischizophrenic drugs act mainly by blocking cortical DA receptors (22).

For some time we have been interested in evaluating which transmitter pathways control the activity in the ascending DA pathways. It is well known that there exists a descending striato- (and/or pallido-) nigral gamma-aminobutyric acid (GABA) pathway (15,20). Furthermore, large amounts of substance P–containing nerve terminals have been observed in the zona reticulata of the substantia nigra (17). The primary concern was to understand the possible interactions between GABA and DA neurons. In order to do this, we performed the following types of experiments, which are summarized in this chapter:

A. Effect of presumable GABAergic drugs on DA turnover in various parts of the forebrain. The GABAergic drugs used are: β-(p-chlorphenyl)-GABA (Lioresal®, Baclofen®), amino-oxyacetic acid (AOAA), γ-hydroxy-butyrolactone (GBL), 5-ethyl-5-phenyl-2-pyrrolidinone (EPP), and ibotenic acid.

B. The effects of presumable GABA receptor blocking agents such as picrotoxin and bicuculline on DA turnover in various parts of the forebrain.

C. The effects of the DA receptor agonist apomorphine on GABA turnover in limbic areas, striatum, and ventral tegmentum.

D. The effect of 6-OH-DA–induced lesions of the ascending DA pathways on GABA turnover in limbic areas, striatum, and ventral tegmentum.

---

* Parts of the findings have been reported at the Sixth International Congress of Pharmacology (13), Helsinki, Finland, July 20–25, 1975.

PRESUMABLE GABAERGIC DRUGS AND DA TURNOVER

DA turnover changes were evaluated by studying the DA fluorescence disappearance after tyrosine hydroxylase inhibition using α-methyltyrosine methylester (6). The DA stores were measured by means of quantitative microfluorimetry (9) on paraffin sections prepared according to the routine Falck-Hillarp technique for demonstration of DA stores or on Vibratome sections as described by Hökfelt et al. (18). The results on AOAA, GBL, Lioresal®, and EPP have previously been reported (10,11,13,16), but those on ibotenic acid have not.

The drugs can be characterized briefly in the following way. Lioresal® is a GABA analogue that may have some GABAmimetic activity (29). γ-Hydroxybutyrolactone may be a precursor to GABA, but this has recently been disputed (24). AOAA is a well-known GABA transaminase inhibitor (35). EPP is a cyclic GABA analogue which according to pharmacological evidence possesses GABAergic activity (23,26). Ibotenic acid is also a GABA analogue which according to neurophysiological evidence has GABAmimetic activity (19).

Lioresal® was used in doses of 5 to 20 mg/kg, GBL in doses of 300 to 600 mg/kg, AOAA in a dose of 25 mg/kg, EPP in doses of 50 to 200 mg/kg, and ibotenic acid in doses of 4 to 10 mg/kg. All injections were made i.p. and usually 15 min before H44/68 (250 mg/kg, i.p., 1 or 2 hr before killing). With the doses and time intervals used, no changes in DA levels were observed 15 min to 2 hr after injection with the exception of 600 mg/kg of GBL, which clearly increased DA levels in agreement with previous results (1,4,14,31,36). Furthermore, EPP (200 mg/kg) increased DA levels in the tuberculum olfactorium 2 hr after injection. The effects of ibotenic acid have so far been studied only in the limbic cortex.

Lioresal® (5 to 20 mg/kg), GBL (300 mg/kg), AOAA (25 mg/kg), and EPP (100 to 200 mg/kg) were found to reduce DA turnover selectively in the limbic system (subcortical and cortical regions), leaving the nigro-neostriatal DA system unaffected. The subcortical limbic regions studied were nucleus accumbens and tuberculum olfactorium, and the limbic cortical region was entorhinal cortex. The most marked effects on DA turnover were obtained when giving the GABAergic drugs to rats that had been pretreated with pimozide (1 mg/kg, i.p., 2 hr before H44/68), a DA receptor blocking agent (5). These latter results in pimozide-treated rats can be explained on the basis that descending GABA tracts mediate the inhibitory feedback on ascending mesencephalic DA tracts. Thus, if this is true, blockade of DA receptor by treatment with pimozide should reduce activity in the descending GABA tracts and subsequently in GABA receptor activity in the mesencephalon. Under these conditions, a GABAergic drug would be expected to cause a marked increase in GABA receptor activity and thus a clear-cut reduction in DA turnover.

Some of the findings obtained with Lioresal® (10 mg/kg) are illustrated in Fig. 1. The slopes (b values) are not changed by Lioresal® in nucleus caudatus (anterior or posterior), whereas in both areas of tuberculum olfactorium [diffuse and dotted fluorescence (25)], a marked reduction in DA turnover is observed. As seen from the 97% confidence intervals, the slope values in the caudatus are not significantly different from zero. Also, there is a clear trend for a reduction of amine turnover in the accumbens DA terminals exhibiting dotted fluorescence. The DA nerve terminals of the median eminence, however, reacted differently from those in the forebrain. As seen in Fig. 2, Lioresal® (10 mg/kg) given to pimozide-pretreated rats (same rats as in Fig. 1) increased the DA turnover in the lateral external layer (LPZ) of the median eminence. Also, the turnover in the NE nerve

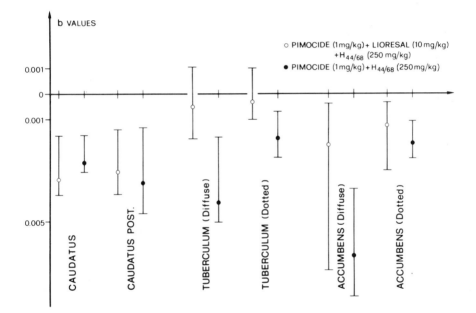

FIG. 1. Effect of Lioresal® on the H44/68-induced DA disappearance in various forebrain regions of the rat after pimozide (pimocide) pretreatment. Pimozide was given i.p. 2 hr before H44/68 (0.5, 1, 2, and 4 hr before killing). Lioresal® was given 15 min before H44/68. Routine Falck-Hillarp procedure has been used in combination with quantitative microfluorimetry to obtain and measure DA fluorescence. On the x-axis the various DA terminal–rich regions and the two types of treatment are shown. Anterior and posterior parts of caudatus have also been compared as well as the dotted and diffuse DA fluorescence in the nucleus accumbens and tuberculum olfactorium. On the y-axis the slopes (b) of the exponential DA fluorescence disappearance are shown based on observations collected at 0, 0.5, 1, 2, and 4 hr ($N = 4$–5). The 97% confidence intervals are shown (calculated according to nonparametrical procedures, Sen's test). Note that after Lioresal® treatment the slopes in the tuberculum olfactorium are not significantly different from zero. Note also a possible difference between the effect of Lioresal® on the slopes in the two parts studied in the nucleus accumbens.

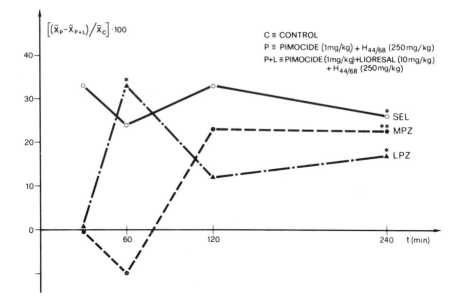

FIG. 2. Effect of Lioresal® on the H44/68-induced DA disappearance in the median eminence after pimozide (pimocide) pretreatment. Same rats as shown in Fig. 1. SEL, mainly NA nerve terminals; MPZ, medial palisade zone, mixture of DA and NE nerve terminals; LPZ, mainly DA nerve terminals, see Fuxe et al. (12). On the x-axis the time after H44/68 injection is shown. On the y-axis the mean difference between the two groups is plotted in percentage of untreated group means. Mann-Whitney U-test. * $p < 0.05$; ** $p < 0.01$. Acceleration of DA disappearance is observed in both NE- and DA-rich areas of the median eminence.

terminals of the subependymal layer (SEL) was increased (Fig. 2). NE turnover has also been found to be increased by Lioresal® (10–20 mg/kg) in biochemical studies on cortex cerebri and the rest of the brain (*unpublished data,* this laboratory).

The same pattern of DA turnover changes in the forebrain was observed after AOAA, GBL, and EPP (Fig. 3). Furthermore, EPP also increased DA turnover in the median eminence after pretreatment with pimozide. All the drugs were found to reduce DA turnover in the entorhinal cortex after pimozide pretreatment. This also holds for ibotenic acid in a dose of 10 mg/kg (Fig. 4), whereas 4 mg/kg was ineffective.

As expected, a reduction of neostriatal DA turnover was obtained when the dose of GBL was increased and when the time interval between the AOAA and H44/68 injections was increased, which leads to increased accumulations of GABA when DA turnover is studied (see also ref. 21).

Since the same spectrum of DA turnover changes was observed after all the presumable GABAergic drugs, it seems possible that the reduction of DA turnover observed in the limbic system was because of increases in GABA receptor activity. However, the obvious question is why no reduc-

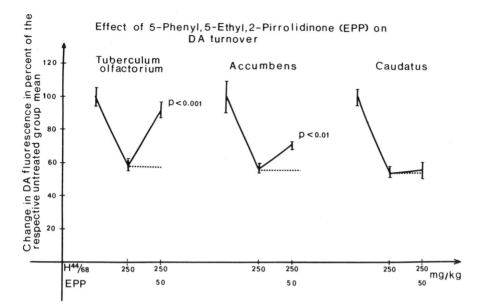

FIG. 3. Effect of EPP on the H44/68-induced DA fluorescence disappearance in the fore-brain. EPP (50 mg/kg) was given i.p. 15 min before H44/68 (250 mg/kg, i.p., 2 hr). On the x-axis the treatments and areas are shown. On the y-axis the values are given in percent of untreated group means. Means ± SEM. Student's t-test. N = 5.

tion was observed in the neostriatum in view of the high levels of glutamic acid decarboxylase activity present in the substantia nigra, especially in the zona reticulata (see Table 1), indicating a dense innervation by GABA terminals. There exists lower, but still high, levels of GAD activity in the DA cell group medial to the substantia nigra (A10, according to 8) (Table I), which gives rise to at least large parts of the DA innervation of the limbic system. Several explanations are certainly possible. One is that the excitatory input to the substantia nigra is stronger and more difficult to counteract by means of activation of inhibitory GABA receptors. In support of this view, there probably exists a very dense excitatory substance P input to the zona reticulata of the substantia nigra, whereas the substance P terminal network in the A10 group is sparse (17).

As in Table 1, GAD activity is higher in the nucleus accumbens and tuberculum olfactorium than in the nucleus caudatus. Thus, it is possible that there exists a stronger presynaptic inhibitory GABAergic input on the DA nerve terminals in the limbic system compared with that in the neostriatum. Such a difference could certainly contribute to the selective reduction of limbic DA turnover observed.

Recently, it has been shown that Lioresal® may block substance P receptors (30). In view of this evidence it also has to be seriously considered

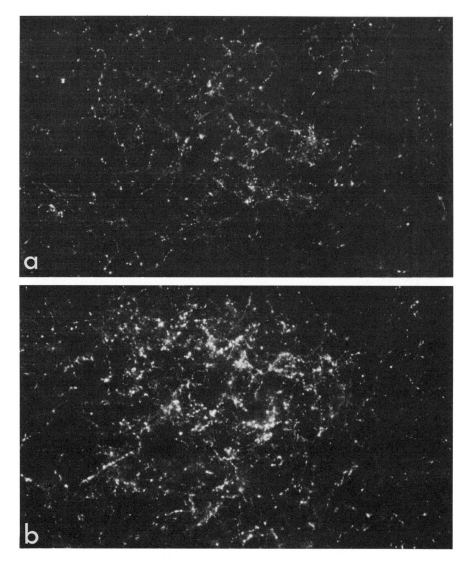

FIG. 4. Effect of ibotenic acid on the H44/68-induced DA disappearance in entorhinal cortex after pimozide pretreatment. Fluorescence microphotographs of DA nerve terminals in entorhinal cortex using a modified Falck-Hillarp procedure (T. Hökfelt, *unpublished data*). **a:** Pimozide (1 mg/kg) was given i.p. 2 hr before H44/68 (250 mg/kg, i.p., 1 hr before killing). **b:** Same treatment as in Fig. 4a except that ibotenic acid was given i.p. in a dose of 10 mg/kg 15 min before H44/68. Ibotenic acid causes a reduction of the pimozide-induced increase in DA fluorescence disappearance after H44/68 treatment (×300).

TABLE 1. *Distribution of GAD activity in the DA and 5-HT cell-rich and DA nerve terminal-rich areas of the brain*

Areas	GAD activity[a]	
	μmoles/g dry weight/hr (means ± SEM)	% of that in caudatus
DA nerve terminal–rich areas		
Nucleus caudatus	93 ± 6 (6)	100
Tuberculum olfactorium	199 ± 28 (6)	213
Nucleus accumbens	190 ± 6 (6)	204
DA cell body–rich areas		
Substantia nigra		
Compacta		
Caudal	395 ± 148 (6)	424
Middle	372 ± 48 (3)	400
Cranial	350 ± 36 (4)	268
Reticulata		
Caudal	383 ± 38 (3)	411
Middle	523 ± 76 (3)	562
Cranial	536 ± 10 (4)	576
A10 region		
Caudal	108 ± 3 (4)	116
Middle	196 ± 6 (2)	210
Cranial	163 ± 22 (4)	175
Corpus callosum	17 ± 4 (3)	18
Nucleus raphe dorsalis		
Caudal	187 ± 15 (3)	201
Middle	174 ± 28 (3)	187
Cranial	200 ± 15 (3)	215
Nucleus raphe medianus		
Caudal	119 ± 42 (3)	127
Middle	69 ± 21 (3)	74
Cranial	84 ± 16 (3)	90

[a] GAD activity was determined by measuring $^{14}CO_2$ produced by decarboxylation of ^{14}C-glutamate (3) using a micromodification in order to be able to measure activity in the freeze-dried cryostate sections from the various regions studied. Number of determinations in parentheses.
From M. Perez de la Mora, K. Fuxe, T. Hökfelt, and Å. Ljungdahl, *unpublished data.*

that Lioresal® could selectively reduce limbic DA turnover via blockade of excitatory substance P receptors. Thus, it may be easier to block the small substance P input to the A10 group than the very large substance P input to the substantia nigra. It therefore becomes important to investigate if EPP and ibotenic acid also have substance P receptor blocking activity.

Whatever the mechanism for the selective reduction observed in limbic DA turnover after treatment with the presumable GABAergic drugs, the effects observed may have important potential implications. Thus, it has been postulated that presumable GABAergic drugs may have a role in the treatment of schizophrenia (10,11,13,16) provided that the reduction of limbic DA turnover observed also means a reduction of DA receptor activity as well, the neuronal consequences of which are not counteracted by the GABAergic drugs themselves. So far, results from controlled clinical trials on combined treatment with neuroleptics and GABAergic drugs are not available. It is of interest to note, however, that Lioresal® (4 mg/kg) has been found to block the disruptive effects of amphetamine on discriminative avoidance responses without interfering with motor performance (2). However, in higher doses (10 to 20 mg/kg) Lioresal® reduces motor performance, causes hypotonia, and reduces *d*-amphetamine–induced rotational behavior (K. Fuxe, *unpublished data*).

EFFECTS OF PROBABLE GABA RECEPTOR BLOCKING AGENTS ON DA TURNOVER

The most well-known GABA receptor blocking agents are bicuculline and picrotoxin (19). In view of the results with GABAergic drugs discussed above, these drugs would be expected to increase DA turnover in the forebrain. Nevertheless, picrotoxin in total i.p. doses of 4 to 5 mg/kg was found to reduce DA turnover in the nucleus accumbens (Fig. 5), whereas no effects were observed in the nucleus caudatus. The DA levels were not affected.

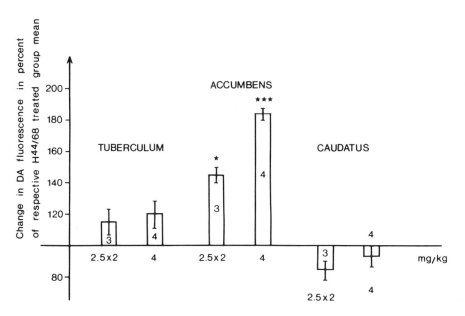

FIG. 5. Effect of picrotoxin on H44/68-induced DA disappearance in the forebrain. Picrotoxin was given i.p. in a dose of 4 mg/kg or in 2 doses of 2.5 mg/kg. The first injections were made immediately before the H44/68 injection (250 mg/kg, i.p., 2 hr). On the x-axis the areas and the two experimental groups with picrotoxin are shown. Means ± SEM. Number of rats is shown in the bars. Student's t-test. *$p < 0.05$; ***$p < 0.001$.

A trend for a reduction of DA turnover was also present in the tuberculum olfactorium. With bicuculline (total dose of 3 mg/kg, i.p.) also, unexpected effects were observed. Thus, a significant reduction ($p < 0.01$) was present in the tuberculum olfactorium. The tyrosine-hydroxylase inhibitor alone (α-methyltyrosine methylester, H44/68, 25 mg/kg, i.p., 2 hr) caused a DA depletion down to 67.7 ± 3.4 (means $\pm$ SEM, $N = 5$) in percent of untreated group mean value (100 ± 2.4, $N = 5$). After combined treatment with bicuculline (2×1.5 mg/kg, i.p., 1-hr interval, the first injection given immediately before H44/68) and H44/68, the depletion of DA was completely counteracted (102 ± 12.3 in percent of untreated group mean value). The DA turnover in nucleus accumbens and nucleus caudatus was not significantly affected by bicuculline (M. Perez de la Mora, K. Fuxe, T. Hökfelt, and Å. Ljungdahl, *unpublished data*).

It is not easy to explain these interesting results. It should be pointed out that GABA neurons are present at practically all levels of the central nervous system, in form of both "long" systems as described above and interneurons. All these systems may be differentially sensitive to the drugs. Furthermore, complex direct or indirect interactions may exist between such GABA systems, further complicating the interpretation. Another

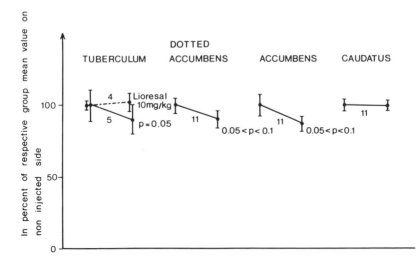

FIG. 6. Effect of unilateral stereotaxic injections of picrotoxin into the ventral tegmental area on the H44/68–induced DA fluorescence disappearance in the forebrain. Picrotoxin (0.5 μg/0.5 μl) was slowly infused into the ventral tegmental area with the rat in fluothane-air anesthesia (coordinates: 4.4 mm behind bregma; 0.9 mm lateral of the midline; and 7.4 mm below the surface of the brain; the König-Klippel atlas was used). The rat usually showed ipsilateral rotational behavior (cf. 32). Immediately after injection H44/68 was given (250 mg/kg, i.p.). Lioresal® was administered i.p. 15 min before picrotoxin. On the x-axis the areas are shown. Accumbens, diffuse DA fluorescence in nucleus accumbens. On the y-axis DA values on the injected side are shown in percent of those on the innervated side. Means $\pm$ SEM. Numbers indicate numbers of rats. Student's paired t-test.

possibility is that these drugs, because they are convulsants, have marked effects on the neuronal activity in large parts of the brain, although sub-convulsive doses are used. These general effects may then override any enhancing action that these drugs may have had on DA turnover. In favor of this latter possibility, it was found that the glycine antagonist strychnine in doses of 0.5 to 0.75 mg/kg reduced DA turnover in the tuberculum olfactorium (M. Perez de la Mora, K. Fuxe, T. Hökfelt, and Å. Ljungdahl, *unpublished data*). These results may offer a neurochemical explanation for the therapeutic effect of electroconvulsive treatment in schizophrenia, since limbic DA receptor activity may be reduced.

In order to evaluate the role of the GABA terminals around the DA cell groups in the midbrain, we infused picrotoxin (0.5 μl) slowly into the ventral tegmental area (Fig. 6). With this low amount of picrotoxin there occurs a small but significant acceleration of DA turnover in tuberculum olfactorium and a trend for acceleration in nucleus accumbens. The DA levels were not affected nor was the DA turnover in nucleus caudatus. The small preferential effects in the limbic areas may be explained on the basis that it is more difficult to block the larger GABA input to the substantia nigra DA cells than the smaller GABA input to the A10 DA nerve cells. Under all conditions the results support the view that GABA receptors may control activity in the mesolimbic DA systems.

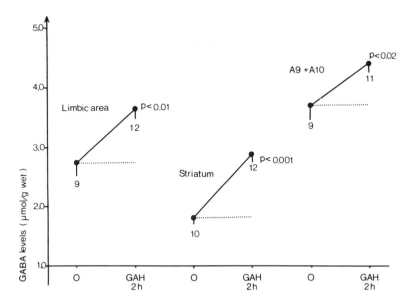

FIG. 7. Effect of GAH on GABA levels in limbic areas (nucleus accumbens and tuberculum olfactorium), striatum, and A9 + A10 DA cell body area. GAH (160 mg/kg, i.p.) was given 2 hr before killing. On the x-axis the various regions are shown. Means ± SEM. Numbers of animals are indicated at each point. Student's t-test.

EFFECTS OF APOMORPHINE ON GABA TURNOVER

In order to establish the existence of GABA-DA interactions, investigators have studied the effects of the DA receptor agonist apomorphine on GABA turnover. The model used to study changes in GABA turnover was to measure the accumulation of GABA after inhibition of the GABA transaminase (GABA) with the help of 1-γ-glutamylhydrazide (GAH). As seen in Fig. 7, GAH (160 mg/kg, 2 hr) increases GABA levels in the striatum, the "limbic" areas (nucleus accumbens and tuberculum olfactorium), and the ventral tegmentum. In Fig. 8 and Table 2 apomorphine is shown to increase the GAH-induced accumulation of GABA in the three regions studied

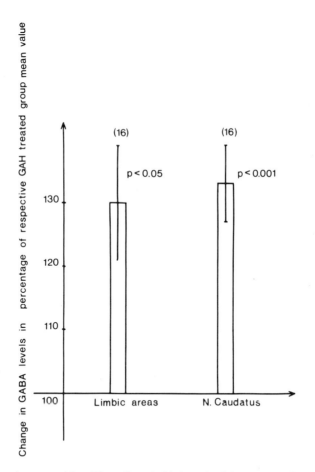

FIG. 8. Effects of apomorphine (10 mg/kg ×2, 2 hr) on the GAH-induced GABA accumulation in limbic areas (tuberculum olfactorium and nucleus accumbens) and striatum. Apomorphine was given i.p. the first injection being made 5 min before GAH and the second injection 1 hr after GAH (160 mg/kg, i.p., 2 hr before killing). On the x-axis the two areas are shown. Means ± SEM. Number of rats is shown in parentheses. Student's t-test (27).

TABLE 2. *Effect of apomorphine on the GAH-induced increase in GABA levels in the ventral tegmentum*

Treatment	Ventral tegmentum GABA levels
Control	3.73 ± 0.24^{a} 100 (5)
GAH	4.74 ± 0.11^{b} 127 (7)
Apomorphine + GAH	5.42 ± 0.23^{c} 145 (10)

Apomorphine (10 mg/kg, i.p.) was given 5 min before and 1 hr after GAH (160 mg/kg, 2 hr). Values are given in μmoles/g wet tissue (means $\pm$ SEM). p values from t-test after variance analysis.
$^{a\text{-}b}p < 0.05$.
$^{b\text{-}c}p < 0.05$ (27).

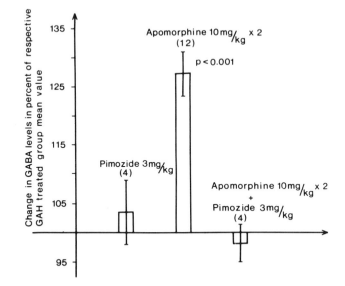

FIG. 9. Effect of apomorphine and pimozide on the accumulation of GABA in the midbrain DA cell body area after GAH treatment. For details on drug treatment, see text to Fig. 8. Pimozide was given i.p. 2.5 hr before GAH. The values are given in percentage of respective GAH-treated group mean. Means $\pm$ SEM; number of rats in parentheses. All comparisons have been made with the group treated with GAH alone. Student's t-test. GABA levels (μmoles/g wet weight) for the GAH-treated control group was 5.66 ± 0.28 ($N = 11$) in the apomorphine experiments and 6.12 ± 0.20 ($N = 4$) in the experiments with pimozide and apomorphine + pimozide (26).

(see refs. 27 and 28), suggesting that apomorphine increases GABA turnover in these three regions since GABA levels were not affected. A DA receptor activation is probably involved since the effects were abolished by pimozide (Fig. 9). These results therefore support the view that DA-GABA interactions exist in various parts of the brain. Thus, DA receptors may control activity in GABA interneurons and collaterals in the limbic system and basal ganglia. The descending GABA pathways may in turn be part of the inhibitory feedback system controlling activity in the ascending DA pathways.

EFFECT OF 6-OH-DA–INDUCED LESIONS OF THE ASCENDING DA PATHWAYS ON GABA TURNOVER

In these unpublished experiments (M. Perez de la Mora, K. Fuxe, T. Hökfelt, and Å. Ljungdahl), the degree of DA denervation was measured by means of quantitative microfluorimetry in the nucleus caudatus, tuberculum olfactorium, and nucleus accumbens. In the same animals the accumulation of GABA after inhibition of GABA-T with GAH (160 mg/kg, 2-hr) was measured. By means of intraindividual correlation coefficients [Spearman's rank correlation coefficient (r_s)], it could be shown that the GABA turnover in the striatum and ventral tegmentum was inversely related to the degree of DA denervation in the nucleus caudatus. The GABA turnover in the tuberculum olfactorium, on the other hand, was inversely related to the degree of denervation in the tuberculum olfactorium. Thus, these studies underline the existence of GABA-DA interactions linking the limbic DA neurons mainly to the limbic GABA neurons and the nigroneostriatal DA neurons to GABA neurons in the basal ganglia.

In conclusion, the present studies give biochemical and experimental evidence based on pharmacological studies on DA and GABA turnover and on lesions of DA pathways that important GABA-DA interactions exist in the forebrain and midbrain. The understanding of such interactions may lead to the development of new treatments of mental disorders (10,13,16).

Future work in this field, however, has to analyze the possible substance P receptor blocking activity of the GABAergic drugs.

ACKNOWLEDGEMENTS

This work has been supported by a grant (MH25504-02) from NIH and grants (04X-715 and 04X-2887) from the Swedish Medical Research Council, M. Bergvall's Stiftelse, and funds from the Karolinska Institute.

Ibotenic acid was generously supplied by Professor Engster, Zurich.

REFERENCES

1. Aghajanian, G. K., and Roth, R. H. (1970): γ-Hydroxybutyrate-induced increase in brain dopamine: localization by fluorescence microscopy. *J. Pharmacol. Exp. Ther.,* 175:131–137.

2. Ahlenius, S., Carlsson, A., and Engel, J. (1975): Antagonism by baclophen of the d-amphetamine-induced disruption of a successive discrimination in the rat. *J. Neurotransmission,* 36:327–333.
3. Alberts, R. W., and Brady, R. O. (1959): The distribution of glutamic decarboxylase in the nervous system of the rhesus monkey. *J. Biol. Chem.,* 234:926–928.
4. Andén, N.-E., and Stock, G. (1973): Inhibitory effect of gammahydroxybutyric acid and gammaaminobutyric acid on the dopamine cells in the substantia nigra. *Naunyn Schmiedeberg's Arch. Pharmacol.,* 279:89–92.
5. Andén, N.-E., Butcher, S., Corrodi, H., Fuxe, K., and Ungerstedt, U. (1970): Receptor activity and turnover of dopamine and noradrenaline after neuroleptics. *Eur. J. Pharmacol.,* 11:303–314.
6. Andén, N.-E., Corrodi, H., and Fuxe, K. (1969): Turnover studies using synthesis inhibition. In: *Metabolism of Amines in the Brain,* edited by G. Hooper, pp. 38–47. Macmillan, London.
7. Andén, N.-E., Dahlström, A., Fuxe, K., Olson, L., and Ungerstedt, U. (1966): Ascending monoamine neurons to the telencephalon and diencephalon. *Acta Physiol. Scand.,* 67:313–326.
8. Dahlström, A., and Fuxe, K. (1964): Evidence for the existence of monoamine containing neurons in the central nervous system. I. Demonstration of monoamines in the cell bodies of brain stem neurons. *Acta Physiol. Scand.,* 62:1–55.
9. Einarsson, P., Jonsson, G., and Hallman, H. (1975): Quantitative microfluorimetry of formaldehyde-induced fluorescence of dopamine in the caudate nucleus. *Med. Biol.,* 53:15–25.
10. Fuxe, K., Agnati, L., Hökfelt, T., Jonsson, G., Lidbrink, P., Ljungdahl, Å., Löfström, A., and Ungerstedt, U. (1975): The effect of dopamine receptor stimulating and blocking agents on the activity of supersensitive dopamine receptors and on the amine turnover in various dopamine nerve terminal systems in the rat brain. *J. Pharmacol.,* 6:117–129.
11. Fuxe, K., Hökfelt, T., Agnati, L., Ljungdahl, Å., Perez de la Mora, M., and Johansson, O. (1975): Further studies on the inhibitory gabaergic control of mesolimbic dopamine neurons. Possibility of improving treatment of schizophrenia by combined treatment with neuroleptics and GABAergic drugs. Abstract read at the Sixth International Congress of Pharmacology, Helsinki, Finland.
12. Fuxe, K., Hökfelt, T., Jonsson, G., and Löfstrom, Å. (1973): Recent morphological and functional studies on hypothalamic dopaminergic and noradrenergic mechanisms. In: *Frontiers in Catecholamine Research,* edited by E. Usdin, pp. 787–794. Pergamon Press, New York.
13. Fuxe, K., Hökfelt, T., Ljungdahl, A., Agnati, L., Johansson, O., and Perez de la Mora, M. (1975): Evidence for an inhibitory gabaergic control of the mesolimbic dopamine neurons: Possibility of improving treatment of schizophrenia by combined treatment with neuroleptics and gabergic drugs. *Med. Biol.,* 53:177–183.
14. Gessa, G. L., Vargiu, L., Crabai, R., Boero, C. C., Caboni, F., and Cambra, R. (1966): Selective increase of brain dopamine induced by gamma-hydroxybutyrate. *Life Sci.,* 5:1921–1930.
15. Hattori, T., Fibiger, H. C., and McGeer, P. L. (1975): Demonstration of a pallidonigral projection innervating dopaminergic neurons. *J. Comp. Neurol.,* 162:487–504.
16. Hökfelt, T., Agnati, L., Fuxe, K., Johansson, O., Ljungdahl, Å., and Löfström, A. (1975): Possible involvement of GABA synapses in the action of neuroleptic drugs on dopamine neurons: In: *Antipsychotic Drugs: Pharmacodynamics and Pharmacokinetics,* edited by G. Sedvall and B. Uvnäs, pp. 227–233. Pergamon Press, Oxford.
17. Hökfelt, K., Kellerth, J.-O., Nilsson, G., and Pernow, B. (1975): Substance P: Localization in the central nervous system and in some primary sensory neurons. *Science,* 190:889–890.
18. Hokfelt, T., Ljungdahl, Å., Fuxe, K., and Johansson, O. (1974): Dopamine nerve terminals in the rat limbic cortex: Aspects of the dopamine hypothesis of schizophrenia. *Science,* 184:177–179.
19. Johnston, G. A. (1976): Physiologic pharmacology of GABA and its antagonists in the vertebrate nervous system. In: *GABA in Nervous System Function, Vol. 5,* edited by E. Roberts, T. N. Chase, and D. B. Tower, pp. 395–411. Raven Press, New York.
20. Kim, J. S., Bak, I. J., Hassler, R., and Okada, Y. (1971): Role of γ-aminobutyric acid

(GABA) in the extrapyramidal motor system. 2. Some evidence for the existence of a type of GABA-rich strionigral neurons. *Exp. Brain Res.,* 14:95–104.

21. Lahti, R. A., and Losey, E. G. (1974): Antagonism of the effects of chlorpromazine and morphine on dopamine metabolism by GABA. *Res. Commun. Chem. Pathol. Pharmacol.,* 7:31–40.

22. Mathysse, S. W., and Kety, S. S. (Eds.) (1975): *Catecholamines and Schizophrenia.* Pergamon Press, Oxford.

23. Meza-Ruiz, G., Tapia, R., Drucker-Colin, R., and González, R. M. (1975): 5-Ethyl, 5-phenyl, 2-pyrrolidinine: A possible GABA-mimetic anticonvulsant. Abstract read at American Society of Neurochemistry, Vancouver.

24. Möhler, H., Patel, A., and Balasz, R. (1974): On the mechanism of action of gamma-hydroxybutyric acid: Lack of conversion to GABA in mouse brain *in vivo. Naunyn Schmiedeberg's Arch. Pharmacol.,* 282:67.

25. Olson, L., Seiger, Å., and Fuxe, K. (1972): Heterogeneity of striatal and limbic dopamine innervation: Highly fluorescent islands in developing and adult rats. *Brain Res.,* 44:283–288.

26. Perez de la Mora, M., and Tapia, R. (1973): Anticonvulsant effect of 5-ethyl, 5-phenyl, 2-pyrrolidinone and its possible relationship to γ-aminobutyric acid-dependent inhibitory mechanisms. *Biochem. Pharmacol.,* 22:2635–2639.

27. Perez de la Mora, M., Fuxe, K., Hökfelt, T., and Ljungdahl, Å. (1975): Effect of apomorphine on the GABA turnover in the CA cell group rich area of the mesencephalon. Evidence for the involvement of an inhibitory gabaergic feedback control of the ascending DA neurons. *Neurosci. Lett.,* 1:109–114.

28. Perez de la Mora, M., Fuxe, K., Hökfelt, T., and Ljungdahl, Å. (1976): Further evidence that apomorphine increases GABA turnover in the DA cell body rich and DA nerve terminal rich areas of the brain. *Neurosci. Lett.,* 2:239–242.

29. Pierau, F.-K., Matheson, G. K., and Wurster, R. D. (1975): Presynaptic action of β(4-chorophenyl)-GABA. *Exp. Neurol.,* 48:343–351.

30. Saito, K., Konishi, S., and Otsuka, M. (1975): Antagonism between Lioresal and Substance P in rat spinal cord. *Brain Res.,* 97:177–180.

31. Stock, G., Magnusson, T., and Andén, N.-E. (1973): Increase in brain dopamine after axotomy or treatment with gammahydroxybutyric acid due to elimination of the nerve impulse flow. *Naunyn Schmiedeberg's Arch. Pharmacol.,* 278:347–361.

32. Tarsy, D., Pycock, C., Meldrum, B., and Marsden, C. D. (1975): Rotational behavior induced in rats by intranigral picrotoxin. *Brain Res.,* 89:160–165.

33. Thierry, A. M., Stinus, L., Blanc, G., and Glowinski, J. (1973): Some evidence for the existence of dopaminergic neurons in the rat cortex. *Brain Res.,* 50:230–234.

34. Ungerstedt, U. (1971): Stereotaxic mapping of the monoamine pathway in the rat brain. *Acta Physiol. Scand.,* 82:1–48.

35. Wallach, D. P. (1961): Studies on the GABA pathway. The inhibition of γ-aminobutyric acid-α-ketoglutaric acid transminase *in vitro* and *in vivo* by U7524 (amino-oxyacetic acid). *Biochem. Pharmacol.,* 5:323–331.

36. Walters, J. R., Roth, R. H., and Aghajanian, G. K. (1973): Dopaminergic neurons, similar biochemical and histochemical effects of γ-hydroxybutyrate and acute lesions of the nigro-striatal pathway. *J. Pharmacol. Exp. Ther.,* 186:630–639.

Psychopathology a
by C. Shagass, S. G.
Raven Press, New

The Biochemical Organization o
and Schizophrenia

J. R. Smythies

Department of Psychiatry and the Neurosciences Program, U... ...sity of Alabama Medical Center, Birmingham, Alabama 35294

INTRODUCTION

My purpose is to review certain aspects of the biochemical organization of the brain insofar as they are relevant to the problem of the etiology of psychosis, in particular, schizophrenia. The focus of interest over the last decade has been on the different transmitter systems in the brain, their synthesis, release, action at receptors, and inactivation. Our current concepts of the etiology of disorders of psychiatric interest such as Parkinson's disease, schizophrenia, and manic-depressive psychosis center on possible disorders in these systems and in those depending on dopamine, serotonin, norepinephrine, and GABA in particular.

I will first review briefly the basic anatomy and behavioral concomitants of these systems as far as they are known. The first three amines listed above share several common anatomical features. Their cell bodies are concentrated in sharply delineated nuclei in the brainstem, but the axons spread widely and the terminal branches form a close network, particularly in the cerebral cortex, so that a local stimulus in the brainstem can lead to widespread release of a specific chemical. The main nucleus of the dopamine system is the substantia nigra. From there, three different pathways supply an extensive dopaminergic innervation to (a) the corpus striatum, (b) the limbic system (nucleus accumbens, olfactory tubercule, and entorhinal cortex), and (c) the cerebral cortex. The main nucleus of the norepinephrine system is the locus ceruleus, and in the serotonin system it is the raphe nucleus. The main efferent pathways of these run via the medial forebrain bundle to the forebrain.

Various lines of animal experiments and of psychopharmacological research suggest the following tentative functions for these systems. The norepinephrine (NE) system [and possibly to some extent also the dopamine (DA) system] may be involved with positive reinforcement. It is thought that whenever a positively rewarding stimulus is received by the organism, the NE system is activated and the widespread release of NE throughout the brain carries the message: "positive reinforcement received—imprint

...ver you are doing as it is likely to lead to good results." Likewise, it ...possible that the release of another as yet unidentified transmitter may ...signal: "negative reinforcements received – do not repeat whatever you are doing."

This formulation is based on the following facts:

• Drugs such as amphetamine and cocaine that potentiate brain NE cause euphoria.

• Drugs such as reserpine that lower brain NE levels can cause severe depression in normal subjects.

• Animals on self-stimulation schedules work hard to receive microinjections of NE into the positive reward areas of the brain.

• Antidepressant drugs such as the tricyclics block the reuptake of NE into the synaptic terminal, or, as in the case of the monoamine oxidase inhibitors (MAOIs), inhibit the breakdown of NE by the MAO present within the terminal.

The brain dopamine system seems to be concerned with posture and movement regulation and perhaps with motivational systems. The evidence is as follows:

First, human Parkinson's disease, or paralysis agitans, is the result of the degeneration of dopamine-containing neurons in the substantia nigra, leading to a profound fall of the dopamine levels in the corpus striatum. The resulting symptoms are the familiar rigidity and tremor and also the akinesia and a poverty of movement and of emotional expression over and above that explicable on grounds of the rigidity alone.

Second, animals given chemicals that block the synthesis of dopamine develop a peculiar akinetic state in which they do not move although they are in no sense paralyzed.

Third, phenothiazines, butyrophenones, and related drugs that have potent antipsychotic properties have in common antidopamine capacities. This is relevant to the dopamine hypothesis of schizophrenia I shall be discussing further below.

Evidence concerning the possible functions of the serotonin (5-HT) system in the brain comes from two main sources:

First, the main group of hallucinogens, such as *d*-LSD, mescaline, and DOM, appear to act on 5-HT systems, although there is still not general agreement on whether they act as 5-HT agonists or antagonists. Reactions to these drugs, particularly during "bad trips," include profound disturbances of perception, of the interpetation of the environment, and of thinking. Presumably 5-HT mechanisms may be involved in these functions.

Second, the drug parachlorphenylalanine (PCPA) blocks the synthesis of 5-HT and leads to disturbances of sleep and control of sexual impulses, and, in man, to psychotic states. There is evidence that both 5-HT and NE are involved in the regulation of sleep, and 5-HT may be involved in control of instinctual mechanisms as well. These three transmitters also have other functions in the brain—for example, dopamine is concerned in the release of hypothalamic hormones and NE in appetite regulation.

Other neurotransmitters of likely importance are acetylcholine, histamine, GABA, glutamate, glycine, and probably a number of polypeptides such as substance P, angiotensin, bradykinin, and enkephaline. The function of these is obscure and their relation to psychosis is uncertain. Anticholinergics such as atropine cause a toxic delirium. Some putative GABA agonists such as muscimol are psychotomimetic, but this drug may act at loci other than the GABA receptor. Then again, drugs (e.g., nalorphine) that are partial agonists/antagonists at the opiate receptor are also psychotomimetic, which is odd because pure agonists and pure antagonists lack this property. Schizophrenics are resistant to the toxic effects of histamine, but the significance of this remains quite obscure, as does the role of histamine in the brain. GABA, glycine, and serotonin have also been linked to anxiety-reducing systems via possible modes of action of the benzodiazepines. But we are still vastly ignorant as to the real functions of these systems in the brain. However, this body of knowledge has enabled us to understand much more about parkinsonism than we did before, and it led to one of the rare achievements in medicine—the rational development of an effective treatment, L-DOPA. It is also contributing greatly to our understanding of bipolar depressive illness as Schildkraut reviews elsewhere in this volume. But what about schizophrenia?

FACTS AND CANDIDATE FACTS ABOUT SCHIZOPHRENIA

Let us look quickly at the present state of our knowledge concerning possible biochemical malfunctions in schizophrenia. In spite of 50 years of effort, although grossly underfinanced, by a small number of dedicated workers (small in comparison with the number of workers in other areas of medical research), all that we have to show is a handful of disconnected facts, a number of sketchy hypotheses, and a reasonably effective treatment (for some). Nevertheless, this is progress of a kind because only a few years ago we had no facts and no effective treatment. Let us look at the facts first; we can categorize these into (a) established facts and (b) statements about which there is no general agreement but for which there is a certain amount of evidence (candidate facts).

Fact 1

The data of Heston, Rosenthal, Kety (1), and others has shown unequivocally that a genetic factor is present in chronic process schizophrenia (but not in acute schizophreniform reactions), and that environmental factors (including intrauterine factors and birth trauma) are also important.

Fact 2

In 1961 Polin, Cardon, and Kety (2) discovered that a certain proportion ($\approx$40%) of chronic schizophrenic patients react to ingested L-methionine (20 g/day) plus a MAOI with an acute psychotic reaction. This finding has now been confirmed by ten groups of workers (3). We (4) replicated these results at Edinburgh using L-methionine alone. The question has been raised as to whether this reaction represents a specific exacerbation of the schizophrenic psychosis or a superimposed nonspecific toxic psychosis. We paid careful attention to this point in our study and concluded that the former was the predominant reaction. In several instances, specific hallucinations and delusions that occurred during the early years of the patient's illness but had not been reported later recurred. However, in two cases an initial delirious response was seen with disorientation and clouding of consciousness. This lasted approximately 2 days before reverting to the "acute schizophreniform" reaction (on continued methionine). This reaction comes on rapidly, usually within 12 hr, and usually recedes rapidly when methionine administration is stopped. Furthermore, the reaction had an all-or-none character—40% of the patients responded fully and 60% failed to respond at all. How can we explain this finding? First, we would like to know how normal people respond to methionine. No large study has been carried out to answer this question. However, approximately 20 years ago Himsworth, Sherlock, and others gave doses up to 10 g/day without any reports of such a reaction. (This reaction must, of course, be distinguished from hepatic coma induced by methionine in patients with liver disease with portocaval shunts.) We do not know whether we are dealing with two subclassifications of schizophrenia—methionine-sensitive and methionine-resistant—or whether different patients can pass through these phases at different times, although the former seems more likely.

Thus, we have one fact in search of an explanation. I will return to consider what the explanation may be.

Fact 3

The phenothiazines, butyrophenones, and related drugs used in psychiatry have a special therapeutic effect in psychoses—that is, they are antipsychotic and not merely tranquilizers. The relevant sites of action are thought to be catecholamine, and particularly dopamine, receptors, which they block. This fact is relevant to the dopamine hypothesis of schizophrenia discussed below.

Fact 4

Many studies (5) have shown that chronic schizophrenic patients are remarkably tolerant of histamine whether ingested or given by intradermal injection. Furthermore, reactivity increases (as measured on the size of wheal produced by intradermal histamine) as recovery from the psychotic episode occurs.

Fact 5

One case diagnosed clinically as schizophrenic (6) of a hebephrenic type was shown to have a specific defect in one of the enzymes of the 1-carbon cycle — 5,10-methylenetetrahydrofolate reductase — leading to raised blood and urine homocysteine but normal methionine. Most "ordinary" homocysteinurics (in whom the disease is caused by defects in the enzyme that links homocysteine to serine to form cystathionine) do not show psychotic features but are severely mentally retarded. However, certain families of homocysteinurics (the original Belfast family, a Limerick family, and five families discovered in Canada by Perry) seem to be loaded with schizophrenia as well; possibly the occurrence of homocysteinuria in a family may increase the expressivity of a concomitant schizophrenogenic gene.

Fact 6: Candidate

Chronic schizophrenics, as well as other psychiatric patients, may have lower-than-normal levels of platelet MAO (7). The level found in chronic schizophrenics was approximately one-half that found in normal controls. Acute schizophrenics, on the other hand, as well as unipolar depressives, had normal values, whereas bipolar patients had intermediate (still significantly depressed) values. Furthermore, in a series of 95 normal controls, the platelet MAO level significantly corresponded with high scores on the MMPI F Scale (overall psychopathology) and the Zuckerman Z Scale (sensation seeking or impulsive feelings): in females the paranoia scale (only) so correlated. These findings have been confirmed by Meltzer and Stahl (8) but not by Friedhoff (9). Moreover, brain MAO may or may not correlate with platelet MAO.

Fact 7: Candidate

A recent double-blind controlled study produced evidence to support Dohan's (10) hypothesis that schizophrenics may share a property in common with patients with celiac disease — namely, intolerance of wheat gluten proteins. In their study Singh and Kay (11) reported that wheat flour added to a gluten-free diet produced clinical deterioration in 14 chronic schizophrenic patients whereas soy flour did not. Many patients with celiac disease have psychiatric symptoms of a schizoid paranoid character. Wheat gluten is particularly rich in glutamate and proline moieties.

How then can we account for this bevy of disconnected facts? There are four hypotheses currently in the field. These are not necessarily competitive and indeed may be complementary. "Schizophrenia" it is widely agreed represents a syndrome within which many different genotypes may end up with similar clinical pictures: further, the neurochemical disorder(s) in the schizophrenias may well be complex in each case or subsection. The primary genetic fault in one system may lead to reverberations in other systems.

Specific Hypotheses

TRANSMETHYLATION HYPOTHESIS

The transmethylation hypothesis was first formulated in 1952 by Harley-Mason and Osmond and Smythies (12). It was based on the observation that mescaline is a chemical relative (0-methylated) of the catecholamines (NE and DA) (Fig. 1). We therefore suggested that schizophrenia might result from an aberration in catecholamine metabolism with the production in the body of mescaline-like psychotoxins, such as 3,4-dimethoxyphenyl-ethylamine (DMPEA). This was before anything was known about the metabolism of catecholamines. Then in 1957 Axelrod discovered that one normal route of catecholamine metabolism is a via 3-O-methylation by the enzyme catechol-O-methyltransferase (COMT) to produce metanephrine and related compounds. Interestingly enough, Harley-Mason had actually drawn the formula of metanephrine in our 1952 paper as a possible metabolite of epinephrine. Later it was found that COMT can O-methylate catecholamine in the 4 position (Fig. 1) as a minor product but not in the 3 and 4 positions. In 1962 Friedhoff and van Winkle (13) reported the occurrence of DMPEA in human urine, and this was confirmed by Creveling and Daly (14) using a definitive mass spectrographic method. DMPEA itself does not appear to be hallucinogenic, and it has been claimed to come from exogenous sources, possibly tea. It is therefore unlikely to be an endogenous psychotogen. In 1935 Slotta and Muller (15) reported that schizophrenics show an abnormal response to the 2,3,4 isomer of mescaline. This is normally considerably weaker than mescaline (3,4,5), but Slotta and Muller claim that in schizophrenics it is more potent than mescaline as a hallucinogen. If this report could be confirmed, it would be of considerable interest.

More recently, attempts have been made to implicate the hallucinogenic tryptamines such as dimethyltryptamine (DMT) and O-methylbufotenine (OMB) (Fig. 2) as pathogenic factors in schizophrenia. Claims have been made of identification of DMT by gas chromotography-mass spectrometry in human blood or urine, but it is premature to judge whether this has any relationship to schizophrenia. Thus, to date, no convincing data have been presented linking endogenous or even exogenous psychotoxins with schizophrenia.

The other "plank" alleged to support the transmethylation hypothesis

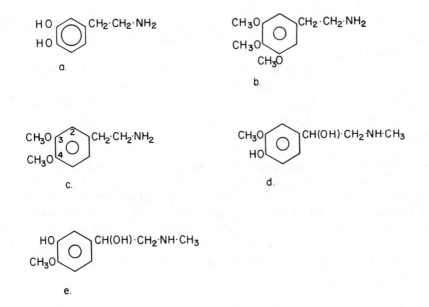

FIG. 1. a: Dopamine. b: Mescaline. c: DMPEA. d: Metanephrine. e: 4-OMe isomer of metanephrine.

is the methionine effect described above. Methionine, via its derivative S-adenosyl methionine (SAM), is the origin of the methyl groups for all known transmethylation reactions in the body. Thus a methionine load might increase an ongoing methylation reaction and consequently brain levels of the alleged methylated psychotoxin. In one such test measuring the excretion of methylated catecholamine metabolites in rats, it failed to do so (17).

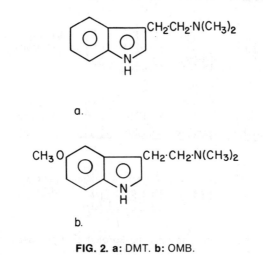

FIG. 2. a: DMT. b: OMB.

Moreover, methionine might be expected to have other effects, e.g., disturbances in the 1-carbon cycle and blockade of the uptake of the amino acids into neurons.

In a series of experiments carried out in Alabama by John Beaton (18), it was found that L-methionine (250 mg/kg) produces behavioral and EEG changes in rodents similar to those produced by LSD and amphetamines. In rats we have used a discriminative Sidman Avoidance Test. The rat is placed in a Skinner box in the dark. At 20 sec a light comes on and at 30 sec a shock is delivered and is repeated every 5 sec until a lever press is made. A lever press at any time during the schedule resets the schedule to the beginning. Responses made while the rat is in the dark are called "premature responses," those made while the light is on are called "efficient responses," and those made after shock are called "late responses." A well-trained rat emits most of its responses during the "efficient" period as this yields maximum remission of shock for minimum effort. Analysis of the response distribution within the 10-sec efficient period reveals a peak at 26 to 27 sec ("shift to the right").

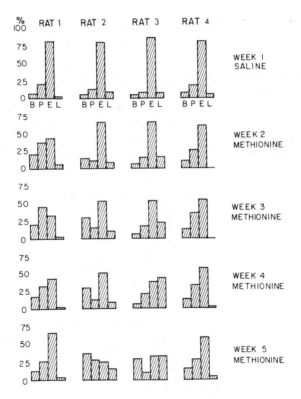

FIG. 3. The effect of L-methionine (250 mg/kg/day) on rats. Measures were summed daily for 1 week.

Different classes of drugs affect this behavior in different ways. Hallucinogens increase both premature and late responses (at the expense of efficient responses), and the distribution of responses within the efficient period becomes random. Amphetamines differ in that they do not cause any increase in late responses (early only), and the peak of responding during the efficient period shifts markedly to the left—to 21 to 22 sec—i.e., the rat presses the lever as soon as the light comes on (a typical "stimulus-bound" amphetamine response). Figure 3 shows the reaction of four rats to L-methionine on this test. Rats 1, 2, and 3 show a clear-cut "hallucinogenic" response, and rat 4, a clear-cut "amphetamine" response. Further studies showed that these effects are closely related—lower doses (125 mg/kg) tend to yield an amphetamine response and higher doses (250 mg/kg) a hallucinogenic response. Figure 4 shows that this effect is completely prevented by simultaneous administration of L-serine (250 mg/kg); other agents such as betaine (another methyl donor), L-serine alone, and cysteine had no effect.

Methionine also causes significant reduction of REM sleep in mice—this effect too is prevented by L-serine (Fig. 5). Examination of part of the one-carbon cycle (Fig. 6) suggested a reason for the protective effect of L-serine. If we hypothesize that these psychotoxic effects of methionine in rodents are owing to the production in the brain of toxic homocysteine, then this toxicity might be prevented by giving an equal amount of L-serine. However, we also found that the methionine effect in rodents could be prevented by giving

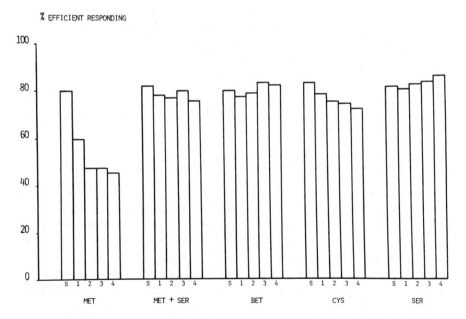

% EFFICIENT RESPONDING

FIG. 4. Inhibition of the methionine (MET) effect in rats by serine (SER)—only the "effective" responses shown. BET, betaine; CYS, cysteine.

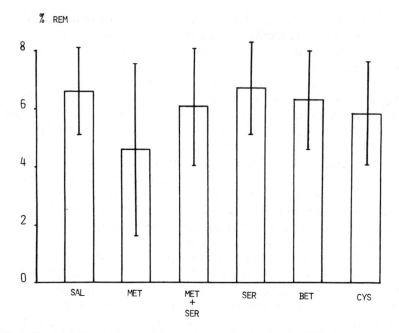

FIG. 5. The inhibition of the methionine-induced reduction in REM sleep by serine.

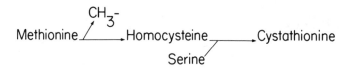

FIG. 6. Part of the one-carbon cycle.

glucose or glycine instead of serine. Since all these compounds are gluco-neogenic, this suggested an alternative hypothesis.

REDUCED TRYPTOPHAN UPTAKE HYPOTHESIS

Wurtman and Fernstrom (19) have recently shown that brain 5-HT levels are a direct function of brain tryptophan levels and that one factor modulating the latter is the amount of glucose ingested by the following mechanism. Glucose ingested leads to insulin secretion. A common amino acid uptake mechanism in the brain is used by tryptophan and other neutral amino acids (leucine, valine, etc.). This mechanism is blocked by insulin for the uptake of all neutral amino acids except tryptophan. Therefore, raised insulin levels lead to increased tryptophan uptake into the brain (and hence raised brain 5-HT) by inhibiting the uptake of these competing amino acids. The most active inhibitor of the uptake of the other amino acids is methionine. Therefore, the hypothesis is as follows: First, the behavioral disruption induced by methionine is due, in part, to blockade of tryptophan uptake leading to reduced 5-HT levels (*vide* PCPA effect). Second, gluconeogenic agents such as serine, glycine, and glucose counter this effect by causing insulin release, which blocks uptake of competing neutral amino acids and allows the blocked tryptophan uptake to recover. Nicotinamide may also affect this system. Beaton has found that at a dose of 25 mg/kg nicotinamide produces a significant increase in REM sleep in mice: Scherer and Krämer (20) report that it increases brain 5-HT. Nicotinamide is the end product of tryptophan metabolism via the kynurenine pathway. High doses of nicotinamide could lead to end-product inhibition of this pathway with consequent augmentation of the alternative pathway to 5-HT.

If certain schizophrenics suffer from a relative central 5-HT insufficiency, then measures designed to raise central 5-HT levels (increased ingestion simultaneously of tryptophan, serine, and nicotinamide, and possibly giving insulin) might be beneficial. The deleterious effect of wheat gluten in these cases might be because of proline overload (acting like methionine). Thus the transmethylation hypothesis has developed two offshoots—the one-carbon cycle hypothesis and the reduced tryptophan uptake hypothesis. Animal experiments to disentangle these possibilities are currently underway. We screened the methionine used in our experiments for possible contaminant toxins (such as methionine sulfoximine) by gas chromatography and did not detect any.

DOPAMINE HYPOTHESIS

The fourth hypothesis is the dopamine hypothesis reviewed recently by Snyder (21). This depends on the following facts: (a) Amphetamine produces a paranoid psychosis clinically indistinguishable from schizophrenia. L-DOPA can also induce psychotic reactions in normal people. (b) Amphetamine, L-DOPA, and MAOIs all induce worsening of schizophrenic symptoms. (c) There is a direct correlation between the antischizophrenic action of a drug and its capacity to block dopamine receptors (as measured by binding studies or by inhibition of isolated dopamine-sensitive adenyl cyclase).

All these data suggest that an overactive dopamine system, especially the limbic dopamine system, is present in schizophrenia, and that inhibiting this system by phenothiazines or butyrophenones reduces the psychosis. However, the primary biochemical fault need not be in the dopamine system. This overactivity may be induced by or relative to a primary pathological reduction in some other system—5-HT or some as yet undiscovered system. A comparable situation exists in Parkinson's disease, in which the primary fault is in the nigrostriatal dopamine system leading to a fall of striatal dopamine levels and an uncompensated overactivity of the striatal cholinergic system. Hence, treatment by anticholinergic agents is of benefit in parkinsonian conditions. The primary dopamine lack is not corrected – but the relatively overactive cholinergic system is brought back into balance. The relative levels of activity of the two systems seem more important than their absolute levels.

REFERENCES

1. Kety, S. S. (1976): Genetic aspects of schizophrenia. *Psychiatr. Ann.,* 6:11–32.
2. Polin, W., Cardon, P. V., Jr., and Kety, S. S. (1961): Effects of amino acid feedings in schizophrenic patients treated with iproniazid. *Science,* 133:104–105.
3. Cohen, S. M., Nichols, A., Wyatt, R., and Polin, W. (1974): The administration of methionine to chronic schizophrenic patients. A review of ten studies. *Biol. Psychiatry,* 8:209–225.
4. Antun, F. T., Burnett, G. B., Cooper, A. J., Daly, R. J., Smythies, J. R., and Zealley, A. D. (1971): The effects of 1-methionine (without MAOI) in schizophrenia. *J. Psychiatr. Res.,* 8:63–71.
5. Smythies, J. R. (1973): Schizophrenia. In: *Companion to Psychiatric Studies, Vol. II,* edited by A. Forrest. Livingstone, Edinburgh.
6. Freeman, J. M., Finkelstein, J. D., and Mudd, S. H. (1975): Folate responsive homocysteinuria and schizophrenia. A defect in methylation due to deficient 5, 10 methylene tetrahydrofolate reductase activity. *N. Engl. J. Med.,* 292:492–496.
7. Wyatt, R. J., Belmaker, R., and Murphy D. (1973): Low platelet monoamine oxidase and vulnerability to schizophrenia? *Science,* 179:916–918.
8. Meltzer, H. Y., and Stahl, S. M. (1974): Platelet monoamine oxidase activity and substrate preferences in schizophrenic patients. *Res. Commun. Chem. Pathol. Pharmacol.,* 7:419–431.
9. Friedhoff, A. J. (1975): Quoted in: Biochemical aspects of schizophrenia. *Psychoneuroendocrinology,* 1:199–201.
10. Dohan, F. C. (1966): Cereals and schizophrenia: data and hypothesis. *Acta Psychiatr., Scand.,* 42:125–152.
11. Singh, M. M., and Kay, S. R. (1976): Wheat gluten as a pathogenic factor in schizophrenia. *Science,* 191:401–402.
12. Osmond, H., and Smythies, J. R. (1952): Schizophrenia. A new approach. *J. Ment. Sci.,* 98:309–315.
13. Friedhoff, A. J., and van Winkle, E. (1962): Isolation and characterization of a compound from the urine of schizophrenics. *Nature,* 194:897–898.
14. Creveling, C. A., and Daly, J. (1967): Identification of 3, 4-dimethoxyphenylethylamine from schizophrenic urine by mass spectrometry. *Nature,* 216:190–191.
15. Slotta, K. H., and Muller, J. (1935): The breakdown of mescaline and substances similar to mescaline in the organism (trans). *Hoppe-Seyler's Z. Physiol. Chem.,* 238:14–22.
16. Gillin, J. C., Kaplan, J., Stillman, R., and Wyatt, R. J. (1976): The psychedelic model of schizophrenia: the case of N, N-dimethyltryptamine. *Am. J. Psychiatry,* 133:203–207.
17. Antun, F., Eccleston, D., and Smythies, J. R. (1973): Transmethylation processes in schizophrenia. In: *Brain Chemistry and Mental Disease,* edited by B. T. Ho and W. M. McIsaac. Plenum Press, New York.
18. Beaton, J. (1975): Methylation and schizophrenia. *Ala. J. Med. Sci.,* 12:193–202.
19. Wurtman, R. J., and Fernstrom, J. D. (1975): Control of brain monamine synthesis by diet and plasma amino acids. *Am. J. Clin. Nutr.,* 28:638–647.
20. Scherer, B., and Krämer, W. (1972): Influence of niacinamide administration on brain 5 HT and possible mode of action. *Life Sci.,* 11(Part I):189.
21. Snyder, S. H. (1976): The dopamine hypothesis of schizophrenia: focus on the dopamine receptor. *Am. J. Psychiatry,* 133:197–202.

Psychopathology and Brain Dysfunction, edited by C. Shagass, S. Gershon, and A. J. Friedhoff. Raven Press, New York © 1977.

Norepinephrine Metabolism in Subtypes of Depressive Disorders

Joseph J. Schildkraut, Paul J. Orsulak, Jon E. Gudeman, *Alan F. Schatzberg, *William A. Rohde, Richard A. LaBrie, Jane F. Cahill, *Jonathan O. Cole, and *Shervert H. Frazier

*Department of Psychiatry, Harvard Medical School; Neuropsychopharmacology Laboratory, Massachusetts Mental Health Center, Boston, Massachusetts 02115; *McLean Hospital, Belmont, Massachusetts 02178*

The observation that drugs which could alter affective state in man had profound effects on catecholamine disposition and metabolism in brain initially prompted our studies of catecholamine metabolism in the affective disorders (depressions and manias) more than a decade ago. An original focus of much of this research was to examine the changes in the urinary excretion of norepinephrine and its metabolites in relation to drug administration and changes in affective state. These findings have been reviewed previously (25,27).

The possibility that abnormalities in norepinephrine metabolism might occur in some but not necessarily all depressions, and that biochemical measures related to catecholamine metabolism might help to differentiate among the subtypes of depressive disorders was suggested more than 10 years ago in a review of the catecholamine hypothesis of affective disorders (24). This chapter summarizes selected aspects of our recent research on catecholamine metabolism in the affective disorders, emphasizing those findings which suggest that the examination of norepinephrine metabolism in patients with depressive disorders may provide a biochemical basis for classifying different types of depressions.

STUDIES OF 3-METHOXY-4-HYDROXYPHENYLGLYCOL EXCRETION AND CHANGES IN AFFECTIVE STATE IN BIPOLAR MANIC-DEPRESSIVE DISORDERS

Many lines of evidence now suggest that in several different species including man, 3-methoxy-4-hydroxyphenylglycol (MHPG) or its sulfate conjugate is the major metabolite of norepinephrine and normetanephrine in the brain (5,17,21–23,39), and that most norepinephrine originating in the brain is excreted in the urine as MHPG (12). However, MHPG which is excreted in the urine may also come, in part, from the peripheral sympathetic nervous system (1), and the fraction of urinary MHPG that in fact derives from norepinephrine originating in the brain remains problematic (3,14); but recent data suggest that in man the contribution from brain may be substantial (11).

In longitudinal studies of individual patients with naturally occurring or amphetamine-induced manic-depressive (i.e., bipolar) episodes, our research and that of other investigators (2,7,9,34,36,38) has shown that the levels of urinary MHPG are relatively lower during depressions and higher during manic or hypomanic episodes than after clinical remissions. However, not all studies concur with these findings (4,37).

The relationship between MHPG excretion and clinical state that we have observed in manic-depressive patients is illustrated in Fig. 1, which summarizes the changes in MHPG excretion in a manic-depressive patient studied longitudinally through five successive drug-free periods that were defined by differences in clinical state. During the initial period summarized here, the patient was mildly depressed. After this MHPG excretion decreased and the patient became severely depressed. During treatment with electroconvulsive therapy (ECT) there was a gradual increase in MHPG excretion and the depression gradually subsided. Following ECT, there was a further increase in MHPG excretion and the patient became transiently hypomanic. Subsequently, MHPG excretion decreased as the hypomania subsided and the patient again became mildly depressed. These

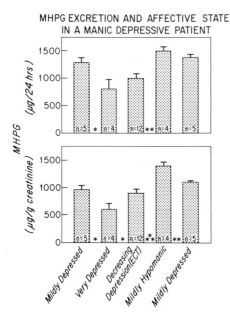

FIG. 1. MHPG excretion was determined in a bipolar manic-depressive patient studied through 5 successive drug-free periods defined by differences in clinical state. MHPG is expressed both in $\mu g/24$ hr and $\mu g/g$ creatinine. n, number of urine samples analyzed in each period. $*p < 0.05$; $**p < 0.01$; $***p < 0.001$ for differences in MHPG between adjacent periods. (Data from ref. 34.)

data show the close association between MHPG excretion and changes in affective state that we observed in patients with bipolar manic-depressive disorders.

However, all depressions are not clinically or biologically homogeneous (24), and all depressed patients do not excrete comparably low levels of MHPG (15,16). Our recent research has, therefore, explored the possibility that the urinary excretion of MHPG and other catecholamine metabolites might provide a biochemical basis for differentiating among the depressive disorders.

STUDIES OF MHPG EXCRETION IN SUBTYPES OF DEPRESSIVE DISORDERS

In our initial preliminary study (32,33), we examined MHPG excretion in a small group of patients with certain clinically defined subtypes of depressive disorders (29). All patients were studied during a clinical depression when they were receiving no psychoactive drugs. Since we have found MHPG excretion to vary with clinical state in bipolar manic-depressive disorders, we were particularly interested in comparing MHPG excretion in bipolar manic-depressive depressions and other clinically defined types of depressive disorders that might represent biologically different entities. Because most bipolar manic-depressive depressions present as endogenous depressive syndromes and it is most unusual for bipolar patients to show chronic characterological depressive syndromes (i.e., dysphoric depressive syndromes), unipolar chronic characterological depressions were selected as the principal comparison group in this initial study. This was done in order to minimize the likelihood of having patients with clinically latent bipolar disorders (i.e., bipolar patients who had not yet manifested their first hypomanic or manic episode) in the comparison group.

In this initial study of 12 patients, we found that MHPG excretion was significantly lower in 5 patients with bipolar manic-depressive depressions than in 5 patients with unipolar chronic characterological depressions. We also observed low MHPG excretion in 1 patient with a schizoaffective depression and intermediate levels of MHPG in 1 patient with a unipolar recurrent endogenous depression (32).

In this series of depressed patients, these differences in MHPG excretion were not related to differences in retardation, agitation, or anxiety (26). Similarly, other investigators (13) have reported the absence of an association between MHPG excretion and marked retardation or agitation in depressed patients.

We have subsequently replicated and extended our findings of differences in MHPG excretion in different subtypes of depressive disorders in another series of 25 depressed patients with clear-cut schizoaffective, bipolar manic-depressive, unipolar endogenous, unipolar chronic characterological, or

TABLE 1. *MHPG excretion in depressive disorders*

Sample	Bipolar manic-depressive and schizoaffective	Unipolar endogenous	Unipolar chronic characterological and nonspecific
Initial	1176 ± 145 (N = 6)	1551 (N = 1)	1803 ± 89[a] (N = 5)
Replication	1235 ± 98 (N = 9)	1728 ± 196[b] (N = 8)	1821 ± 152[a] (N = 8)
Total	1211 ± 80 (N = 15)	1709 ± 174[c] (N = 9)	1814 ± 96[c] (N = 13)

MHPG was determined in 2–10 separate 24-hr urine samples obtained from each patient. The average value for each patient was used to compute the group means and SEM presented in this table. MHPG is expressed in μg/24 hr. *N*, number of patients.
  [a] $p < 0.01$, [b] $p < 0.05$, [c] $p < 0.001$ for comparisons between bipolar manic-depressive and schizoaffective group versus unipolar chronic characterological and nonspecific group, or unipolar endogenous group.

unipolar nonspecific depressive syndromes.[1] (Excluded were patients with histories of chronic asocial or eccentric behaviors, patients with histories of amphetamine or barbiturate abuse, and patients with depressions that could not be uniquely classified according to our system for classifying depressive disorders.) Since MHPG excretion was comparably reduced in patients with schizoaffective and bipolar manic-depressive depressions, these two groups were combined in the analysis of data. Similarly, since there were no differences in MHPG excretion in patients with unipolar chronic characterological or unipolar nonspecific depressions, these two groups were combined for the purposes of data analysis.

Table 1 presents the data on MHPG excretion in the initial sample of 12 patients, the replication sample of 25 patients, and the total sample of 37 patients. As shown in Table 1, the replication sample also showed significantly lower MHPG excretion in the schizoaffective and bipolar manic-depressive depressions than in the unipolar chronic characterological and unipolar nonspecific depressions. Considering the total sample of 37 depressed patients, we found that 13 of the 15 patients with schizoaffective or bipolar manic-depressive depressions had MHPG levels less than 1,500 μg/day, whereas in 12 of the 13 patients with unipolar chronic characterological or unipolar nonspecific depressions, the levels of MHPG were 1,500 μg/day or higher.

Although the mean MHPG excretion in the group of endogenous de-

---

[1] The term unipolar nonspecific depressive syndrome is used to refer to unipolar depressive disorders that fit no specific syndrome (e.g., endogenous or chronic characterological) in our nosological system (29).

pressions was higher than in the group of schizoaffective and bipolar manic-depressive depressions, three of the nine patients with unipolar endogenous depressions had MHPG levels below 1,500 μg/day. This suggests that the group that we identify clinically as unipolar endogenous depressions may be biochemically heterogeneous, with some patients in this group bearing a biochemical similarity to the schizoaffective and bipolar manic-depressive depressions. (As noted above, one might expect that some of the patients, classified as unipolar because there was no prior history of hypomania or mania, might subsequently become hypomanic or manic at some time in the future, particularly when the disorder presents as an endogenous depressive syndrome.)

The highly significant differences ($p < 0.001$) in MHPG excretion between the schizoaffective and bipolar manic-depressive depressions versus the unipolar chronic characterological and nonspecific depressions could not be explained by sex differences, since the various diagnostic groups were well balanced with respect to sex distribution. Moreover, there were no significant differences in age, severity of depression [assessed on the modified Hamilton Depression Rating Scale (8)], urine volume, or creatinine excretion.

We also measured the urinary excretion of norepinephrine, normetanephrine (NMN), epinephrine, metanephrine (MN), and 3-methoxy-4-hydroxymandelic acid (VMA) in these patients. Although the urinary excretion of norepinephrine tended to be lower in schizoaffective and bipolar manic-depressive depressions than in the unipolar endogenous depressions or unipolar chronic characterological and nonspecific depressions, these differences were of only borderline statistical significance. There were no other statistically significant differences in normetanephrine, epinephrine, metanephrine, or VMA excretion among these diagnostic groups of depressive disorders. Thus, of the urinary catecholamines and metabolites that we measured, only MHPG showed highly significant differences among these subgroups of depressive disorders.

Our findings on the relationship between MHPG excretion and the clinical classification of depressive disorders have recently been supported by the work of two other groups of investigators, although somewhat different systems of classification were used in each of these studies. Goodwin et al. (6) have confirmed our findings of relatively lower MHPG excretion in bipolar depressions than in unipolar depressions; and similar findings of low MHPG in patients with bipolar depressions have been reported by Maas and Jones and their associates (10,13). The relative lowering of MHPG excretion in schizoaffective and bipolar manic-depressive depressions may be related to the recent observation that platelet monoamine oxidase activity was decreased in patients with some types of schizophrenias (19,31), as well as in patients with bipolar manic-depressive disorders (18), but relatively increased in other types of depressive disorders (20).

In summary, our findings suggest that there may be a biologically related group of depressive disorders with relatively low MHPG excretion (of which bipolar manic-depressive depressions represent a clinically identifiable subgroup) and a biologically related group of depressive disorders with relatively high MHPG excretion (of which unipolar chronic characterological depressions represent a clinically identifiable subgroup).

CATECHOLAMINES AND CLASSIFICATION OF DEPRESSIONS: PRELIMINARY APPLICATION OF MULTIPLE DISCRIMINANT FUNCTION ANALYSIS

Although in our studies (Table 1) MHPG was the only catecholamine metabolite that showed a highly significant difference in levels when values in bipolar manic-depressive and unipolar chronic characterological depressions were compared, we could not rule out the possibility that the other urinary metabolites might also contain information that would be useful in differentiating these two types of depressive disorders. In order to explore this possibility, we examined the data obtained from the first 10 patients studied (i.e., 5 with bipolar manic-depression and 5 with unipolar chronic characterological depressions) by means of multiple discriminant function analysis. Complete biochemical data were available on a total of 41 urine samples from these patients (i.e., 3 to 6 samples per patient). We used the biochemical data from each urine sample as a discrete incident (weighting the number of observations from each subject so that all subjects contributed equally to the analysis).[2] In this analysis, the six catecholamines and metabolites, including norepinephrine, normetanephrine, epinephrine, metanephrine, VMA, and MHPG, as well as various sums and ratios involving the six basic variables, were potential predictors (30).

A discrimination equation was developed in a "stepwise" procedure in which the variable entered into the equation at each step was the one with the largest contribution to discrimination when the information shared with items already entered was partialed out. This equation was determined by an analytic procedure that obtained the best least-squares "fit" of the data and, therefore, was not influenced by the investigators' theoretical framework.

As shown in Table 2, the equation for "depression-type" (D-type) score was of the form:

$$\text{D-type score} = C_1 (\text{MHPG}) + C_2 (\text{VMA}) + C_3 (\text{NE}) + C_4 \frac{(\text{NMN} + \text{MN})}{(\text{VMA})} + C_0$$

---

[2] The heuristic advantages and statistical limitations of such analyses of repeated measures on the same subject (termed "incidence analysis") are discussed elsewhere (R. LaBrie, *unpublished observations*).

TABLE 2. *Discrimination equation for D-type score*

$$\text{D-type score} = C_1 \, (\text{MHPG}) + C_2 \, (\text{VMA}) + C_3 \, (\text{NE}) + C_4 \, \frac{(\text{NMN} + \text{MN})}{(\text{VMA})} + C_0$$

Coefficients and constant	Standardized coefficients
$C_1 = 3.734 \times 10^{-4}$	0.438
$C_2 = -2.303 \times 10^{-4}$	-0.454
$C_3 = 1.035 \times 10^{-2}$	0.420
$C_4 = -4.217$	-0.389
$C_0 = 0.918$	—

In this formulation, low scores (< 0.5) are related to bipolar manic-depressive depressions and high scores (> 0.5) are related to unipolar chronic characterological depressions. Although this equation was generated mathematically to provide the best least-squares fit of the data, we have proposed a biologically meaningful rationale to account for the terms that were selected (30).

Preliminary validation of this discrimination equation has been obtained in a sample of 25 additional depressed patients whose biochemical data had not been used to derive the equation. In this validation sample, all of the patients with schizoaffective or bipolar manic-depressive depressions had D-type scores below 0.5 (in fact, the largest D-type score in this subgroup was 0.381), whereas all of the patients with unipolar chronic characterological or unipolar nonspecific depressions had D-type scores above 0.5 (Table 3 and Fig. 2).

In addition to the patients with schizoaffective or bipolar manic-depressive depressions, three of the eight patients with "unipolar" endogenous depressions also had D-type scores below 0.5 (Table 3). Such D-type scores below 0.5 may conceivably help to identify, from within the group of unipolar endogenous depressions, those patients with a biochemical similarity or predisposition to bipolar manic-depressive (or schizoaffective) disorders even though the patient may not have had overt episodes of hypomania or mania (or other forms of excited states).

TABLE 3. *D-type scores in depressive disorders: preliminary validation sample*

D-type scores	Bipolar manic-depressive and schizoaffective	Unipolar endogenous	Unipolar chronic characterological and nonspecific
Mean ± SEM	0.237 ± 0.032	0.545 ± 0.089	0.651 ± 0.033
Range	0.142–0.381	0.252–0.942	0.534–0.757
	($N = 9$)	($N = 8$)	($N = 8$)

D-type scores were computed using the biochemical data from 2–6 separate 24-hr urine samples obtained from each patient. The average D-type score for each patient was used to compute the group means ± SEM presented in this table. *N*, number of patients.

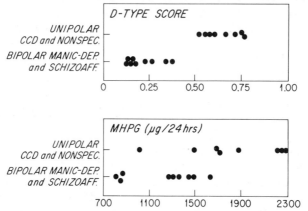

FIG. 2. Individual values of the D-type scores and MHPG excretion are plotted for the group of schizoaffective or bipolar manic-depressive depressions and the group of unipolar chronic characterological (CCD) or nonspecific depressions in the preliminary validation sample.

This possibility is illustrated by the case of a 60-year-old man who was studied biochemically during his fourth endogenous depressive episode. Since he had never had a prior episode of hypomania or mania, at the time of the biochemical studies he was considered to have a unipolar endogenous depressive disorder. However, his D-type score (0.381) was in the range usually seen in schizoaffective or bipolar manic-depressive depressions. One year after the biochemical studies were performed, this patient experienced his first hypomanic episode. Thus, it is possible that the D-type score may be of use in identifying depressed patients with a latent predisposition to bipolar manic-depressive illness before the appearance of the first overt manic or hypomanic episode.

Figure 2, which compares individual values of the D-type scores and MHPG excretion in the group of schizoaffective or bipolar manic-depressive depressions and the group of unipolar chronic characterological or nonspecific depressions in the preliminary validation sample, shows that there was no overlap and a very wide separation of the D-type scores in these two groups, whereas there was some overlap and less separation of the MHPG levels. Thus, although additional studies using a larger sample are needed to further validate and refine this equation for obtaining D-type scores, the present findings suggest that this equation may provide an even more precise discrimination between these types of depressive disorders than does urinary MHPG alone. In this regard, it is intriguing to speculate that the discrimination equation, by including the contribution of various urinary catecholamine metabolites of peripheral origin, may be correcting for that fraction of urinary MHPG that derives from the periphery rather than the brain.

PRELIMINARY EXAMINATION OF PLATELET MONOAMINE OXIDASE ACTIVITY IN CONJUNCTION WITH MHPG EXCRETION IN DEPRESSIVE DISORDERS

We have recently begun to examine platelet monoamine oxidase activity in conjunction with MHPG and other urinary catecholamine metabolites in our studies of patients with depressive disorders. Up to the present time we have analyzed data on 25 patients, some of whom were included in previous studies. However, in this phase of our research we included a broader range of clinical diagnostic entities inasmuch as we did not exclude patients with histories of chronic asocial, eccentric, or bizarre behavior; patients with histories of prior amphetamine or barbiturate abuse; or patients with depressions that could not be uniquely classified according to our system of classification (29).

Preliminary findings suggest that the measurement of platelet monoamine oxidase activity (using tryptamine as substrate) may enable us to make clinically relevant distinctions within the group of depressed patients with relatively low MHPG excretion (i.e., less than 1,500 μg/day). The study of Murphy and Weiss (18) reporting low platelet monoamine oxidase activity in bipolar affective disorders, in conjunction with our findings of relatively low MHPG excretion in depressed patients with bipolar manic-depressive disorders, suggests that there should be a subgroup of depressive disorders with low MHPG excretion and low platelet monoamine oxidase activity that includes bipolar manic-depressive depressions as well as other biologically related disorders; and our preliminary findings support this possibility. However, as shown in Table 4, our data further suggest that the occurrence of relatively high platelet monoamine oxidase activity (i.e., greater than 7 nmoles tryptamine deaminated per hour per milligram protein) in conjunction with low MHPG excretion (less than 1,500 μg/day) may help to discriminate a further subgroup of depressive disorders, characterized clinically by histories of chronic asocial, eccentric, or bizarre behavior and the propensity for psychotic disorganization (clinically distinguishable from hypomanic or manic states), particularly when treated with tricyclic antidepressant drugs.

As shown in Table 4, five of the six patients with urinary MHPG less than 1,500 μg/day and platelet monoamine oxidase activity greater than 7 nmoles tryptamine deaminated per hour per milligram protein had histories of chronic asocial, eccentric, or bizarre behavior, and four of these six patients (including the one without chronic asocial behavior) had experienced psychotic disorganization when treated with tricyclic antidepressant drugs. In contrast, none of the seven patients with low MHPG excretion

TABLE 4. *Chronic asocial behavior and psychotic disorganization on tricyclic antidepressants in depressed patients with low MHPG excretion and high platelet MAO activity*

	Chronic asocial behavior[a,b]	Psychotic disorganization on tricyclic antidepressants[b]
MHPG < 1,500[c]		
MAO > 7.0[d]	5/6	4/6
MAO < 7.0	0/7	1/7
MHPG > 1,500		
MAO > 7.0	2/6	0/6
MAO < 7.0	0/6	0/6

[a] Chronic asocial behavior includes deterioration in functioning, extreme social isolation, or odd, bizarre, eccentric behavior of at least several years' duration.
[b] Fraction of patients showing this manifestation.
[c] MHPG excretion is expressed in μg/24 hr.
[d] Platelet MAO activity is expressed in nanomoles of tryptamine deaminated per hour per milligram of platelet protein.

and low platelet MAO activity had histories of chronic asocial, eccentric, or bizarre behavior, and only one of these seven patients had a history of psychotic disorganization on tricyclic antidepressants. Of the remaining twelve subjects (i.e., with MHPG greater than 1,500 μg/day) only two had histories of chronic asocial, eccentric, or bizarre behavior, and none manifested psychosis during treatment with tricyclic antidepressants (Table 4).

The patients in the subgroup with relatively low MHPG excretion and relatively high platelet monoamine oxidase activity had frequently received clinical diagnoses (at other facilities) in the schizophrenia spectrum including schizophrenia and schizoid or schizoaffective disorders, and the term "borderline" was sometimes used to describe them. It should be emphasized, however, that our research classification of "schizoaffective disorders" does not include patients with histories of chronic asocial, eccentric, or bizarre behavior (29),[3] and such patients were not included among the "schizoaffective disorders" that we grouped with bipolar manic-depressive disorders in our studies demonstrating low D-type scores in these disorders (Table 3). Further analyses are in progress to determine D-type scores in the group of patients with low MHPG excretion and high

---

[3] According to our research classification, depressive disorders with histories of chronic asocial behavior (which includes deterioration in functioning, extreme social isolation, or odd, bizarre, eccentric behavior of at least several years' duration) plus evidence of a well-documented schizophrenic psychosis, characterized by thought disorders and delusions or hallucinations that are not affect consonant, are termed "true schizophrenia-related depressive disorders." Depressive disorders with histories of chronic asocial behavior but without evidence of overt psychosis are termed "schizoid-affective disorders." As we use it, the term "schizoaffective disorder" is restricted to depressive or manic disorders without histories of chronic asocial behavior but with histories of psychotic manifestations (including transient micropsychotic episodes) that are not solely affect consonant.

platelet MAO activity, but preliminary data on four patients suggest they may not have low D-type scores.

Thus, our preliminary findings suggest that depressed patients with relatively low MHPG excretion and relatively high platelet monoamine oxidase activity may constitute a biochemically identifiable and clinically relevant subgroup of depressive disorders that includes patients with histories of chronic asocial, eccentric, or bizarre behavior and a propensity for psychotic disorganization, particularly when treated with tricyclic antidepressants. In contrast, depressed patients with low MHPG excretion and relatively low platelet monoamine oxidase activity may constitute another subgroup of depressive disorders that includes bipolar manic-depressive and related disorders. Further studies will clearly be required to confirm these preliminary findings.

CONCLUSION

In summary, we have observed that MHPG excretion was higher during hypomanias or manias, intermediate during well intervals, and lower during depressions in longitudinal studies of patients with bipolar manic-depressive disorders. In cross-sectional comparisons of groups of patients with various clinically defined subtypes of depressive disorders, examined before treatment with antidepressant drugs or ECT, we have observed that MHPG excretion was significantly lower in patients with schizoaffective or bipolar manic-depressive depressions than in patients with unipolar chronic characterological or unipolar nonspecific depressions. Extending these findings, our studies (using multiple discriminant function analysis) suggest that an equation, which includes other measures related to catecholamine metabolism in addition to MHPG, may provide a more precise discrimination among these subtypes of depressive disorders than does urinary MHPG alone.

Moreover, recent preliminary findings suggest that the measurement of platelet monoamine oxidase activity may enable us to make clinically relevant distinctions within the group of depressed patients with relatively low MHPG excretion. Our findings, together with those of other investigators, suggest that there is a subgroup of depressive disorders with low MHPG excretion and low platelet monoamine oxidase activity that includes bipolar manic-depressive depressions as well as other biologically related disorders. However, our recent preliminary findings also suggest that another subgroup of depressive disorders, characterized clinically by chronic asocial, eccentric, or bizarre behavior and a propensity for psychotic disorganization, particularly on tricyclic antidepressants, may be discriminated on the basis of relatively high platelet monoamine oxidase activity occurring in conjunction with relatively low MHPG excretion.

The present findings suggest that various measures related to catecholamine metabolism may provide a clinically useful biochemical basis for classifying the depressive disorders. Although further studies will be required to confirm this, these findings do provide support for the possibility, suggested a number of years ago (24), that biochemical measures related to catecholamine metabolism may help to differentiate among the subtypes of depressive disorders.

Although our findings provide further evidence that alterations in central norepinephrine metabolism may be of importance in the underlying pathophysiology of at least some types of depressive disorders, many other biochemical abnormalities, including alterations in serotonin metabolism, also have been observed in these complex biological states (28,35). The basic physiological implications and possible practical clinical applications of these biochemical findings remain to be explored.

ACKNOWLEDGMENTS

This work was supported in part by USPHS Grant No. MH-15413 and by a grant from the Benevolent Foundation of Scottish Rite Freemasonry, Northern Jurisdiction, U.S.A. The authors wish to thank Mr. Edwin Grab, Ms. Patricia Platz, Ms. Sandra Lipchus, Mr. Vincent DaForno, and Ms. Barbara Keeler for their technical assistance.

REFERENCES

1. Axelrod, J., Kopin, I. J., and Mann, J. D. (1959): 3-Methoxy-4-hydroxyphenylglycol sulfate, a new metabolite of epinephrine and norepinephrine. *Biochim. Biophys. Acta*, 36:576–577.
2. Bond, P. A., Jenner, F. A., and Sampson, G. A. (1972): Daily variations of the urine content of 3-methoxy-4-hydroxy-phenylglycol in two manic-depressive patients. *Psychol. Med.*, 2:81–85.
3. Breese, G. R., Prange, A. J., Jr., Howard, J. L., Lipton, M. A., McKinney, W. T., Bowman, R. R., and Bushnell, P. (1972): 3-Methoxy-4-hydroxyphenylglycol excretion and behavioral changes in rat and monkey after central sympathectomy with 6-hydroxy-dopamine. *Nature [New Biol.]*, 240:286–287.
4. Bunney, W. E., Jr., Goodwin, F. K., Murphy, D. L., House, K. M., and Gordon, E. K. (1972): The "switch-process" in manic-depressive illness. *Arch. Gen. Psychiatry*, 27:304–309.
5. Glowinski, J., Kopin, I. J., and Axelrod, J. (1965): Metabolism of (H³) norepinephrine in rat brain. *J. Neurochem.*, 12:25–30.
6. Goodwin, F. K., Beckmann, H., and Post, R. M. (1975): Urinary methoxy-4-hydroxyphenylglycol in subtypes of affective illness. Scientific Proceedings, pp. 96–97. Annual Meeting of the American Psychiatric Association.
7. Greenspan, K., Schildkraut, J. J., Gordon, E. K., Baer, L., Aranoff, M. S., and Durell, J. (1970): Catecholamine metabolism in affective disorders. III. MHPG and other catecholamine metabolites in patients treated with lithium carbonate. *J. Psychiatr. Res.*, 7:171–183.
8. Hamilton, M. (1960): A rating scale for depression. *J. Neurol. Neurosurg. Psychiatry*, 23:56–62.
9. Jones, F. D., Maas, J. W., Dekirmenjian, H., and Fawcett, J. A. (1973): Urinary catecholamine metabolites during behavioral changes in a patient with manic-depressive cycles. *Science*, 179:300–302.
10. Jones, F. D., Maas, J. W., Dekirmenjian, H., and Sanchez, J. (1975): Diagnostic subtypes

of affective disorders and their urinary excretion of catecholamine metabolites. *Am. J. Psychiatry*, 132:1141–1148.

11. Kopin, I., and Ebert, M. (1974): Recent preliminary studies of the metabolism of catecholamines in the periphery and brain of human subjects. Reported at the Symposium on the Biological Deficit in the Affective Disorders, Munich, October.

12. Maas, J. W., and Landis, D. H. (1968): *In vivo* studies of metabolism of norepinephrine in central nervous system. *J. Pharmacol. Exp. Ther.*, 163:147–162.

13. Maas, J. W., Dekirmenjian, H., and Jones, F. (1973): The identification of depressed patients who have a disorder of norepinephrine metabolism and/or disposition. In: *Frontiers in Catecholamine Research—Third International Catecholamine Symposium*, edited by E. Usdin and S. Snyder, pp. 1091–1096. Pergamon Press, New York.

14. Maas, J. W., Dekirmenjian, H., Garver, D., Redmond, D. E., Jr., and Landis, D. H. (1972): Catecholamine metabolite excretion following intraventricular injection of 60H-dopamine. *Brain Res.*, 41:507–511.

15. Maas, J. W., Fawcett, J. A., and Dekirmenjian, H. (1968): 3-Methoxy-4-hydroxyphenylglycol (MHPG) excretion in depressive states: pilot study. *Arch. Gen. Psychiatry*, 19:129–134.

16. Maas, J. W., Fawcett, J. A., and Dekirmejian, H. (1972): Catecholamine metabolism, depressive illness and drug response. *Arch. Gen. Psychiatry*, 26:252–262.

17. Mannarino, E., Kirshner, N., and Nashold, B. S., Jr. (1963): Metabolism of C[14] noradrenaline by cat brain *in vivo*. *J. Neurochem.*, 10:373–379.

18. Murphy, D. L., and Weiss, R. (1972): Reduced monoamine oxidase activity in blood platelets from bipolar depressed patients. *Am. J. Psychiatry*, 128:1351–1357.

19. Murphy, D. L., and Wyatt, R. J. (1972): Reduced monoamine oxidase activity in blood platelets from schizophrenic patients. *Nature*, 238:225–226.

20. Nies, A., Robinson, D. S., Ravaris, C. L., and Davis, J. M. (1971): Amines and monoamine oxidase in relation to aging and depression in man. *Psychosom. Med.*, 33:470.

21. Rutledge, C. O., and Jonason, J. (1967): Metabolic pathways of dopamine and norepinephrine in rabbit brain *in vitro*. *J. Pharmacol. Exp. Ther.*, 157:493–502.

22. Schanberg, S. M., Breese, G. R., Schildkraut, J. J., Gordon, E. K., and Kopin, I. J. (1968): 3-Methoxy-4-hydroxyphenylglycol sulfate in brain and cerebrospinal fluid. *Biochem. Pharmacol.*, 17:2006–2008.

23. Schanberg, S. M., Schildkraut, J. J., Breese, G. R., and Kopin, I. J. (1968): Metabolism of normetanephrine-H[3] in rat brain—identification of conjugated 3-methoxy-4-hydroxyphenylglycol as major metabolite. *Biochem. Pharmacol.*, 17:247–254.

24. Schildkraut, J. J. (1965): The catecholamine hypothesis of affective disorders: a review of supporting evidence. *Am. J. Psychiatry*, 122:509–522.

25. Schildkraut, J. J. (1972): Neuropharmacological studies of mood disorders. In: *Disorders of Mood*, edited by J. Zubin and F. A. Freyhan, pp. 65–92. Johns Hopkins University Press, Baltimore.

26. Schildkraut, J. J. (1973a): Catecholamine metabolism and affective disorders: studies of MHPG excretion. In: *Frontiers in Catecholamine Research—Third International Catecholamine Symposium*, edited by E. Usdin and S. Snyder, pp. 1165–1171. Pergamon Press, New York.

27. Schildkraut, J. J. (1973b): Norepinephrine metabolism in the pathophysiology and classification of depressive and manic disorders. In: *Psychopathology and Psychopharmacology*, edited by J. O. Cole, A. M. Freedman, and A. J. Friedhoff, pp. 231–249. Johns Hopkins University Press, Baltimore.

28. Schildkraut, J. J. (1974): Biogenic amines and affective disorders. *Annu. Rev. Med.*, 25:333–348.

29. Schildkraut, J. J., and Klein, D. F. (1975): The classification and treatment of depressive disorders. In: *Manual of Psychiatric Therapeutics*, edited by R. I. Shader, pp. 39–61. Little, Brown and Co., Boston.

30. Schildkraut, J. J., and LaBrie, R. A. (1974): Catecholamines and classification of depressions. New research abstracts, p. 17. Annual Meeting of the American Psychiatric Association.

31. Schildkraut, J. J., Herzog, J. M., Orsulak, P. J., Edelman, S. E., Shein, H. M., and Frazier, S. H. (1976): Reduced platelet monoamine oxidase activity in a subgroup of schizophrenic patients. *Am. J. Psychiatry*, 133:438–440.

32. Schildkraut, J. J., Keeler, B. A., Grab, E. L., Kantrowich, J., and Hartmann, E. (1973): MHPG excretion and clinical classification in depressive disorders. *Lancet*, 1:1251–1252.
33. Schildkraut, J. J., Keeler, B. A., Papousek, M., and Hartmann, E. (1973): MHPG excretion in depressive disorders: relation to clinical subtypes and desynchronized sleep. *Science*, 181:762–764.
34. Schildkraut, J. J., Keeler, B. A., Rogers, M. P., and Draskoczy, P. R. (1972): Catecholamine metabolism in affective disorders: a longitudinal study of a patient treated with amitriptyline and ECT. *Psychosom. Med.* 34:470 (Abs.); plus erratum (1973): *Psychosom. Med.*, 35:274.
35. Schildkraut, J. J., Sachar, E. J., and Baer, L. (1976): Biochemistry of affective disorders. In: *Psychotherapeutic Drugs*, edited by E. Usdin and I. A. Forrest, pp. 275–328. Marcel Dekker, New York.
36. Schildkraut, J. J., Watson, R., Draskoczy, P. R., and Hartmann, E. (1971): Amphetamine withdrawal: depression and MHPG excretion. *Lancet*, 2:485–486.
37. Shopsin, B., Wilk, S., Gershon, S., Roffman, M., and Goldstein, M. (1973): Collaborative psychopharmacologic studies exploring catecholamine metabolism in psychiatric disorders. In: *Frontiers in Catecholamine Research — Third International Catecholamine Symposium*, edited by E. Usdin and S. Snyder, pp. 1173–1179. Pergamon Press, New York.
38. Watson, R., Hartmann, E., and Schildkraut, J. J. (1972): Amphetamine withdrawal: affective state, sleep patterns and MHPG excretion. *Am. J. Psychiatry*, 129:263–269.
39. Wilk, S., and Watson, E. (1973): VMA in spinal fluid: evaluation of the pathways of cerebral catecholamine metabolism in man. In: *Frontiers in Catecholamine Research — Third International Catecholamine Symposium*, edited by E. Usdin and S. Snyder, pp. 1067–1069. Pergamon Press, New York.

Psychopathology and Brain Dysfunction, edited
by C. Shagass, S. Gershon, and A. J. Friedhoff.
Raven Press, New York © 1977.

Receptor Sensitivity Modification—A New Paradigm for the Potential Treatment of Some Hormonal and Transmitter Disturbances*

Arnold J. Friedhoff

*Department of Psychiatry, New York University School of Medicine,
New York, New York 10016*

BACKGROUND

It was first shown by Walter Cannon (1) that the sensitivity of a neuronal receptor to its specific transmitter is increased when the afferents are interrupted, and he called this phenomenon denervation supersensitivity. Carlsson (2) and Klawans et al. (3) have proposed an analogous mechanism as an explanation for the appearance of tardive dyskinesia. Along with Van Winkle, I (4) pointed out in 1964 that all antipsychotic drugs were capable of producing a Parkinson-like syndrome. Inasmuch as parkinsonism is related to a dopamine deficiency, we suggested that antipsychotic drugs might act by interfering with dopaminergic transmission. Carlsson and Lindquist (5) demonstrated directly that antipsychotic drugs block central dopamine receptors. The first study of this phenomenon was reported in a publication that has now become a classic, and this report was the stimulus for a great deal of subsequent work (6,7). The dopamine receptor, when blocked for long periods of time, becomes chemically denervated and this is followed by the development of supersensitivity, in a manner similar to the supersensitivity that occurred in Cannon's preparation. This supersensitivity provides a means by which the receptor can overcome the blocking agent and thus restore function toward normal. This persisting supersensitivity of the receptor may be an endpoint of a normal regulatory system of the receptor cell. Katz and Thesleff (8), in 1957, showed that acetylcholine receptor desensitization could occur in the presence of increased agonist. Thus receptor cells appear to be capable of "tuning" their receptivity up or down to compensate for agonist supply.

More recently, Goldstein et al. (9) showed that hyperinsulinemic, hyperglucagonemic, diabetic patients had a reduced number of insulin and glucagon binding sites demonstrable on peripheral mononuclear leukocytes. This finding may be another example of the production of receptor subsensitivity, rather than supersensitivity. If blocking the agonist from the receptor produces supersensitization, then perhaps increasing the agonist available at

---

* Presidential address to the American Psychopathological Association.

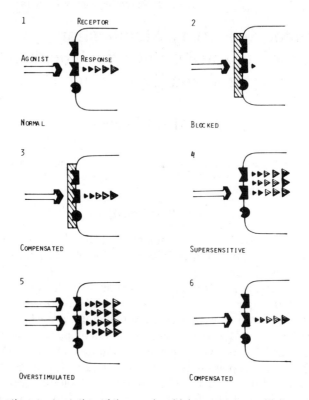

FIG. 1. Schematic representation of the way in which receptor sensitivity can be modified by use of receptor blocking agents. The hatched vertical represents a specific receptor blocker.

the receptor may produce subsensitization. In the case of the leukocytes studied by these investigators, it would appear that the compensation occurred by a reduction in the number of receptor binding sites.

Another group of investigators (10) has shown that thyroid releasing hormone (TRH), when added to a cell culture, reduces the number of TRH binding sites. These investigators also showed that the *reduction* in the number of binding sites was minimal if a protein synthesis inhibitor was added to the medium. Thus the processes for modification of the number of receptor binding sites involve active protein synthesis and are therefore presumably under genetic control.

In 1974 Tarsy and Baldessarini (11) showed that apomorphine, a dopaminergic agonist, induced stereotyped gnawing behavior in rats after pretreatment with alpha-methyl-*p*-tyrosine, reserpine, chlorpromazine, or haloperidol, all of which interfere with dopaminergic function. They demonstrated that this behavioral stereotype was probably specifically related to supersensitization of the dopaminergic receptor because apomorphine is believed to be a specific dopaminergic agonist. Supersensitization did not

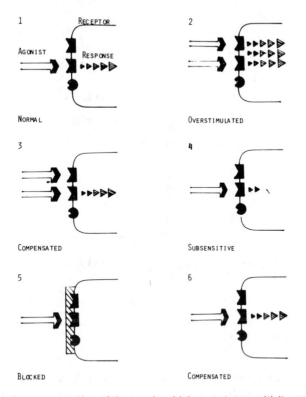

FIG. 2. Schematic representation of the way in which receptor sensitivity can be modified by manipulation of agonist supply. The arrows to the left of the receptor represent the specific agonist.

occur when nondopamine blockers such as phenobarbital were used as a pretreatment, even though behavioral depression was produced as with the antipsychotic drugs. Interestingly, they found that detectable supersensitization did not occur with less than 11 days of pretreatment. Thus changes in receptor sensitivity setpoint appear to require intensive and prolonged treatment. The stepwise production of the compensatory increase in receptivity resulting from blockade of a receptor (that is, agonist underavailability) is illustrated in Fig. 1, as is the reversal of the supersensitivity by overstimulation. In this figure it can be seen that a blocking agent produces a compensatory increase in receptor responsivity. When the blocker is removed, the unblocked receptor is supersensitive (Fig. 1–4). If the supersensitive receptor is overstimulated by increasing the supply of agonist above normal, a compensatory decrease in receptivity occurs so that when the agonist supply is returned to normal the receptor responds in a normal fashion.

Figure 2 shows the steps involved in the production or reversal of subsensitivity. If the agonist supply is excessive the receptor is overstimulated

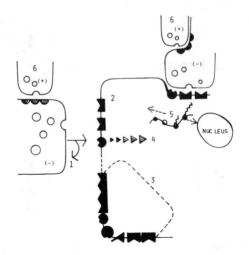

FIG. 3. Possible regulatory mechanisms in the modification of neuronal sensitivity. **1:** Change in reuptake system. **2:** Local change in receptor molecule. **3:** Change in number of receptor sites: (a) proliferation of synapses; (b) change in receptor binding sites on existing synaptic membrane. **4:** Change in associated response mechanisms, i.e., cyclic AMP synthesis and/or degradation, protein kinase activity, phosphorylation of membrane. **5:** Change in nuclear regulation of protein systhesis (modified gene expression). **6:** Change in balance with other neuronal systems.

(Fig. 2–2). The receptor compensates by decreasing its sensitivity so that when the agonist supply is returned to normal the receptor is subsensitive. If the subsensitive receptor is blocked the sensitivity is increased to compensate for the blockade. When the blocker is removed the receptor response is normalized.

From reports that these changes can be demonstrated on diverse receptors such as those for insulin, glucagon, TRH, and dopamine, it appears that the paradigm may be a general one referable to many types of receptors. Figure 3 presents a schematic representation of possible modes by which receptor sensitivity modification (RSM) can occur in neuronal receptors. This regulation of sensitivity may occur in the receptor cell or it may result from an interaction and modulation of that cell by other cells, including the presynaptic neuron or synapsing inhibitory or excitatory neurons. In both hormonal and neuronal receptors, modulation of receptor sensitivity by agents other than the specific agonist may also occur (12,13).

It seems likely that the postsynaptic dopaminergic receptor cells, and possibly receptor cells of other types, have a control mechanism whose function is to establish a receptor sensitivity setpoint in response to persistent changes in receptor agonist supply. This particular control mechanism would serve to adapt the receptor cell to long-term changes.

If receptor changes in tardive dyskinesia are typical of changes in receptor sensitivity in other receptors, then these changes in setpoint, once firmly established, would not readily reverse themselves spontaneously, inasmuch as tardive dyskinesia often persists for years, or may remain permanently, after withdrawal of the offending dopaminergic blocking agent.

We have proposed the following general hypothesis for control of receptor sensitivity: (a) that receptor cells can change receptor setpoint, either increasing or decreasing the sensitivity; (b) that these changes occur in the direction of restoring homeostasis, so that a receptor blocker will provoke the cell to increase the sensitivity of its receptor, whereas an oversupply of agonist would stimulate the cell to reduce its own sensitivity; (c) that these processes proceed with a slower time course than the phasic nervous activity; (d) that the adaptive processes must be under active regulatory control; and (e) that persistent changes in sensitivity reflect an enduring change in regulatory processes in the cell.

DEVELOPMENT OF THE PARADIGM AND TEST OF THE HYPOTHESIS

A study of tardive dyskinesia that we initiated several years ago has proven to be our first test of this hypothesis. The early cases of tardive dyskinesia that we saw were not as severe as some that we saw subsequently, and initially I felt that the syndrome was difficult to define. Alpert and Diamond (14), in our laboratory, had developed a sensitive device for measuring finger tremor and felt that this could be applied to the diagnosis of tardive dyskinesia, and might also be used to measure change in that condition. Although I was not enthusiastic about studying tardive dyskinesia because of my lack of conviction that it was a definite syndrome, Alpert and associates (15,16) sustained their interest and found a characteristic tremor associated with tardive. This led them to conceive of the idea of treating tardive patients with L-DOPA in an attempt to decrease the sensitivity of their dopamine receptors. During that same period I had become interested in the mechanism involved in the development of tolerance to depressant drugs, including ethanol, and proposed a negative feedback model of tolerance based on the development of compensatory changes in enzyme activity (17,18). Our present hypothesis regarding RSM is an amalgamation of my ideas about tolerance with Alpert's ideas about tardive dyskinesia and has resulted from discussions between Alpert and me over a number of years.

In order to continue our investigations of tardive dyskinesia, we decided to measure finger tremor by the technique that we had used in 1963 to demonstrate that L-DOPA had a normalizing effect on parkinsonism. This tremor, present in everyone, is dramatically altered in parkinsonian patients. It is detectable only by using rather high amplification and is not the tremor that is observed grossly in many patients with parkinsonism. Using this objective technique we were able to show a significant normalization of tremor in parkinsonian patients who were administered small doses of

L-DOPA (19). At that time we believed that L-DOPA was probably an extremely toxic drug so that we administered pathetically small doses. Although we published our report (19) several years before the discovery that L-DOPA, in very large doses, had dramatic therapeutic effects in the treatment of many Parkinson's disease patients (20), we cannot take too much credit for its discovery. Our conclusion, because of the low doses we used, was that L-DOPA had a beneficial effect in parkinsonism but that it was probably not a practical therapeutic agent because the magnitude of its effects was small.

When we studied tardive dyskinesia we turned again to the tremor test as an objective means for measuring changes in this condition. In 1967 Alpert et al. (15) published a review of their findings regarding finger tremor, and over the next several years Alpert (21) devised techniques for doing both frequency and intensity analysis of resting finger tremor. The tremor in tardive dyskinesia is characteristic of the syndrome (Fig. 4) and reverts to a normal tremor when clinical symptoms disappear. Thus it can be used as a quantitative measure of change in tardive symptoms.

In early 1970 a patient (J. H.) who suffered from intractable tardive dyskinesia was referred to our Special Studies Center. The tardive symptoms persisted even though the patient had been drug-free for several years. At that time we decided that this was an excellent opportunity to test our ideas for an experimental treatment since the patient had been in extreme distress with his tardive symptoms for a long time and was eager to volunteer for a test of a new approach, and we knew of no successful conventional treatment. Also, we had an excellent objective method for measuring changes in tardive symptoms. We decided, in line with our subsequent general hypothesis, that if dopamine receptor supersensitization and, therefore, tardive symptoms resulted from blockade of the dopaminergic receptor by an antipsychotic drug, then perhaps we could tune down the sensitivity of the receptor by overstimulating it, by the administration of L-DOPA which would be transformed to dopamine.

We predicted that the patient's condition would initially worsen from the L-DOPA since the dopamine would be stimulating the already supersensitive dopaminergic receptor. As the receptor adapted, the patient's condition should begin to improve. We felt that after withdrawal of the L-DOPA, the patient should be substantially improved. We could not predict how long the improvement would last, if it occurred. Figure 1, which is a general model, also depicts the approach to the tardive patients.

We treated J. H. with gradually increasing doses of L-DOPA up to 3 g/day. As we anticipated, the patient's tardive symptoms worsened with each increment in dose. However, after several days at each fixed dose, the worsening effect ceased. When we stopped the treatment after 3 weeks, the patient was virtually symptom-free for the first time. Some small further improvement continued for several months post-DOPA, as though the DOPA

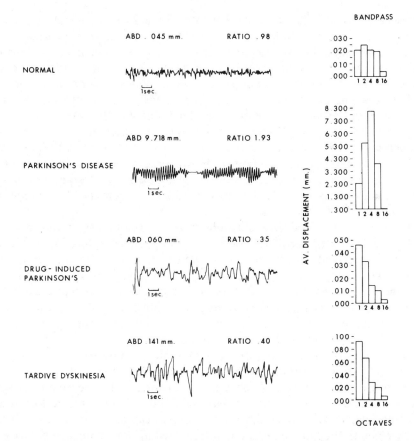

FIG. 4. Comparisons of some extrapyramidal tremor waveforms. ABD, average beam displacement, a measure (in millimeters) of the average distance of the finger oscillations from the null point. Average displacement of the finger in each of 5 octave passbands (1–2 Hz, 2–4 Hz, 4–8 Hz, 8–16 Hz, and 16–32 Hz) is indicated in the bar graph to the right of each tracing. Time (1 sec) is indicated as a horizontal line. (From ref. 21.)

had initiated a recovery process. We have followed this patient for 2 years post-treatment, during which time his symptoms have not returned. We have since studied a small number of other subjects and have seen the same dramatic improvement and identical course of response in some but not all of them. Details of these clinical studies will be published elsewhere (22).

DISCUSSION

Until the present time we have made a limited number of clinical observations of the effect of L-DOPA on tardive dyskinesia. We have not ruled out the possibility of placebo effects or spontaneous remissions. However, one patient was drug-free for several years during which time his tardive symptoms persisted. In the same patient after 3 weeks of L-DOPA treatment followed by abrupt withdrawal of DOPA, the symptoms disappeared. Many controls remain to be carried out before definitive conclusions can be made. However, it is our distinct impression that L-DOPA administration followed by L-DOPA withdrawal reverses tardive dyskinesia symptoms, and we believe that the best hypothesis at present is that this occurs by decreasing the sensitivity of the receptor by overstimulating it with L-DOPA.

At present, as I stated earlier in this chapter, there are several experimental and clinical studies, including our own, which support the idea that receptor sensitivity can be modified. However, data are still limited and our understanding of the mechanism of this phenomenon is even more limited. The paradigm has potential implications for the treatment of a number of different kinds of conditions.

It has been proposed that schizophrenia or some of its symptoms may result from increased sensitivity of the dopaminergic receptor. The evidence for this is derived mainly from observations that antipsychotic drugs can block the receptor through decreasing receptivity. It is reasoned that if blocking agents produce therapeutic improvement, then perhaps the initial problem is in some way related to increased sensitivity of receptors in one or more central dopaminergic systems. Direct evidence for this in schizophrenic subjects has not been forthcoming.

In a study of brains from autopsy of schizophrenic patients compared with brains from a normal control group, Carenzi et al. (23) concluded that there might be a subgroup of schizophrenic patients who are extremely sensitive to dopamine stimulation. It has been found that there is a dopamine-specific adenyl cyclase in the dopaminergic regions of mammalian brain (24). When the dopamine receptor is stimulated by dopamine, adenyl cyclase is activated and generates cyclic AMP. The amount of cyclic AMP formed is believed to be a measure of the sensitivity of the receptor to dopamine. Carenzi et al. (23) investigated the possibility that schizophrenics would have greater responsiveness than normals, that is, have supersensitive receptors. Although they failed to confirm this, the study was confounded by the fact that the schizophrenics but not the normals had been treated with antipsychotic drugs, which are dopamine-blocking agents. They did find, however, that the baseline adenyl cyclase activity – that is, the unstimulated level – was not significantly correlated with the stimulated activity in normals but highly correlated in schizophrenics.

Although it is difficult to interpret the significance of this finding, it does raise the possibility that as a result of drugs, schizophrenia, or both, the receptor-linked adenyl cyclase is different in schizophrenic subjects. If there is increased sensitivity of the dopaminergic receptor in schizophrenics, then the RSM principle can be applied to the treatment of these patients. Alternatively, the dopamine-blocking action of antipsychotic drugs may be the means for producing a compensatory effect rather than for reversing a primary deficit. In that event RSM might be effective even in the absence of a supersensitive receptor.

We are presently involved in a study of schizophrenics using the RSM approach and are treating schizophrenic patients with L-DOPA for a limited period of time. Our hypothesis is that these patients will initially worsen somewhat, as has been shown previously (25), but that persistent treatment with L-DOPA and subsequent withdrawal of this drug after several weeks will produce a long-lasting improvement. It should be noted that the tardive patients we treated with L-DOPA were also schizophrenic and have been out of hospital without medication for up to 4 years.

The RSM principle also has implications for the treatment of various metabolic and hormonal disturbances. By increasing or decreasing the sensitivity of hormone receptors or receptors for hormone-releasing or -inhibiting factors, it might be possible to modify the levels of various hormones or their effect on their target cells.

There is growing laboratory evidence that the sensitivity of receptor cells can be modified by changing the environment of the receptor cell, but at present the evidence that this procedure has clinical application is scanty. Nonetheless, we are encouraged by our own clinical and laboratory observations. This chapter was written with the hope that it will stimulate other studies directed toward a further definition of the therapeutic potential of the receptor sensitivity modification approach.

ACKNOWLEDGMENTS

This work was supported by the author's Research Scientist Award No. MH14024 and Program Project Grant MH08618. The author thanks Jeannette Miller for her help and ingenuity in the design and rendering of the figures.

REFERENCES

1. Cannon, W. B., and Rosenbleuth, A. (1949): *The Supersensitivity of Denervated Structures; A Law of Denervation.* Macmillan, New York.
2. Carlsson, A. (1970): Biochemical implications of dopa induced action on the central nervous system with particular reference to abnormal movements. In: *L-dopa and Parkinsonism,* edited by A. Barbeau and F. H. McDowell, p. 205, F, A. Davis Co., Philadelphia.
3. Klawans, H. L., Slaki, M. M., and Shenker, D. (1970): Theoretical implications of the use of L-DOPA in Parkinsonism. *Acta Neurol. Scand.,* 46:409–441.
4. Friedhoff, A. J., and Van Winkle, E. (1964): Biological O-methylation and schizophrenia. *Psychiatr. Res.,* 19:49.
5. Carlsson, A., and Lindquist, M. (1963): Effect of chlorpromazine or haloperidol on formation of 3-methoxytyramine and normetanephrine in mouse brain. *Acta Pharmacol. Toxicol.,* 20:140–143.
6. Anden, N. E., Roos, B. E., and Werdinius, B. (1964): Effects of chlorpromazine, haloperidol and reserpine on the levels of phenabic acids in rabbit corpus striatum. *Life Sci.,* 3:149–158.

7. Von Rossum, M. M. (1966): Significance of dopamine receptor blockade for mechanism of action of neuroleptic drugs. *Arch. Int. Pharmacodyn. Ther.,* 160:492–494.
8. Katz, B., and Thesleff, S. (1957): A study of 'desensitization' produced by acetylcholine at the motor endplate. *J. Physiol.,* 138:63–80.
9. Goldstein, S., Blecher, B., Binder, R., Perinno, P. V., and Recant, L. (1975): Hormone receptors 5. Binding of glucagon and insulin to human circulatory mononuclear cells in diabetic mellitus. *Endocrinol. Res. Commun.,* 2:367–376.
10. Hinkle, P. M., and Tashjian, H. A., Jr. (1975): Thyrotropin-releasing hormone regulates the number of its own receptors in the GH_3 strain of pituitary cells in culture. 14(17):3845–3851.
11. Tarsy, D., and Baldessarini, R. J. (1974): Behavioral supersensitivity to apomorphine following chronic treatment with drugs which interfere with the synaptic function of catecholamines. *Neuropharmacology,* 13:927–940.
12. Vreeburg, J. T. M., Schretten, P. J. M., and Baum, M. J. (1975): Specific, high affinity binding of 17β-estradiol in cytosols from several brain regions and pituitary of intact and castrated male rats. *Endocrinology,* 97:969–977.
13. Reel, J. R., and Shih, Y. (1975): Estrogen-inducible uterine progesterone receptors. Characteristics in the ovarectomized immature and adult hamster. *Acta Endocrinol. (Kbh.),* 80:344–354.
14. Alpert, M., and Diamond, F. (1967): Regularity of tremor in extrapyramidal disease. In: *Progress in Neurogenetics,* edited by A. Barbeau, pp. 404–405. Excerpta Medica, New York.
15. Alpert, M., Lomask, M., and Friedhoff, A. J. (1966): Instrumentation for the recording and predictive analysis of physiological tremor. In: *Instrumentation Methods for Predictive Medicine,* edited by T. B. Weber and J. Poyer, p. 159. Instrument Society of America, Los Angeles.
16. Alpert, M. (1967): The parameters of physiological and pathological tremor. Proceedings of the First NIMH Workshop on Tardive Dyskinesia, St. Louis.
17. Friedhoff, A. J., Miller, J. C., and Sandler, M. E. (1971): Effect of repeated courses of ethanol and phenobarbital on microsomal enzymes. In: *Recent Advances in Studies of Alcoholism,* edited by N. K. Mello and J. H. Mendelson, pp. 59–71. U.S. Government Printing Office, Washington, D.C.
18. Friedhoff, A. J. (1970): The influence of ethanol on activity of detoxifying enzymes. In: *Proceedings of the Committee of Problems of Drug Dependence,* pp. 6489–6495. National Academy of Science and National Research Council, Washington, D.C.
19. Friedhoff, A. J., Hekimian, L., Alpert, M., and Tobach, E. (1963): Dihydroxyphenylalanine in extrapyramidal disease. *J.A.M.A.,* 184:285–286.
20. Cotzias, G. C., Van Woert, M. H., and Schiffler, L. M. (1967): Aromatic amino acids and modification of parkinsonism. *N. Engl. J. Med.,* 276:374–379.
21. Alpert, M. (1975): Tremography as a measure of extrapyramidal function in study of the dopamine hypothesis. In: *Catecholamines and Behavior,* edited by A. J. Friedhoff, pp. 167–185. Plenum Press, New York.
22. Alpert, M., and Friedhoff, A. J. (1976): L-DOPA in the treatment of putative hyperdopaminergic conditions. In preparation.
23. Carenzi, A., Gillin, C. G., Guidotti, A., Schwartz, M. A., Trabucchi, M., and Wyatt, R. J. (1975): Dopamine sensitive adenylylcyclase in human caudate nucleus. *Arch. Gen. Psychiatry,* 32:1056–1059.
24. Kebabian, J. W., and Greengard, P. (1971): Dopamine-sensitive adenylcyclase: Possible role in synaptic transmission. *Science,* 174:1346.
25. Angrist, B., Sathananthan, G., and Gershon, S. (1973): Behavioral effects of L-DOPA in schizophrenic patients. *Psychopharmacologia,* 31:1.

Psychopathology and Brain Dysfunction, edited by C. Shagass, S. Gershon, and A. J. Friedhoff. Raven Press, New York © 1977.

Basic Mechanisms of Seizures: Neurophysiological and Biochemical Etiology

Dixon M. Woodbury and John W. Kemp

Department of Pharmacology, University of Utah College of Medicine, Salt Lake City, Utah 84132

Ideally, the best model in which to study the mechanisms of seizures is man himself. However, except in EEG recordings, depth electrode studies, and occasional biopsies of epileptogenic foci, this is difficult to do. This is the case because detailed analysis of the basic neurophysiological and biochemical mechanisms of seizures involves work on the brain itself and sometimes removal of brain samples, and this is not possible to do in humans. Consequently, experimental models of epilepsy must be used instead. The relevance of such studies is clearly related to the degree to which the experimental models approximate the disease in humans. The ideal model for studying the basic mechanisms of seizures is one that closely approximates human epilepsy and yet is readily available, inexpensive, and easy to work with. No model at present meets all these criteria, but all models are potentially useful for studying at least one aspect of the mechanisms of seizures. However, because of the variety of clinical types of epilepsy with different types of onset and manifestations, it is essential to have models in animals that mimic the different forms in man, that is, focal and generalized seizure types. The purpose of this chapter is to discuss some of the various experimental models and how study of them helps to elucidate the basic mechanisms of seizures. In using these models, it is important to realize that, as Ajmone-Marsan (2) stated, "the gap between . . . an experimental situation and the focal form of human epilepsy, a clinical entity characterized by exquisitely chronic features, is only apparent and . . . once an epileptic process has become established, its sporadic electrical manifestations, at least in their main qualitative aspect, appear to be rather stereotyped, and there is no convincing evidence for the existence of important differences in their underlying basic mechanisms that might be related to its type of development." Thus the basic properties of seizures, regardless of etiology, are similar and any one model can be used to study these properties. Nevertheless, it is important to study the mechanisms by which the seizure in each model is initiated because the mechanisms may be different for each one, and this gives us information on the various ways in which seizures start.

A simple classification of the various experimental models of epilepsy is
presented in Table 1. The models shown are those that have been most used
for study of seizure mechanisms and, therefore, ones in which the majority
of our current knowledge of the neuropathological, neurophysiological, and
biochemical properties of seizures has been obtained. Two classes of models
are used: those for inducing local epileptogenic activity acutely and chronically, and those for inducing generalized epileptogenic seizures. By definition, human epilepsies are recurrent, self-sustained paroxysmal disorders of
brain function characterized by excessive discharge of cerebral neurons.
Among the many models for producing local epileptiform seizures in animals, the only one that fulfills the criterion of prolonged "spontaneous"
recurrence is the topical or intracerebral application of alumina gel (57).
Because it produces a long-lasting chronic epileptogenic lesion, it is the
method of choice for the reproduction of a lesion resembling very closely
that seen in man. However, it is most useful in primates and requires elabo-

TABLE 1. *Experimental models of epilepsy useful for elucidation of mechanisms of seizure initiation, spread, and arrest*

I. Models for inducing local epileptogenic activity
  A. Acute models
      Topical convulsant metals: cobalt, tungstic acid gel
      Topical freezing
      Topical convulsant drugs: penicillin, ouabain, strychnine,
                        conjugated estrogens, etc.
      Focal electrical stimulation
  B. Chronic models
      Topical convulsant metals: alumina cream
II. Models for inducing generalized epileptogenic activity
  A. Sensory-precipitated models (genetic)
      Photogenic seizures—*Papio papio*
      Audiogenic seizures—mice
  B. Electrically induced seizures
  C. Chemically induced seizures
      Stimulate excitatory systems—pentylenetetrazol
      Block inhibitory systems
        Block glycine receptors—strychnine
        Block GABA receptors—picrotoxin, penicillin, bicuculline
      Block electrolyte transport systems in neurons and/or glia and/or
        Elevate extracellular ion concentrations
      Cation—ouabain, lithium, high potassium perfusion
      Anion—thiocyanate, perchlorate, low chloride perfusion,
        high bicarbonate
  D. Withdrawal seizure models
      Acute
      CO_2 withdrawal seizures
      Chronic
        Barbiturate withdrawal seizures
        Alcohol withdrawal seizures
        Benzodiazepine withdrawal seizures
        Bromide withdrawal seizures

rate secondary techniques to obtain good results. This is very costly, hence for biochemical studies requiring tissue samples, less elaborate and expensive acute models have been used and are satisfactory for studying seizure mechanisms as described above. The agents of choice for such acute models, as shown in Table 1, are local freezing, cobalt, or penicillin. Local electrical stimulation with implanted electrodes in either cortical or subcortical sites is particularly useful for studying the neurophysiological mechanisms of seizures. Biochemical and neuropathological studies of generalized seizures are often best done in genetic models of epilepsy such as photomyoclonus in baboons (*Papio papio*) and audiogenic seizures in mice, and by use of chemically induced generalized seizures such as with pentylenetetrazol, strychnine, and picrotoxin, which usually act by different synaptic mechanisms involving excitatory and inhibitory systems.

In this chapter the emphasis is on the correlation of neuroanatomical, neurophysiological, and biochemical data obtained in various local and generalized models in an attempt to elucidate some of the basic mechanisms by which seizures occur. Particular emphasis is on data from focal seizure models, studies of monovalent anion-induced convulsions to bring in the role of glial cells in seizure processes, and investigations on the production of generalized seizures by pentylenetetrazol to emphasize the usefulness of isolated systems and lower classes of organisms in understanding the mechanisms of seizures in mammals.

SEIZURES WITH LOCAL ONSET

Briefly, the pathophysiological events in epilepsy can be considered in three steps: (a) the abnormalities that generate the discharge of an epileptogenic focus; (b) the local spread and the changes that precipitate the interictal activity into a seizure; (c) the propagation of discharge during a major seizure; and (d) the events that arrest the seizure.

Abnormalities That Generate the Discharge of an Epileptogenic Focus

PATHOLOGICAL CHANGES

The pathological changes that occur in epileptogenic foci produced by various experimental focal procedures are summarized in Table 2. Glial proliferation is characteristic of such lesions, as is loss of nerve cells and impairment in local cerebral circulation (see ref. 43 for summary). An impressive feature of such lesions observed in epileptogenic foci in man and in experimental animals by Westrum et al. (60) was, in addition to the glial proliferation, the marked abnormalities in dendritic structure. The dendritic trees were deformed and denuded of spines as compared to normal tissue. These changes were thought to result in a denervation type of supersensi-

TABLE 2. *Summary of pathological changes in epileptogenic foci of animals and man*

Primary focus
   Glial proliferation (gliosis)
   Diminution in nerve cells
   Impairment in local cerebral circulation
   Abnormalities in dendritic structure
      Deformed—less branching
      Denuded of spines—irregular varicose-like swelling
  These changes are thought to result in denervation type of supersensitivity as a result of reduced synaptic input (de-afferentation). Spines are concerned mainly with inhibitory synapses, hence loss would lead to increase in excitatory input.

Secondary focus
   Mild glial proliferation
   Some dendritic spine changes
  Both of these changes appear to be secondary to trans-callosal degeneration.

tivity as a result of reduced synaptic input (partial deafferentation) (57). There was an overall decrease in neuronal elements, and the remaining neurons were of intermediate-to-small size, an observation that was thought to be important since small cells are easier to discharge than larger ones (27). There was less dendritic branching, and the course of the apical shaft and its branches was frequently distorted in different planes. Dendrites were marked by irregular varicose-like swelling on both the large shafts and the finer branches. The dendritic surfaces were relatively smooth along most of their course and were almost completely divested of their normal dendritic spines. The changes extended out from the focus a short distance and then gradually disappeared. This geographical distribution of the anatomical changes correlated well with the physiological changes where abnormal patterns of firing showed a similar transition to normal activity as one moved radially from the focus. Similar changes have been observed by Scheibel and Scheibel (46).

    Pathological changes in the secondary focus projected from the primary side are minimal as compared with those in the primary focus (Table 2). Mild glial proliferation is present (54,55,59,61), as well as some small changes in the dendritic spines. Both these changes appear to be secondary to transcallosal degeneration as a result of the lesion in the primary area (61). Often no changes or only a mild glial proliferation is seen in secondary foci that have become independently active, and it is evident from the morphological as well as the neurophysiological evidence discussed below that partial denervation is not a necessary condition for establishing a chronic epileptic focus. The role of glial cell proliferation in epileptogenic foci is discussed below.

NEUROPHYSIOLOGICAL EVENTS

[See excellent summary by Merlis (39).] The main neurophysiological changes that occur in epileptogenic foci of animals and man are summarized in Table 3 for both the primary and secondary foci. A number of different experimental models of the local epileptic process have been studied intensively. Regardless of what method is used — acute topical application of chemical agents such as strychnine, pentylenetetrazol, or penicillin, or use of more chronic agents such as freezing or alumina cream — each is characterized by the sporadic occurrence of large potentials recorded from the cortical surface or scalp as *spikes or sharp waves*. Coincidental with these there is, in some cells, a *paroxysmal depolarization shift* (PDS), on which there may appear a burst of axon spikes (Fig. 1). The PDS is a graded potential, frequently so large as to inactivate the spike-generating mechanism by excessive depolarization. It is frequently followed by a prominent hyperpolarization or inhibitory postsynaptic potential (IPSP), attributed to recurrent inhibition. Extending outward from the focus, hyperpolarization becomes more prominent, and at the periphery many of the neurons generate IPSPs that are not preceded by PDSs. This is called "surround inhibition" and it presumably serves to limit the spread of the discharge. Neurons generating PDSs appear to be otherwise normal. In the intervals between paroxysmal discharges they may generate normal excitatory postsynaptic potentials

TABLE 3. *Summary of neurophysiological changes in epileptogenic foci of animals and man*

Primary focus
  Acute
    Surface recordings: spikes and/or sharp waves, large slow waves
    Intracellular recordings: paroxysmal depolarization shift (PDS) — bursts of axon spikes may appear on PDS
    PDS frequently followed by a prominent hyperpolarization or IPSP, attributed to recurrent inhibition
    Outward from focus — hyperpolarization, not preceded by PDS — surround inhibition — limits spread of discharge
  PDS represents a large EPSP due to synaptic activation
    Extracellular recordings — spikes from units firing; high-frequency bursts
  Chronic
    Generally less active
    PDS less frequent
    "Epileptic neuron" — hyperactive through partial denervation
Secondary focus
  Propagation from primary focus via association tracts to homologous region of opposite hemisphere evokes a secondary spike
  If independently active is "mirror focus"
    Also present in limbic and other subcortical nuclei
    Synaptically related to a primary subcortical focus
  Activity of neurons in mirror focus does not differ from that of neurons in primary focus
  Thus, partial denervation is not a necessary condition for establishing a chronic epileptic focus

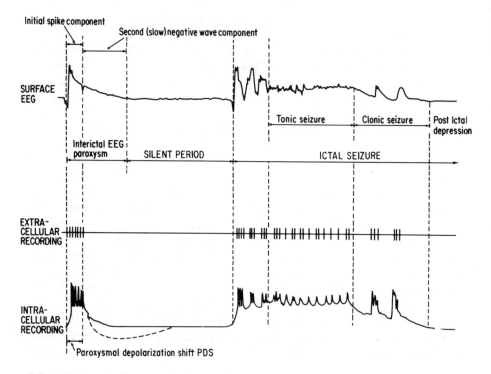

FIG. 1. Schematic diagram of relations between EEG discharge and microelectrode recordings from a neuron in a penicillin focus. (From ref. 5 with permission of publisher.)

(EPSPs) and spike potentials. A PDS is thought to be a large EPSP as a result of synaptic activation by an as yet unknown mechanism. Part of the effect may be owing to the depression of recurrent inhibition. However, a PDS is not present in all epileptogenic discharges. This is especially the case in the chronic focus produced by alumina cream or by freezing. In freezing lesions PDSs were recorded by Goldensohn (22) in only approximately 14% of neurons and even less frequently by Ward (57) in the alumina cream focus. The chronic focus appears to be less active than the acute one, probably, as discussed below, because more glial cell proliferation has occurred. The partial denervation sensitivity as a result of changes in dendritic structure, as described by Ward and colleagues (i.e., "epileptic neurons"), and which results in generation of repetitive firing with abnormal sites of spike generation, can explain the sequence of events that occur in the epileptic focus. Final proof of the hypothesis, however, is still lacking.

The interictal cortical spike may propagate via association tracts to the homologous region of the opposite hemisphere and evoke a secondary spike. If this secondary spiking becomes independently active, as it often does in chronic preparations, it is called a mirror focus and may persist even after the primary focus becomes inactive or is ablated [see Wilder (61)]. Mirror foci can also be established in limbic and other subcortical nuclei that are synaptically related to a primary subcortical focus. The activity of neurons in the secondary focus, recorded by microelectrodes, does not differ from that in the primary focus. It is, therefore, evident that at least for the mirror focus partial denervation is not a necessary condition for establishing a chronic epileptic focus. The secondary focus seems to result in some manner from bombardment by neurons of the primary focus so that they become independently epileptic. This phenomenon, as originally described by Goddard and co-workers (20,21), is related to kindling, which is the development of an epileptic response to repeated minimal electrical stimulation of various regions of the brain. The mechanism(s) of kindling is not known. A schematic diagram of the relations between EEG discharge and microelectrode recordings from a neuron in a penicillin focus is shown in Fig. 1 (5).

BIOCHEMICAL CHANGES

A summary of the biochemical changes observed in epileptogenic foci (primary and secondary) taken from animals and man is shown in Table 4. Changes in the primary focus are those either in the actual area of the lesion or in the immediately surrounding area, where maximal paroxysmal discharges are measured by microelectrode recording. The changes in the area of the lesion are those to be expected from destruction of neurons and their replacement by glial cells. Thus, there is a decrease in protein, usually but not always of oxidative metabolism, RNA synthesis, K^+, total lipid and phospholipid, cholesterol, and various fatty acids because of neuron loss; and an increase in Na^+, water, probably Cl^-, Ca^{2+}, Mg^{2+}, carbonic anhydrase, DNA, CO_2 fixation, and some fats—changes that reflect the glial proliferation since most of the changes in these substances involve glial cell metabolism. Thus, glial edema occurs as reflected in the increase in Na^+, Cl^-, and water. The rise in DNA reflects the increase in glial cell number inasmuch as neurons do not divide in the adult. Also, the glial cell proliferation is reflected by the increase in carbonic anhydrase, an enzyme found only in glial cells (17). The enzyme is also involved in CO_2 fixation, which explains the increase in this parameter. The changes in the amino acids, cyclic AMP, acetylcholinesterase, and some specific fatty acids in the primary focus appear to reflect changes in synaptic function since all these are involved in neurotransmission or in synaptic membrane function. Of particular interest are the decrease in glutamic and aspartic acids (excitatory neurotransmitters) and of GABA (an inhibitory transmitter) and the increase in glycine (an inhibitory neurotransmitter in the spinal cord) (4,52,53). The amino acid changes are found both at the lesion site and in the immediately adjacent active discharge area and occur before the seizures.

TABLE 4. *Summary of biochemical changes in epileptogenic foci of animals and man*

	Primary focus	Area adjacent to lesion	Secondary focus
Electrolytes			
Water	Increased		Very slightly increased
Na^+	Increased		Slightly increased
K^+	Decreased		Slightly decreased
Ca^{2+}	Increased		No change
Mg^{2+}	Increased		No change
Cl^-	—		—
$H^{14}CO_3^-$ space	Decreased		Decreased
Na^+-K^+-ATPase	Increased (8 hr), normal (24 hr), or decreased		Increased
Carbonic anhydrase	Increased		Increased
Synaptosome K^+ transport	Decreased		Decreased
DNA	Increased		Slightly increased
RNA Synthesis	Decreased		Decreased
Proteins	Decreased		Little change
Amino acids			
Glutamic acid	Decreased		Decreased or no change
Glutamine	Increased		No change
Aspartic acid	Decreased		Decreased or no change
GABA	Decreased		Decreased or no change
Glycine	Increased		No change
Taurine	Decreased		
Alanine	No change		
Serine	No change		
Glutamic acid decarboxylase	Decreased		Transient small decrease
Cholinesterases			
Acetyl	Increased		
Cholineacetylase	Decreased		Decreased → no change
Cyclic AMP	Increased		Increased
CO_2 fixation	Increased		Increased
Lactic dehydrogenase	Decreased		Increased
Oxidative metabolism	No change or decrease		No change
Lipids			
Total lipid	Decreased	No change	No change
Free cholesterol	Decreased	No change	No change
Total phospholipid	Decreased	No change	No change
Cholesterol esters	Increased	Increased	No change
Triglycerides	Increased	No change	No change
Phosphatidyl ethanolamine	Decreased	Decreased	No change
Oleic, arachidonic, and nervonic acids	Decreased	Decreased	No change
Lignoceric acid	Increased	Increased	Slightly increased
Palmitoleic acid	No change	Decreased	Decreased
Ganglioside sialic acid			Increased

There was a clear correlation between the severity of epilepsy and the extent to which the concentration of these amino acids deviated from normal. These data were interpreted to mean that epileptogenic cortex suffers from impaired energy metabolism. Glutamic and aspartic acids are linked to the tricarboxylic acid cycle by transamination and dehydrogenation, and thus they serve as secondary energy substrates of the CNS and also are intermediate steps in the transfer of glucose carbons into amino acids and protein. It is thought that glucose oxidation and amino acid metabolism become uncoupled during chronic epileptogenic activity. The imbalance in taurine and glycine also indicates inhibition of protein synthesis, as has been observed for such primary focal lesions (Table 4).

It appears quite probable that the later decrease in GABA content, which is secondary to the low content of its precursor, glutamic acid, throughout the cortex as well as at the primary focus is an important factor in maintaining the hyperexcitable condition in the brain of animals in which chronic epileptogenic seizures have been produced. This later decrease in GABA concentration would release its strong inhibitory effect on the cortex and result in an increase in excitability, a change that can probably explain the diminished inhibitory control seen in a focus and that appears to contribute to the spread of epileptic discharge. The prior decrease in glutamic acid content in the lesion area appears to be caused by increased liberation of this dicarboxylic amino acid early in the sequence of events leading to a focal discharging lesion and is probably partly responsible for the development of a pool of hyperactive neurons [see Jasper (31)].

The origin of the increase in glycine is not known, but certain data suggest that it may result from both inhibition of protein synthesis and its enhanced catabolism that results from the neuronal hyperexcitability in the focus. The increase in glutamine concentration similarly seems to be the result of ongoing hyperexcitability and enhanced protein breakdown in the focal region.

In both the primary and secondary foci, Escueta and Appel (14) have shown that synaptosomes isolated from these areas have decreased ability to transport K^+ actively. Thus these epileptic areas have impaired K^+ metabolism, and this coupled with reports of decreased Na^+-K^+-ATPase activity in the focus indicated defects in the Na^+-K^+ active transport system in synaptic terminals. Such defects obviously can lead to enhanced excitability and seizures as is the case for local application of ouabain, a selective inhibitor of Na^+-K^+-ATPase. Although the mechanism of the failure of the Na^+-K^+ pump in the synaptosomal membranes from epileptogenic foci is not known, it appears to result from the pathological change in the neurons induced by the seizure-provoking agent. It is likely that the changes in some of the lipid components (phospholipids, fatty acids, etc.) in the membrane (8), noted in Table 4, may be involved.

In the secondary focus the biochemical changes are generally similar to those observed in the primary focus but are quantitatively less marked.

Again the changes are characteristic of glial proliferation as described for the primary focus. The significance of this in terms of the hyperexcitability of the secondary focus is described below. The lack of or only small changes in amino acids and other transmitter substances and their enzymes indicate that the spiking activity in the secondary focus is not related to transmitter levels in any simple way. Studies on the release and synthesis of these amino acids in the mirror focus are obviously necessary.

ROLE OF GLIAL CELLS IN EPILEPTOGENIC FOCI

Buffering of Potassium

Before proceeding to the problem of the local spread and the changes that precipitate the interictal activity into a seizure, it is necessary to discuss the role of the glial cells in the seizure process. This is important since glial proliferation is one of the major events in the development of the focus. That glial proliferation is present is indicated by the anatomical studies already discussed and by the increase in DNA and carbonic anhydrase, a glial marker. What is the effect of the glial proliferation? Many workers [see review by Somjen (49)] have demonstrated an important role of glial cells in K^+ homeostasis in the brain. During excessive nervous activity or in seizures, a marked increase in extracellular potassium (Ko^+) occurs (16,28,40,44). However, this increase is generally ameliorated by K^+-stimulated active uptake of K^+ by glial cells (26), so the change is only transient. Nevertheless, during this rise in Ko^+ glial depolarization takes place, since glial cells generally behave as K^+ electrodes and are exquisitely sensitive to Ko^+ concentrations (34,42). The increase in Ko^+ activates Na^+-K^+-ATPase in the glial cell membrane and promotes Ko^+ active uptake into these cells.

During the large increase in spiking activity that occurs in an epileptic focus, Ko^+ rises rapidly as K^+ is lost from the hyperactive neurons and leaks into the narrow interstitial channels between the neurons and glia. As shown by many workers (3,10,13,35,41,56), hyperactivity of neurons is a stimulus for glial proliferation, presumably as a mechanism to increase the capacity of these cells to modulate the marked elevation of Ko^+ and possibly other electrolytes. Therefore, the lower epileptogenicity of chronic focal lesions as compared to acute lesions might well be owing to glial proliferation and, as a result, enhanced ability of glial cells to "buffer" Ko^+.

The experiments of Glötzner (19) summarized in Table 5 provide evidence that glial cells modulate the increase in Ko^+ that occurs in a chronic epileptogenic focus. Cats were injected with aluminum hydroxide into the motor cortex and tested 6 weeks later when spiking activity was present. Intracellular electrodes were inserted in glial cells and the membrane properties of these cells determined in the scar and compared to those of normal

TABLE 5. *Membrane properties of neuroglia in epileptogenic gliosis*

	Glial membrane time constant (τ) (mean $\pm$ SD)	Input resistance (Ri) (mean $\pm$ SD)
Cat neocortex Normal glial cells	482 $\pm$ 65 μsec	12.4 $\pm$ 4.7 MΩ
Glial cells in scar of aluminum hydroxide–induced epileptogenic focus	255 $\pm$ 98 μsec	2.0 $\pm$ 1.3 MΩ

From ref. 19.

glial cells. A striking difference in membrane properties was found (Table 5). In the focus the glial membrane time constant (τ) was 255 $\pm$ 98 μsec and the input resistance (Ri) was 2.0 $\pm$ 1.3 MΩ. These values equal approximately one-half and one-sixth, respectively, the values found for glial cells in normal tissue of 482 $\pm$ 65 μsec for τ and 12.4 $\pm$ 4.7 MΩ for Ri. Calculation of these data by Glötzner (19) in terms of specific membrane resistance and surface area indicated that the glial cells in the focus had an increase of the safety factor for the rate of removal of K$^+$ from the extracellular fluid as compared to its rate of release from the neurons during activity.

From these results, Glötzner concluded that the neuroglial buffering system in the focus is able to transport even more K$^+$ away from sites of K$^+$ release than it does under normal conditions. If K$^+$ were allowed to accumulate in the interstitial channels to a sufficiently high level, the resulting depolarization of neurons and glia would lower their excitability thresholds of neurons and/or increase the effectiveness of synaptic transmission, and thereby cause seizure discharges. Such an accumulation of Ko$^+$ does not normally occur because it is prevented by the glial cell modulation system, which is sensitive to Ko$^+$. Glötzner's data suggest an adaptive response of this system during chronic epileptogenesis to ameliorate the enhanced Ko$^+$ accumulation caused by hyperactivity of the neurons. This adaptive response would limit the spread of the seizure discharge, which is at least partly caused by Ko$^+$ accumulation as described later (11).

ROLE OF CARBONIC ANHYDRASE

In addition to buffering Ko$^+$, glial cells appear to play an important role in the modulation of acid-base changes in the extracellular fluid. This process uses the glial enzyme carbonic anhydrase and probably a Mg-ATPase that is activated by HCO$_3^-$ ion. This enzyme is part of the system involved in the transport of monovalent anions (Cl$^-$, I$^-$, HCO$_3^-$, etc.) across glial cell membranes. The role of carbonic anhydrase in epileptogenic foci can be eluci-

dated in animals implanted with cobalt in the frontal cortex (38). When this
is done spiking activity is generated in the region of the focus, in the parietal
cortex on the ipsilateral side, and in the secondary focus on the contralateral
side. Such activity begins 5 days after implantation and reaches a peak at 12
days. By 19 days the spiking has decreased, and by 30 to 40 days it has almost disappeared. Accompanying the increased spiking activity is a gliosis
characterized by a marked increase in carbonic anhydrase, the time course
of which follows *pari-passu* with spiking activity in the electrocorticogram
(ECoG). The changes with time in days of carbonic anhydrase activity in the
secondary focus located in the left frontal cortex as compared with the right
occipital cortex in which no spiking activity occurs are shown in Fig. 2,
taken from the observations of McQueen and Woodbury (38). There is a
marked and significant increase in carbonic anhydrase activity at 5 and 12
days after cobalt implantation and a slight increase at 19 days. These values
are significantly increased as compared to the same tissue obtained from
control animals at the same time. These authors found a direct correlation
between spiking activity and carbonic anhydrase activity in the various
regions of the brain and at various times after implantation, particularly in
the secondary focus where few pathological changes are produced.

   In Table 6 is shown the effect of cobalt implantation in the right frontal
cortex of the rat on the total free $^{14}CO_2$ space, $^{14}CO_2$ fixation, and carbonic
anhydrase activity in the projected (secondary) focus of the left frontal

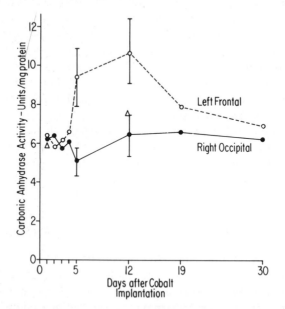

FIG. 2. Effect of implantation of cobalt in the right frontal cortex of rats on carbonic anhydrase activity in the left frontal (projected focus) cortex and right occipital cortex at
various days after implantation. See text for discussion. (From ref. 38.)

TABLE 6. *Effect of cobalt implantation in the right frontal cortex of the rat in the projected (mirror) focus of the left frontal cortex*

Treatment	Total free CO_2 space (%)	$\dfrac{\% CO_2 \text{ fixed in brain}}{\% \text{ total free } CO_2 \text{ space}}$	Carbonic anhydrase activity units/mg protein
Controls	43.8	0.60	5.0 ± 0.41
Projected focus	34.0^a	0.81^a	10.7 ± 1.6^a

[a] Significantly different from controls.
Samples removed 12 days after cobalt implantation.

cortex as compared with the same tissue from control animals not implanted with cobalt. The samples were removed 12 days after cobalt implantation at the peak of the spiking activity in the ECoG. Compared to the same area in control animals, the secondary focus in the frontal cortex had a 23% lower total free $^{14}CO_2$ space, a 44% greater rate of $^{14}CO_2$ fixation, and a 114% increase in carbonic anhydrase activity. These data suggest that carbonic anhydrase regulates the total free CO_2 concentration in glial cells and also the incorporation of CO_2 into various metabolic products (CO_2 fixation), such as tricarboxylic acid cycle intermediates, glutamic and aspartic acids, pyrimidines and purines, and fatty acids. Enhanced CO_2 fixation would, therefore, increase synthesis of proteins and nucleic acids and result in glial growth and proliferation. The decrease in free CO_2 space suggests that carbonic anhydrase also regulates CO_2 movement into and out of glial cells and that increased amounts accelerate its removal from the brain and thereby prevent its accumulation. Such an accumulation could occur in the focus where metabolic production of CO_2 is increased as a result of the enhanced neuronal activity if carbonic anhydrase were not increased to handle the greater metabolic load of CO_2. Accumulation of CO_2 results in blocking of synaptic transmission and, in high concentration, can produce seizures (63,64,66).

The effects of acetazolamide (Diamox®), a selective inhibitor of carbonic anhydrase, on the activity of this enzyme in the primary and secondary foci induced by cobalt as related to its effects on spiking activity add further evidence to a modulating role of glial cell carbonic anhydrase on neuronal excitability. These results are shown in Fig. 3. Acetazolamide given acutely or chronically inhibited carbonic anhydrase to normal or below normal levels and enhanced seizure activity. On withdrawal of acetazolamide after chronic administration, carbonic anhydrase activity returned to levels higher than those produced by cobalt implantation alone, and this was accompanied by suppression of both spiking in the ECoG and clinical seizure activity. Thus chronic administration of a carbonic anhydrase inhibitor induces increased activity of carbonic anhydrase in glial cells. This can explain the previously observed development of tolerance to the anticonvulsant effect of acetazolamide. Acetazolamide also inhibits CO_2

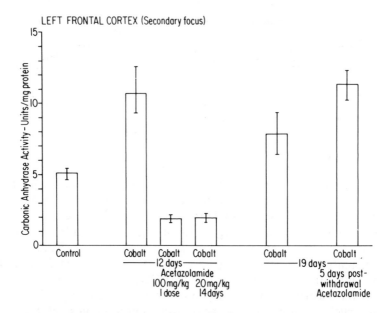

FIG. 3. Effects of acute and chronic administration of acetazolamide and its withdrawal on the increased carbonic anhydrase activity in the secondary focus of the left frontal cortex induced by a cobalt-induced epileptogenic focus in the right frontal cortex of rats. See text for discussion. (From ref. 38.)

fixation in brain (D. M. Woodbury, *unpublished observations*). These data suggest a role of glial cells in the modulation of increased neuronal activity no matter how induced. This regulatory system involves control of HCO_3^--H_2CO_3-CO_2 metabolism and distribution in the brain by glial cell carbonic anhydrase. Inhibiting the enzyme by acetazolamide or other carbonic anhydrase inhibitors compromises the modulating system and increases neuronal excitability. In the chronic cobalt lesion the increased neuronal activity enhances CO_2 production, which appears to cause an adaptive increase in carbonic anhydrase activity. This increase in activity, however, is not only *not* prevented by chronic inhibition of the carbonic anhydrase but is actually enhanced, and this results in modulation of the excessive neuronal activity present in the cobalt brain and causes tolerance to develop to the inhibitor. It is evident from these observations that glial cells have a significant role as modulators of neuronal activity by regulating the concentrations of K^+ and of the CO_2-HCO_3^--H_2CO_3 system in the interstitial ionic milieu.

GLIAL ANION TRANSPORT SYSTEMS

The evidence just presented suggests that glial cells, in addition to regulating the cation content of the extracellular space of the brain, particularly

K^+, also regulate the anion content of this fluid. This is accomplished by actively transporting monovalent anions using carbonic anhydrase and HCO_3-activated Mg-ATPase. Inhibition of this system, as is the case for inhibition of the cation system (e.g., with ouabain), has dire consequences on neuronal excitability and can result in seizures. This monovalent anion transport system is selective for glial cells and has the ability, like the choroid plexus, to transport actively chloride, iodide, bromide, thiocynate, perchlorate, and bicarbonate into glial cells (6,7,18,32,65). The system is K^+ dependent and is carrier mediated since the transported monovalent anions compete for the carrier system. In Table 7 is shown the distribution of radioactive iodide, thiocyanate, perchlorate, and bromide with and without added carrier (5 mEq/kg) in brain and CSF of adult rats. The values given are the ratios of the concentration of the specific anion in the brain cells or CSF as compared to its concentration in the extracellular space in the case of the brain or in the plasma in the case of the CSF. In the brain of the control rats the ratio is greater than 1.0 for iodide and thiocyanate, and in the case of perchlorate the ratio is also greater than the predicted ratio for passive distribution of monovalent anion (approximately 0.25). Thus the three anions are transported into cells against an electrical gradient. The bromide ratio is less than the predicted passive ratio, hence it appears to be transported out of the cells. A large load of carrier blocks this transport and the anions are then distributed passively across the cell membrane in accordance with the membrane potential. All these anions including bromide are also transported out of the CSF across the choroid plexus, and the system is blocked by carrier loading.

The distribution of radioactive perchlorate ion with and without loading in the brain and CSF of rats during maturation is shown in Table 8. In rats 3 days old, an age when no functional glial cells are present, radioactive perchlorate is passively distributed in the brain and carrier loading has little effect on its distribution, nor does it influence brain excitability. The active anion transport system appears after 10 days of age when glial cells develop, and at this time carrier loading blocks this transport. Also at this time

TABLE 7. *Distribution of radioactive anions with and without carrier (5 mEq/kg) in brain and CSF of adult rats*

Radioactive anion	Ratio: Brain cell anion / Extracellular anion		Ratio: CSF anion / Plasma anion	
	Control	Carrier loaded	Control	Carrier loaded
Iodide	1.30	0.22	0.02	0.42
Thiocyanate	1.33	0.19	0.06	0.74
Perchlorate	0.71	0.15	0.10	0.80
Bromide	0.15	0.25	0.78	1.00

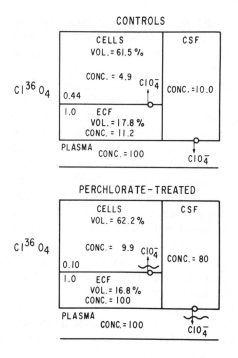

FIG. 4. Scheme of the distribution of $^{36}ClO_4^-$ in brain cells, interstitial space, and CSF relative to plasma in normal and perchlorate-treated (5 mEq/kg) rats. (From ref. 65 with permission of publisher.)

perchlorate and thiocyanate begin to produce prominent excitatory effects on the nervous system as described below. A schematic diagram of the relative distribution of radioactive perchlorate between brain cells, interstitial fluid, CSF, and plasma with and without carrier loading is shown in Fig. 4 (65). Note that in the scheme for the perchlorate-treated group, the ratio between cells and interstitial fluid approaches that for passive distribution. The cell values are for the overall distribution of perchlorate in all the cells of the brain (neurons and glia). However, the transport system is in the glia and these anions seem to be passively distributed across neurons as is evident from the data in 3-day-old rats (Table 8) in which no functional glial cells are present. Also, resolution of radioactive perchlorate uptake

TABLE 8. *Effects of a 5 mEq/kg load of perchlorate on distribution of ^{36}Cl-perchlorate in brain and CSF of rats during maturation*

Age (days)	Ratio: $\dfrac{\text{Brain cell } ^{36}ClO_4^-}{\text{Extracellular } ^{36}ClO_4^-}$		Ratio: $\dfrac{\text{CSF } ^{36}ClO_4^-}{\text{Plasma } ^{36}ClO_4^-}$	
	Control	Perchlorate	Control	Perchlorate
3	0.07	0.17	0.82	0.92
9	0.16	0.13	0.61	0.88
16	0.45	0.18	0.30	0.74
Adult	0.43	0.15	0.12	0.80

curves allows separation of the glial and neuronal uptake components and calculation of the glial and neuronal cell concentrations. The results from such calculations show active transport into glial cells and passive distribution across neurons. Carrier loading blocks the glial transport but does not alter the distribution across neurons.

The evidence for active transport of radioactive chloride into glial cells has been presented by Bourke, Tower, and colleagues (6,7,18). Its transport into glial cells is K^+ dependent, but that into neurons is not (18). As is the case for the transport of perchlorate, iodide, and thiocyanate, chloride transport into glial cells is blocked by large loads of these same anions, as is shown in Table 9 taken from the results of Gill et al. (18) for cultured astrocytes. In addition, the system is inhibited by acetazolamide, showing the involvement of carbonic anhydrase, and by 2,4-dinitrophenol and fluoride, evidence that the process is energy dependent.

The effect of inhibition of the glial anion system by large loads (5 mEq/kg) of the various monovalent anions on brain excitability, as assessed by the ratio of the tonic extensor to the tonic flexor (E/F ratio) component of the maximal electroshock seizure, is shown in Fig. 5. The E/F ratio was increased 750% by thiocyanate, 100% by perchlorate, and decreased approximately 45% by bromide and 50% by iodide. Thus thiocyanate and perchlorate exert marked excitatory effects on the CNS, whereas bromide and iodide exert anticonvulsant effects. In Table 10 is shown the dose-effect relation for the convulsive and lethal effects of perchlorate, alone and in combination with acetazolamide in rats. The convulsive dose 50 (CD_{50}) for perchlorate is 9 mEq/kg and the lethal dose 50 (LD_{50}) is 12 mEq/kg. When acetazolamide (10 mg/kg) was given in combination with perchlorate,

TABLE 9. *Inhibition of ^{36}Cl uptake into astrocytes*

Inhibitor (10 mM)	5–8 mM K^+ control at 10 min (%)
Acetazolamide	$41 \cdot 2$ ($66 \cdot 2$)[a]
Perchlorate	$34 \cdot 1$
Thiocyanate	$28 \cdot 2$
Bromide	$25 \cdot 9$
Iodide	$41 \cdot 2$
2,4-Dinitrophenol	$12 \cdot 2$
Fluoride	$11 \cdot 4$

[a] Value for 5 mM acetazolamide given in parentheses. Cultured cells on small glass cover slips were incubated at 37°C for 10 min in media containing 144 mM Cl^- plus ^{36}Cl (2×10^6 cpm/ml), 5–8 mM K^+ and $142 \cdot$ mM Na^+, in the presence of [^3H]inulin as a measure of extracellular fluid (from ref. 18).

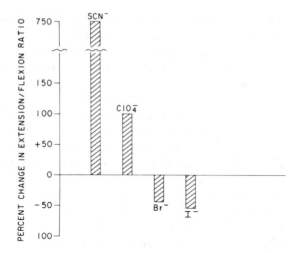

FIG. 5. Effect of various monovalent anions (5 mEq/kg) on the extensor/flexor (E/F) ratio of rats. Ordinate is the percent change in E/F rates from the pretreatment control value.

the CD_{50} decreased to 7.5 mEq/kg and the LD_{50} to 10 mEq/kg. Thus inhibition of carbonic anhydrase enhanced both the convulsive and the lethal effects of perchlorate. It is evident, therefore, that inhibition of glial cell anion transport results in seizures in adults, but not in neonatal animals in which no functional glial cells are present. The observation of Ransom (45) that seizures can be produced in rats when the cortical surface is irrigated with low chloride concentration solutions also demonstrates the importance of anions in the regulation of brain excitability. In addition, it shows that irrigation of the cortex with solutions of high chloride concentration prevents the seizures induced by elevation of Ko^+. High bicarbonate concentration solutions also cause seizures. How inhibition of anion transport into glial cells causes seizures is not clear, but it may be owing either to elevation of Ko^+, since anion transport is K^+ dependent, or to accumulation of HCO_3^- in the extracellular space, since HCO_3^- appears to be transported into glial cells by this same system.

Kimmelberg and Bourke (33) have characterized a HCO_3^--activated Mg-ATPase (HCO_3-ATPase) in brain and have found that it is located in the mitochondria of both glial and neuronal cells. It is postulated to play

TABLE 10. *Convulsive and lethal effects of perchlorate alone and in combination with acetazolamide in rats*

	CD_{50}	LD_{50}
Perchlorate	9.0 mEq/kg	12.0 mEq/kg
Perchlorate + acetazolamide (10 mg/kg)	7.5 mEq/kg	10.0 mEq/kg

some role in anion transport. That this is the case is suggested by its in-hibition by thiocyanate, perchlorate, and other monovalent anions. The effects of these anions on HCO_3-ATPase are shown in Fig. 6. Thiocyanate completely inhibited this enzyme at a concentration of 12 mм/liter, and perchlorate at a concentration of 16 mм/liter. Bromide and iodide were much less effective and inhibited HCO_3-ATPase only approximately 15% at concentration of 10 mм/liter. The inhibition of the enzyme by perchlorate was found to be uncompetitive, an indication of a multienzyme system, which probably involves inhibition of both HCO_3-ATPase and Mg-ATPase.

In Table 11 is shown a comparison of the concentrations of perchlorate ion in various body fluids 15 min after injection of 5 or 10 mм/kg with the concentration that inhibits HCO_3-ATPase *in vitro*. At 5 mм/kg body weight, the fluid concentrations of perchlorate in plasma, CSF, and brain cell are 14, 3, and 0.6 mм/liter, respectively. At these concentrations, the HCO_3^--ATPase in brain would be 93% inhibited at the concentration of perchlorate in plasma, 30% inhibited at the concentration in CSF, and 5% inhibited at the concentration observed in brain cells. At 10 mм/kg, the concentration of perchlorate in these fluids is calculated to be 28 mм/liter for plasma, 13 mм/liter for CSF, and 2 mм/liter for brain cells. The HCO_3^--ATPase in brain would be inhibited 100% at the concentration in plasma, 92% at the concentration in CSF, and 20% at the concentration in brain cells. At 5 mм/kg perchlorate produces an increase in the E/F ratio but no seizures, whereas at 10 mм/kg perchlorate produces seizures in 100% of animals and

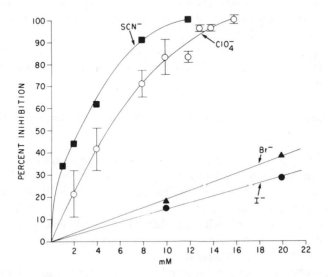

FIG. 6. Inhibition of HCO_3^--ATPase activity in the cerebral cortex of rats by thiocyanate, perchlorate, bromide, and iodide ions. Ordinate is percent inhibition of the enzyme and abscissa is concentration of the indicated anion.

TABLE 11. *Comparison of the concentrations of perchlorate ion in various body fluids of rats with the concentration that inhibits brain HCO$_3$-ATPase* in vitro, *and with its effects on brain excitability*

Fluid	Perchlorate concentration 15 min after administration	
	At 5 mM/kg	At 10 mM/kg
Plasma	14 mM/liter	28 mM/liter
CSF	3 mM/liter	13 mM/liter
Brain cell	0.6 mM/liter	2 mM/liter
In vitro inhibition of HCO$_3^-$-ATPase at plasma conc.	93%	~100%
In vitro inhibition of HCO$_3^-$-ATPase at CSF conc.	30%	92%
In vitro inhibition of HCO$_3^-$-ATPase at brain cell conc.	5%	20%
Brain excitability	↑ E/F ratio no seizures	100% seizures

17% of the animals die. The results suggest that the effect of perchlorate to inhibit HCO$_3$-ATPase and to increase excitability and produce seizures correlates best with its concentration in CSF, which is also the brain extracellular concentration. This is also the concentration that inhibits anion transport into glial cells. The ability of perchlorate and thiocyanate to elicit seizures appears to be related to their capacity to inhibit HCO$_3^-$-ATPase, an enzyme, together with carbonic anhydrase, involved in glial cell anion transport processes. The ability of acetazolamide to enhance both the seizure-evoking effects and the inhibition of anion transport by perchlorate appears to be owing to its inhibition of carbonic anhydrase. Hence it is evident that inhibition of both enzymes results in a greater effect than blockade of either enzyme alone.

Local Spread and the Changes That Precipitate the Interictal Activity into a Seizure

As described by Merlis (39), "Any focus discharging sporadic spikes may develop a self-sustained discharge of rhythmic potentials, i.e., a local seizure. In the development of seizure activity, cells generating PDSs may demonstrate a progressive decrease in the hyperpolarization which follows PDS, with the development of after-depolarizations and, finally, rhythmic depolarizations." The paroxysmal discharges activate recurrent and surround inhibitory receptors, which tend to delimit the discharge. However, by some as yet unknown mechanism these inhibitory influences are dissipated, the IPSPs are converted to EPSPs, and an ictal episode occurs. Since this episode is highly synchronous, a combination of recurrent excitatory and inhibitory systems appears to be involved (50). Convulsant drugs applied locally probably act by increasing potency of the excitatory system and reducing inhibitory input, a response that produces a hypersynchronous discharge [see Merlis (39)].

The experiments of Dichter et al. (11) provide some evidence on the mechanism of transition from the interictal state to seizures. They recorded from glial cells during penicillin-induced interictal discharges and seizures in the cat hippocampus. The changes in glial cell membrane potentials were used as an index of changes in local extracellular K^+ concentrations, as discussed above. They observed that K^+ accumulated in the extracellular space during an interictal discharge and interpreted these results to indicate that the K^+ accumulation is a result of the neuronal activity underlying the discharge. However, since it has been shown that such an accumulation can depolarize cells and thereby lower their excitability thresholds or increase the effectiveness of synaptic transmission, Dichter et al. (11) presented evidence that the interictal K^+ accumulation may play a causative role in the transition from interictal spiking to seizure activity. Furthermore, such accumulation around neurons might enable many neurons to become synchronized during paroxysm. After each isolated interictal discharge, the excess K^+ in the extracellular space returns to neurons via the Na^+-K^+ pump, enters the glial cells also actively, or diffuses away into the large volumes of extracellular fluid and the glial membrane potential returns to its previous value. However, when the excitability of the focus increases as interictal discharges occur more frequently, the hippocampal cortex is unable to clear the accumulated K^+ adequately. Thus, as each interictal discharge occurs, more K^+ is released from neurons into the already loaded extracellular space. The consequence of this is an even greater increase in excitability leading to a seizure. Thus they hypothesized that a seizure will tend to develop when subsequent interictal discharges occur before the cortex (presumably the glial cells) has had the chance to clear all the extra K^+ in the extracellular space from previous discharges.

Various internal and external factors that affect excitability are also important in precipitating interictal discharge into a seizure. Such factors as blood sugar level, endocrine balance, nutritional changes, temperature, and water and salt balance affect the threshold for seizures and are important factors in altering the susceptibility of the brain to seizures. A discussion of these factors has been presented by Woodbury (62).

Propagation of Discharge During a Major Seizure

The seizure discharge may propagate (spread) to other areas of the brain, by either a rapid or a slow process. The rapid spread of discharge involves all synaptically related neurons available to the epileptogenic focus. However, not all routes are of equal importance in the spread of the epileptic discharge. The propagation of discharge involves local spread, presumably using short internuncial cortical neurons, spread to the contralateral homologous region (mirror focus) via transcallosal and other interhemispheric or subcortical pathways, and spread via corticofugal pathways to the mesencephalon, where presumably by involvement of the reticular substance the spread is projected diffusely to the entire telencephalon, as well as to the spinal cord. However, the generalization of seizures also involves a number of other subcortical centers in addition to the reticular activating system (see refs. 1, 30, and 39 for summaries).

Spread of the discharge to other regions usually requires a high-frequency drive from the primary focus, which appears to involve post-tetanic potentiation. This excessive bombardment causes the other areas to become independently active, and this serves to initiate discharges in still other areas with diffuse spread of seizure activity.

A seizure discharge in a cortical epileptic focus may spread to neighboring cortex at a slow rate. This is the case for the jacksonian motor seizure in which the wave creeps across the cortex at a rate of only a few millimeters per minute. This slow spread of activity appears to be related to the spreading depression of Leão (36) and involves accumulation of K^+ in the extracellular fluid and depolarization of both glia and neurons. Grafstein (23) presented evidence to suggest that the K^+ released during excessive activation of clusters of neurons leads to depolarization of the same and adjacent neurons, thus leading to further release of K^+ and the recruitment of more and more neurons into the process. This leads to diffuse spread of the seizure discharge, and this is followed by profound postictal depression as a result of the spreading depression. As expected from the role of glial cells in K^+ homeostasis, the accumulated K^+ in spreading depression would depolarize glia as well as neurons and cause stimulation of the K^+ transport system in the glia. This would then reduce Ko^+ and lead to recovery from the spreading depression. Measurements with potassium-selective electrodes have shown that during spreading depression Ko^+ levels in the cortex rise to very high values (see ref. 49 for summary).

Events That Arrest the Seizure

Although the seizure focus is always present, ictal episodes are only occasional and short-lived events in the behavior of an epileptogenic focus. It is essential, therefore, to consider the various processes that delimit focal firing and that terminate a seizure once it has been initiated. The most important methods for carrying out these processes appear to be inhibitory mechanisms, accumulation of metabolic products that inhibit seizure activity, and glial uptake of Ko^+ and released neurotransmitters. The intrinsic cortical inhibitory mechanisms, i.e., recurrent and surround inhibition, have been discussed above and appear to be the most important processes to restrain a focus from firing and to arrest an ongoing seizure discharge. Extracortical inhibitory systems also exert some measure of control as well. For example, stimulation of portions of the cerebellum suppresses interictal spiking activity in the penicillin- or cobalt-induced cortical focus, and cerebellar ablations facilitate the spike activity (12,29). Also, stimulation of the caudate suppresses the acute cortical penicillin focus (see ref. 39 for summary). Whether the same or similar inhibitory systems are operative to terminate seizures in parts of the cortex other than the sensory or motor areas is not known. During severe tonic-clonic seizures, respiratory arrest occurs briefly and there is a transient hypoxia and hypercapnia. Also since intense muscular activity takes place during the seizure, lactic acid accumulates in the plasma. This results in a mixed systemic metabolic and respiratory acidosis. In experimental animals, possibly in man, CO_2 accumulates in brain to a level sufficiently high to block seizure discharges (58,64). The seizure arrest may be partly owing to accumulation of CO_2. The hypoxia and increased CO_2 accumulation also cause increased cerebral blood flow, which in man may be sufficient to prevent CO_2 accumulation in brain, but this has not been proved.

The role of glial cells in modulating Ko^+ has already been described, as has their ability to adapt to chronic neuronal hyperexcitability. Thus this K^+-modulating system appears to play an important role in delimiting focal spread as already discussed and in arresting ongoing seizure activity. In addition, the ability of glial cells actively to take up neurotransmitters released as a result of neuronal activity may be important in terminating seizures (25,47).

SEIZURES WITH GENERALIZED ONSET

Seizures may be generalized from the start, in the form of myoclonic jerks, tonic seizures, or tonic-clonic seizures. In many examples there is widespread and diffuse neuronal involvement — such as diffuse degenerative disease, metabolic disturbance, or toxic state, in which there may be a diffuse increase in excitability of neurons — and explosively rapid involvement of cortex and subcortex. But such diffuse disturbance is not essential, and generalized seizures have been elicited by focal electrical stimulation of mesial thalamus or midbrain (see discussion in ref. 39 and summary of the mechanism of action of convulsants in ref. 15).

Pentylenetetrazol

One of the drugs that produces generalized seizures which mimic an absence-type seizure in man, as validated by electrocorticographic recording and clinical seizures, is pentylenetetrazol (PTZ). Drugs that prevent PTZ seizures are those that are effective in the treatment of absence epilepsy.

Therefore, an understanding of its mechanism of action should give a clue to the processes by which generalized seizures, such as absence, are triggered. From the preceding discussion on mechanisms of focal epilepsy it is evident that initiation of seizures involves effects on cell membranes and is related to active or passive movement of ions across these membranes. It is difficult in the intact brain to separate the effects of convulsant drugs on cell membranes with regard to whether they influence active transport or membrane permeability.

Since there is evidence that PTZ may alter both these parameters (9), we decided to use a model system that could sort out these effects. One of the systems in which this can be done is the short-circuited skin of the frog or the short-circuited skin of the frog or the short-circuited urinary bladder of the toad. In these preparations there is a net transfer of Na^+ across the epithelial cells as a result of an active Na^+ transport system located in the cell membrane facing the outside surface of the epithelial cells of the skin or the serosal side of the bladder cells. When the membranes are short-circuited by applying a voltage in the opposite direction from the one occurring normally across the cells, a current flows because of active Na^+ movement across the cells from the mucosal to the serosal side. Effects of substances on Na^+ permeability (mucosal side) and active transport (serosal side) can thus be elucidated in this model.

Since some data in animals suggested that PTZ seizures affect K^+ movements, the effects of this excitatory convulsant on the short-circuit current (SCC) of the toad bladder were tested (24). In order to do this a series of tetrazol derivatives related to PTZ was tested. The CD_{50} of these agents in mice was measured and compared with the previous data of Stone (51). The results of these tests are shown in Table 12 (24). Trimethylenetetrazol (C_3) was least potent and heptamethylenetetrazol (C_7) was most potent. These analogues differ from PTZ in the length of the carbon chain attached to the tetrazol ring. In Fig. 7 is shown the effect of the C_3 to C_7 tetrazol analogues on the SCC of the toad urinary bladder. C_7 was the most effective and C_3 the least effective of the series. In Table 13 is shown a comparison of the ratio of effect on SCC of equimolar concentrations (5 mM) of PTZ and

TABLE 12. $CD_{50}s$ of various tetrazol derivatives

Tetrazol derivative	No. of mice tested	Approximate i.p. CD_{50} (mg/kg)	Approximate i.p. $CD_{50}{}^a$ (mg/kg)
Trimethylenetetrazol	20	900	1,000
Tetramethylenetetrazol	20	250	250
Pentamethylenetetrazol	20	50	50
Hexamethylenetetrazol	20	40	40
Heptamethylenetetrazol	20	30	30

[a] From Stone (51).
From ref. 24 with permission of publisher.

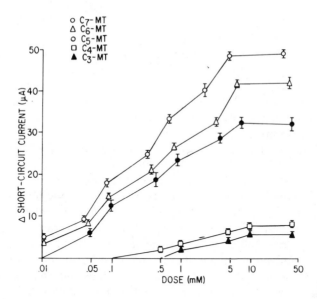

FIG. 7. Comparison of the dose-effect curves for various tetrazol analogues with PTZ. Absolute changes in SCC are expressed along the ordinate. Concentration is shown along the abscissa. Each point represents the mean value obtained in 4 experiments. Vertical bars denote ±SE. C_3MT, trimethylenetetrazol; C_4-MT, tetramethylenetetrazol; C_5-MT, (PTZ) pentamethylenetetrazol; C_6-MT, tetramethylenetetrazol; C_7-MT, heptamethylenetetrazol. See text for discussion. (From ref. 24 with permission of the publisher.)

the various tetrazol derivatives with the ratio of CD_{50} obtained in mice. It is clear from this table that a strong correlation exists between the convulsive potency of these derivatives and the increase in SCC measured in the isolated toad bladder. This suggests that the mechanisms of their effect in the two systems may be the same.

TABLE 13. *Comparisons of the ratios of effects on SCC of equimolar doses of PTZ and various tetrazol derivatives with the ratios of $CD_{50}s$ obtained in mice*

Tetrazol derivative	$\dfrac{\text{PTZ } CD_{50}{}^a}{\text{derivative } CD_{50}{}^a}$	$\dfrac{\Delta SCC \text{ derivative}^b}{\Delta SCC \text{ PTZ}^b}$
Trimethylenetetrazol	0.06	0.13 ± 0.02^c
Tetramethylenetetrazol	0.20	0.21 ± 0.01
Hexamethylenetetrazol	1.25	1.27 ± 0.03
Heptamethylenetetrazol	1.67	1.71 ± 0.07

[a] These values are derived from Fig. 8.
[b] Average changes produced in four different bladder lobes by 5 mM of each tetrazol.
[c] Values shown are means ± SE.
From ref. 24 with permission of publisher.

Further studies demonstrated that the increase in SCC produced by these convulsants was not owing to an increase in Na^+ permeability of the mucosal membrane as is the case for phenytoin and vasopressin. In addition, we (24) tested the effects of PTZ on SCC in toad bladders exposed to high or low concentrations of K^+ in the medium bathing the serosal surface of the bladder. These results demonstrated that PTZ had no effect on SCC in the presence of high K^+ concentration in the medium, whereas PTZ increased SCC when K^+ was removed from the medium. We therefore suggested that the effects of PTZ on SCC might be mediated by the effect of PTZ on potassium permeability. Thus its effects on ^{22}Na, ^{36}Cl, and ^{42}K fluxes across the short-circuited toad bladder were assessed. PTZ did not influence ^{22}Na nor ^{36}Cl flux across epithelial cells. It did, however, increase ^{42}K flux from the mucosal to serosal side, and this increase accounted completely for the increase in SCC. We concluded that PTZ appears to increase SCC by increasing the permeability of the serosal-side membrane to potassium.

The effects of trimethadione, dimethadione, ethosuximide, and diazepam, drugs effective against PTZ convulsions in animals and useful in the therapy for absence seizures in man, were tested on the increase in SCC induced by PTZ in the toad bladder. It was shown that all these drugs inhibited the increase in SCC produced by PTZ. The ratio of the inhibitory effects of these drugs against the PTZ increase in SCC and their effectiveness to prevent PTZ-induced seizures in animals is the same for all of these anti-PTZ drugs. Also, the relative ratios of these drugs in preventing seizures in man are the same as for inhibiting the PTZ-induced increase in SCC. Thus the increase in permeability to K^+ produced by PTZ in the toad bladder correlates with its effects to produce convulsions in animals and man. The question, then, is how does PTZ produce seizures in brain by increasing K^+ permeability? PTZ is thought to stimulate both excitatory as well as inhibitory synapses (37). However, it produces seizures by excitation of cerebral structures relatively unopposed by inhibition. Its effect to increase K^+ permeability would result in hyperpolarization of excitatory neurons and thereby increase the release of sufficient amounts of excitatory transmitter(s) in those areas lacking inhibitory input to cause seizures.

An additional action, for which there is some evidence, could be on glial cells. A PTZ-induced increase in K^+ permeability of the glial cell membranes, cells that have characteristics similar to those of epithelial cells, could cause rapid and massive release of K^+ into the extracellular space where its accumulation would depolarize neurons to such an extent that seizures would result, particularly if it occurred in concert with enhanced excitatory transmitter release from neuronal hyperpolarization.

Strychnine and Picrotoxin and the GABA and Glycine Receptors

Although a large number of convulsant drugs are known, the mechanism of action of only a few of these has been worked out. Strychnine causes

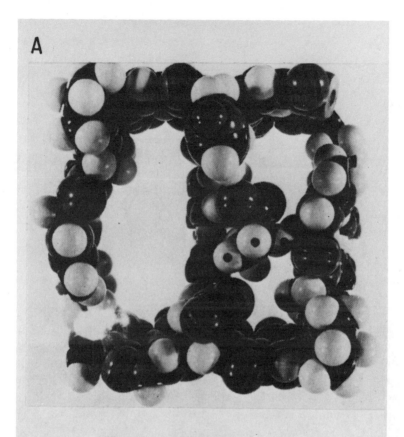

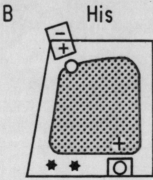

FIG. 8. A: A Corey-Pauling-Kaltun (CPK) model of glycine bound in its model receptor. Glycine is $^+NH_3$-CH_2-COO^-. **B:** Diagram of how strychnine fills the glycine receptor. Two stars indicate where the two methoxy groups of brucine fit; circle in the square represents Asp. (Modified from ref. 48 and used with permission of the publisher.)

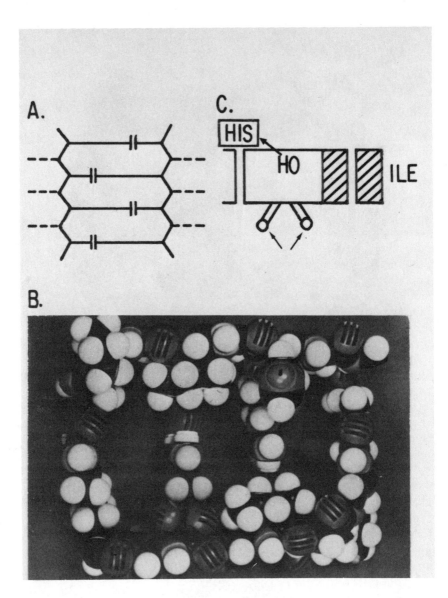

FIG. 9. Models of the GABA receptor and the mode of binding of drugs to it. **A:** An Arg-Glu grid showing the 4 rungs in the GABA receptor and the right- and left-hand secondary chains described in the text. The short apposed amino acid is Glu and the long one is Arg. **B:** CPK model of the postulated GABA receptor. **C:** Diagram of suggested mode of binding of picrotoxin in the GABA receptor. Arrows indicate the correct hydrogen bonds from Arg NHs to carbonyl Os. (Modified from ref. 48 and used with permission of publisher.)

convulsions by blockade of postsynaptic inhibitory pathways, thus releasing excitatory pathways that fire excessively on sensory stimulation. The neurotransmitter for postsynaptic inhibition is glycine, and it acts on the postsynaptic membrane via the glycine receptor. Strychnine blocks the glycine receptor. According to Smythies (48) the glycine receptor has three rungs in its primary structure consisting of Arg-Glu; Glu-Arg; Glu-Arg, and secondary chains with the sequences -Gly-x-Gly-Pro-x-Asp-x and -Gly-x-Gly-Pro-x-His-x. Glycine binds to its model receptor with its amino group caught between Asp and Glu, its carboxyl group between His and Arg, and there is a lipophilic contact between its single methylene group and an adjacent Gly moiety in the receptor protein in addition (Fig. 8A). According to Smythies (48), the strychnine molecule fills the receptor cup almost completely with an ionic bond from its protonated amino N to Asp and a hydrogen bond from His to its carbonyl O (Fig. 8B). The effect of glycine on the glycine receptor is to increase Cl^- permeability of the postsynaptic membrane. The increase in Cl^- permeability results in an IPSP and hyperpolarization of the membrane. Strychnine blocks the increase in Cl^- permeability and the resulting IPSP induced by glycine.

Picrotoxin, like strychnine, causes seizures by release of inhibitory control, but in this case the effect is blockage of the GABA receptor. GABA is an inhibitory mediator in higher cortical centers, in the cerebellum, and also in some subcortical areas. The primary structure of the GABA receptor, as postulated by Smythies (48), has four rings consisting of Glu-Arg; Arg-Glu; Glu-Arg; Glu-Arg; the secondary chains have the sequence on the right side of -x-His-x-Val(or Ile)-Pro-Gly-x-Gly- (on E chain), and on the left side of -x-Gly-x-Gly-Pro-x-Ile-x-Asp-x (on F chain) (Fig. 9A and B shows a model of this receptor). GABA binds in its receptor with its carboxyl group caught between three protons (two from Arg of rung 3 and one from His), its amino group binds to the Glu of rung 2 (repelling Arg of rung 2), and its α-methylene group binds lipophilically to the adjacent Ile. Picrotoxin binds to the GABA receptor as shown in Fig. 9C. Its square upper section fits into the rectangular "inside" of the F secondary chain with extensive lipophilic interactions and a hydrogen bond from OH to His. The two carboxyl oxygens jut down with the correct locations and bond angles to receive hydrogen bonds from the two spare protons in the two Args (of rungs 2 and 3) in the floor of the receptor.

GABA acts on its receptor to increase Cl^- permeability and produce an IPSP. Picrotoxin blocks these effects of GABA on the receptor. Smythies (48) has classified many other convulsants as to their effects to block either glycine or GABA receptors.

SUMMARY

The study of seizure mechanisms is best carried out in experimental models that resemble human epilepsy as closely as possible. Both local and generalized models are used. Local foci induced by implantation of alumina cream, cobalt, or tungstic acid or by local freezing or application of penicillin are characterized by neuronal loss, glial proliferation, and abnormalities in dendritic structure, which include loss of dendritic spines with resultant deafferentation and supersensitivity. Spikes and large slow waves are observed in the surface EEG, and intracellular recordings show a paroxysmal depolarizing shift with bursts of axon spikes. This is frequently followed by a hyperpolarization particularly in the area outward from the focus. Biochemically the lesion and its surrounding areas and the secondary (mirror) focus are characterized by glial edema, decreased protein synthesis and oxidative metabolism, decreased K^+ transport and Na-K-ATPase, defects in neurotransmitters, and an increase in carbonic anhydrase, a glial enzyme. These changes are compatible with the pathological alterations and the increased neuronal activity. Glial proliferation represents an adaptive response to the increased neuronal discharge such that the spread of the discharge is limited. Glial cells in a focus have a greater ability to modulate changes in extracellular K^+, Cl^-, HCO_3^-, and CO_2 and thereby regulate the ionic composition of the neuronal environment. In addition, glial cells actively transport the monovalent anions chloride, bicarbonate, iodide, thiocyanate, perchlorate, and bromide by a system that involves HCO_3^--activated ATPase and carbonic anhydrase. Inhibition of this anion transport system by thiocyanate and perchlorate produces seizures that are enhanced by acetazolamide. The increase in excitability produced by increasing doses of thiocyanate and perchlorate correlates with the degree to which they inhibit HCO_3^--ATPase.

Generalized seizures can be induced by drugs such as pentylenetetrazol, which stimulate excitatory systems; by drugs such as strychnine, picrotoxin, bicuculline, and penicillin, which inhibit inhibitory systems; or by drugs such as ouabain and thiocyanate, which block electrolyte transport systems in neurons and/or glia. In the case of pentylenetetrazol, experiments in isolated systems such as the toad bladder demonstrate that it increases K^+ permeability. Such an effect *in vivo* could cause loss of K^+ from cells and its accumulation in extracellular fluid, an effect which, if exerted on all cells (particularly glia), could cause generalized seizures by depolarization of neuronal membranes. Blockade of inhibitory synapses involving the GABA receptor by substances such as picrotoxin, penicillin, and bicuculline produces seizures by competition for the receptor. Also inhibitory glycine receptors can be blocked competitively by strychnine.

Although a considerable amount of information has been accumulated on the neurophysiological and biochemical mechanisms of seizures, much is still to be learned. Particular areas needing attention are the role of glia and their interactions with neurons, the mechanisms of dendritic spine loss in epileptogenic foci, and the sequence of events leading to supersensitivity, neurotransmitter changes in the focus, the nature of excitatory and inhibitory receptors, and the mechanisms whereby recurrent and surround inhibition is overcome to induce a seizure discharge. Further studies on the mechanisms of seizure arrest are also needed.

ACKNOWLEDGMENTS

Unpublished data presented in this paper were supported by Program-Project Grant No. 5-PO1-NS-04553 from the National Institute of Neurological Diseases and Stroke. One of us (D.M.W.) is a Research Career Awardee (5-K6-NS-13,388) of the National Institute of Neurological Diseases and Stroke.

REFERENCES

1. Aird, R. D., and Woodbury, D. M. (1974): *The Management of Epilepsy.* Charles C. Thomas, Springfield, Ill.
2. Ajmone-Marsan, C. (1969): Acute effects of topical epileptogenic agents. In: *Basic Mechanisms of the Epilepsies,* edited by H. H. Jasper, A. A. Ward, Jr., and A. Pope, pp. 299–319. Little, Brown and Co., Boston.
3. Altman, J., and Das, G. D. (1964): Autoradiographic examination of the effects of enriched environment on the rate of glial multiplication in the adult rat brain. *Nature,* 204:1161–1163.
4. Ashcroft, G. W., Dow, R. C., Emson, P. C., Harris, P., Ingleby, J., Joseph, M. H., and Mc-Queen, J. K. (1974): A collaborative study of cobalt lesions in the rat as a model for epilepsy. In: *Epilepsy. Proceedings of the Hans Berger Centenary Symposium,* edited by P. Harris and C. Mawdsley, pp. 115–124. Churchill Livingstone, Edinburgh.
5. Ayala, G. F., Matsumoto, H., and Gumnit, R. J. (1970): Excitability changes and inhibitory mechanisms in neocortical neurons during seizures. *J. Neurophysiol.,* 33:73–85.
6. Bourke, R. S. (1969): Evidence for mediated transport of chloride in cat cortex *in vitro. Exp. Brain Res.,* 8:219–231.
7. Bourke, R. S., and Nelson, K. M. (1972): Further studies on the K^+-dependent swelling of primate cerebral cortex *in vivo:* The enzymatic basis of the K^+-dependent transport of chloride. *J. Neurochem.,* 19:663–685.
8. Cendella, R. J., and Craig, C. R. (1973): Changes in cerebral cortical lipids in cobalt-induced epilepsy. *J. Neurochem.,* 21:743–748.
9. DeRobertis, E., Rodriquez de Lores, Arnaiz G., and Alberici, M. (1969): Ultrastructural neurochemistry. In: *Basic Mechanisms of the Epilepsies,* edited by H. H. Jasper, A. A. Ward, Jr., and A. Pope, pp. 137–158. Little, Brown and Co., Boston.
10. Diamond, M. C., Law, F., Rhodes, H., Lindner B., Rosenzweig, M. R., Krech, D., and Bennett, E. L. (1966): Increases in cortical depth and glial numbers in rats subjected to enriched environment. *J. Comp. Neurol.,* 128:117–126.
11. Dichter, M. A., Herman, C. J., and Selzer, M. (1972): Silent cells during interictal discharges and seizures in hippocampal penicillin foci. Evidence for the role of extracellular K^+ in the transition from the interictal state to seizures. *Brain Res.,* 48:173–183.
12. Dow, R. C. (1965): Extrinsic regulatory mechanisms of seizure activity. *Epilepsia,* 6:122–140.
13. Dropp, J. J., and Sodetz, F. J. (1971): Autoradiographic study of neurons and neuroglia in autonomic ganglia of behaviorally stressed rats. *Brain Res.,* 33:419–430.
14. Escueta, A. V., and Appel, S. H. (1972): Brain synapses. An *in vitro* model for the study of seizures. *Arch. Intern. Med.,* 129:333–344.
15. Esplin, D. W., and Zablocka-Esplin, B. (1969): Mechanisms of action of convulsants. In: *Basic Mechanisms of the Epilepsies,* edited by H. H. Jasper, A. A. Ward, Jr., and A. Pope, pp. 167–183. Little, Brown and Co., Boston.
16. Fertiziger, A. P., and Ranck, J. B. (1970): Potassium accumulation in interictal space during epileptiform seizures. *Exp. Neurol.,* 26:571–585.

17. Giacobini, E. (1962): A cytochemical study of the localization of carbonic anhydrase in the nervous system. *J. Neurochem.,* 9:169–177.
18. Gill, T. H., Young, O. M., and Tower, D. B. (1974): The uptake of ^{36}Cl into astrocytes in tissue culture by a potassium-dependent, saturable process. *J. Neurochem.,* 23:1011–1018.
19. Glötzner, F. L. (1973): Membrane properties of neuroglia in epileptogenic gliosis. *Brain Res.,* 55:159–171.
20. Goddard, G. V. (1967): Development of epileptic seizures through brain stimulation at low intensity. *Nature,* 214:1020–1021.
21. Goddard, G. V., McIntyre, D. C., and Leech, C. K. (1969): A permanent change in brain function resulting from daily electrical stimulation. *Exp. Neurol.,* 25:295–330.
22. Goldensohn, E. (1969): Discussion. Experimental seizure mechanisms. In: *Basic Mechanisms of the Epilepsies,* edited by H. H. Jasper, A. A. Ward, Jr., and A. Pope, pp. 289–298. Little, Brown and Co., Boston.
23. Grafstein, B. (1956): Mechanism of spreading cortical depression. *J. Neurophysiol.,* 19:154–171.
24. Gross, G. J., and Woodbury, D. M. (1972): Effects of pentylenetetrazol on ion transport in the isolated toad bladder. *J. Pharmacol. Exp. Ther.,* 181:257–272.
25. Henn, F. A., and Hamberger, A. (1971): Glial cell function: uptake of transmitter substances. *Proc. Natl. Acad. Sci. U.S.A.,* 68:2686–2690.
26. Henn, F. A., Haljamäe, H., and Hamberger, A. (1972): Glial cell function: active control of extracellular K^+ concentration. *Brain Res.,* 43:437–443.
27. Henneman, E., Somjen, G., and Carpenter, D. O. (1965): Functional significance of cell size in spinal motoneurons. *J. Neurophysiol.,* 28:560–580.
28. Hotson, J. R., Sypert, G. W., and Ward, A. A., Jr. (1973): Extracellular potassium concentration changes during propagated seizures. *Exp. Neurol.,* 38:20–26.
29. Hutton, J. R., Frost, J. D., and Foster, J. (1972): The influence of the cerebellum in cat penicillin epilepsy. *Epilepsia,* 13:401–408.
30. Jasper, H. H. (1969): Mechanisms of propagation: extracellular studies. In: *Basic Mechanisms of the Epilepsies,* edited by H. H. Jasper, A. A. Ward, Jr., and A. Pope, pp. 421–438. Little, Brown and Co., Boston.
31. Jasper, H. H. (1972): Application of experimental models to human epilepsy. In: *Experimental Models of Epilepsy,* edited by D. P. Purpura, J. K. Penry, D. B. Tower, D. M. Woodbury, and R. D. Walter, pp. 585–601. Raven Press, New York.
32. Kemp, J. W., and Woodbury, D. M. (1975): The effect of perchlorate and acetazolamide on brain excitability. Abstracts of Sixth International Congress of Pharmacology, Helsinki, Finland, p. 617.
33. Kimmelberg, H. K., and Bourke, R. S. (1973): Properties and localization of bicarbonate-stimulated ATPase activity in rat brain. *J. Neurochem.,* 20:347–359.
34. Kuffler, S. W., and Nicholls, J. G. (1966): The physiology of neuroglial cells. *Ergeb. Physiol.,* 57:1–90.
35. Kulenkampff, H. (1952): Das verhalten der neuroglia in den vorderhörner des rückenmarks der weissen maus unter dem reiz physiologischer tatigkeit. *Z. Anat. Entwicklungsgesch.,* 116:304–312.
36. Leão, A. A. P. (1944): Spreading depression of activity in the cerebral cortex. *J. Neurophysiol.,* 7:359–390.
37. Lewin, J., and Esplin, D. W. (1961): Analysis of the spinal excitatory action of pentylenetetrazol. *J. Pharmacol. Exp. Ther.,* 132:245–250.
38. McQueen, J. K., and Woodbury, D. M. (1976): Carbonic anhydrase activity and cyclic AMP levels during the development of cobalt-induced epilepsy in the rat. *Epilepsia (submitted for publication).*
39. Merlis, J. (1974): Neurophysiological aspects of epilepsy. In: *Epilepsy. Proceedings of the Hans Berger Centenary Symposium,* edited by P. Harris and C. Mawdsley, pp. 5–19. Churchill Livingstone, Edinburgh.
40. Moody, W. J., Futamachi, K. J., and Prince, D. A. (1974): Extracellular potassium activity during epileptogenesis. *Exp. Neurol.,* 42:248–262.
41. Murray, M. (1968): Effects of dehydration on the rate of proliferation of hypothalamic neuroglia cells. *Exp. Neurol.* 20:460–468.

42. Orkand, R. K. (1969): Neuroglial-neuronal interactions. In: *Basic Mechanisms of the Epilepsies,* edited by H. H. Jasper, A. A. Ward, Jr., and A. Pope, pp. 737–746. Little, Brown and Co., Boston.

43. Pope, A. (1969): Perspectives in neuropathology. In: *Basic Mechanisms of the Epilepsies,* edited by H. H. Jasper, A. A. Ward, Jr., and A. Pope, pp. 773–781. Little, Brown and Co., Boston.

44. Prince, D. A., Lux, H. D., and Neher, E. (1973): Measurement of extracellular potassium activity in cat cortex. *Brain Res.,* 50:489–495.

45. Ransom, B. (1974): The behavior of presumed glial cells during seizure discharge in cat cerebral cortex. *Brain Res.,* 69:83–99.

46. Scheibel, M. E., and Scheibel, A. B. (1968): On the nature of dendritic spines – report of a workshop. *Commun. Behav. Biol.,* 1:231–265.

47. Schrier, B. K., and Thompson, E. J. (1974): On the role of glial cells in the mammalian nervous system. Uptake, excretion, and metabolism of putative neurotransmitters by cultured glial tumor cells. *J. Biol. Chem.,* 249:1769–1780.

48. Smythies, J. R. (1974): Relationship between the chemical structure and biological activity of convulsants. *Annu. Rev. Pharmacol.,* 14:9–21.

49. Somjen, G. G. (1975): Electrophysiology of neuroglia. *Annu. Rev. Physiol.,* 37:163–190.

50. Spencer, W. A., and Kandel, E. R. (1969): Synaptic inhibition in seizures. In: *Basic Mechanisms of the Epilepsies,* edited by H. H. Jasper, A. A. Ward, Jr., and A. Pope, pp. 575–603. Little, Brown and Co., Boston.

51. Stone, W. E. (1970): Convulsant actions of tetrazole derivatives. *Pharmacology,* 3:367–370.

52. Van Gelder, N. M., and Courtois, A. (1972): Close correlation between changing content of specific amino acids in epileptogenic cortex of cats and severity of epilepsy. *Brain Res.,* 43:477–484.

53. Van Gelder, N. M., Sherwin, A. C., and Rasmussen, T. (1972): Amino acid content of epileptogenic human brain: focal versus surrounding regions. *Brain Res.,* 40:385–393.

54. Velasco, M., Velasco, F., Estrada-Villanueva, F., and Olivera, A. (1973): Alumina cream-induced focal motor epilepsy in cats. Part 1. Lesion size and temporal course. *Epilepsia,* 14:3–14.

55. Velasco, M., Velasco, F., Lozoya, X., Feria, A., and Gonzalez-Licea, A. (1973): Alumina cream-induced focal motor epilepsy in cats. Part 2. Thickness and cellularity of cerebral cortex adjacent to epileptogenic lesions. *Epilepsia,* 14:15–27.

56. Vernadakis, A., Valcana, T., Curry, J. J., Maletta, G. J., Hudson, D., and Timiras, P. S. (1967): Alterations in growth of brain and other organs after electroshock in rats. *Exp. Neurol.,* 17:505–516.

57. Ward, A. A., Jr., (1969): The epileptic neuron: chronic foci in animals and man. In: *Basic Mechanisms of the Epilepsies,* edited by H. H. Jasper, A. A. Ward, Jr., and A. Pope, pp. 263–288. Little, Brown and Co., Boston.

58. Ward, J. R., and Call, L. S. (1949): Changes in blood chemistry in rats following electrically-induced seizures. *Proc. Soc. Exp. Biol. Med.,* 70:381–382.

59. Westmoreland, B. F., Herman, M., Hanna, G., and Bass, N. (1971): Cobalt-induced secondary epileptogenesis in the cerebral cortex of the albino rat: a neurophysiologic, morphologic, and microchemical study. *Epilepsia,* 12:280.

60. Westrum, L. E., White, L. E., and Ward, A. A., Jr. (1964): Morphology of the experimental epileptic focus. *J. Neurosurg.,* 21:1033–1046.

61. Wilder, B. J. (1972): Projection phenomena and secondary epileptogenesis – mirror foci. In: *Experimental Models of Epilepsy,* edited by D. P. Purpura, J. K. Penry, D. B. Tower, D. M. Woodbury, and R. D. Walter, pp. 85–111. Raven Press, New York.

62. Woodbury, D. M. (1969): Role of pharmacological factors in the evaluation of anticonvulsant drugs. *Epilepsia,* 10:121–124.

63. Woodbury, D. M., and Esplin, D. W. (1959): Neuropharmacology and neurochemistry of anticonvulsant drugs. *Proc. Assoc. Res. Nerv. Ment. Dis.,* 37:24–56.

64. Woodbury, D. M., and Karler, R. (1960): Role of carbon dioxide in the nervous system. *Anesthesiology,* 21:686–703.

65. Woodbury, D. M., Johanson, C. E., and Brondsted, H. (1974): Maturation of the blood-brain and blood-cerebrospinal fluid barriers and transport systems. In: *Narcotics and the*

Hypothalamus, edited by E. Zimmerman and R. George, pp. 225–250. Raven Press, New York.

66. Woodbury, D. M., Rollins, L. T., Gardner, M. D., Hirschi, W. C., Hogan, J. R., Rallison, M. L., Tanner, G. S., and Brodie, D. A. (1958): Effects of carbon dioxide on brain excitability and electrolytes. *Am. J. Physiol.,* 192:79–90.

Psychopathology and Brain Dysfunction, edited
by C. Shagass, S. Gershon, and A. J. Friedhoff.
Raven Press, New York © 1977.

All That Spikes Is Not Fits

Janice R. Stevens

*Division of Neurology, University of Oregon School of Medicine,
Portland, Oregon 97201*

If we can accept that the principle of a selective filter applies universally and
that only abnormally strong and properly patterned excitation gets through
to the next stage, then the problem is to find effective stimulus situations.
Horridge (22)

Enhanced neuronal excitability or coherence leading to rapid bursting
discharge or synchronous polarization underlies the EEG spike. The brain's
capacity for these modes of activity under conditions requiring absolute
command of neural circuitry suggests that the EEG spike is a manifestation
of a special language used by the nervous system for communication of imperative messages. Normal when confined to certain axial nuclei of the brain
during sleep and photic and sexual excitation, and compensatory in response
to deafferentation, hypoxia, and other threats to function, this powerful
transmission mode must have certain advantages to have persisted throughout our evolutionary history.

An electroencephalographer who reports spike or spike-wave activity in
the EEG always takes the risk that the referred patient may be diagnosed
as epileptic on the basis of his report. Epilepsy, defined as recurrent episodes of convulsion, or disturbed consciousness, perception, or behavior
associated with excessive neuronal discharge, is nearly always associated
with spikes in the EEG during frank seizures. Although we are accustomed
to thinking of spike and spike-wave activity, like epilepsy itself, as an abnormality to be rid of, there are several situations in which spikes appear
normally from the surface and depth electroencephalogram in animals and
man. Among these are the sharp spike-like transients commonly superimposed on K complexes and delta waves of slow-wave sleep of normal
children, the 14 and 6/sec positive spikes recorded over temporal regions
during light sleep in adolescents and young adults, and paroxysmal spike-
wave response to intense photic stimulation found not only in patients with
epilepsy but in a significant percentage of normal girls and young women.
A striking feature of each of these various "normal spikes" is its relationship to chronological age, with a quite remarkable predilection for the peri-
adolescent period. Desynchronized (rapid eye movement) sleep, and thus
by inference the monophasic sharp waves in the EEG known as ponto-

geniculate-occipital (PGO) spikes associated with this state, is also strikingly related to ontogeny and brain maturation, displaying a steady decline from birth to around 12 years of age in man and a similar association with maturation in animals.

The EEG spike, defined as a transient potential with rapid rise and fall over a period of 50 to 75 msec, is generally considered to represent the envelope of temporally and spatially summed synaptic events that result from synchronous activation of numerous synapses on the same neuron or group of neurons (30). The outstanding characteristic of the *epileptic* spike is the capacity for excitation and propagation from a primary focus to distant cortical and subcortical sites. In contrast, spikes associated with the physiologic states of sleep do not propagate over ever-wider areas of cerebrum, but like the single spikes of sensory-evoked potentials, reflect signal transmission by physiologic synchronization which is limited to closely associated neurons.

PHOTOCONVULSIVE RESPONSE

The waking brain is normally excitable to photic stimuli, as is evident from the occurrence of visual-evoked potentials and photic driving. Exaggeration of the photic driving response, including elicitation of paroxysmal high-voltage waves, spikes, or spike-wave activity in response to regular light flashes, occurs in nearly 50% of patients with bilateral spike-wave epilepsy (17,44). Less well known are the reports from a number of workers (10–12,21,29,37,39,58) that 10 to 15% of normal girls between the ages of 10 and 16 years and 1 to 2% of boys display the photoconvulsive response. The age distribution and genetic characteristics of the photoconvulsive response in the nonepileptic population are strikingly similar to those of petit mal epilepsy, a disorder in which photoconvulsive response is found not only in nearly 50% of probands, but also in parents and siblings who never manifest clinical seizures. In contrast, only 3% of patients with focal epilepsy demonstrate a paroxysmal EEG response to intermittent photic stimulation. As in the general population, age-related susceptibility is striking, with the incidence of spike-wave trait among seizure-free siblings of patients with petit mal epilepsy rising precipitously to nearly 50% between the ages of 4.5 and 16.5 years, and falling to less than 10% by age 30 (33) (Fig. 1).

Whether the remarkable predilection for photoconvulsive response to occur predominantly in females in early adolescence and throughout the reproductive period relates to a sex-linked genetic trait, to sexually dimorphic cerebral target cells, or to the interaction of the 3 cps spike-wave trait with female hormone activity is unknown. Woolley and Timiras (59) have noticed decreased threshold for electrically induced convulsions in association with a rise in estrogen at the onset of sexual maturation or during estrus in the rat, and increased excitability of a number of sensory systems has been observed in conjunction with physiologic fluctuation of gonadal

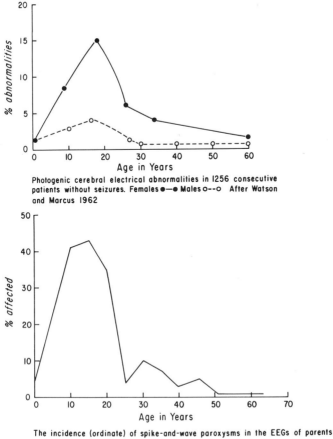

Photogenic cerebral electrical abnormalities in 1256 consecutive patients without seizures. Females ●—● Males o--o After Watson and Marcus 1962

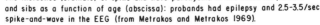

The incidence (ordinate) of spike-and-wave paroxysms in the EEGs of parents and sibs as a function of age (abscissa): probands had epilepsy and 2.5–3.5/sec spike-and-wave in the EEG (from Metrakos and Metrakos 1969).

FIG. 1. Graphic representation of age distribution and paroxysmal EEG response to photic stimulation and 3 cps spike-wave activity. (From refs. 33 and 58.)

steroids (54). The high incidence of photoconvulsive response among apparently normal young women in the Northern Hemisphere countries where systematic studies have been accomplished suggests that the trait may confer some advantages that have survival value. This conjecture is supported by investigations of cerebral excitability to light in other species.

The photoconvulsive response has been discovered in only one species other than man, the Senegalese baboon *Papio papio,* first described by Killam et al. (25). Although a high percentage of these animals displays the photoconvulsive response, there is a striking difference in the incidence of the response, which is closely related to the animals' age, sex, and terrain (2,4). Thus, no baboons under the age of 6 months exhibit the response, and maximum incidence is found in females between the ages of 6 months and 4 years, just as in the human female prepubertal and adolescent periods (2). Furthermore, although nearly 70% of the animals captured in the southwest part of Senegal exhibit the photoconvulsive response to stroboscopic flicker, a similar response was obtained from only 15% of baboons captured in the northeastern part of the country and none of the animals of the same species from the extreme eastern areas exhibit the response (2). The eastern part of Senegal is an unforested desert and savannah of scrub bushes and thorn trees in which direct sunlight is the rule. In contrast, the southwest Casamance valley from which the animals with a high incidence of convulsive response derive has high rainfall, rich foliage, and thick forests. It is of particular interest that *Papio papios* which inhabit these shaded forests show the greatest photoconvulsive response (PCR) to green light, the spectrum reflected from the leaves of a jungle habitat (42). As in man, PCR in this species is obtained preferentially through the sclera, i.e., with the eyes closed, and may, in response to the bright stroboscopic light of the laboratory, lead to a generalized convulsion (36).

In his natural habitat, *Papio papio* is distinguished by a remarkable anatomical feature, namely, pale eyelids in a face otherwise deeply pigmented brown to black. (Fig. 2). Nature does not choose her colors lightly. Nor is natural selection likely to choose a genotype with photoconvulsive capacity unless this trait has survival value. The occurrence of the PCR in baboons living in Southwest Senegal suggests that the pale eyelids may be part of a special adaptation that has survival value for animals inhabiting dark forests to provide augmented access of diffused light through the lids to sclera and retina in order to reach photically excitable central cerebral structures that depend on photic activation for a physiologic purpose. The occurrence of exaggerated cerebral response to flickered light in members of this species indicates that there is a sex, age, and geographically related increase in excitability of the pathway that transmits diffused light from retina to intracranial sites that respond to such stimuli.

That focal cerebral excitation by diffused light serves some homeostatic function in the cerebral economy is suggested by evidence of a reciprocal relationship between ambient light exposure and threshold for PCR in this species. Thus, Wada and collaborators (57) noted a steady increase in the threshold for PCR in baboons permitted to self-stimulate with light and a markedly augmented rate of self-stimulation after a period of reduced light exposure. In contrast, housing in brightly lit quarters decreased the subsequent tendency for *Papio papio* to self-stimulate. These data suggest that the PCR in this species is an augmented neuronal response of structures that require light stimulation to maintain normal function. The higher incidence of PCR in animals living in deeply shaded environments or following ambient light deprivation in the laboratory is consistent with considerable experimental evidence that increased excitability is a general property of

FIG. 2. Note pale eyelids of *Papio papio*, the photosensitive baboon. Photo by CNRS, Marseille.

neuronal aggregates partially deprived of afferent stimulation (50) and that durations of spike discharges and interspike intervals are systematically related in patients with generalized epilepsy (48). Although Fischer-Williams et al. (14) reported that the spike-wave response to light in *Papio papio* originates in the supplementary motor area and frontal eye field, Wada et al. (57) have recently shown that the earliest spike response to flickered light in this species commences in brainstem reticular area just lateral to median raphe. It is then of particular interest that the PCR in *Papio papio* is abolished by feeding with 5-hydroxytryptophan, the precursor of serotonin, or by lysergic acid diethylamide (LSD). In contrast, parachlorophenylalanine (PCPA), which blocks the formation of serotonin from tryptophan, lowers the convulsive threshold (32,55).

We have speculated that the functional significance of the photoconvulsive response in *Papio papio* and in young women in northern climates may relate to the effect of light and season on the maturation of sexual activity in many species via the function of the pineal gland (45).

It has long been known that light regulates onset of sexual maturation in many species via suppression of pineal function (40). Pinealectomy induces permanent estrus in the immature rat, whereas pinealomas are frequently accompanied by precocious puberty in man. Melatonin, one of the hormones secreted by the pineal, is regulated by light-sensitive neurohumoral systems

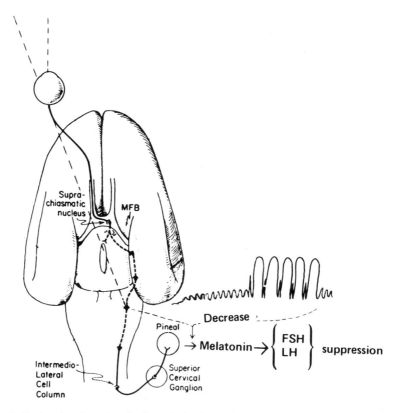

FIG. 3. Retinopineal and retinohypothalamic pathways (adapted from ref. 34). Light-induced impulses leave the primary visual pathway and traveling via a multisynaptic route close to medial forebrain bundle (MFB) reach superior cervical ganglion to synapse on norepinephrine neurons, which send axons to pineal gland. Entrainment to light of the circadian rhythm for pineal serotonin *N*-acetyltransferase is maintained by a retinohypothalamic pathway that projects from suprachiasmatic nuclei caudally via MFB to the intermediolateral cell column of the upper thoracic cord and then to sympathetic ganglion (35). It is postulated that augmented central conduction to light occurs at a critical period in all females. This increased photic susceptibility is diagrammatically illustrated by the spike-wave response. It is further postulated that the synchronous electrical discharge may suppress melatonin and thus release FSH and LH.

that commence in the retina and pass via the accessory optic tract and medial forebrain bundle through reticular formation and superior cervical ganglion to pineal gland. A second pathway branches from the optic chiasm to enter the hypothalamus directly and regulates the rate-limiting enzyme for conversion of serotonin to N-acetylserotonin, the direct precursor of melatonin (34,35) (Fig. 3). Melatonin is selectively concentrated in the hypothalamus and midbrain, exerts an antigonadotropic effect by suppression of the pituitary hormones follicle-stimulating hormone (FSH) and luteinizing hormone (LH), and may regulate other hormones directly or by altering sleep (1,8). Exposure to constant light accelerates or precipitates onset of estrus in the rat, and secretion of melatonin is suppressed by light in man as well as in birds and rodents (28,60). Activation of a light-sensitive neuroendocrine system in species living under conditions of constant ambient light would require relatively increased conductivity of photically initiated impulses at the required time or season. The photoconvulsive response may thus represent a laboratory-induced exaggeration of age-related susceptibility to photic excitation, which is especially marked in certain individuals but is common to all members of the species. This hypothesis suggests that photoconvulsive response should be much less common in populations residing in bright sunlight, and, indeed, there is a negligible incidence of the PCR in normal natives of Senegal (J. J. Papy, *personal communication,* 1976). Furthermore, the evoked response to light, in contrast to other sensory evoked potentials, is consistently larger in girls and young women of the Northern Hemisphere than in males of similar age, but it does not show this discrepancy in Israel, also a land of constant bright sunlight (E. Gershon and M. Buchsbaum, *this volume*).

EEG SPIKES AND SLEEP CYCLES

A second condition in which spikes occur from nonepileptic individuals, also closely related to light, is sleep. Characterized by onset of the burst-pause form of discharge from many subcortical nuclei, it is not surprising that sleep is accompanied by emergence of EEG spike activity. Frequently used as an activating procedure for the detection of epileptic activity in the EEG laboratory, it is common to record sharp and spike transients superimposed on K complexes and delta waves in the EEGs of normal children during slow-wave sleep.

Rhythmic spikes of positive sign are also recorded over the temporal and parietal regions of either hemisphere during light sleep of normal adolescents and young adults. Although originally reported to occur in individuals with a high incidence of behavior or autonomic disorders, more extensive surveys have since indicated that these 14 and 6/sec positive spikes are distributed in normal young persons in numbers equal to or even greater than in individuals with suspected nervous or mental disturbances. Maximum negativity of these potentials at nasopharyngeal electrodes suggests origin of the positive spikes in subcortical regions.

A third common type of spike-like transient associated with normal sleep are the pontogeniculate-occipital "spikes" or PGO waves, initially recorded during paradoxical sleep in lateral geniculate and pontine nuclei of the cat by Bizzi and Brooks (5). With a duration of 150 to 250 ms, these striking potentials are longer than the 50 to 75 ms required by definition of EEG "spikes," but like other members of that genre they represent bursts of rapidly firing units in pontine reticular formation and geniculate body (23). Great interest has been attached to these potentials because they regularly precede the rapid eye movements of desynchronized sleep. Dement and his collaborators (9) have demonstrated an obligatory rebound of REM sleep and PGO waves after deprivation, suggesting that the PGO spike and associated tonic and phasic phenomena of desynchronized sleep fulfill necessary biologic tasks. Desynchronized sleep has an age distribution that is almost the reciprocal of the PCR, occupying a much higher proportion of total sleep time in young mammals and steadily declining until a plateau is reached around the age of sexual maturity (13).

Like the photoconvulsive response, PGO waves are markedly increased by reserpine and PCPA, and suppressed by serotonin precursors and by catecholamine potentiation (24). REM rebound following deprivation is decreased or absent in patients with schizophrenia and following electroconvulsive therapy (9,62). Desynchronized sleep is also abolished after establishment of kindled seizures as was recently shown in the cat by Tanaka and Naquet (52) and in our own laboratory by T. Marx (*unpublished observations*).

In contrast, REM deprivation decreases convulsive threshold and increases epileptiform activity in the EEG of patients with manifest or latent epilepsy and lowers the threshold for photically as well as electrically induced seizures (3,41). This evidence of reciprocity between REM cycles and epileptiform activity is further manifest by suppression of interictal spike activity during REM cycles and by the occurrence of generalized seizure activity at the time of anticipated REM during sleep (47). The data suggest that the extremely high rates of discharge of brainstem neurons at essentially convulsive levels during REM cycles and during epileptiform activity may share some similar functions. More specifically, the burst type of discharge of individual units recorded in brainstem and lateral geniculate neurons in the REM state, and the spikes during slow wave sleep of childhood indicate locally synchronous patterns of polarization and firing that may code or transfer information associated with activation of specific circuits.

REM periods are significantly increased not only by REM deprivation but by light deprivation in rats raised in darkness (15). Furthermore, REM periods increase in length toward the end of the dark cycle in the early morning hours in man (13).

The rather striking parallels between increased REM activity and decreased threshold for photoconvulsive response after periods of light or REM deprivation suggest that both REM and PCR are associated with essential activities of structures in the light-sensitive pathway and may even fulfill similar functions. As with PCR, a relationship between REM and reproductive function is suggested by the steady decline in duration of REM periods until onset of puberty, the occurrence during REM sleep of penile erection, the increase in REM during pregnancy and reported disturbances following oöphorectomy or adrenalectomy (6,38). Slow-wave sleep, and superimposed sharp waves and spikes, also exhibits a dramatic decline as the growth rate decreases during childhood and is associated with secretion of growth hormone in periods interrupted by the briefer REM cycles (51).

The EEG spike, recorded with gross electrodes and representing rapid bursts of firing or synchronous polarization in closely proximate units of specific subcortical nuclei during slow-wave and REM sleep, may thus represent a powerful mode of information transmission or amplification that appears to be particularly associated with maturation and reproduction, including hormone release during sleep and in response to changes in light and season.

High-voltage spike activity is recorded in amygdala after copulation in the rabbit and is assumed to relate to the reflex ovulation that immediately follows coitus in this animal (16). In this volume Heath draws attention to the high-voltage synchronous spike-wave activity that occurs from amygdala and septal region during coitus and sexual climax in man. Electrical stimulation of the ventral tegmental area or medial forebrain bundle induces dopamine fluorescence in tuberal dopamine neurons and influences the hypothalamic secretion of gonadotropic releasing factors in the rat, whereas electrical stimulation of amygdala induces ovulation in the estrous rabbit (27).

The closely related septum and medial forebrain bundle are also the regions preferred for self-stimulation by animals and man. Thus has nature assured a powerful mode of reinforcement and simultaneously used the central response to trigger appropriate endocrine functions after reproductive activity.

PATHOPHYSIOLOGY OF EEG SPIKE ACTIVITY

Chronic bilateral spike-wave epilepsy and the photoconvulsive response can be induced in the cat by lesions in the lateral reticular formation and tegmentum of the midbrain (46). Recently we have induced bilateral or propagated spike activity by placing small quantities of 6-hydroxydopamine (Fig. 4), which destroys catecholamine terminals and fibers, in midbrain tegmentum of animals previously stimulated repeatedly in the ventral teg-

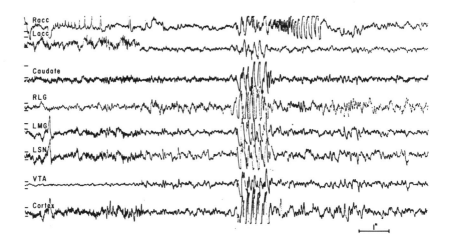

No Behavioral Change

FIG. 4. Focal spikes in nucleus accumbens septi and bilateral synchronous, diffuse spike-wave activity 48 hr after 6-hydroxydopamine administration (30 μg) in ventral tegmental area (VTA) and medial reticular formation of the cat. No clinical signs accompanied these paroxysmal discharges. Racc, right accumbens; lacc, left accumbens; RLG, right lateral geniculate; LMG, left medial geniculate; LSN, left substantia nigra. (From ref. 49.)

mental area with small electric currents or with the GABA-blocking agent bicuculline (49). Corcoran et al. (7) have reported similar facilitation of kindling following ventricular 6-hydroxydopamine. Augmentation of central monoamine activity by low doses of amphetamine or by tricyclic antidepressant agents generally inhibits bilateral spike-wave discharges in the EEG, including the photoconvulsive response, whereas depletion of catecholamines and blocking by neuroleptic agents augment epileptic discharge (31). The potential importance of central monoamine system inhibition of bilateral spike-wave activity is underlined by a recent report from Shaywitz, Cohen, and Bowers (43) indicating that acid metabolites of serotonin and dopamine are significantly reduced in spinal fluid of some individuals with generalized epilepsy.

The data suggest that structural or functional deficits in central monoamine elaboration are associated with some genetic or acquired epilepsies and that the synchronous intense discharge of neuronal units represented by photoconvulsive response or seizures and interictal spike discharge may have a restitutive function in potentiating the generation of transmitter. In relating such a restitutive effect to photically responsive pathways, it is interesting to recall that Ulett et al. (53) reported a number of years ago that therapeutic results with photically induced convulsions were equal to, and at 6 months' follow-up actually superior to, the effects of electroconvulsive therapy in a group of patients with depression and schizophrenia.

SPIKES AND SCHIZOPHRENIA

It is well known that EEG spikes are recorded with greater frequency in individuals with behavior disorders and psychosis than in the general population. Subcortical spike activity has been reported from amygdala, paraseptal region, and head of caudate nucleus in schizophrenic man by Heath and other investigators (19,20). In our experience, 20 to 25% of patients with acute schizophrenia have slow or paroxysmal sharp activity over the temporal regions of the scalp, although frank spikes are rare. Abrupt changes in blink rate, which must indicate altered synchrony of firing in units of the 7th cranial nerve nucleus, are often a striking aspect of sudden behavioral change in schizophrenic subjects and may reflect subcortical spike activity (R. G. Heath, *this volume*).

The efficacy of dopamine antagonists in the treatment of schizophrenic disorders has recently directed interest toward corpus striatum, and in particular to the limbic striatum, as the two major sites of dopamine terminals in the cerebrum. Because of many phenomenologic similarities in the auras and automatisms of psychomotor epilepsy and the subjective symptoms and stereotypies of schizophrenia, we have been particularly interested in dopamine regulation in the mesolimbic system, which originates in the ventral tegmental nuclei of midbrain and terminates in limbic striatal structures that receive projections from amygdala, hippocampus, and temporal cortex. Dopamine regulation in striatum is partially subserved by inhibitory, probably GABA-coded feedback from postsynaptic receptors of striatal interneurons (26,61). Experimental blockade of this inhibitory feedback on ventral tegmental dopamine cells in waking, unrestrained cats produces a remarkable behavioral state of hypervigilance, searching, hiding, fear, and repeated orienting activity during which spikes are recorded from the ipsilateral nucleus accumbens, essentially the same region from which Heath recorded spike activity in schizophrenic man (49). Similar spike activity and changed behavior were also induced after kindling of ventral tegmental area (Fig. 5).

Goddard, McIntyre, and Leech (18) gave the name kindling to the behavioral and physiologic changes associated with progressive permanent decline in convulsive threshold after daily focal cerebral stimulation with a fixed current. Although initially unassociated with afterdischarge, repeated application of a low-voltage alternating current to a single cerebral site elicited progressively prolonged afterdischarges and finally frank convulsions. Kindled animals, like man with generalized epilepsy, demonstrate widespread reorganization of cerebral activity, manifest as chronic diffuse

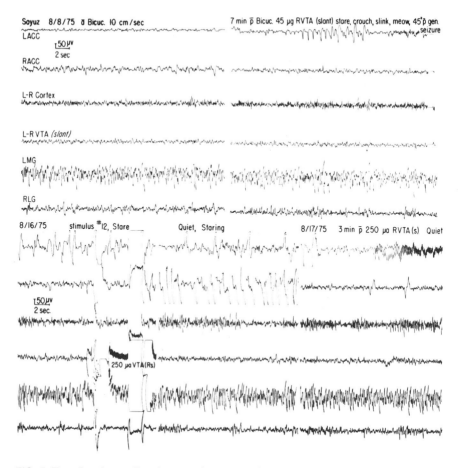

FIG. 5. Top: Random spikes from nucleus accumbens after instillation of bicuculline, 30 μg in the VTA of waking, unrestrained cat, are accompanied by stereotypic hiding and searching behaviors. **Bottom:** Daily electrical stimulation (kindling) of VTA of same animal in same site after electrical stimulation with 250-μA, square-wave 1-ms pulses at 80 cps for 2 sec. Propagation of seizure discharge occurred only after destruction of the catecholamine system with 6-hydroxydopamine in medial reticular formation. Abbreviations as in Fig. 4.

spontaneous spike and spike-wave activity and increased evoked potentials at sites distant from the stimulated focus even in the absence of frank seizures. The development of spontaneous convulsions in the final stage of kindling is always associated with spread of spike discharge to medial reticular formation (56). In addition to spontaneous convulsions and widespread EEG changes, REM sleep is diminished or lost after kindling and animals may develop pathological interictal behavior (52).

In contrast to the ease with which seizures can be kindled in cortical and amygdala sites, kindling of seizures is extremely difficult or impossible from ventral tegmental area and other structures in the central catecholamine pathway. Recently we have attempted to develop chronic hyperactivity in the mesolimbic dopamine system by repeated electrical stimulation employing the kindling model. Daily electrical stimulation of the ventral tegmental area, origin of the mesolimbic dopamine system, in cats chronically implanted with electrodes failed to elicit convulsions but was associated with a progressive state of chronic fear and withdrawal and the intermittent occurrence of nonpropagating spike activity in nucleus accumbens and medial geniculate nucleus (Fig. 5). Both the location and random monophasic appearance of these spikes bear a striking resemblance not only to the spike activity by bicuculline instillation in ventral tegmental area but to the spikes recorded from limbic forebrain in response to systemic hallucinogens or from schizophrenic man (19).

The data presented suggest that the physiologic EEG spikes that occur during sleep or in response to intense light flashes are signals of focal synchrony of closely associated units that normally code or pulse information, particularly to neuroendocrine and "reward" systems. Activity of central monoamine pathways, by regulating neural synchrony in these same systems, restricts spread of physiologic spikes to other areas. Epileptic activity is fostered by agents and states that decrease or disturb this central monoamine regulatory activity. An outstanding quality of the spike mode of transmission is the uncompromising fashion in which the spike-coded message preempts access to cerebral circuitry by swamping and displacing ongoing activity. In contrast to seizures, the high-voltage spikes from septum, striatum, and geniculate bodies must fail to propagate to systems that regulate consciousness and motor behavior if they play an essential role in release of substances vital to survival of the individual and the species. These pathways are normally inhibited by a catecholamine network that opposes propagation, and destruction of the catecholamine pathways permits wide dissemination of discharge.

Evolution of the burst mode of transmission, which we recognize by the EEG spike, and the risk it carries of seizure discharge, must have certain advantages for survival. In particular, the low threshold for epileptic discharge in limbic structures and the tendency for limbic spike activity to be confined to that system suggest a functional role for the associated synchronous neuronal discharge. If the neural events associated with physiologic EEG spike activity have a function in the release of substances or behavior vital to survival of the individual and species, spike activity recorded from septum, amygdala, and brainstem under physiologic conditions must fail to propagate to systems that regulate consciousness and motor behavior or be restricted to periods in which these are in abeyance, such as sleep. Manifest by intense brainstem and forebrain discharges that occur in sleep and in relation to ovulation, lactation, and sexual climax, the spike mode of message transmission guarantees delivery of information vital to survival of the species, but it also carries the risk of seizures or psychosis if wide propagation occurs. The EEG spike, representing bursts of firing or synchronous polarization in closely proximate units, may thus represent a powerful mode of information transmission or amplification which is particularly associated with maturation and reproduction, including hormone release during sleep and in response to changes in light, season, and sexual activity.

ACKNOWLEDGMENT

Supported in part by MH 18055, National Institutes of Health, and Epilepsy Foundation of America.

REFERENCES

1. Anton-Tay, F. (1971): Pineal brain relationships. The pineal. *Ciba Found. Symp.*, 213–227.
2. Balzamo, E., Bert, J., Menini, Ch., and Naquet, R. (1975): Excessive light sensitivity in Papio papio. Its variation with age, sex, and geographic origin. *Epilepsia*, 16:269–276.
3. Bergonzi, P., Chiurulla, C., and Cianchetti, C. (1972): Privazione della IVa fase di sonno negli epilettici. (Deprivation of the fourth sleep phase in epileptics.) *Riv. Neurol.*, 42:506–512.
4. Bert, J., and Naquet, R. (1969): Variations geographiques de la photosensibilite chez le babouin Papio papio. *Rev. Neurol. (Paris)*, 121:364–365.
5. Bizzi, E., and Brooks, D. C. (1963): Functional connections between pontine reticular formation and lateral geniculate nucleus during deep sleep. *Arch. Ital. Biol.*, 101:666–680.
6. Colvin, G. B., Whitmoyer, D., Lisk, R. D., Walter, D. O., and Sawyer, C. H. (1968): Changes in sleep-wakefulness in female rats during circadian and estrous cycles. *Brain Res.*, 7:173–181.
7. Corcoran, M. E., Fibiger, H. C., McCaughran, J. A., and Wada, J. A. (1974): Potentiation of amygdaloid kindling and metrazol induced seizures by 6-hydroxydopamine in rats. *Exp. Neurol.*, 45:118–133.
8. Cramer, H., Rudolph, J., Consbruch, U., and Kendel, K. (1974): On the effects of melatonin on sleep and behavior in man. *Adv. Biochem. Psychopharmacol.*, 11:187–191.
9. Dement, W., Henry, A., Cohen, H., and Ferguson, J. (1967): Studies of the effect of REM deprivation in humans and in animals. In: *Sleep and Altered States of Consciousness*, edited by S. S. Kety, E. V. Evarts, and H. L. Williams, pp. 456–468. Williams & Wilkins, Baltimore.
10. Doose, H., Gerken, H., Hein-Volpel, K. F., and Volzke, E. (1969): Genetics of photosensitive epilepsy. *Neuropaediatrie*, 1:56–73.
11. Doose, H., Gerken, H., Horstman, T., and Volzke, E. (1973): Genetic factors in spike-wave absences. *Epilepsia*, 14:57–75.
12. Eeg-Olofsson, O., Petersen, I., and Sellden, U. (1971): The development of the electroencephalogram in normal children from the age of 1 through 15 years: paroxysmal activity. *Neuropaediatrie*, 2:375–404.
13. Feinberg, I. (1975): Changes in sleep cycle patterns with age. *J. Psychiatr. Res.*, 10:283–306.
14. Fischer-Williams, M., Poncet, J., Neche, D., and Naquet, R. (1968): Photosensitive epilepsy in the baboon, *Papio papio. Rev. Neurol. (Paris)*, 118:206–209.
15. Fishman, R., and Roffwarg, H. P. (1972): REM sleep inhibition by light in the Albino rat. *Exp. Neurol.*, 36:166–178.
16. Ganong, W. F., and Lorenzen, L. (1967): Brain neurohumors and endocrine function. In: *Neuroendocrinology, Vol. II*, edited by W. F. Ganong and L. Martini, pp. 583–640. Academic Press, New York.

17. Gastaut, H., Roger, J., and Gastaut, Y. (1948): Les formes experimentales de l'épilepsie humaine: 1. L'épilepsie induite par la stimulation lumineuse intermittente rythmée ou épilepsie photogenique. *Rev. Neurol.* (*Paris*), 80:161–183.
18. Goddard, G. V., McIntyre, D., and Leech, C. (1969): A permanent change in brain function resulting from daily electrical stimulation. *Exp. Neurol.*, 25:295–330.
19. Heath, R. G. (1962): Common characteristics of epilepsy and schizophrenia: Clinical observation and depth electrode studies. *Am. J. Psychiatry*, 118:1018–1026.
20. Heath, R. G. (1975): Brain function and behavior. I. Emotion and sensory phenomena in psychotic patients and in experimental animals. *J. Nerv. Ment. Dis.*, 160:159–175.
21. Hedenstrom, I. V. (1969): Sensitivity to photic stimulation in the relatives of epileptics. *J. Am. Med. Wom. Assoc.*, 24:227–229.
22. Horridge, G. A. (1968): *Interneurons, Their Origin, Action, Specificity, Growth and Plasticity*. W. H. Freeman Co., London.
23. Jacobs, B. L., McGinty, D. L., and Harper, R. M. (1973): Brain single unit activity during sleep-wakefulness—a review. In: *Brain Unit Activity During Behavior*, edited by I. Phillips, pp. 155–164. Charles C. Thomas, Springfield, Ill.
24. Jouvet, M. (1967): Mechanism of the states of sleep: A neuropharmacological approach. In: *Sleep and Altered States of Consciousness*, edited by S. S. Kety, E. V. Evarts, and H. L. Williams, pp. 86–126. Williams & Wilkins, Baltimore.
25. Killam, K. F., Killam, E. K., and Naquet, R. (1967): An animal model of light sensitive epilepsy. *Electroencephalogr. Clin. Neurophysiol.*, 22:497–513.
26. Kim, J. S., Bak, I. J., Hassler, R., and Okada, Y. (1971): Role of γ-aminobutyric acid (GABA) in the extrapyramidal motor system. II. Some evidence for the existence of GABA-rich strio-nigral neurone. *Exp. Brain Res.*, 14:95–104.
27. Lichtensteiger, W. (1974): Extrahypothalamic influences on the tubero-infundibular dopamine neurones and the secretion of luteinizing hormone (LH) and prolactin. In: *Neurosecretion—the Final Endocrine Pathway*, edited by F. Knowles and L. Vollrath, pp. 229–240. Springer-Verlag, New York.
28. Lynch, H. J., Wurtman, R. J., Moskowitz, M. A., Archer, M. C., and Ho, M. H. (1975): Daily rhythm in human urinary melatonin. *Science*, 187:169–171.
29. Marcus, E. M., Watson, C. W., and Bowker, R. (1960): The relation of seizures, endocrine and maturational factors to the genetic trait: light-evoked EEG abnormality. *Proc. Am. Acad. Neurol.*, 12:28.
30. Matsumoto, H., Ayala, F. F., and Gumnit, R. J. (1969): Neuronal behavior and triggering mechanism in cortical epileptic focus. *J. Neurophysiol.*, 32:688–703.
31. Meldrum, B., Anlezark, G., and Trimble, M. (1975): Drugs modifying dopaminergic activity and behaviour, the EEG and epilepsy in *Papio papio. Eur. J. Pharmacol.*, 32:203–213.
32. Meldrum, B. S., Balzamo, E., Wada, J. A., and Vuillon-Cucciuttolo, G. (1972): Effects of L-tryptophan, L-3,4 dihydroxyphenylalanine and tranylcypromine on the electroencephalogram and on photically induced epilepsy in the baboon, *Papio papio. Physiol. Behav.*, 9:615–621.
33. Metrakos, K. O., and Metrakos, J. D. (1961): Genetics of convulsive disorders. II. Genetic and electroencephalographic studies in centrencephalic epilepsy. *Neurology* (*Minneap.*), 11:474–483.
34. Moore, R. Y., and Klein, D. C. (1974): Visual pathways and the central neural control of a circadian rhythm in pineal serotonin N-acetyltransferase activity. *Brain Res.*, 71:17–33.
35. Moore, R. Y., Heller, A., Wurtman, R. J., and Axelrod, J. (1967): Visual pathway mediating pineal response to environmental light. *Science*, 155:220–233.
36. Naquet, R., and Meldrum, B. S. (1972): Photogenic seizures in baboons. In: *Experimental Models of Epilepsy*, edited by D. P. Purpura, J. K. Penry, D. B. Tower, D. M. Woodbury, and R. D. Walter, pp. 373–406. Raven Press, New York.
37. Nekhorcheff, I. (1950): La stimulation lumineuse intermittente chez l'enfant normal. *Rev. Neurol.* (*Paris*), 83:601–602.
38. Petre-Quadens, O., and de Lee, C. (1970): Eye movements during sleep. A common criterion of learning capacities and endocrine activity. *Dev. Med. Child Neurol.*, 12:730–740.
39. Rabendeng, G. O., and Klepel, H. (1970): Photoconvulsive and photomyoclonic responses:

age dependent variations of genetically determined photosensitivity. *Neuropaediatrie,* 2:164-172.

40. Rowan, W. (1925): Relation of light to bird migration and developmental changes. *Nature,* 115:494-495.
41. Scollo-Lavizzari, G. (1972): Sleep deprivation and photosensitive epilepsy. *Electroencephalogr. Clin. Neurophysiol.,* 33:354-359.
42. Serbenescu, T., Naquet, R., and Menini, C. (1972): Various physical parameters which influence photosensitivity in Papio papio. In: *Experimental Models of Epilepsy,* edited by D. P. Purpura, J. K. Penry, D. B. Tower, D. M. Woodbury, and R. D. Walter. Raven Press, New York.
43. Shaywitz, B. A., Cohen, D. J., and Bowers, M. B., Jr. (1975): Reduced cerebrospinal fluid 5-hydroxyindoleacetic acid and homovanillic acid in children with epilepsy. *Neurology (Minneap.),* 25:72-79.
44. Stevens, J. R. (1962): Central and peripheral factors in epileptic discharge, clinical studies. *Arch. Neurol.,* 7:330-338.
45. Stevens, J. R. (1976): Computer analysis of the telemetered EEG in the study of epilepsy and schizophrenia. *Acta Neurochir. Suppl. 23:*71-84.
46. Stevens, J. R., Nakamura, Y., Milstein, V., Okuma, P., and Llinas, R. (1964): Central and peripheral factors in epileptic discharge: Part II. Experimental studies in the cat. *Arch. Neurol.,* 11:463-476.
47. Stevens, J. R., Lonsbury, B. L., and Goel, S. L. (1972): Seizure occurrence and interspike interval. Telemetered electroencephalogram studies. *Arch. Neurol.,* 26:409-419.
48. Stevens, J. R., Lonsbury, B. L., Kodama, H., and Mills, L. (1971): Ultradian characteristics of spontaneous seizure discharges recorded by radiotelemetry in man. *Electroencephalogr. Clin. Neurophysiol.,* 31:313-325.
49. Stevens, J. R., Wilson, K., and Foote, W. (1974): GABA blockade, dopamine and schizophrenia. Experimental studies in the cat. *Psychopharmacologia,* 39:105-119.
50. Sypert, G. W., and Ward, A. A., Jr. (1967): The hyperexcitable neuron: Micro-electrode studies of the chronic epileptic focus in the intact, awake monkey. *Exp. Neurol.,* 19:104-144.
51. Takahashi, K., Takahashi, S., Azumi, K., Honda, Y., Utena, H. (1971): Changes of plasma growth hormone during nocturnal sleep in normals and in hypersomnic patients. *Adv. Neurol. Sci.,* 14:743-754.
52. Tanaka, T., and Naquet, R. (1975): Kindling effect and sleep organization in cats. *Electroencephalogr. Clin. Neurophysiol.,* 39:449-454.
53. Ulett, G. A., Smith, K., and Gleser, G. C. (1956): Evaluation of convulsive and subconvulsive shock therapies utilizing a control group. *Am. J. Psychiatry,* 112:795-802.
54. Vernikos-Danellis, J. (1972): Effects of hormones on the central nervous system. In: *Hormones and Behavior,* edited by S. Levine. Academic Press, New York.
55. Wada, J. A., Balzamo, E., Meldrum, B. S., and Naquet, R. (1972): Behavioral and electrographic effects of L-5-hydroxytryptophan and D,L-parachlorophenylalanine on epileptic Senegalese baboon (*Papio papio*). *Electroencephalogr. Clin. Neurophysiol.,* 33:520-526.
56. Wada, J. A., Sato, M., and Ohsawa, T. (1973): Photosensitivity and deep cerebral structures in epileptic Senegalese baboon *Papio papio*. 8th International Congress EEG, September 1-7, 1973, Marseilles, *Electroencephalogr. Clin. Neurophysiol.,* 34:786.
57. Wada, J. A., Terao, A., and Booker, H. E. (1972): Longitudinal correlative analysis of epileptic baboon, *Papio papio. Neurology (Minneap.),* 22:1272-1285.
58. Watson, C. S., and Marcus, E. M. (1962): The genetics and clinical significance of photogenic cerebral electrical abnormalities, myoclonus, and seizures. *Trans. Am. Neurol. Assoc.,* 87:251-253.
59. Woolley, D. E., and Timiras, P. S. (1962): Estrus and circadian periodicity and electroshock convulsions in rats. *Am. J. Physiol.,* 202:379-382.
60. Wurtman, R. J., Axelrod, J., Chu, E. W., and Fischer, J. E. (1964): Mediation of some effects of illumination on the rat estrus cycle by the sympathetic nervous system. *Endocrinology,* 75:266-272.
61. Yoshida, J., and Precht, W. (1971): Monosynaptic inhibition of neurons of the substantia nigra by caudate-nigral fibers. *Brain Res.,* 32:225-228.
62. Zarcone, V., Gulevich, G., Pivik, T., and Dement, W. (1968): Parial REM phase deprivation and schizophrenia. *Arch. Gen. Psychiatry,* 18:194-202.

Psychopathology and Brain Dysfunction, edited by C. Shagass, S. Gershon, and A. J. Friedhoff. Raven Press, New York © 1977.

Relationship Between Paroxysmal Electroencephalographic Dysrhythmia and Suicide Ideation and Attempts in Psychiatric Patients

*Frederick A. Struve, **Kishore R. Saraf, ***Robert S. Arko, †Donald F. Klein, and ‡Dorothy R. Becka

*Hillside Division Clinical-Research Electroencephalographic Laboratory, Long Island Jewish-Hillside Medical Center, Glen Oaks, N.Y. 11004; **Research Department, Long Island Jewish-Hillside Medical Center, Glen Oaks, New York 11004, and Department of Psychiatry, Health Science Center, State University of New York at Stony Brook, Stony Brook, N.Y. 11790; ***Child Development Center, Coney Island Hospital, Brooklyn, N.Y. 11235, and College of New Rochelle, New Rochelle, N.Y. 10801; †New York State Psychiatric Institute, and The College of Physicians and Surgeons, Columbia University, New York, New York 10032; ‡Riverside, Illinois, 60546*

It may be perplexing to find a chapter focusing on suicide included in a volume on psychopathology and brain dysfunction. That suicidal intent represents a symptomatic aspect of psychopathology of grave importance to the practitioner is clear. Equally well recognized is its status as a major public health concern. However, the deep roots of tradition have tended to shield the suicide act from biologically oriented scrutiny. Concern with its mystery and tragedy — once confined to philosophical, religious, and literary contemplation — has evolved into contemporary efforts to understand self-destruction almost exclusively within the conceptual frameworks of modern sociological, psychological, and psychoanalytical theory. It cannot be denied that the genesis of suicidal distress is, in fact, frequently embedded in a quagmire of complex intrapsychic and psychosocial variables and that emphasis on functional-dynamic explanatory systems has seemed inherently both theoretically sensible and clinically useful. Although it may be unreasonable to expect biological assessment techniques to provide etiologically clear explanations of suicide, the possibility that their use may aid recognition of unsuspected variables capable of exerting an influencing or modifying effect on the development of self-destructive urges seems to have been neglected. With sparse exception (2–4,18,28,36,43,51) investigations of what might be construed as "organic" aspects of suicide are virtually absent from the mainstream of literature in this field.

Our interest in electroencephalographic correlates of suicide began as a purely serendipitous venture. Informal observation of "abnormal" admission EEGs in a handful of patients who later committed suicide aroused our curiosity and interest in systematic investigation. Existing precedents suggesting the plausibility of an EEG-suicide relationship were sketchy, inconclusive, and contradictory. Certainly the topic does not receive discussion in available reference works on electroencephalography (5,9–11,16,17,22,25,34,44,54). Although a fair amount of electroencephalographic literature has been concerned with psychiatric dysfunction, only incidental references to suicide have occurred and studies explicitly designed to focus sharply on this issue were not found.

RELATED INVESTIGATIONS

Perusal of Volume 2 of the Gibbs' Atlas (9) suggests that suicide is not an immediately obvious correlate of EEG dysrhythmia. In this early work a massive amount of material pertaining to patients with a variety of seizure disorders and electroencephalographic seizure patterns is presented. Buried and obscured by all of these data is the fact that all patients except those displaying infantile spasms (hypsarhythmia), myoclonic seizures, and thalamic-hypothalamic dysfunction are rated for "suicidal tendencies" and the numerical data given. By abstracting this item from the entire volume, we find the incidence of "suicidal tendencies" among 12,222 patients to be only 0.9%–a figure less than impressive. Patients with a purely anterior temporal spike focus ($N = 1,675$) have an incidence of suicide distress of 2.7%. More recently a well-organized study by Tucker et al. (52) contrasted 95 acute psychiatric inpatients with abnormal EEGs with 45 similar patients with normal EEGs on a variety of symptom items. Both subject groups had similar age and sex distributions. Psychiatric ratings and EEG interpretation were kept independent and adequate interrater reliabilities were presented. Although several interesting significant relationships occurred, the incidence of suicidal ideas (and the related variable of depression) did not differ significantly between the normal and abnormal EEG patients. Subdivision of abnormal EEG findings into the trichotomy of (a) diffuse, (b) paroxysmal, and (c) focal did not alter these negative results. Whether or not sleep EEG recordings were taken is not specified. Joyce Small and associates have been producing a continuing excellent series of EEG-behavior investigations within a psychiatric population, and some of their data pertain to suicide. Of special merit is the thoroughness of the EEG evaluations secured, which include wake and sleep studies plus activation with hyperventilation and photic stimulation. Contrasting psychiatric patients with specific dysrhythmias with control patients without these EEG findings, they found no salient association between suicidal behavior and 14 and 6/sec positive spikes (40,41) or the psychomotor variant pattern (41). Patients displaying the 6/sec spike-and-wave pattern (37,41) were found to have significantly *fewer* suicide attempts than psychiatric patients with normal EEGs.

An especially germane study of this issue is provided by Flood and Seager (8). These investigators conducted a retrospective examination of hospital charts of 73 psychiatric patients who had committed suicide along with a similar review of 73 nonsuicide random controls and 70 controls matched for age, sex, diagnosis, hospital, and general admission period. Over half of the patients in each group had clinical EEGs recorded as part of their hospital work-up. Analyses indicated a lack of any tendency for those in the suicide group to have a differentially high incidence of EEG abnormality as contrasted with either control group. Unfortunately, specific information concerning EEG methodology and the discrete types of findings was not made available.

In an early clinical report by Weil (53), the plausibility of an EEG-suicide relationship is suggested. Basically he presented a small series of temporal lobe seizure patients with "paroxysmal depressive reactions" that were relieved by anticonvulsant therapy. Of special interest is a follow-up study patient for which Weil states "we obtained . . . serial EEGs over years which showed no temporal lobe spiking as long as the patient was free of emotional depression . . . the temporal lobe spikes reoccurred, however, as soon as the patient slipped back into a depressive episode which, at times, reached suicidal depth." The clearly contiguous association between spiking and depressive-suicidal symptoms in this case is interesting. In an earlier study from our laboratory Greenberg and Pollack (12) found that schizophrenic patients with 14 and 6/sec positive spikes were judged to be of significantly greater suicidal risk than similarly diagnosed patients with normal EEGs. However, literature reviews of the 14 and 6 pattern (15,19,31) have not mentioned any salient association between suicide and this EEG finding, and this relationship was not found by Small and associates in their studies (40,41) of 14 and 6 spiking in psychiatric patients.

In a study (39) in which 60 psychiatric patients with photoconvulsive EEG responses and 20 patients with photomyoclonic responses were matched for age, sex, and education with psychiatric patients with normal resting and activated EEGs, Small found among other things that the incidence of suicide attempts correlated significantly ($p < 0.01$) with positive EEG evidence of photoconvulsive response. In another study by this investigator (38), 45 psychiatric patients with the small sharp spike EEG pattern (and *no* other abnormal EEG feature) were contrasted with psychiatric controls with pure normal EEGs. The small sharp spike dysrhythmia was significantly related ($p < 0.01$) to diagnoses of manic-depressive and psychotic-depressive reactions, and histogram data showed prior suicide attempts to be three times as frequent among the abnormal EEG group as with normal EEG controls. Recently the implications of these findings have been expanded into a provocative study (42) of the possibility that this EEG signal may be a correlative indicator of "familial transmission of manic-depressive disease." The relationship of small sharp spikes to affective disorder has not been confirmed by a recent study (26), although marked differences in patient population are suggested as relevant to the discrepancy. A clinically thoughtful and detailed investigation by Davies and associates (6) contrasted schizophrenics with and without phenothiazine-related EEG abnormalities on an exhaustive list of symptomatic, developmental, and neurological variables. All EEGs were interpreted without knowledge of clinical ratings. Patients were trichotomized into those with normal EEGs ($N = 50$), nonparoxysmal EEG findings consisting of slow-wave dysfunctions ($N = 31$), and paroxysmal EEG findings ($N = 33$). Although several important relationships emerged, a 2×3 contingency contrasting presence or absence of impulsively suicidal behavior against the three EEG categories just failed to reach significance ($p < 0.10$). However, since the raw data array indicates this symptom to be twice as frequent in the paroxysmal EEG group (27.3%) as in the normal (10%) or nonparoxysmal group (12.9%), we reanalyzed these data according to our own methodology. When normal and nonparoxysmal groups are combined into one class to be contrasted with paroxysmal EEG patients, the impulsive suicidal trait is related to the latter group at an acceptable level of significance (uncorrected $\chi^2 = 4.606$, df $= 1$, $p = 0.03$). The sample size and expected cell frequencies do not require Yates correction (33).

The above data have been derived from investigations of findings in the electroencephalogram. A tangential view of this issue is provided by examining groups known to have a markedly high incidence of paroxysmal EEG abnormalities. Unfortunately, only limited work is available in this area. Jovanovic (21) has observed that psychotic-depressive episodes are common – but certainly not universal – among psychomotor epileptics. He offers no discussion of suicidal behavior at all. Studies specifically focusing on suicide in epileptic populations (1,7) have found that as many as one-third of such patients may have made prior suicide attempts, and incidence figures for completed suicides among epileptics have been reported by some authors (14,27,32,50) to be higher than actuarial expectations derived from the general population. Of interest in this context is a controlled investigation recently performed by Gunn (13). Briefly, 158 epileptic prisoners were matched for age, sex, institution, length of time institutionalized, and length of sentence with 180 nonepileptic prisoners. These groups were contrasted regarding presence of various psychiatric symptoms and type of psychiatric diagnosis, if any. Whereas the absolute incidence of suicide ideation among all subjects was low, suicidal thoughts were significantly more frequent ($p < 0.005$) among the epileptic prisoners. Similarly, those with epilepsy displayed significantly greater ($p < 0.025$) affective symptomatology. Subsidiary data are presented arguing against the possibility that observed differences were related to anticonvulsant medication.

Studies of this type contain serious conceptual confounds that render their support of EEG-suicide hypotheses tenuous. To argue that the secondary personal, social, and economic consequences of suffering from seizures cannot contribute to development of psychiatric problems and depressive affect would be foolish. Gunn (13) has stressed that the studies mentioned, including his own, involve epileptics who arrive at the hospital, prison, or colony through social selection procedures and are thus atypical. Also in such surveys the possibility of additional brain damage secondary to seizure injury is almost never examined.

HILLSIDE PILOT STUDIES

Our initial study (48) of EEG-suicide relationships was retrospective. Without knowledge of EEG results or the purpose of the study (which was disguised), two experienced raters evaluated the case histories of 219 consecutively admitted psychiatric patients for degree of (a) suicide ideation, (b) suicide acts, (c) assaultive and/or destructive ideation, (d) assaultive and/or destructive acts, and (e) temper dyscontrol. Based on these ratings the following five subject groups were formed: (a) control group — no significant suicidal or aggressive behavior; (b) suicide ideation only — suicidal thoughts without attempts or assaultive tendencies; (c) suicide ideation plus acts — combined ideation and overt attempts but with no significant assaultive or temper ratings; (d) assaultive-destructive — as item implies but without suicidal behavior or thoughts; and (e) mixed suicidal-assaultive. No significant age differences existed among these groups.

An important feature of this subject grouping is that it allows one to focus on patients with suicidal behavior who do not display outward-directed aggressive behavior. Failure to establish a pure suicidal grouping uncontaminated by other aggressive behaviors would invite conceptual confusion because it has been strongly implied that relationships between aggressive violence and brain dysfunction may exist (6,20,29–31,35,52).

Wake and sleep EEG studies are routinely secured on all newly admitted patients. Concerning this study, all EEGs were secured and interpreted long before the study was even conceptualized, and interpretations were made without knowledge of the patients' psychiatric history or symptoms. Our ongoing investigation of reliability of electroencephalographic interpretation bracketed this study. The results, summarized elsewhere (47), indicate that interinterpreter agreement at our laboratory has been consistently high. Cases ($N = 12$) that failed to contain a sleep tracing or for which interpretation was felt to be questionable were omitted from analyses. All EEGs were classified for purposes of analyses as either *nonparoxysmal* (i.e., normal or generalized slowing) or *paroxysmal* (i.e., suddenly or paroxysmally emerging transients of various types).

The clinical subject groupings and EEG categorizations were made independently by different personnel without cross communication of any kind. A series of 2×2 contingencies contrasting nonparoxysmal versus paroxysmal EEGs with the control group versus each symptom group demonstrated, for males and females considered separately, a highly significant positive relationship between paroxysmal EEGs and (a) suicide ideation only, (b) suicide ideation plus acts, and (c) pure assaultive-destructive acts. Separate analyses also indicated that paroxysmal EEGs were significantly more frequent among patients with mixed suicidal-assaultive symptomatology than among controls. Since when they are found to occur at all EEG-behavior relationships usually involve overt behavioral symptoms of dyscontrol, our finding that paroxysmal EEGs may relate to ideational aspects of suicide alone is especially intriguing.

Preliminary results of our present investigation have been presented elsewhere (49), and they serve to replicate the above findings. A total of 535 consecutively admitted psychiatric patients aged 14 to 49 were individually interviewed and rated on a variety of scaled items pertaining to present and past aspects of suicide ideation and attempts. Because we have recognized the conceptual necessity of treating outwardly directed aggressive behavior separately, all patients were also rated for degree of assaultive-destructive acts and temper dyscontrol. Ratings were secured without knowledge of EEG results, and interrater reliability was assessed and found to be adequate. Wake and sleep EEGs were routinely secured as before and were interpreted with no knowledge of the clinical interview findings or the patient's history. Reliability of EEG interpretation was separately assessed and found to be adequate. At the point in time these data were presented, these procedures resulted in a control group ($N = 83$) with no significant suicidal or assaultive symptoms, a suicide ideation only group ($N = 50$), and a suicide ideation plus attempt group ($N = 49$). Mixed suicidal-assaultive data had not been analyzed. Also, males and females were combined and had not been considered separately.

Results indicated a statistically significant association between presence of paroxysmal EEG abnormality and suicide ideation alone ($p < 0.05$) and suicide ideation plus attempts ($p < 0.025$). In spite of the statistical replication that occurred, we noted at that time that the phenomena did not appear as robust as we had previously found and that the significance levels required larger than expected sample sizes.

PRESENT INVESTIGATION

Method

SUBJECT SELECTION

Subjects consisted of 1,199 psychiatric patients aged 14 to 49 consecutively admitted to the Hillside Division of Long Island Jewish-Hillside Medical Center, a 200-bed inpatient psychiatric hospital. All patients were voluntary admissions for a variety of acute psychiatric conditions. All patients were initially entered into the study. Subjects were dropped from the investigation for a variety of reasons concerning which we could not exercise experimental control. Sources of attrition included the following: (a) subject discharged or eloped before data collection, (b) subject refused to be interviewed, (c) subject was confused or psychotic to the degree that interview information was deemed unreliable, and (d) subject refused the EEG or the EEG examination was incomplete or unreliable. A total of 698 patients was completely evaluated with all data being usable.

SUICIDE INTERVIEW

Without any knowledge of the EEG results, two of the investigators (K.R.S. and R.S.A.) interviewed all patients individually. At its conclusion each interview was rated on a 4-point scale in terms of impression of overall adequacy. Interviews thus judged to be inadequate (i.e., no confidence in ratings; subject confused; subject tried to mislead or produce what he thought interviewer wanted to hear, offered minimal cooperation or refused, etc.) were noted and the subject dropped from the study.

The interviewers rated all subjects on the following variables using an 8-point scale for each item: present illness and past history of (a) frequency of suicide ideation, (b) intensity of suicide ideation, (c) duration of ideation, (d) degree of "reactivity" of ideation,[1] (e) ability to control (dismiss) thoughts, (f) subject's concern over ideation, and (g) degree of formulation of suicide plans. If actual suicide attempts had occurred, similar ratings were made for past and present number of attempts, seriousness (medical hazard) of attempt, and degree of reactivity of attempt. To screen out subjects with other-directed aggressive behaviors, we also made 8-point ratings for presence and degree of assaultive-destructive ideation, assaultive-destructive acts, and simple temper dyscontrol.

During data collection two samples obtained involved patients being interviewed jointly by both investigators. After these interviews, the investigators filled out the rating form independently and without cross communication, and their results were compared for reliability purposes. Estimates of interrater reliability of symptom ratings are shown in Table 1 for items pertaining to present illness behavior. Coefficients of equal magnitude were obtained for ratings of past symptomatic behavior. Interrater reliabilities are deemed adequate for study purposes.

---

[1] The term "reactivity" needs explanation. "Reactive" suicidal behavior is clearly in response to some known precipitating event such as loss of a job, rejection by a boy or girl friend, or removal from a school program. Nonreactive ideation is that which insidiously arises out of a chronic long-term matrix of failure, disappointment, depressive affect, etc.

TABLE 1. *Interrater reliability of selected variables*

Item	Sample 1		Sample 2	
	N	r	N	r
Suicide ideation frequency	18	0.95	30	0.99
Suicide ideation intensity	18	0.77	30	0.93
Suicide plan formulation	18	0.92	30	0.91
Suicide ideation duration	18	0.94	30	0.99
Control of ideation	18	0.87	30	0.88
Subject concern with suicide	18	0.89	30	0.91
Suicide ideation reactivity	18	0.69	30	0.93
Suicide attempts				
Number	18	0.99	30	1.00
Seriousness	18	0.98	30	0.98
Reactivity	18	0.87	30	0.97
Assaultive-destructive ideation	18	0.77	30	0.92
Assaultive-destructive acts	18	0.84	30	0.93
Temper dyscontrol	18	0.87	30	0.95

EEG PROCEDURE

All EEGs were taken awake and asleep and with hyperventilation. Numerous previous studies have indicated that sleep recording is essential in recording a variety of paroxysmal dysrhythmias, and two empirical studies (45,46) of the value of sleep recording in our own population confirm these observations. Any EEG that failed to contain a sleep tracing and was otherwise normal was omitted from data analysis to reduce potential error from false-negative EEGs. All EEGs were secured with either a Grass Model 6–10 channel or Grass Model 8–10 channel instrument using disk scalp electrodes. Monopolar technique using linked ear, single ear, or contralateral ear reference was employed. All tracings were obtained by technicians trained to evaluate the recording interpretively as it is being obtained.

All EEGs were interpreted by one of the authors (F.A.S.) without prior knowledge of the results of the suicide rating interview or the patient's psychiatric history. All EEGs were interpreted using the Gibbs' classification scheme (9,10) for categorizing EEG abnormality. For purposes of this study all EEGs were categorized as either normal, nonparoxysmal abnormal, or paroxysmal abnormal.[2] All data analyses involved EEGs dichotomized as normal or nonparoxysmal versus paroxysmal.

---

[2] In our usage the term "paroxysmal EEG" denotes those EEG patterns characterized by an episodic disruption of normal background activity as opposed to those dysrhythmias (i.e., generalized and focal slowing, amplitude asymmetry, etc.) that are more or less continual in the tracing. Paroxysmal findings encountered in the present study consist of the following: (a) nonspecific diffuse spike and wave, (b) focal spiking, (c) diffuse paroxysmal slow, (d) paroxysmal runs of slow, (e) psychmotor variant, (f) small sharp spikes, (g) 6/sec spike and wave,

TABLE 2. *Interrater reliability of EEG interpretation*

	Rater B			
	Paroxysmal	Nonparoxysmal normal	Paroxysmal	Nonparoxysmal normal
Rater A Paroxysmal	97	7	111	4
Nonparoxysmal normal	2	119	22	149

Sample 1: $N = 225$, $X^2y = 186.8$, df = 1, $p < 0.001$, $\phi = 0.91$.
Sample 2: $N = 286$, $X^2y = 190.1$, df = 1, $p < 0.001$, $\phi = 0.82$.

Special attention was given to reliability of EEG interpretation. One of the authors (D.R.B.) independently and without knowledge of interview data, patient history, or previous EEG interpretation read two large samples ($N = 225$ and 286, respectively) of EEGs. Thus co-interpretation was secured on 511 subjects. During this part of the study EEG technicians were instructed not to underline or mark the tracings in any way. The results of our assessment of EEG interinterpreter reliability are shown in Table 2. The reliability figures are deemed adequate. Cases of disagreement in EEG interpretation were resolved by jointly reviewing the tracing and arriving at a consensus interpretation following the suggestions of Klein and Cleary (23,24).

Interview ratings and EEG data were kept by a research assistant, and the two sets of data were joined only when all data collection for a subject was completed.

Results

CLINICAL GROUPS

Based on the results of the suicide interviews and ratings, all subjects were assigned to one of five study groups as follows:

1. Control ($N = 168$)—Absence of significant suicide, assaultive, or temper symptoms. Subjects with a rare, isolated suicide thought of negligible intensity were accepted in this group.
2. Pure suicide ideation ($N = 115$)—Subjects displayed current suicide ideation of minimal, moderate, or marked degree. They had never made a suicide attempt or gesture and had no significant assaultive or temper dyscontrol.
3. Suicide ideation plus attempts ($N = 187$)—In addition to ideation, subjects

(h) retained alpha, (i) 14 and 6 positive spikes, and (j) rare fast. In this context the term "paroxysmal" does not always imply or denote epileptic activity, and the reader is cautioned against making any such unwarranted inference.

had made one or more suicide attempts or gestures. They had no significant assaultive or temper dyscontrol.

4. Mixed suicide-assaultive ($N = 189$) — Subjects displayed suicide ideation and/or attempts and also displayed greater than minimal assaultive-destructive or temper dyscontrol.

5. Pure assaultive-destructive ($N = 37$) — Subjects in this group had never made a suicide attempt and displayed no significant suicide ideation.

t-Tests that were performed indicated no significant age differences among the control group and any of the symptom groups. The subject groups were formed on an *a priori* basis without knowledge of the EEG results. Since the pure assaultive-destructive grouping was of small sample size and of only tangential relevance to our primary concern with suicide, it was not given further consideration.

Our initial analysis considered the differential incidence of paroxysmal EEGs between the control group and the first three symptom groups for all subjects regardless of age or sex. The results of this analysis are shown in Table 3 where a significant statistical association is observed among paroxysmal EEGs and suicide ideation alone, suicide ideation combined with attempts, and mixed suicide-assaultive symptomatology. In groups B and C assaultive-temper symptomatology has been carefully screened out and does not account for the observed relationships. The association between paroxysmal EEG dysrhythmia and suicide ideation without overt behavioral expressivity which was found in our pilot study (48) remains.

The 14 and 6 positive spike pattern is the most frequently encountered EEG finding in our population, and we examined it separately to determine its relationship to the control and symptom groups. Table 4 displays the distribution of this EEG finding across subject groups for different age and sex samples. Abundantly evident is the lack of discernible association between the positive spike pattern and suicide. This result is consistent with relevant literature reviews (15,19) and the experimental studies by Small and associates (40,41) but is in conflict with the earlier report by Greenberg and Pollack (12).

Because of the ubiquity of the 14 and 6 pattern and its lack of relationship

TABLE 3. *Incidence of paroxysmal EEGs in control and symptom groups — all subjects*

	A Control	B Suicide ideation	C Ideation- attempts	D Mixed suicide- assaultive
Sample size	168	115	187	189
% Paroxysmal EEG	25.6	40.0	44.4	44.4

A vs B: $X^2 = 6.571$, df $= 1$, $p = 0.005$, $\phi = 0.19$.
A vs C: $X^2 = 13.646$, df $= 1$, $p < 0.0005$, $\phi = 0.20$.
A vs D: $X^2 = 13.788$, df $= 1$, $p < 0.0005$, $\phi = 0.13$.

TABLE 4. *Distribution of 14 and 6 positive spikes across symptom groups (various age and sex samples)*

	% 14 and 6 positive spikes			
Sample	Control	Suicide ideation	Ideation-attempts	Mixed suicide-assaultive
All subjects	18.2	19.1	21.9	28.0
All subjects age 19+	18.3	15.3	19.3	24.4
Females age 19+	13.0	7.0	19.1	18.4
Males age 19+	23.2	23.8	19.6	28.2

to symptom groups, the data in Table 3 were reanalyzed with the positive spike pattern omitted from the paroxysmal EEG category and considered as normal. The results of this analysis are shown in Table 5 where it can be seen that although the absolute incidence of paroxysmal EEGs is not high in any group, the differentially higher incidence of such findings in the symptom groups as contrasted with the control group continues to generate high levels of statistical significance. Paroxysmal EEGs are almost three times as frequent in the suicide ideation group as in the control subjects.

We next attempted to examine these data at different age levels. An analysis identical to that shown in Table 5 was carried out for a combined male and female sample aged 19 and above. The results (not displayed because of space considerations) were nearly identical to those found in Table 5. The incidence figures for paroxysmal EEGs across groups were nearly equivalent to those shown before and the significance levels remained unchanged. However, comparable analyses for subjects aged 14 to 18 failed to produce significant relationships between paroxysmal EEGs and any of the suicide symptom groups. Analyses of these younger patients suffered because the sample size involved was only approximately one-quarter of the total patient sample, and considerably more striking control versus symptom group differentials would be needed for significance. Instead, the differentially

TABLE 5. *Incidence of paroxysmal EEGs (omitting 14 and 6) in control and symptom groups – all subjects*

	A Control	B Suicide ideation	C Ideation-attempts	D Mixed suicide-assaultive
Sample size	168	115	187	189
% paroxysmal	7.7	20.9	22.5	16.4

A vs B: $X^2 = 10.358$, df = 1, $p < 0.005$, $\phi = 0.19$.
A vs C: $X^2 = 14.649$, df = 1, $p < 0.0005$, $\phi = 0.20$.
A vs D: $X^2 = 6.179$, df = 1, $p = 0.007$, $\phi = 0.13$.

TABLE 6. *Incidence of paroxysmal EEGs (omitting 14 and 6) in control and symptom groups—females aged 19+*

	A Control	B Suicide ideation	C Ideation- attempts	D Mixed suicide- assaultive
Sample size	61	42	99	49
% paroxysmal	9.8	30.9	23.2	24.5

A vs B: $X^2 = 7.373$, df $= 1$, $p = 0.004$, $\phi = 0.27$.
A vs C: $X^2 = 4.564$, df $= 1$, $p = 0.02$, $\phi = 0.17$.
A vs D: $X^2 = 4.263$, df $= 1$, $p = 0.02$, $\phi = 0.20$.

higher incidence of paroxysmal EEGs in the symptom groups as contrasted with the control group, although present, was of smaller magnitude among the adolescent as opposed to adult patients.

The relationship of paroxysmal EEGs (omitting 14 and 6 positive spikes) to suicidal symptomatology in males and females aged 19 and above considered separately is shown in Tables 6 and 7. These analyses suffer from the effect of a one-half reduction in overall sample size. The data for females (Table 6) continue to reflect a statistically significant positive relationship among paroxysmal EEGs and suicide ideation alone, suicide ideation combined with overt attempts, and mixed suicidal-assaultive symptomatology. A similar state of affairs occurs for males also (Table 7), but for reasons that remain obscure the relationship of paroxysmal EEGs to mixed suicide-assaultive symptoms is reduced to a trend.

These data are viewed as, in substance, successfully confirming our previous pilot study. As we had noted, the data relationships are not as robust as our pilot study data would have suggested and the need for rather large sample sizes to make the phenomena manifest is apparent. We could not demonstrate relationships among adolescents and they may not exist.

TABLE 7. *Incidence of paroxysmal EEGs (omitting 14 and 6) in control and symptom groups—males aged 19+*

	A Control	B Suicide ideation	C Ideation- attempts	D Mixed suicide- assaultive
Sample size	69	43	46	78
% paroxysmal	4.3	14.0	17.4	10.3

A vs B: $X^2 = 3.308$, df $= 1$, $p = 0.034$, $\phi = 0.17$.
A vs C: $X^2 = 5.428$, df $= 1$, $p = 0.01$, $\phi = 0.22$.
A vs D: $X^2 = 1.846$, df $= 1$, $p = 0.09$, $\phi = 0.11$.

TABLE 8. *Incidence of psychotropic medication in control and symptom groups – males and females aged 19+*

Psychotropic medication	A Control	B Suicide ideation	C Ideation-attempts	D Mixed suicide-assaultive
No	52	37	67	65
Yes	73	46	70	57

A vs B: $X^2 = 0.181$, df = 1, p = ns.
A vs C: $X^2 = 1.407$, df = 1, p = ns.
A vs D: $X^2 = 3.378$, df = 1, p = ns.

However, sample sizes for our younger patients were restrictively small. Findings from all subjects considered as a whole are maintained in analyses of male and female samples considered separately.

To assess the possibility that medication effect might contribute to the obtained results, we reinspected the records of all patients aged 19 and above for presence or absence of psychotropic medication at the time of EEG evaluation. This information was available in reliable form for 96% of this patient sample. Electroencephalographic evaluations were secured free of psychotropic medication in 47.3% of the patients. The remaining patients were receiving phenothiazines, antidepressants, or lithium – either alone or in combination. Eleven patients were receiving diazepam (Valium®) alone. The presence or absence of psychotropic medication was then compared across control and suicide symptom groups. The results of this analysis are shown in Table 8, where it can be seen that no statistically significant differential incidences of medication use between control and symptom groups are found.

NUMERICAL ANALYSIS

The following analysis does not depend on the formation of clinical groups. As such it is free of experimenter decision making processes. For all symptoms studied, rating scale distributions for paroxysmal and nonparoxysmal EEG subjects are contrasted and the data allowed to speak for themselves.

Since previous results failed to reveal salient EEG-suicide associations within patients aged 14 to 18, the present analysis was confined to all patients aged 19 and above. These patients were dichotomized into those with paroxysmal EEG findings ($N = 86$) and those with nonparoxysmal EEGs ($N = 335$). The 14 and 6 positive spike pattern was omitted from consideration entirely, and patients with 14 and 6 spiking as the only finding were omitted from this analysis. Interview ratings (8-point scale) for ten aspects of suicidal behavior assessed both for current illness and past history were card punched along with the EEG categorizations. For each variable rated, the difference in distribution of ratings between paroxysmal and nonparoxysmal EEG groups was assessed using *t*-tests. The results of these tests are shown in Table 9. Those patients with paroxysmal EEGs appear to report suicidal ideation of significantly greater frequency and intensity than do nonparoxysmal EEG groups, and for the current illness at least such ideation is of longer duration. Among paroxysmal EEG subjects the tendency for suicidal ideation to develop in reaction to some discrete stimulus or precipitating event (i.e., reactivity) is statistically highly significant; yet, paradoxically — and for reasons that remain obscure — this is not true for actual suicide attempts. Subjects with these EEG findings are significantly less able to dismiss suicidal thoughts from their mind when they occur and tend to make somewhat more suicide attempts for the current illness than patients with normal or nonparoxysmal EEGs. It is unclear why those patients with paroxysmal EEGs are less concerned over their suicide ideation than are other patients.

It must be pointed out that the numerous significant differences displayed in Table 9 do not reflect true qualitative differences between EEG groups in

TABLE 9. *Differences (t-tests) between nonparoxysmal and paroxysmal EEG subject groups on suicide interview items*

Item rated	Nonparoxysmal mean	Paroxysmal mean	*t*	*p*
Suicide ideation (current illness)				
1. Frequency	3.0	3.8	2.36	0.009
2. Intensity	3.0	3.5	1.29	0.098
3. Duration	3.3	4.0	1.77	0.039
4. Plan formulation	1.4	1.4	0.06	0.475
5. Ability control thoughts	1.9	2.4	1.73	0.042
6. Subject's concern over	4.5	2.6	2.06	0.02
7. Reactivity	1.4	2.3	3.77	0.0001
Suicide attempts (current illness)				
8. Number	0.7	0.9	1.78	0.038
9. Seriousness	1.5	1.6	0.27	0.391
10. Reactivity	1.2	1.4	1.07	0.144
Suicide ideation (past history)				
11. Frequency	0.8	1.4	3.13	0.0009
12. Intensity	0.8	1.5	2.80	0.003
13. Duration	0.9	0.9	0.34	0.365
14. Ability control thoughts	0.7	1.1	1.69	0.046
15. Subject's concern over	0.6	0.9	1.87	0.031
16. Reactivity	0.7	1.1	2.06	0.02
Suicide attempts (past history)				
17. Number	0.2	0.3	0.79	0.213
18. Seriousness	0.5	0.7	1.29	0.099
19. Reactivity	0.4	0.6	0.72	0.233

All tests are one-tailed.

terms of how suicidal symptoms are expressed. This is because the distributions of item ratings are based on all adult patients including the control group subjects who have an absence of suicide symptoms and a preponderance of normal EEGs. This would have the effect, for the nonparoxysmal EEG group, of differentially reducing the mean rating for each item assessed. The data in Table 9 reflect the empirical finding that patients with paroxysmal EEG signals simply have significantly more ratings on a variety of suicidal behaviors than do nonparoxysmal EEG patients, thus supporting by different analyses the clinical group results shown earlier.

In order to assess true qualitative differences in the expression of suicide symptomatology between patients with and without paroxysmal EEG patterns, one must confine analyses to only those patients who display suicidal behavior. Toward this end, we reanalyzed the data in Table 9 omitting all patients who did not display suicidal symptoms. The remaining patients 19 years of age and above all displayed suicidal symptomatology and they were dichotomized into 70 patients with paroxysmal EEGs and 211 patients with nonparoxysmal EEGs. As before, the 14 and 6 pattern was omitted from data analysis. For each interview item, the difference in rating scale distributions between EEG groups was assessed using analysis of covariance with sex as the covariate. Suicidal patients with paroxysmal EEGs displayed significantly greater "reactivity" of present suicide ideation ($F = 5.61$, df $= 1,277$, $p < 0.02$, two-tailed), whereas similar patients without paroxysmal EEGs had significantly higher ratings on degree of plan formulation ($F = 3.75$, df $= 1,275$, $p < 0.05$, two-tailed). Both of these items were present illness ratings. Concerning past illness episodes, trends were found for paroxysmal EEG suicidal patients to display a greater frequency ($p = 0.07$) and greater intensity ($p = 0.06$) of suicide ideation. No other significant differences or trends between suicidal patients with and without paroxysmal EEG features were uncovered by this analysis.

EEG PATTERNS

Of necessity, all previous analyses have considered the variety of discrete paroxysmal dysrhythmias encountered as a single group. Subdividing the data by type of discrete EEG finding would have resulted in samples of insufficient size for meaningful statistical analyses. In this section an effort is made to look at each separate paroxysmal EEG pattern encountered during the study in terms of its degree of association with suicidal symptomatology. The 14 and 6 positive spike pattern was considered previously (see Table 4) and will not be reintroduced at this point. In order to maximize our samples of EEG findings, we considered subjects of all ages, both male and female. Subjects with normal EEGs and with nine types of paroxysmal EEG findings were identified. For each group the number and percentage of patients displaying suicidal symptomatology (ideation and/or attempts) were computed as well as similar incidence figures for actual suicide attempts. We did not separate assaultive-temper symptoms from these data. The results of these procedures are displayed in Table 10. Although the samples of each discrete EEG pattern are relatively small, it can be seen that the incidence of suicidal symptoms in many EEG classifications is impressive when contrasted with the corresponding incidence figure for normal EEG patients. This is not true, however, when one focuses only on suicide attempts. In this latter situation only four EEG patterns (6/sec spike and wave, rare fast, focal spikes, and psychomotor variant) appear to be associated with an incidence of suicide attempts noticeably elevated over that of normal EEG patients. Some EEG patterns (i.e., small sharp spikes and runs of slow) appear to have a high association with suicide ideation but are no more predictive of suicide attempts than would be a normal EEG. Others such as rare fast seem strongly associated with both ideation and actual overt attempts. The data shown in Table 10 must be viewed with extreme caution and with the recognition that they do not represent empirical fact. These are incidence statistic data and as such are dependent for stability on subsample sizes considerably in excess of those presented.

An interesting observation regarding the data array in Table 10 is that the incidence of suicidal symptoms in each of the nine categories of paroxysmal EEG findings is greater than the incidence of such symptomatology within a normal EEG population. If one assumes that paroxysmal EEGs bear no relationship to suicide, then this state of affairs should not exist and one would expect that some EEG classifications would have a higher, some a lower, and some a similar incidence of suicide as compared to that in the normal EEG group. In other words, if one conceives of the data in Table 10 as ten samples drawn from the general psychiatric population (much as ten samples could be drawn based on height or hair length), the observed

TABLE 10. *Percentage incidence of suicidal symptoms and suicide attempts only in patients with various EEG patterns*

	Sample size	All suicide symptoms		Only suicide attempts	
		N	%	N	%
Normal EEG	418	275	65.8	179	42.8
6/sec spike and wave	30	23	76.7	18	60.0
Diffuse spike and wave	18	14	77.8	7	38.9
Rare fast	14	12	85.7	10	71.4
Diffuse paroxysmal slow	16	15	93.8	7	43.8
Small sharp spikes	15	15	100.0	7	46.7
Focal spikes	9	9	100.0	6	66.7
Psychomotor variant	8	8	100.0	5	62.5
Paroxysmal runs of slow	5	5	100.0	2	40.0
Retained alpha	1	1	100.0	1	100.0

TABLE 11. Incidence of suicidal symptomatology in EEG categories

	Normal	6/sec spike wave	Diffuse spike wave	Rare fast	Paroxysmal slow	Small sharp spikes	Focal spikes	Psychomotor variant	Runs of slow
No suicide symptoms	(1) 143	(0) 7	(0) 4	(0) 2	(0) 1	(0) 0	(0) 0	(0) 0	(0) 0
Suicide symptoms	(0) 275	(1) 23	(1) 14	(1) 12	(1) 15	(1) 15	(1) 9	(1) 8	(1) 5

Weighted kappa = 0.1209, X^2 = 21.08, df = 1, $p < 0.00001$.
Conventional X^2 = 26.69, df = 8, $p < 0.001$.
Weight matrix for weighted kappa is shown at upper left in parentheses.

ranking would be expected only if paroxysmal EEGs were in some way positively related to suicide. The probability that the observed data ranking could result from chance can be obtained by use of a weighted kappa. The results of this analysis are shown in Table 11 where it is apparent that the data array in Table 10 cannot be easily attributed to chance.

Discussion

These results provide substantial confirmation of our previous pilot findings (48) suggesting the existence of a significant positive relationship between paroxysmal EEG signals and suicidal behavior. These observed relationships cannot be attributed to a possible EEG correlation with aggressive behavior in general because in both studies patients with other-directed aggressive behaviors were kept separate from those with pure suicidal symptomatology. The possibility that psychotropic medication use influenced the results is not tenable. At the time of EEG evaluation, there was no significant differential incidence of psychotropic medication use between control and symptom groups.

Both studies taken together increase the viability of the empirical proposition that, among adult psychiatric patients, paroxysmal EEG dysrhythmia is significantly related to (a) suicide ideation existing alone without attempts, (b) suicide ideation combined with overt attempts, and (c) mixed suicide-assaultive symptomatology. These positive relationships hold for older males and females considered separately, but the existence of such relationships among young adolescent patients remains in doubt, since we could not demonstrate EEG-suicide relationships in this age range. However, our negative results for adolescents are mitigated both by the smaller sample size and the increased base rate of paroxysmal EEG findings, in young patients in general, which render discernment of differential incidences more difficult.

The incidence of paroxysmal EEG findings is significantly elevated among suicidal as contrasted with nonsuicidal patients. However, the absolute incidence of paroxysmal EEG dysrhythmia is not high, and inspection of Tables 3, 5, 6, and 7 indicates that the clear majority of suicidal patients have normal EEGs. Clearly, paroxysmal EEG dysrhythmia can exert, at best, a contributory influence on only a minority of the total population displaying self-destructive thought and action.

We can also focus on those select cases displaying electroencephalographic dysrhythmia and attempt to see to what extent suicidal behavior might occur as a correlative symptom. Although the results vary depending on the specific type of EEG finding, a general review of Table 10 indicates that the overwhelming majority of patients with paroxysmal EEG findings display some type of suicidal behavior. Therefore, adult psychiatric patients with paroxysmal EEGs may be at high risk for suicidal behavior, but they constitute a relatively small proportion of all psychiatric patients with suicidal symptomatology.

It seems plausible that some restrictions on the generality of these findings exist. Almost all of our patients with paroxysmal EEGs displayed some degree of suicidal preoccupation. If this state of affairs existed for the universe of people with paroxysmal EEGs, one suspects that the phenomena would have sufficient salience that they would have been noted and documented long ago. It is not plausible to imagine that the well-controlled adult epileptic with an abnormal EEG who is under adequate medical supervision, married, employed, and raising a family – of which there are a great many – necessarily spends his idle moments contemplating self-destruction. Similarly, it is doubtful that the accident patient with a post-traumatic asymptomatic paroxysmal EEG finding incurs any unusual suicide risk. The electroencephalographic literature does not discuss suicide or remark on its unusual prevalence. These considerations suggest that the relationships we observe stem from an obscure interaction between cerebral dysrhythmia and psychiatric disturbance.

In just what manner paroxysmal EEG dysrhythmias influence the development and expression of suicidal impulses is not clear. That such EEG dysrhythmias directly cause suicidal behavior is doubtful. Episodic behavioral dyscontrol involving impulsive, often aggressive, behaviors has been viewed as possibly related to cerebral dysrhythmia (6,20,29–31), and our results suggest the inclusion of some suicidal behaviors within this concept. Cerebral dysrhythmia may impair emotional and behavioral controls during high situational stress thus making suicidal behavior – as well as other ineffective behavioral reactions – more likely. As such, paroxysmal EEG findings may reflect an ill-defined neurophysiological handicap that must then interact with the psychiatric patient's already increased vulnerability to stress in order to enhance the prospects of self-destructive feelings emerging.

Another possibility is that such EEG abnormalities reflect a pathophysiology that predisposes to the development of depressive affect, of which suicidal symptomatology is but a secondary manifestation. This concept is given some plausibility by the recent studies of Small and associates (38,42) who have demonstrated an association between the small sharp spike EEG signal and depressive affect, as well as the early case study presented by Weil (53) in which marked depression and EEG spiking covaried over time. Relationships among depressive affect, EEG abnormality, and suicide are complex and poorly understood. However, future studies designed to examine interrelationships among these variables may be of considerable value. Although the link between depression and suicide is accepted, attempts to examine both the incidence and qualitative aspects of suicide in depressive patients with and without paroxysmal EEG dysrhythmias may be rewarding.

A prime concern in much suicidology research is the use of various predictors in the delineation of high-risk patient populations. The present study has been concerned with the issue of suicide-EEG associations within a "general" psychiatric population. Future studies should expand this survey approach by attempting to focus on how these relationships appear when examined separately within patient groups known to represent high and low suicide risks. More precise empirical relationships might emerge through more careful stratification of patient samples by age, sex, diagnoses, and qualitative type of suicide behavior. Expansion of electroencephalographic assessment by inclusion of nasopharyngeal recording, photic stimulation, and other activation techniques may warrant consideration.

We have collapsed a variety of paroxysmal EEG patterns into one group. This tactic is a two-edged sword that may obscure as well as enhance data relationships. Certainly it is possible that different EEG findings may relate differently to suicide, and this issue deserves further clarifying study. In agreement with Small et al. (40,41), we found that 14 and 6 positive spikes were unrelated to suicide (see Table 4). That all our patients with small sharp spikes displayed suicidal ideation is consistent with reports by Small and co-workers (38,42). Although our samples are not large (Table 10), the 6/sec spike-and-wave and psychomotor variant patterns yielded a substantial incidence of suicide symptoms, in apparent conflict with earlier reports (37,41). The incidence of suicide behavior in our patients with nonspecific diffuse spike-and-wave discharges was not impressive. If sufficient numbers of patients with each subtype of EEG abnormality could be studied, eventually it would be possible to rank various EEG patterns in terms of their relative "suicidogenic" potential, just as some types of EEG findings are much more "epileptogenic" than others.

A pragmatic issue in need of further study is the extent to which qualitative differences in the manifestation of self-destructive behavior exist between suicidal patients with and without paroxysmal EEG patterns. Our initial attempt to search for such differences resulted in a paucity of positive findings. For the present illness period, suicidal patients with paroxysmal EEGs displayed suicide ideation of significantly greater "reactivity" as contrasted with similar patients with normal EEGs. Conversely, those with normal EEGs displayed ideation that included a suicide plan of action more highly formulated than those of patients with EEG abnormality. This may reflect the postulated impulsiveness and tendency to overreact to stress stimuli of paroxysmal EEG patients suggested earlier. No differences in frequency, intensity, duration, ability to control thoughts, and degree of concern over ideation were found between EEG groups. Differences in number of actual suicide attempts, seriousness of attempts, and reactivity of attempts were not found. However, it is possible that additional analyses that focus only on patients making attempts (i.e., omitting cases that only display ideation) will suggest differences not apparent at present. As mentioned before, more refined age, sex, and diagnostic sample stratification would be worthwhile in detecting EEG-related qualitative suicide differences specific to some subgroups and not to others.

Such additional knowledge could eventually have pragmatic clinical consequences, but at present these results have more theoretical significance than practical utility. All suicidal behavior must be taken seriously, and EEG results offer no firm aid to clinical decision. Since anticonvulsant medication has from time to time been used — with conflicting results and opinion — to alleviate symptoms of behavioral dyscontrol in patients with abnormal EEGs, the question of its value in reducing suicidal distress in patients with abnormal EEGs arises. Although our data suggest that this issue deserves investigation, there is no supporting evidence that this particular use of anticonvulsants is justified. Extension of our findings into the decision making processes and treatment considerations of clinical practice is premature.

Suicide is a complex phenomenon the genesis of which is no doubt related to many contributing influences. Our investigations suggest that biological variables may interact with the more accepted psychosocial antecedents of suicide. As such, continuing biologically oriented scrutiny of this problem may be of contributory value.

ACKNOWLEDGMENTS

Dr. Donald C. Ross provided valuable statistical consultation throughout the study. Mrs. Lillian Pike performed an enormous amount of work tabulating all of the data and performing endless data analyses. The study could not have been completed without her effort. Mrs. Patricia Ramsey provided frequent statistical advice and assistance. Mr. Carlton Farnum and Mrs. Joan Trotman secured excellent EEGs on all patients, and Mrs. Z. Susan Feigenbaum, R.N., supervised laboratory operation during the study. Mrs. Terry Handler organized the often difficult subject scheduling procedures and provided ongoing secretarial support. This work was supported, in part, by Grant MH20662 from the National Institute of Mental Health, USPHS, and Long Island Jewish-Hillside Medical Center Internal Grant Funds.

REFERENCES

1. Barande, R. (1958): Contribution a Petude de l'etat dangereux chez les epileptiques. *Soc. Int. Criminol. Bull.,* 39–75.
2. Bunney, W. E., Jr., and Fawcett, J. A. (1965): Possibility of a biochemical test for suicidal potential. *Arch. Gen. Psychiatry,* 13:232–239.
3. Bunney, W. E., Jr., and Fawcett, J. A. (1968): Biochemical research in depression and suicide. In: *Suicidal Behaviors: Diagnosis and Management,* edited by H. L. P. Resnik, pp. 144–159. Little, Brown and Co., Boston.
4. Bunney, W. E., Jr., Fawcett, J. A., Davis, J. M., et al. (1969): Further evaluation of urinary 17-hydroxycorticosteroids in suicidal patients. *Arch. Gen. Psychiatry,* 21:138–150.
5. Cohn, R. (1949): *Clinical Electroencephalography.* McGraw-Hill, New York.

6. Davies, R. K., Neil, J. F., and Himmelhoch, J. M. (1975): Cerebral dysrhythmias in schizophrenics receiving phenothiazines: Clinical correlates. *Clin. Electroencephalogr.,* 6:103–115.
7. Delay, J., Deniker, P., and Barande, R. (1957): Le suicide des epileptiques. *Encephale,* 46:401–436.
8. Flood, R. A., and Seager, C. P. (1968): A retrospective examination of psychiatric case records of patients who subsequently committed suicide. *Br. J. Psychiatry,* 114:443–450.
9. Gibbs, F. A., and Gibbs, E. L. (1952): *Atlas of Electroencephalography, Vol. 2: Epilepsy.* Addison-Wesley Press, Reading, Mass.
10. Gibbs, F. A., and Gibbs, E. L. (1964): *Atlas of Electroencephalography, Vol. 3: Neurological and Psychiatric Disorders.* Addison-Wesley Press, Reading, Mass.
11. Glaser, G. H. (Ed.) (1963): *EEG and Behavior.* Basic Books, New York.
12. Greenberg, I. M., and Pollack, M. (1966): Clinical correlates of 14&6/sec. positive spiking in schizophrenic patients. *Electroencephalogr. Clin. Neurophysiol.,* 20:197–200.
13. Gunn, J. (1973): Affective and suicidal symptoms in epileptic prisoners. *Psychol. Med.,* 3:108–114.
14. Henriksen, B., Juul-Jensen, P., and Lund, M. (1970): The mortality of epileptics. In: *Life Assurance Medicine: Proceedings of the 10th International Congress of Life Assurance Medicine,* edited by R.O.C. Brackenridge, pp. 139–148. Pitman, London.
15. Henry, C. E. (1963): Positive spike discharges in the EEG and behavior abnormality. In: *EEG and Behavior,* edited by G. H. Glaser, pp. 315–344. Basic Books, New York.
16. Hess, R. (1969): *EEG Handbook, 2nd Ed.* Sandoz Monographs, Sandoz, Ltd.
17. Hill, D., and Parr, G. (Eds.) (1963): *Electroencephalography.* Macmillan, New York.
18. Hoch-Liget, C. (1966): Adrenal cholesterol concentration in cases of suicide. *Br. J. Exp. Pathol.,* 47:594–598.
19. Hughes, J. R. (1965): A review of the positive spike phenomenon. In: *Applications of Electroencephalography in Psychiatry,* edited by W. P. Wilson. Duke University Press, Durham, N.C.
20. Jonas, A. (1965): *Ictal and Subictal Neurosis: Diagnosis and Treatment.* Charles C. Thomas, Springfield, Ill.
21. Jovanovic, U. J. (1974): *Psychomotor Epilepsy: A polydimensional study.* Charles C. Thomas, Springfield, Ill.
22. Kiloh, L. G., and Osselton, J. W. (1966): *Clinical Electroencephalography.* Butterworths, London.
23. Klein, D. F., and Cleary, T. A. (1967): Platonic true scores and error in psychiatric rating scales. *Psychol. Bull.,* 68:77–80.
24. Klein, D. F., and Cleary, T. A. (1969): Platonic true scores: Further comment. *Psychol. Bull.,* 71:278–280.
25. Kooi, K. A. (1971): *Fundamentals of Electroencephalography.* Harper & Row, New York.
26. Koshino, Y., and Niedermeyer, E. (1975): The clinical significance of small sharp spikes in the electroencephalogram. *Clin. Electroencephalogr.,* 6:131–140.
27. Krohn, W. (1963): Causes of death among epileptics. *Epilepsia,* 4:315–322.
28. Levy, B., and Hansen, E. (1969): Failure of the urinary test for suicide potential: Analysis of urinary 17-OHCS steroid findings prior to suicide in two patients. *Arch. Gen. Psychiatry,* 20:415–418.
29. Maletzky, B. M. (1973): The episodic dyscontrol syndrome. *Dis. Nerv. Syst.,* 34:178–185.
30. Mark, V., and Ervin, F. (1970): *Violence and the Brain.* Harper & Row, New York.
31. Monroe, R. R. (1970): *Episodic Behavioral Disorders: A Psychodynamic and Neurophysiologic Analysis.* Harvard University Press, Cambridge, Mass.
32. Prudhomme, C. (1941): Epilepsy and suicide. *J. Nerv. Ment. Dis.,* 94:722–731.
33. Roscoe, J. T., and Byars, J. A. (1971): An investigation of the restraints with respect to sample size commonly imposed on the use of the chi square statistic. *J. Am. Stat. Assoc.,* 66:755–759.
34. Schwab, R. S. (1951): *Electroencephalography in Clinical Practice.* W. B. Saunders Co., Philadelphia.
35. Schwade, E. D., and Geiger, S. G. (1960): Severe behavior disorders with abnormal electroencephalograms. *Dis. Nerv. Syst.,* 21:616–620.

36. Shaw, D. M., Camps, F. E., and Eccleston, E. G. (1967): 5-Hydroxytryptamine in the hind brain of depressive suicides. *Br. J. Psychiatry,* 113:1407–1411.
37. Small, J. G. (1968): The six per second spike and wave: A psychiatric population study. *Electroencephalogr. Clin. Neurophysiol.,* 24:561–568.
38. Small, J. G. (1970): Small sharp spikes in a psychiatric population. *Arch. Gen. Psychiatry,* 22:277–284.
39. Small, J. G. (1971): Photoconvulsive and photomyoclonic responses in psychiatric patients. *Clin. Electroencephalogr.,* 2:78–88.
40. Small, J. G., and Small, I. F. (1964): Fourteen and six per second positive spikes in psychiatry. *Arch. Gen. Psychiatry,* 11:645–650.
41. Small, J. G., Sharpley, P., and Small, I. F. (1968): Positive spikes, spike-wave phantoms, and psychomotor variants. *Arch. Gen. Psychiatry,* 18:232–238.
42. Small, J. G., Small, I. F., Milstein, V., and Moore, D. F. (1975): Familial associations with EEG variants in manic-depressive disease. *Arch. Gen. Psychiatry,* 32:43–48.
43. Snyder, S. H. (1975): Biology. In: *A Handbook For the Study of Suicide,* edited by S. Perlin, pp. 113–129. Oxford University Press, New York.
44. Strauss, H., Ostow, M., and Greenstein, L. (1952): *Diagnostic Electroencephalography.* Grune & Stratton, New York.
45. Struve, F. A., and Honigfeld, A. (1970): Routine electroencephalograms of psychiatric patients awake and asleep. *Clin. Electroencephalogr.,* 1:80–83.
46. Struve, F. A., and Pike, L. E. (1974): Routine admission electroencephalograms of adolescent and adult psychiatric patients awake and asleep. *Clin. Electroencephalogr.,* 5:67–72.
47. Struve, F. A., Becka, D. R., Green, M. A., and Howard, A. (1975): Reliability of clinical interpretation of the electroencephalogram. *Clin. Electroencephalogr.,* 6:54–60.
48. Struve, F. A., Klein, D. F., and Saraf, K. R. (1972): Electroencephalographic correlates of suicide ideation and attempts. *Arch. Gen. Psychiatry,* 27:363–365.
49. Struve, F. A., Saraf, K. R., Arko, R. S., Klein, D. F., and Becka, D. R. (1973): Further investigation of electroencephalographic correlates of suicide ideation and attempts: Preliminary results. Fourth Annual Conference of the Indian Psychiatric Society, West Zone, Bombay, India, September 29–30.
50. Taylor, D. C., and Falconer, M. A. (1968): Clinical, socioeconomic, and psychological changes after temporal lobectomy for epilepsy. *Br. J. Psychiatry,* 114:1247–1261.
51. Trautman, E. C. (1961): The suicidal fit: A psychobiologic study on Puerto Rican immigrants. *Arch. Gen. Psychiatry,* 5:76–83.
52. Tucker, G. J., Detre, T., Harrow, M., and Glaser, G. H. (1965): Behavior and symptoms of psychiatric patients and the electroencephalogram. *Arch. Gen. Psychiatry,* 12:278–286.
53. Weil, A. A. (1954): Depressive reactions in temporal lobe uncinate seizures. *Electroencephalogr. Clin. Neurophysiol.,* 6:701.
54. Wilson, W. P. (Ed.) (1965): *Applications of Electroencephalography in Psychiatry.* Duke University Press, Durham, N.C.

Psychopathology and Brain Dysfunction, edited by C. Shagass, S. Gershon, and A. J. Friedhoff. Raven Press, New York © 1977.

CNS Sequelae of Electroseizure Therapy: Risks of Therapy and Their Prophylaxis

Max Fink

Department of Psychiatry, Health Sciences Center, State University of New York, Stony Brook, New York 11790

INTRODUCTION

Epilepsy is a frightening illness, for which robust therapies are generally prescribed. In the neurological literature the negative effects of seizures are emphasized, and concern is great to prevent them. In folklore seizures are marks of ill-omen, and epileptics are often segregated.

Yet in clinical psychiatry seizures are induced under controlled conditions for their effects on behavior. Since the mid-1930s, various methods have been used to elicit grand mal convulsions in mentally ill patients. Seizures are induced a number of times a week, and a treatment course may consist of four to eight seizures for depressive illnesses, and up to thirty seizures for patients with more severe psychoses (61). The principal effects of repeated seizures (EST) are reductions in depressive affects, suicidal preoccupation, and delusional thoughts. Insomnia, anorexia, weight loss, irritability, and loss of libido are also responsive to EST. The efficacy and safety of EST for appropriate psychiatric disorders are well described (29–31,52,110).

There is a discrepancy in attitudes between the psychiatrists who use EST and the public and many professionals who do not. Anxiety concerning the hazards and potential misuses of EST has led to legal restrictions in its use in some jurisdictions. A review of the criticism of EST reveals that few deny the efficacy of EST for depressive psychosis, although there is less assurance in other conditions (31). The principal causes of concern are the risks of impairment of memory and recall functions after EST, and alleged abuses, particularly the use of EST to diminish complaining, negativistic, and hostile behavior. This latter use is poorly documented—as to both the efficacy of EST as well as its incidence—and it is beyond the scope of this chapter to discuss the efficacy, safety, or legality of such applications. Impairment of memory and the associated complications of spontaneous seizures, brain damage, and death are neurologic sequelae ascribed to EST, and the present report examines these effects to answer the questions:

- What are the CNS risks of EST?
- Are the neurological effects central to the therapeutic process of EST?
- Can these neurological effects be reduced and modified?

The evaluation of EST is complicated by historical factors. In the early decades treatments were given without sedation, patients being brought to the treatment room, placed on a pallet, held by two to four aides, and treated. Missed seizures occurred, and patients experienced the panic and pain of unmodified electric currents or subconvulsive pentylenetetrazole (Metrazol®). Treatment today is modified by the use of special electrode placements, muscle relaxants, sedatives, anesthesia, and hyperoxygenation so that missed seizures, panic, fracture, and death are exceedingly rare. These modifications have been gradually introduced over four decades. As it became known that the cerebral seizure is necessary for the therapeutic response, and that neither the motor convulsion, nor fear, nor memory loss is essential, treatments were modified and the use of sedation, anesthesia, and muscle paralysis using succinylcholine was generally accepted. Memory loss was also reduced by nondominant unilateral placement of electrodes and by hyperoxygenation before and after the seizure.

The principal studies of the neurologic sequelae of EST were done during the initial enthusiasm for the treatment, when amnesia, apnea, hypoxia, and punishment were believed to be part of the therapeutic process. Instead of reducing their effects, these states were encouraged, with inestimable effects on neurologic functions. These data, although derived from different methods of treatment, are discussed in this chapter, and their relevance for present methods reviewed.

SEQUELAE OF EST

The principal neurologic complications of EST are memory impairment, spontaneous seizures, organic psychosis, and "brain damage." These effects are similar to those seen after head trauma, to which EST has been compared (28). In addition, death, fear and panic, and headache are also associated with EST.

Impairment of Memory

The most widely known and extensively studied sequel of EST is memory impairment (19,20,44,102). There is amnesia for each seizure and for the events of the immediate post-treatment period. Retrograde amnesia also occurs and may extend for hours and occasionally for days before EST. The extent varies with the number of seizures, their frequency, and the age of the subject (21,36,65).

During a treatment, performance on memory tasks decays with each successive seizure. After the first seizure, impairment is measurable for a few hours; after four to six seizures, impaired performance is measurable for 24 to 48 hr and longer; and after eight to ten seizures, impairment is measurable for 4 to 7 days.

Impairment in memory tasks involves a variety of functions. The functions are defined by the tasks used in their measurement or by the different theoretic constructs regarding the memory processes (20). Immediate, intermediate, and remote memory are all affected, as are the processes of retention and recall. The learning of new material is affected, as is the normal process of "forgetting" or the decay of learned material. Different modalities respond to seizures differently. Studies of unilateral electrode placements emphasize the differential impact of EST on the learning and recall of visual or auditory information, in both verbal and nonverbal modes. Yet regardless of the task, modality, or process studied, the temporal pattern after EST shows increasing disruption in performance with successive treatments. Impairment is greatest proximal to the seizure and improves after each seizure, with progressive recovery of performance when seizures are terminated. Measures taken a few weeks after the last treatment usually show scores on memory tests to be equal to or better than the scores before EST. Within a few months of the last treatment, memory functions reach pre-illness levels for the recall of life events (102–105).

Memory impairment is largely the consequence of the seizures, although the mode of induction may influence the type and degree of impairment. In comparisons of seizures induced electrically (EST) with seizures occurring after administration of the inhalant flurothyl, changes in scores are usually found to be equivalent during and immediately after equal numbers of treatments (34,66,94,101). After the treatment course, there may be a greater improvement after flurothyl (68,97,100). Laurell (68) found equivalent effects on immediate and delayed recall tests but less retrograde amnesia for flurothyl, suggesting that the electric current had a small but measurable effect on forgetting. Differences in the degree of memory impairment are also described with changes in current characteristics during EST. An example is the decrease in memory impairment when brief, pulsed stimuli are used to induce a seizure (70) or when threshold currents are used (33).

Missed seizures are an identifiable difficulty with these analyses. Small and Small (97,98) and Laurell (68) considered the influence of incomplete inductions and suggested that until each seizure is monitored electrographically, the differences between the two therapies must be related to the influence of partial or missed seizures reducing the therapeutic efficacy rather than some other factor inherent in the induction.

In electrical inductions the location of the electrodes has a direct effect on the type and extent of memory loss. Conventional electrode placement is bitemporal, with currents concentrated in the anterior temporal lobes and the brainstem. Seizures may be induced by currents through electrodes on one side of the head—unilateral electrode placement—and these may be placed over the dominant or the nondominant hemisphere. The clinical efficacy of treatments using unilateral electrodes is approximately equal to that of bilateral placements, but the effects on memory are less extensive (16–18). Further, the impact on memory tasks differs depending on whether electrodes are placed over the dominant or the nondominant hemisphere. When electrodes are placed over the nondominant hemisphere, impairment is greater in visual nonverbal tasks than on verbal tasks; verbal tasks are selectively impaired when electrodes are over the dominant hemisphere. Moreover, the degree of impairment is less with nondominant EST than with bilateral EST or dominant EST (8,14,15,21,43,53).

It is useful to consider that these evaluations may be confounded by reports that the depressive illness itself, in the absence of EST, is associated with measurable amnesia that improves when the illness subsides (106).

Spontaneous Seizures

Spontaneous seizures are convulsions that occur outside the treatment setting days or weeks after the last treatment (83). Fifty-one cases had been reported before 1955, when Blumenthal (11) added twelve cases. He estimated the incidence of spontaneous seizures after EST to be 0.5%, similar to that recorded for epilepsy in the population. Karliner (63) reported six additional cases in patients without a history of epilepsy. He noted that the seizures remitted within 3 years and viewed their appearance as evidence of persistent brain dysfunction. More recently, Assael, Halperin, and Alpern (6) reported a single case of a 30-year-old woman without a personal or family history of seizures who developed a typical grand mal convulsion 2 weeks after the successful treatment of a catatonic stupor with four incidents of EST. Seizures recurred once or twice weekly until anticonvulsant drugs were given.

It has been suggested that EST may "kindle" an epileptic focus (84). "Kindling" is a phenomenon described in some animal species when small electric currents are passed through implanted electrodes in the brainstem, lowering the threshold to seizures such that incidental stimuli elicit spontaneous seizures (39). Pinel and Van Oot (84) implanted electrodes aimed at the center of the amygdaloid complex and stimulated male rats with forty-five 1-sec, 400-μA, 60-Hz stimulations three times a day, 5 days a week. They then intubated the animals and administered large amounts of alcohol for 45 intubations. When alcohol administration ceased, the withdrawal symptoms were found to be intensified. Similar observations were made using repeated administrations of pentylenetetrazole, and subconvulsive amygdaloid stimulations. From these data they hazard warnings that similar increased sensitivity to seizures may occur in patients receiving EST.

Inherent in the definition of kindling is a lowering of the cerebral threshold, so that a seizure may be elicited by low, incidental stimuli. This explanation is inconsistent, however, with the observations by Brockman et al. (12) and Green (42) who found that the threshold for the currents necessary to elicit a seizure in EST rises during treatment. Green found that the current necessary to elicit a seizure rose in 24 of 39 cases and showed no change in 15. In no case did the threshold for a seizure fall in his series. Brockman et al. (12) found that patients needed greater amounts of intravenous Azozol (hexazole) to induce seizures as treatment progressed. The difference between EST and the animal experiments cited in the studies by Pinel and Van Oot (84) may be in their use of depth electrodes, the absence of anesthesia, the large amplitudes of their currents, the frequency at which the brain was stimulated, and the species used to study the phenomenon.

Organic Psychosis

The characteristics of an organic psychosis are impairment in orientation, memory, intellectual functions, and vigilance, with confusion, perceptual defects, lability of affect, and defective judgment as occasional symptoms. In a technical sense, all induced seizures are associated with an "organic" impairment since memory loss and change in affect are common. But severe organic psychosis has been described in some subjects (60,85). The psychosis disappeared within a few days, and the observers suggested that its appearance should not be interpreted as an adverse sign, particularly that additional seizures should not be given. The attitudes to the organic psychosis after EST may have been conditioned by the earlier experience with insulin coma, in which a prolonged coma resulted in a prolonged confusional state, often with good clinical results when the confusion resolved.

These observations led some authors, notably Glueck et al. (38) and more recently Murillo and Exner (77), to treat severely ill schizophrenic patients three times daily to induce an organic psychosis in a process termed "regressive EST." Glueck and co-workers noted regression to be complete when a patient manifested memory loss, confusion, disorientation, lack of verbal spontaneity, slurring of speech to dysarthria or muteness, and apathy. In this special form of EST, the psychotic state is reversible with the long-term clinical benefits for schizophrenia to be equal to or better than those with drug therapy (77). A detailed description of the recovery process from a severe dementia caused by frequent EST has been reported by Regenstein, Murawski, and Engel (89). They noted that with cessation of EST, mental functions and behavior recovered over a period of more than 1 year.

A modification of regressive EST was suggested by Blachly and Gowing (10) in which multiple seizures (up to six) are induced daily under conditions of hyperoxygenation. It is not clear why this method, termed multiple monitored ECT (MMECT) by these authors, rarely gives the severe organic psychosis noted by Glueck et al. In a series of 40 cases of MMECT, Abrams and Fink (1) noted 2 cases of confusion, and Strain and Bidder (107) reported a single such case, suggesting that oxygenation does not fully protect the patient.

An interesting aspect of the organic psychosis is seen in the syndrome of denial of illness (116). In neurological patients with brain damage, a syndrome of anosognosia, perceptual distortion, and changed language patterns may be elicited by barbiturates and defined as a measure of brain dysfunction (117). The same patterns of denial language and perceptual errors are seen after EST, indicating that the post-EST syndrome is qualitatively similar to other forms of diffuse cerebral dysfunction (57).

Another description of the organic mental syndrome is found in the report by a psychiatrist (86) of his experiences through two courses of EST. He notes the types of memory effects, particularly the differential impact on recent events, the topographical disorientation, and the changes in mood accompanying these treatments in eloquent detail.

An organic mental syndrome is common in EST and is related to the number and frequency of induced seizures. Recovery even after a severe state is common, and oxygenation is a significant factor in this process.

"Brain Damage"

The evidence for sustained pathologic changes with repeated seizures comes from three sources: examination of brain tissues from patients who died after EST and from epileptic patients who died in status epilepticus; examination of tissues from animals subjected to repeated seizures; and results of the psychologic and physiologic tests that are usually interpreted as measures of an organic mental syndrome in man.

HUMAN BRAIN TISSUE

The assessment of the pathology of EST is complicated by the time between EST and the time of death. In some studies tissues are examined after seizures that are clearly proximal to the death, whereas in others EST is a distant event that may or may not be related to the pathologic examination. With this caveat, brain tissues have been reported to show increased gliosis (22), diffuse degeneration (41), petechial hemorrhages in the brainstem with fat embolism (75), and, more commonly, edema and subarachnoid hemorrhage (5,67,69). Will et al. (119) found the brain of a patient who died 15 min after the 12th EST to be edematous and to show neuronal damage and increased lipofuscin pigmentation. Madow (72) reported one case of intraventricular hemorrhage and three who died of cardiovascular disease in four autopsies of patients who died after EST.

These cases raise the question as to the cause of death in EST. The incidence of death varies from none in 8,500 treatments in 870 patients (110) to 0.06, 0.08, 0.3, and 0.8% of patients treated (9,40,51,61). Death is usually ascribed to cardiac complications, frequently occurring after the seizure during the recovery period, and rarely during the seizure itself. The records of death rates show deaths to be higher in the early treatments, which were usually given without modifications. Some early studies used curare or gallamine triethiodide (Flaxedil®) to relax musculature. But both these agents were unpredictable in their onset and duration of action, leading to irregular modification of seizures and the frequent occurrence of "missed" or incomplete seizures. In such events, the passage of electric current was not followed by a seizure or by postictal amnesia. Patients experienced pain, fear, and panic – psychologic events that may contribute to a cardiac death (24). In the pathologic reports cited above, missed seizures were associated as a prelude to a number of deaths (67,74,119).

Missed seizures and subsequent panic, fear, and excitement are no longer a feature of clinical EST. Pretreatment sedation and anesthesia are routine, probably contributing to the reduction in the number of deaths occurring with EST.

These pathologic data may also be compared to the findings in patients who die in status epilepticus, even though it is difficult to separate the lesions that may be the cause of the seizure state from the anatomic changes that result from repeated seizures. A common finding in epileptics is sclerosis of the pyramidal cell layer of Ammon's horn (73), or diffuse necrosis, neurophagia, and gliosis (95). Norman et al. (79) suggest that repeated seizures lead to impaired blood and oxygen supply and that the sequence of pathologic changes is secondary to hypoxia. Oxygenation is another factor in the present treatment procedure which differs from the early EST procedure. Hypoxia and cyanosis were exaggerated to increase memory impairment, since such impairment was believed to be the basis for the therapeutic efficacy of EST. Reports of therapeutic efficacy for EST using unilateral electrode placement without measurable memory impairment have made hypoxia no longer a feature of therapy, and, indeed, hyperoxygenation is encouraged (1,10).

ANIMAL EXPERIMENTAL DATA

When animals are subjected to experimental seizures, punctate hemorrhages and subarachnoid bleeding are seen (5,47). Ferraro et al. (26) found degeneration of brain cells and gliosis in monkeys subjected to 4 to 18 seizures at a rate of 3/week. Ferraro and Roizin (25) studied monkeys receiving an extensive course of 32 to 100 seizures with a follow-up of 30 min to 18 months, and they reported gliosis and cellular degeneration soon after treatment, but none after months. They concluded that these changes were reversible. Hartelius (45) studied the effects of seizures in cats and noted disintegration of nerve cells, neuronal loss, and glial reactions. These changes were not extensive and were related to the age of the animal and the number of seizures. Other workers, however, carrying out equally extensive studies, failed to find either vascular or glial reactions to repeated seizures (7,37,71,78).

It is difficult to determine the relevance of these studies since many of the parameters of the treatment (seizure rate, current strength, physiologic state, age) in animals are not comparable to those in EST in man.

PHYSIOLOGIC INDICES OF ORGANIC BRAIN SYNDROME

The indices frequently used to define an organic impairment of brain function are tests of orientation, memory and recall, confabulation, body image, and psychomotor performance; language measures; and electrophysiologic measures (EEG). These indices are highly intercorrelated and some have been discussed earlier.

The scalp-recorded EEG is a reliable and easily recorded index of cerebral activity. Characteristic patterns have been defined and related to the diagnosis of epilepsy, organic confusional states, and cerebral impairment because of trauma, mass lesions, and cerebrovascular deficiency. These conditions are characterized by diffuse high-voltage slow waves of 2 to 6 Hz in runs and bursts and in focal, asymmetric, or symmetric patterns (48,108).

After EST, EEG slow-wave activity increases, appearing in bursts and runs prominent in the frontal and temporal leads (32). Fast frequencies decrease and disappear (49). The degree of slowing, the increase in amplitudes, the duration of burst activity, and their persistence after the last treatment are directly related to the number and frequency of seizure inductions and to the time of recording in relation to a seizure. After the last seizure the slow waves rapidly disappear, amplitudes decrease, and the mean frequency increases. Within 4 weeks of the last treatment, the EEG is filled with regular, rhythmic alpha activity, usually in amounts greater than those recorded before EST (28,32,109,111,112). Occasionally, slow waves persist and may be recorded up to 10 months after the last treatment (76).

The persistence of increased theta/delta burst activity has been related to the clinical efficacy of the treatment (32). Roth and co-workers (91,92) reported that the early development of bilateral synchronous slow-wave bursts elicited by intravenous thiopental (Pentothal®) was prognostic of a good clinical outcome with EST. Ottosson (80) found that pretreatment with lidocaine reduced the amount of delta/theta activity developed with EST and also reduced the therapeutic efficacy of the seizures. He asserted that the clinical efficacy was related to the duration of the seizure and not to the currents used to induce the seizure—a finding later confirmed in studies of flurothyl and the unilateral placement of electrodes. Ottosson noted that the severity of the memory deficits was related to the intensity of the currents used to elicit a seizure and not to the seizure itself. These studies suggested that there was an association between the duration of the seizure's electrographic effects and the clinical outcome, whereas the memory effects were related more to other factors in the treatment. Analyses find the relationship between EEG slowing and improvement to be coincidental, not causal (112,113). From a theoretic viewpoint, synchronous slow-wave activity in bursts is related to activity of the brainstem, and it is to this region of the brain that much study is directed to understand the basis of the therapeutic process of EST.

Studies of language measures (54,56) and psychomotor performance (58,59) find increasing deficits related to the number and frequency of seizures, and they report a return to pretreatment levels in the weeks after the last seizure. Few studies relate the changes in these measures to therapeutic outcome, although the language measures were the focus of one novel hypothesis of the action of EST. Weinstein et al. (117) found that after amobarbital was administered, speech patterns of neurological patients exhibited the language of denial, and these investigators predicted that the organic mental state elicited by EST was conducive to the expression of explicit and implicit verbal denial—an anosognosia for the illness. Kahn et al. (57) and Kahn and Fink (56) found that denial language patterns did increase during EST, that the denial language was related to pretreatment personality and diagnosis, and that denial early in treatment was prognostic of good clinical outcome. The changes in perception and language, like the changes in memory tasks, are probably additional signs of the organic mental syndrome, whose relationship to therapeutic outcome remains obscure.

MODIFICATION OF NEUROLOGIC EFFECTS

The repeated induction of seizures elicits a defined, although reversible, neurologic syndrome that has many characteristics of the post-traumatic state, including impairment of memory, organic psychosis, and spontaneous seizures. There is limited evidence for persistent brain damage, and death from cerebral causes is occasionally reported. The severity of these effects is related to the number, frequency, and mode of induction of seizures, the clinical diagnosis, and age. Frequency and number of seizures are the most critical.

These sequelae were more severe and more prevalent in the early days of shock therapy—when the techniques were being developed—and when the similarities and distinctions among EST, pentylenetetrazole, insulin coma, psychosurgery, histamine shock, and atropine coma were blurred. Indeed, these different treatment approaches are still confused. Yet in depressive psychoses EST is as effective, or more so, than other treatments; it is as effective as antipsychotic drug therapy in acute schizophrenia; and in chronic schizophrenia its efficacy is suggestive (31). These neurologic sequelae limit its use to instances in which the benefits outweigh the risks. Considering the advances in the understanding of the EST process, the risks may be materially reduced by a more general application of the technical developments of the past two decades.

Panic, fear, and their probable association with death can be reduced by pretreatment sedation, as with secobarbital or diazepam. And anesthesia should be used as it is prophylactic for the pain, discomfort, and panic of a missed seizure.

Fracture and other consequences of muscular contractions may be relieved by succinylcholine. Its proper use provides the patient with a cerebral seizure without motor manifestations.

Sedation and anesthesia may also reduce spontaneous seizures. These seizures have become less frequent during the past few decades; although there are few data for this association, the difficulty to induce kindling in animals pretreated with barbiturates is suggestive that sedatives may reduce this possibility.

Memory dysfunction and other manifestations of organic psychosis remain the chief hazards of EST. Hyperoxygenation, selective locations of EST electrodes, and modifications of the currents used to elicit the seizure should be considered to reduce these manifestations.

The differences in the incidence of organic psychosis after multiple seizures are striking when one compares regressive EST as used by Glueck and multiple monitored ECT of Blachly and Gowing. The principal difference between the techniques lies in the importance Blachly and Gowing place on hyperoxygenation—the need to maintain the patient's color as pink throughout the treatment—and their use of threshold currents. In the descriptions of treatments of the earlier period, patients usually became cyanotic and remained so during and after the seizure until they breathed spontaneously.

The differences in memory effects between unilateral and bilateral electrode placements are well documented (17,18,21,35). Despite the experimental evidence, however, clinical reports emphasize a difference in the clinical response between unilateral and bilateral electrode placements, asserting that unilateral EST is slower and requires more seizures for equal efficacy.[1] It is not clear if the hazards of extra seizures and additional time for a satisfactory clinical response outweigh the benefits of reduced memory deficit, but at the least unilateral EST provides a way to reduce memory dysfunction and organic psychosis. In addition, the selective impairment in

---

[1] These differences may reflect the need for EEG monitoring of seizures since missed seizures with unilateral electrode placements are frequent and difficult to identify, particularly by therapists who may be unfamiliar with the unilateral EST process.

memory in visual, nonverbal tasks with nondominant EST as against impairment in verbal tasks with dominant EST allows the treating practitioner to select dominant or nondominant electrode placements according to the occupation and principal responsibilities of the patients to reduce memory complaints further; that is, selecting dominant EST for craftsmen and artisans, and nondominant for those for whom verbal skills are critical.

Impairment in memory functions may also be reduced by modifying the parameters of the electric currents (13,70,114). These technical aspects are still under investigation, but if their promise is fulfilled, current type may be an additional parameter to reduce the hazards of EST.

SIGNIFICANCE OF NEUROLOGIC EFFECTS

Reviewing the relationships between the many clinical and experimental modifications of EST with clinical outcome, one finds that the seizure is central to the therapeutic process (particularly in depressive psychosis), with the length of seizure best correlated with outcome (42,80). The other features—convulsion, memory loss and organic psychosis, and EEG and language changes, for example—are correlated less well and are regarded as secondary phenomena or side effects. Thus, measures to induce seizures without the convulsion, memory loss, or organic psychosis are clinically useful since they do not reduce the efficacy of the treatment.

The significance of the seizure lies in the persistent biochemical sequelae that are seen as the basis for the clinical efficacy of EST (23,27,28,30,50,64, 80–82,92). These reviewers emphasize that cerebral events occurring in the brainstem, and particularly the hypothalamus, are central to the therapeutic process. The evidence for such opinions comes from various sources.

Depressive psychosis is the clinical entity that responds best to EST. Central to the depressive illness are such vegetative signs as anorexia, insomnia, weight loss, decrease in libido, and amenorrhea. These symptoms show a rapid response to EST, and their early amelioration is a favorable prognostic sign, suggesting that diencephalic stimulation is a factor in the process.

The EEG activity after EST is usually bilateral slow (delta and theta) activity occurring in burst patterns (32). Such activity can be induced by disturbances of midline structures in the vicinity of the third ventricle, notably the hypothalamus (48,108). It is classically seen in clinical epilepsy classified as "centrencephalic." Such activity may be reduced by lidocaine (80) or anticholinergic drugs (27), or it may be enhanced by thiopental (92), with associated changes in clinical activity.

In EST, the principal current density is between the electrodes (46,115). When electrodes are bitemporal, currents are presumed to affect the brainstem directly; with unilateral electrode placement, the effects on the brainstem are presumed to be less extensive. After bilateral EST, the EEG exhibits greater slowing than after unilateral electrode placement; and in the latter, accentuation of slow waves is seen on the side of the electrodes (96,99,112,113). Placing electrodes far anteriorly should reduce current effects in the brainstem and reduce efficacy, as demonstrated by Abrams and Taylor (2). More recently, they (3) treated patients with either bilateral EST or simultaneous unilateral electrode placement to both sides of the head (dominant/nondominant unilateral EST), finding lesser efficacy for simultaneous unilateral electrode placement. Unfortunately, in neither study were EEG controls used; nevertheless, the findings, if confirmed, would suggest that brainstem stimulation is important to the therapeutic process.

While changes in the brainstem seem critical to the therapeutic response, evidence of persistent hypothalamic effects have been sought but have not been elicited. There are transient elevations of plasma ACTH with each seizure, but administration of ACTH to depressed patients is not therapeutic (4,64,82). Studies of cortisol in depression find cortisol secretion elevated with the usual nighttime reduction absent. With improvement after EST, secretion of cortisol is reduced and the diurnal variation returns (93). However, persistent changes in catecholamine levels of the brain, with increases in serotonin, norepinephrine, and dopamine, have been described (64,82). Of special interest is the persistent elevation, up to 6 weeks, of brain monoamine oxidase in rats given electroconvulsive shocks (88). This persistent elevation exhibits a time course consistent with the clinical effects of EST. In an earlier review (7), elevations in the acetylcholine and cholinesterase levels of the brain were suggested as central to both clinical antidepressant activity and bilateral EEG slowing. Some recent reports have not supported this theory (62,64,88), although clinical studies have sought to implicate cholinergic mechanisms in psychosis (55).

Although the biochemical data remain highly speculative, it is probable that seizures stimulate brainstem structures and modify hypothalamic regulatory systems. Elevations in mood and antidepressant activity as well as changes in vegetative symptoms are the principal neurologic sequelae of repeated seizures. The persistent interseizure slow-wave activity of the EEG is an accompanying electrophysiologic reflection of changes in the brainstem, whereas the other neurologic effects, usually defined as the organic mental syndrome, are the more distant and diffuse effects of currents used to stimulate hypothalamic centers. Much attention is placed on the catecholamine or neurohumoral effects of EST, but there is considerable evidence that hypothalamic peptides may have cerebral effects, particularly on mood and memory (87,90,118). (If one were to attempt to encapsulate some present views of EST, it could be by relabeling the treatment as "diencephalic stimulation.")

The action of EST in schizophrenia and mania may also be related to similar mechanisms, but the need for more seizures to achieve a clinical result and the dependence on an organic mental syndrome suggest that the therapeutic process in these conditions involves more diffuse cerebral systems whose nature remains obscure. The reports that insulin coma and leukotomy were more effective in schizophrenia when organic mental syndromes were severe, and the data of regressive and multiple EST, suggest that diffuse brain dysfunction is an important step in the EST process in schizophrenia — a conclusion that is not necessary for depressive psychoses and one that has caused much confusion in clinical practice and research.

SUMMARY

The effects of repeated seizures (EST) are mood elevation, relief of depression, reduction of vegetative (hypothalamic) symptoms, and an organic mental syndrome. The latter is characterized by changes in memory, perception, and language.

Side effects of EST are organic psychoses, spontaneous seizures, brain damage, fear and panic, and, rarely, death. The therapeutic process for depression lies in biochemical events that accompany or result from seizures, and not in the convulsion, memory loss, or other neurologic sequelae. Modifications of the treatment process that maintain therapeutic activity and reduce side effects are sedation, anesthesia, muscle relaxation, selective electrode placements and electric currents, and hyperoxygenation.

The neurologic and biochemical events in the treatment process and their significance are discussed to suggest that EST is effective in depression to the extent that centrencephalic structures and persistent changes in catecholamine and peptide metabolism are stimulated. A different mechanism of action, one more dependent on diffuse cerebral activity, is postulated for the activity in schizophrenia.

ACKNOWLEDGMENTS

Aided in part by grants MH-15561, 20762, and 24020 from the National Institute of Mental Health; and from the International Association for Psychiatric Research, Inc.

REFERENCES

1. Abrams, R., and Fink, M. (1972): Clinical experiences with multiple electroconvulsive treatments. *Compr. Psychiatry,* 13:115–121.

2. Abrams, R., and Taylor, M. A. (1973): Anterior bifrontal ECT: a clinical trial. *Br. J. Psychiatry,* 122:587–590.
3. Abrams, R., and Taylor, M. A. (1976): Diencephalic stimulation and the effects of ECT in endogenous depression. *Br. J. Psychiatry,* 129:482–485.
4. Allen, J. P., Denney, D., Kendall, J. W., and Blachly, P. H. (1974): Corticotrophin release during ECT in man. *Am. J. Psychiatry,* 131(11):1225–1228.
5. Alpers, B. J., and Hughes, J. (1942): Changes in the brain after electrically induced convulsion in cats. *Arch. Neurol. Psychiatry,* 47:385–398.
6. Assael, M. I., Halperin, B., and Alpern, S. (1967): Centrencephalic epilepsy induced by electrical convulsive treatment. *Electroencephalogr. Clin. Neurophysiol.,* 23:195.
7. Barrera, S. E., Lewis, N. L. C., Pacella, B. L., and Kalinowsky, L. (1942): Brain changes associated with electrically induced seizures. *Trans. Am. Neurol. Assoc.,* 31:31.
8. Berent, S., Cohen, B. D., and Silverman, A. J. (1975): Changes in verbal and non-verbal learning following a single left or right unilateral electroconvulsive treatment. *Biol. Psychiatry,* 10:95–100.
9. Beresford, R. H. (1971): Legal issues relating to ECT. *Arch. Gen. Psychiatry,* 25:100–102.
10. Blachly, P. H., and Gowing, D. (1966): Multiple monitored electroconvulsive treatment. *Compr. Psychiatry,* 7:100–109.
11. Blumenthal, I. J. (1955): Spontaneous seizures and related electroencephalographic findings following shock therapy. *J. Nerv. Ment. Dis.,* 122:581–588.
12. Brockman, R. J., Brockman, J. C., Jacobson, U., Gleser, G. C., and Ulett, G. A. (1956): Changes in convulsive threshold as related to type of treatment. *Confin. Neurol.,* 16:97–104.
13. Carney, M. W. P., and Sheffield, B. (1973): Electroconvulsion therapy and the diencephalon. *Lancet,* 1:1505–1507.
14. Cohen, B. D., Noblin, C. D., and Silverman, A. J. (1968): Functional asymmetry of the human brain. *Science,* 168:475–477.
15. Costello, C. G., Belton, G. P., Abra, J. C., and Dunn, B. E. (1970): The amnesic and therapeutic effects of bilateral and unilateral ECT. *Br. J. Psychiatry,* 116:69–78.
16. D'Elia, G. (1972): Unilateral electroconvulsive therapy. *Acta Psychiatr. Scand. (Suppl.),* 215:1–98.
17. D'Elia, G. (1974): Unilateral electroconvulsive therapy. In: *Psychobiology of Convulsive Therapy,* edited by M. Fink, S. Kety, J. McGaugh, and T. A. Williams, pp. 21–34. V. H. Winston & Sons, Washington, D.C.
18. D'Elia, G., and Raotma, H. (1975): Is unilateral ECT less effective than bilateral ECT? *Br. J. Psychiatry,* 126:83–89.
19. Dornbush, R. L. (1972): Memory and induced ECT convulsions. *Semin. Psychiatry,* 4:47–54.
20. Dornbush, R. L., and Williams, M. (1974): Memory and ECT. In: *Psychobiology of Convulsive Therapy,* edited by M. Fink, S. Kety, J. McGaugh, and T. A. Williams. V. H. Winston & Sons, pp. 199–208. Washington, D.C.
21. Dornbush, R. L., Abrams, R., and Fink, M. (1971): Memory changes after unilateral and bilateral convulsive therapy. *Br. J. Psychiatry,* 119:75–78.
22. Ebaugh, F. G., Barnacle, C. H., and Neuberger, K. T. (1943): Fatalities following electric convulsive therapy: report of two cases, with autopsy. *Arch. Neurol. Psychiatry,* 49:107–117.
23. Elithorn, A. (1962): The treatment of depression. In: *Aspects of Psychiatric Research,* edited by D. Richter, J. M. Tanner, L. Taylor, and O. L. Zangwill, pp. 420–440. Oxford University Press, London.
24. Engel, G. L. (1976): Psychologic factors in instantaneous cardiac death. *N. Engl. J. Med.,* 294:664–665.
25. Ferraro, A., and Roizin, L. (1949): Cerebral morphologic changes in monkeys subjected to a large number of electrically induced convulsions (32–100). *Am. J. Psychiatry,* 106:278–284.
26. Ferraro, A., Roizin, L., and Helfand, M. (1946): Morphologic changes in the brain of monkeys following convulsions electrically induced. *J. Neuropathol. Exp. Neurol.,* 5:285–308.
27. Fink, M. (1958): Effect of anticholinergic agent, diethazine, on EEG and behavior:

significance for theory of convulsive therapy. *Arch. Neurol. Psychiatry,* 80:380–387.
28. Fink, M. (1966): Cholinergic aspects of convulsive therapy. *J. Nerv. Ment. Dis.,* 142:475–484.
29. Fink, M. (1972): The therapeutic process in ECT. *Semin. Psychiatry,* 4:39–46.
30. Fink, M. (1974): Clinical progress in convulsive therapy. In: *Psychobiology of Convulsive Therapy,* edited by M. Fink, S. Kety, J. McGaugh, and T. A. Williams, pp. 271–278. V. H. Winston & Sons, Washington, D.C.
31. Fink, M. (1976): Efficacy and safety of induced seizures (EST) in man: a cost-benefit analysis. *Arch. Gen. Psychiat. (in press).*
32. Fink, M., and Kahn, R. L. (1957): Relation of EEG delta activity to behavioral response in electroshock: quantitative serial studies. *Arch. Neurol. Psychiatry,* 78:516–525.
33. Fink, M., Kahn, R. L., and Green, M. (1958): Experimental studies of the electroshock process. *Dis. Nerv. Syst.,* 19:113–118.
34. Fink, M., Kahn, R. L., Karp, E., Pollack, M., Green, M. A., Alan, B., and Lefkowits, H. J. (1961): Inhalant-induced convulsions. *Arch. Gen. Psychiatry,* 4:259–266.
35. Fovlon, L. (1973): Electrochoc bilatéral ou unilatéral? Une revue critique de la littérature. *Acta Psychiatr. Belg.,* 73:356–378.
36. Fromholt, P., Christensen, A., and Stromgren, L.-S. (1973): The effects of unilateral and bilateral electroconvulsive therapy on memory. *Acta Psychiatr. Scand.,* 49:466–478.
37. Globus, J. H., van Harreveld, A., and Wiersma, C. A. G. (1943): The influence of electric current application on the structure of the brain of dogs. *J. Neuropathol. Exp. Neurol.,* 2:263–276.
38. Glueck, B. C., Jr., Reiss, H., and Bernard, L. E. (1957): Regressive electric shock therapy. *Psychiatr. Q.,* 31:117–135.
39. Goddard, G., McIntyre, D., and Leech, C. (1969): A permanent change in brain function resulting from daily electrical stimulation. *Exp. Neurol.,* 25:295–330.
40. Gomez, J. (1974): Death after E. C. T. *Br. Med. J.,* 1:45.
41. Gralnick, A. (1944): Fatalities associated with electric shock treatment of psychoses: report of two cases, with autopsy observations in one of them. *Arch. Neurol. Psychiatry,* 51:397–402.
42. Green, M. A. (1960): Relation between threshold and duration of seizures and electrographic change during convulsive therapy. *J. Nerv. Ment. Dis.,* 131:117–120.
43. Halliday, A. M., Davison, K., Browne, M. W., and Kreeger, L. C. (1968): A comparison of the effects on depression and memory of bilateral ECT and unilateral ECT to the dominant and non-dominant hemispheres. *Br. J. Psychiatry,* 114:997–1012.
44. Harper, R. G., and Wiens, A. N. (1975): Electroconvulsive therapy and memory. *J. Nerv. Ment. Dis.,* 161:245–254.
45. Hartelius, H. (1952): Cerebral changes following electrically induced convulsions. An experimental study on cats. *Acta Psychiatr. Scand. [Suppl.],* 77:1–128.
46. Hayes, K. J. (1950): The current path in electric convulsion shock. *Arch. Neurol. Psychiatry,* 63:102–109.
47. Heilbrunn, G., and Weil, A. (1942): Pathologic changes in the central nervous system in experimental electric shock. *Arch. Neurol. Psychiatry,* 47:918.
48. Hill, D., and Parr, G. (Eds.) (1963): *Electroencephalography.* Macmillan, New York.
49. Hoagland, H., Malamud, W., Kaufman, I. C., and Pincus, G. (1946): Changes in electroencephalogram and in the excretion of 17-ketosteroids accompanying electroshock therapy of agitated depression. *Psychosom. Med.,* 8:246–251.
50. Holmberg, G. (1963): Biological aspects of electroconvulsive therapy. *Int. Rev. Neurobiol.,* 5:389–412.
51. Haussar, A. E., and Pachter M. (1968): Myocardial infarction and fatal coronary insufficiency during electroconvulsive therapy. *J.A.M.A.,* 11(204):146–149.
52. Ilaria, R., and Prange, A. J. (1975): Convulsive therapy and other biological treatments. In: *The Nature and Treatment of Depression,* edited by F. F. Flach and S. C. Draghi, pp. 271–308. John Wiley & Sons, New York.
53. Inglis, J. (1969): Electrode placement and the effect of ECT on mood and memory in depression. *Can. Psychiatr. Assoc. J.,* 14:463–471.
54. Jaffe, J., Kahn, R. L., and Fink, M. (1960): Changes in verbal transactions with induced altered brain function. *J. Nerv. Ment. Dis.,* 130:235–239.

55. Janowsky, D. S., Davis, J. M., El-Yousef, K., and Sekerke, H. J. (1972): A cholinergic-adrenergic hypothesis of mania and depression. *Lancet,* 2:632–635.
56. Kahn, R. L., and Fink, M. (1958): Changes in language during electroshock therapy. In: *Psychopathology of Communication,* edited by P. H. Hoch and J. Zubin. Grune & Stratton, New York.
57. Kahn, R. L., Fink, M., and Weinstein, E. A. (1956): Relation of amobarbital test to clinical improvement in electroshock. *Arch. Neurol. Psychiatry,* 76:23–29.
58. Kahn, R. L., Pollack, M., and Fink, M. (1960a): Social attitude (California F Scale) and convulsive therapy. *J. Nerv. Ment. Dis.,* 130:187–192.
59. Kahn, R. L., Pollack, M., and Fink, M. (1960b): Figure-ground discrimination after induced altered brain function. *Arch. Neurol.,* 2:547–551.
60. Kalinowsky, L. B. (1945): Organic psychotic syndromes occurring during electric convulsive therapy. *Arch. Neurol. Psychiatry,* 53:269–273.
61. Kalinowsky, L., and Hippius, H. (1972): *Pharmacological, Convulsive and Other Treatments in Psychiatry.* Grune & Stratton, New York.
62. Karczmar, A. G. (1974): Brain acetylcholine and seizures. In: *Psychobiology of Convulsive Therapy,* edited by M. Fink, S. Kety, J. McGaugh, and T. A. Williams. pp. 251–270. V. H. Winston & Sons, Washington, D.C.
63. Karliner, W. (1956): Epileptic states following electroshock therapy. *J. Hillside Hosp.,* 5:1–9.
64. Kety, S. (1974): Biochemical and neurochemical effects of electroconvulsive shock. In: *Psychobiology of Convulsive Therapy,* edited by M. Fink, S. Kety, J. McGaugh, and T. A. Williams, pp. 285–294. V. H. Winston & Sons, Washington, D.C.
65. Korin, H., Fink, M., and Kwalwasser, S. (1956): Relation of changes in memory and learning to improvement in electroshock. *Confin. Neurol.,* 16:88–96.
66. Kurland, A., Hanlon, T. F., Esquibel, A. J., Krantz, J. C., and Sheets, C. S. (1959): A comparative study of hexafluorodiethyl ether (Indoklon) and electroconvulsive therapy. *J. Nerv. Ment. Dis.,* 129:95–98.
67. Larsen, E. F., and Vraa-Jensen, G. (1953): Ischaemic changes in the brain following electroshock therapy. *Acta Psychiatr. Scand.,* 28:75–80.
68. Laurell, B. (1970): Flurothyl convulsive therapy. *Acta Psychiatr. Scand. (Suppl.),* 213:5–79.
69. Liban, E., Halpern, L., and Rozanski, J. (1951): Vascular changes in the brain in a fatality following electroshock. *J. Neuropathol. Exp. Neurol.,* 10:309–318.
70. Liberson, W. T. (1953): Current evaluation of electric convulsive therapies. In: *Psychiatric Treatment,* pp. 199–231. Williams & Wilkins, Baltimore.
71. Lidbeck, W. L. (1944): Pathologic changes in the brain after electric shock: An experimental study on dogs. *J. Neuropathol. Exp. Neurol.,* 3:81.
72. Madow, L. (1956): Brain changes in electroshock therapy. *Am. J. Psychiatry,* 113:337–347.
73. Marjerrison, J. H., and Corsellis, J. A. N. (1966): Epilepsy and the temporal lobes. *Brain,* 89:499–530.
74. Martin, P. A. (1949): Convulsive therapies: review of 511 cases at Pontiac State Hospital. *J. Nerv. Ment. Dis.,* 109:142–157.
75. Meyer, A., and Teare, L. (1949): Cerebral fat embolism after electrical convulsion therapy. *Br. Med. J.,* 2:42–44.
76. Mosovich, A., and Katzenelogen, S. (1948): Electroshock therapy, clinical and electroencephalographic studies. *J. Nerv. Ment. Dis.,* 107:517–530.
77. Murillo, L. G., and Exner, J. E., Jr. (1973): The effects of regressive ECT with process schizophrenics. *Am. J. Psychiatry,* 130:269–273.
78. Neuberger, K. T., Whitehead, R. W., Rutledge, E. K., and Ebaugh, F. G. (1942): Pathologic changes in the brains of dogs given repeated electric shocks. *Am. J. Med. Sci.,* 204:381–387.
79. Norman, R. M., Sandry, S., and Corsellis, J. A. N. (1974): The nature and origin of pathoanatomical change in the epileptic brain. In: *Handbook of Clinical Neurology,* edited by P. T. Vinken and G. W. Bruyn, pp. 611–620. North Holland Publishing Co., Amsterdam.

80. Ottosson, J.-O. (1960): Experimental studies of the mode of action of electroconvulsive therapy. *Acta. Psychiatr. Scand. (Suppl.),* 35:1–141.
81. Ottoson, J.-O. (1962): Seizure characteristics and therapeutic efficiency in electroconvulsive therapy: an analysis of the antidepressive efficiency of grand mal and lidocaine-modified seizures. *J. Nerv. Ment. Dis.,* 135:239–251.
82. Ottoson, J.-O. (1974): Systemic biochemical effects of ECT. In: *Psychobiology of Convulsive Therapy,* edited by M. Fink, S. Kety, J. McGaugh, and T. A. Williams, pp. 209–220. V. H. Winston & Sons, Washington, D. C.
83. Pacella, B. L., and Barrera, S. E. (1945): Spontaneous convulsions following convulsive shock therapy. *Am. J. Psychiatry,* 101:783–788.
84. Pinel, J. P. J., and Van Oot, P. H. (1975): Generality of the kindling phenomenon: some clinical implications. *Can. J. Neurol. Sci.,* 2:467–475.
85. Polatin, P., Strauss, H., and Altman, L. (1940): Transient organic mental reactions during shock therapy of the psychoses: a clinical study. *Psychiatr. Q.,* 14:457–466.
86. Psychiatrist, Practicing (1965): The experience of electro-convulsive therapy. *Br. J. Psychiatry,* 111:365–367.
87. Prange, A. J., Jr., Wilson, I. C., Lara, P. P., Alltop, L. B., and Breese, G. R. (1972): Effects of thyrotrophin-releasing hormone in depression. *Lancet,* 2:999–1002.
88. Pryor, G. T. (1974): Effect of repeated ECS on brain weight and brain enzymes. In: *Psychobiology of Convulsive Therapy,* edited by M. Fink, S. Kety, J. McGaugh, and T. A. Williams. pp. 171–184. V. H. Winston & Sons, Washington, D. C.
89. Regenstein, Q. R., Murawski, B. J., and Engel, R. P. (1975): A case of prolonged, reversible dementia associated with abuse of convulsive therapy. *J. Nerv. Ment. Dis.,* 161:200–203.
90. Riezen, H. van, and Rigter, H. (1976): Possible significance of ACTH fragments for human mental performance. *Biol. Psychiatry (in press).*
91. Roth, M. (1951): Changes in the EEG under barbiturate anesthesia produced by electroconvulsive treatment and their significance for the theory of ECT action. *Electroencephalogr. Clin. Neurophysiol.,* 3:261–280.
92. Roth, M., Kay, D. W. K., Shaw, J., and Green, J. (1957): Prognosis and pentothal induced electroencephalographic changes in electroconvulsive treatment. *Electroencephalogr. Clin. Neurophysiol.,* 9:225–237.
93. Sachar, E., Roffwarg, H. P., Gruen, P. H., Altemann, N., and Sassin, J. (1976): Neuroendocrine studies of depressive illness. *Pharmakopsychiatr. Neuropsychopharmakol.,* 9:11–17.
94. Scanlon, W. G., and Mathas, J. (1967): Electroencephalographic and psychometric studies of Indoklon convulsive treatment and electroconvulsive treatment (a preliminary report). *Int. J. Neuropsychiatry,* 3:276–281.
95. Sholz, W. (1951): *Die Krampfschadigungen des Gehirns.* Springer, Berlin.
96. Small, I. (1974): Inhalant convulsive therapy. In: *Psychobiology of Convulsive Therapy,* edited by M. Fink, S. Kety, J. McGaugh, and T. A. Williams, pp. 65–78. V. H. Winston & Sons, Washington, D. C.
97. Small, I. F., and Small, J. G. (1968): Ictus and amnesia. *Recent Adv. Biol. Psychiatry,* 10:144–159.
98. Small, J. G., and Small, I. F. (1972): Clinical results: Indoklon vs. ECT. *Semin. Psychiatry,* 4:13–26.
99. Small, J. G., Small, I. F., Perez, H. C., and Sharpley, P. (1970): EEG and neurophysiological studies of electrically induced seizures. *J. Nerv. Ment. Dis.,* 150:479–489.
100. Small, J. G., Small, I. F., Sharpley, P., and Moore, D. M. (1968): A double-blind comparative evaluation of fluorothyl and ECT. *Arch. Gen. Psychiatry,* 19:79–86.
101. Spreche, D. (1964): A quantitative comparison of electroconvulsive therapy with hexaflurodiethyl ether. *J. Neuropsychiatry,* 5:132–137.
102. Squire, L. R., and Chace, P. M. (1975): Memory functions six to nine months after electroconvulsive therapy. *Arch. Gen. Psychiatry,* 32:1557–1568.
103. Squire, L. R., and Miller, P. L. (1974): Diminution of anterograde amnesia following electroconvulsive therapy. *J. Clin. Psychol.,* 125:490–495.
104. Squire, L. R., and Slater, P. C. (1975): Forgetting in very long-term memory as assessed

by an improved questionnaire technique. *J. Exp. Psychol. Hum. Learn. Memory*, 104:50–54.

105. Squire, L. R., Slater, P. C., and Chace, P. M. (1975): Retrograde amnesia: temporal gradient in very long-term memory following electroconvulsive therapy. *Science*, 187:77–79.
106. Sternberg, D. E., and Jarvik, M. E. (1976): Memory functions in depression. *Arch. Gen. Psychiatry*, 33:219–224.
107. Strain, J. J., and Bidder, T. G. (1971): Transient cerebral complication associated with multiple monitored electroconvulsive therapy. *Dis. Nerv. Syst.*, 32:95–100.
108. Strauss, H., Ostow, M., and Greenstein, L. (1952): *Diagnostic Electroencephalography.* Grune & Stratton, New York.
109. Turek, I. S. (1972): EEG correlates of electroconvulsive treatment. *Dis. Nerv. Syst.*, 33:584–589.
110. Turek, I. S. (1976): ECT: Its efficacy and safety. *Dis. Nerv. Sys.* (*in press*).
111. Volavka, J. (1972): Neurophysiology of ECT. *Semin. Psychiatry*, 4:55–65.
112. Volavka, J. (1974): Is EEG slowing relating to the therapeutic effect of convulsive therapy? In: *Psychobiology of Convulsive Therapy*, edited by M. Fink, S. Kety, J. McGaugh, and T. A. Williams, pp. 35–40. V. H. Winston & Sons, Washington, D.C.
113. Volavka, J., Feldstein, S., Abrams, R., Dornbush, R., and Fink, M. (1972): EEG and clinical change after bilateral and unilateral electroconvulsive therapy. *Electroencephalogr. Clin. Neurophysiol.*, 32:631–639.
114. Weaver, L., Ravaris, C., Rush, S., and Paananen, R. (1974): Stimulus parameters in electroconvulsive shock. *J. Psychiatr. Res.*, 10:271–281.
115. Weaver, L., Williams, R., and Rush, S. (1976): Current density in bilateral and unilateral ECT. *Biol. Psychiatry*, 11:303–312.
116. Weinstein, E. A., and Kahn, R. L. (1955): *Denial of Illness.* Charles C Thomas, Springfield, Ill.
117. Weinstein, E. A., Linn, L., and Kahn, R. L. (1952): Psychoses during electroshock therapy: its relation to the theory of shock therapy. *Am. J. Psychiatry*, 109:22–26.
118. de Wied, D. (1974): Pituitary-adrenal-system hormones and behavior. In: *The Neurosciences, Third Study Program*, edited by F. O. Schmitt and F. G. Worden, pp. 653–666. M. I. T. Press, Cambridge.
119. Will, O. A., Jr., Rehfeldt, F. C., and Neumann, M. A. (1948): A fatality in electroshock therapy: report of a case and review of certain previously described cases. *J. Nerv. Ment. Dis.*, 107:105–126.

Psychopathology and Brain Dysfunction, edited by C. Shagass, S. Gershon, and A. J. Friedhoff. Raven Press, New York © 1977.

Neurologic Findings in Recidivist Aggressors

Russell R. Monroe, Barbara Hulfish, George Balis, John Lion, Jeffrey Rubin, Matthew McDonald, and J. David Barcik

Department of Psychiatry, University of Maryland School of Medicine, Baltimore, Maryland 21201

INTRODUCTION

Over the past 20 years the senior author has studied over 800 subjects with *episodic behavioral disorders* defined as any precipitously appearing maladaptive behavior, usually intermittent and recurring, which interrupts the life style and the life flow of the individual (5). Episodic disorders are in turn divided into two subcategories: *episodic inhibitions* of actions such as narcolepsy, cataplexy, akinetic mutism, periodic catatonia, and petit mal status; and *episodic disinhibition* of action. Episodic disinhibition is further divided into *episodic dyscontrol,* representing an abrupt single act, or a short series of acts, with a common intention carried through to completion with at least partial relief of tension or gratification of a specific need; and the *episodic reactions,* representing a more prolonged interruption in the life style, but also characterized by a precipitous onset and an equally abrupt remission as well as a tendency to recur. The dyscontrol acts that characterize the episodic behavioral disorders are usually based on primitive emotions of fear, rage, or sensuous feelings without concern for the effect on the immediate environment or the long-term consequences to the actor or society and are either self- or socially destructive.

The abruptness of the appearance of symptoms, particularly when of short duration and accompanied by confusion and other signs of clouded sensorium, strongly suggests a basic epileptoid mechanism involving circumscribed areas of excessive neuronal discharge, particularly in the limbic system. Electroencephalographic data would add circumstantial support for this hypothesis, which is further validated by the frequent response of such patients to anticonvulsant medication. The senior author has presented elsewhere (6) the concept that the basic mechanism might also be thought of as a maturational retardation, which is compatible with the lowered seizural threshold of the epileptoid hypotheses. He has pointed out that some of the episodic behavioral disorders are undoubtedly learned patterns of responses (motivated or hysteroid episodic disorders) and that clinical experience indicates that most patients fall somewhere between the polar extremes of epileptoid mechanisms on one hand and hysteroid on the other.

Previous studies suggested that between the ages of 5 and 10 the episodic disorders were more frequent in males than females; however, just the opposite was found in serial adult admissions to an acute psychiatric hospital (5): namely, twice as many females as males were found to fit the definition of the episodic behavioral disorders. Further examination of the histories suggests that this reversal might be explained on the basis of how a society copes with the episodic disorders. As an example, it was noted that the women admitted to a mental hospital with this diagnosis usually had committed some atrocious act — e.g., shooting their minister, setting a house on fire, pouring boiling water on their husband, abusing their children — that would have more likely led to incarceration in a penal institution if the act had been committed by a male. This hypothesis, plus the known fact that dyscontrol acts characteristic of the episodic disorders are often of an antisocial nature, led us to investigate the possibility of the episodic behavioral disorder as an explanation for some aggressive recidivism.

THE PRESENT STUDY

Details of the present study will be presented in a monograph now in preparation. The individuals studied were 93 prisoners at Patuxent Institu-

TABLE 1. *Criminal offenses* (N = 93)

Offense	No. of subjects
Assault to murder	7
Rape	10
Attempted rape	2
Assault to rape	1
Carnal knowledge	1
Assault to carnally know	2
Indecent exposure	1
Perverted practice	8
Assault on child	1
Assault and battery	4
Assault	3
Narcotics laws	1
Abduction	1
Robbery	5
Robbery with a deadly weapon	20
Assault to rob	3
Explosives violation	1
Arson	4
Burglary	7
Breaking and entering	3
Housebreaking	2
Storehouse breaking	2
Rogue and vagabond	1
Grand larceny	1
Auto larceny	1
Ambiguous	1
Total	93

tion in Maryland, a unique hospital-prison where, after conviction and sentencing, individuals are determined by the court to be "defective delinquents" and institutionalized on an indeterminate sentence. Most of these individuals have had six or more convictions and have repeatedly transgressed, usually within a matter of weeks or a few months after obtaining parole status from their previous conviction. As can be seen from Table 1, the criminal offenses are largely aggressive acts toward other individuals or sexual trangressions. This population does not include the criminally insane (Table 2). The age range of our population was 19 to 54 with a mean of 29. The data collected that were pertinent for the present study are listed in Table 3.

Data that proved significant correlations with a neurologic scale were the following:

1. Current and Past Psychopathology Scales (CAPPS) (3) and dyscontrol characteristics rated on a scale of severity from 1 to 6 by participating psychiatrists.
2. Global estimate of epileptoid mechanism of the dyscontrol behavior [based on behavioral data alone (5)] rated on a scale of

TABLE 2. *Diagnoses of subject population*

Diagnosis	No. of subjects[a]
A. Mental retardation	
Borderline	1
Mild	2
B. Organic brain syndrome	
Epilepsy	1
C. Psychoses	
Simple	1
D. Neuroses	
Anxiety	1
Hysterical	1
Hypochondriacal	1
E. Personality disorders	
True personality disorders	
Paranoid personality	1
Schizoid personality	10
Explosive personality	10
Antisocial personality	44
Passive-aggressive personality	21
Sex deviations	
Homosexuality	3
Pedophilia	9
Exhibitionism	1
Other sex deviation	4
Alcoholism	
Episodic excessive drinking	13
Habitual excessive drinking	5
Alcohol addiction	1
Narcotic drug dependence	15

[a] Some subjects had multiple diagnoses.

TABLE 3. *Data analysis*

Instrument	No. of items
Current and Past Psychopathology Scale (CAPPS)	121
CAPPS Addenda (Characteristics of Episodic Disorders)	34
Estimated "epileptoid" mechanism	1
Mood Scale	7
Olson Affect Scale	8
Monroe Dyscontrol Scale	1
WAIS: Verbal, Performance, Full Scale, and Subtest	14
MMPI	14
Canter Background Interference Procedure (BIP) and Bender Gestalt	7
Memory for Design	1
Prison Infraction Rating	1
Holtzman Inkblot Technique	22
Porteus Maze Test Quotient and Quality Score	2
Time Estimation Test	1
Slow Writing Test	1
Matching Familiar Figures	2
Draw-A-Line	1
Auditory Discrimination Test	2
Chloralose-"activated" EEG	1
Lion Symptom Check List	1
Group Therapist Rating	13
Total	255

present to absent from 1 to 7 by the psychiatrist who had no knowledge of neurologic or EEG findings.

3. Monroe Dyscontrol Scale, a self-rating scale constructed by Plutchik et al. (9) to evaluate dyscontrol behavior (see Appendix A).

4. Mood Scale rated by the psychiatrist on a scale from 1 to 7 (low to high) on seven separate factors.

5. Olson Affect Scale, an eight-item instrument rated on a scale of 1 to 8 (low to high) by the psychiatrist.

6. Neurological history and physical and mental examinations (4).

7. Canter Background Interference Procedure — Bender Test (1) given by the research psychometrician to determine possible organic central nervous system dysfunction.

8. Holtzman Inkblot Technique given by the research psychometrician consisting of ratings on 22 variables.

9. Draw-A-Line Test created by the research psychometrician to determine any further correlation to a simple 60-sec time estimation task hoping to tap impulse controllability. This task consisted of asking the subject to draw a 1-inch line on blank paper.

10. EEG recordings (including drug activation with alpha chloralose) read by an electroencephalographer and two of the research psychiatrists (7).

11. Infraction ratings that were weighted scores based on the incidence and degree of severity of rule infractions as reported by the custodial officers at the institution (see Appendix B).
12. Group therapist questionnaire rated on a 1 to 6 scale by the institutional staff therapist (see Appendix C).

NEUROLOGICAL SCALE

In earlier analyses of the data using either the electroencephalographic patterns or the Monroe Dyscontrol Scale as the criterion variable, a number of neurologic findings correlated at a level of 0.05 or better on the t-test or analysis of variance. These variables suggested that a scale of neurologic signs and symptoms might correlate with psychiatric, psychometric, or psychotherapeutic characteristics of the dyscontrol syndrome. It was evident that the entire pool of 32 neurological items as rated by the neurologist during examination was not necessary. Therefore, the present neurological scale was developed by selecting certain key items from the following major categories that were scored on a 1 to 6 point scale, indicating absence of findings to severe or definite abnormalities, respectively.

Historical Data

Historical data consisting of evidence of birth trauma, head injury, possible epilepsy, and other central nervous system "insult" seemed important, whereas school problems, "short" fuse, and repetitive dreams did not.

In evaluating birth data, we considered the age of the parent at the time of the patient's birth, the number of children the mother had borne, birth difficulties including prolonged labor, forceps delivery, bleeding or other complications of pregnancy, multiple births, prematurity, resuscitation problems, abnormal Apgar signs, or combinations of these factors.

Head injury was rated as minimal to maximum, i.e., from trauma to facial soft tissues to repeated closed head injuries with periods of unconsciousness.

Epilepsy suspect referred to a range of symptoms from dizziness, lightheadedness, headaches, blurred vision, déjà vu or jamais vu, forgetfulness, size, space, shape, or time distortion, absentmindedness, dropping objects, episodic enuresis, and frequent falls, to a definite history of tonic-clonic convulsions.

Other central nervous system "insult" noted evidence of frontal lobe symptoms such as poor judgment, recent memory impairment, various infections with delirium, or drug abuse to a point of unconsciousness.

Neurologic Symptoms

We evaluated two neurologic symptoms. Hyperacusis was rated on the basis of distractibility, intolerance of high pitches, or cacaphony with an evaluation of the patient's distractibility by extraneous noises during the neurologic examination itself; and photophobia was rated on the basis of intolerance to bright fluorescent lights, as well aversive responses to such lights during the examination including a history of wearing dark glasses, excessive pupillary reaction to a bright light, and spontaneous remarks on questioning regarding intolerance to bright or flashing lights. Hypersensitivity to touch was not important.

Neurologic Signs

Neurologic signs included what we have chosen to call congenital stigmata, as well as apraxia, abnormalities in motor strength, and two areas that seem to correlate negatively with dyscontrol symptoms and EEG abnormalities, namely, coordination and sensations.

Congenital stigmata included small heads, small ears, pectus excavatum, extra toes or fingers, large birthmarks, amblyopic eyes, strabismus, and odd behavior or hyperactivity during the examination.

Apraxia evaluated fine motor dexterity varying from assembling a four-part stapler (for the more intelligent subjects) to simply replacing batteries in a flashlight (for the less intelligent subjects). Drawing, writing, spelling, and reading as tested by the neurologist showed no significant correlations with psychiatric behavioral or electroencephalographic data. This was also true for similar psychometric data.

Motor strength (in the absence of orthopedic reasons) was evaluated in terms of the extremities, with particular emphasis on whether there was a difference between the strength in opposite extremities, tested by the two arms held overhead against resistance, external rotation against resistance, flexion and extension of the elbows and wrists, and grasp. In the lower extremities, there was a test for flexion and extension of the knees and for dorsiflexion of the feet and toes with the patient being asked to hop, first on one foot and then on the other.

Coordination was tested in terms of finger-to-thumb coordination, looking for mirror movements, dysdiadochokinesia, rapid alternating tongue movement, and foot tapping. Sensation was tested for pain (pinprick), vibration, and proprioception, but not for light touch or temperature. Scars, handedness, cranial nerve dysfunction, speech, and reflexes proved unimportant.

It is important to state again that the neurologic scale was developed as a clinical tool to be composed of the algebraic sum of 11 neurological variables: + birth data + head injury + epilepsy suspect + other CNS "insult" + neurologic stigmata + hyperacusis + photophobia + apraxia + motor strength − coordination − sensation.

The descriptive statistics of the neurological scale for the 93 subjects are a range in actual scores from +4 to +20 with a possible range of −3 to +52. The mean was 16.9, and the standard error was 1.12.

Multiple regression analyses suggest that these 11 neurologic variables might be reduced to 7, but future analysis of the data will be necessary before the reduced scale is proven more useful than that reported today.

RESULTS

Pearson product-moment correlations with 255 variables at the level of 0.05 or better are listed in Tables 4 and 5. There proved to be a surprising consistency on the Pearson product-moment analysis among these disparate instruments and different observers who were totally naive regarding the data collected by their peers. With exceptions noted below, the correlations showed a consistency with the clinically evolved concept of the "epileptoid" dyscontrol act.

TABLE 4. *Significant product-moment correlation coefficients of the neurologic scale with items from the modified CAPPS*

Data source	Variable description	Correlation coefficient ($N = 91-93$)
Past history (psychiatrist)	Neurotic traits in childhood	+0.183
	Antisocial traits in childhood	+0.314[a]
	Adolescent friendship patterns	+0.214
	Outpatient treatment	+0.234
	Received treatment for psychopathology	+0.252[a]
	Efforts to improve	+0.174
	Physical health	+0.173
	Amnesia, fugue, dissociative state	+0.216
	Hypochondriasis	+0.171
	Overreacts emotionally	+0.267[a]
	Angry	+0.307[a]
	Violent	+0.278[a]
	Impulsive	+0.390[a]
	Judgment (poor)	+0.271[a]
	Self-defeating	+0.198
	Fluctuation of feeling	+0.208
	Lack of responsibility	+0.222
	Grandiosity	+0.243[a]
	Illusions	+0.179
	Overall severity	+0.187
Current behavior (psychiatrist)	Conversion reaction	+0.218
	Psychophysiological reactions	+0.175
	Grandiosity	+0.272[a]
	Belligerance-negativism	+0.260[a]
Dyscontrol characteristics (psychiatrist)	Premeditated acts	−0.178
	Specificity of affect during act	+0.182
	Prodromal anger	+0.200
	Prodromal autonomic symptoms	+0.174
Global estimate (psychiatrist)	Epileptoid mechanism	−0.395[a]

[a] $p \leq 0.01$ (all others shown, $p \leq 0.05$).

TABLE 5. *Significant product-moment correlation coefficients of the neurologic scale with items from the psychological and clinical variables*

Data source	Variable description	Correlation coefficient ($N = 73$–93)
Mood Scale (psychiatrist)	Fatigue-inertia	−0.173
Affect Scale (psychiatrist)	Level of tension	+0.190
	Emotional lability	+0.248[a]
	Impulsiveness	+0.073[a]
Monroe Scale (self-rating)	Dyscontrol score	+0.310[a]
Infraction Rating (custodial staff)	Prison infraction rating	+0.214
EEG	Chloralose-induced paroxysmal theta	+0.328[a]
Bender BIP (psychologist)	Distractibility	+0.179
	Degree of organicity	+0.190
Holtzman (psychologist)	Form definitiveness (FD)	+0.177
	Animal (A)	+0.172
	Anatomy (At)	+0.213
	Abstract (Ab)	−0.178
Draw-a-Line (psychologist)	Distance estimation	−0.286
Group Behavior Questionnaire (staff therapist)	Participation	−0.249[a]
	Wide range of emotions	+0.341[a]
	Verbal hostility to therapist	+0.234

[a] $p \leq 0.01$ (all others shown, $p \leq 0.05$).

Correlations of the neurological scale at the 0.05 level or better were found with psychiatric history of anger, violent behavior, overreactive emotional behavior, as well as fluctuations of feelings, poor judgment, self-defeating action, lack of responsibility, grandiosity, illusions, hypochondriasis, fugue state, and specific health problems. This was also true for neurotic or antisocial traits in childhood and poor peer relationships during adolescence. It may appear incongruous, but it was predicted on the basis of the early findings that these individuals were more likely to have received specific medical or psychiatric treatment for their problems and were more likely to have made individual efforts or to have shown initiative to help themselves (5).

The current mental status examination revealed correlations with belligerent-negativistic behavior, psychophysiologic and conversion symptoms. Again, as was predicted, there was a correlation between dyscontrol behavior in those with evidence of CNS impairment and absence of premeditation, but contrary to the original predictions we found that such dyscontrol behavior was more likely to be accompanied by specific rather than diffuse affects (5). Correlations with prodromal feelings of anger or physiologic instability were also found.

It is important to note that the estimate by the psychiatrist of an epileptoid mechanism based on behavioral symptoms (see Table 4) correlated with the neurologic scale at the level of 0.001. Correlations on the mood and affect scales were consistent with the psychiatric history in that these individuals were more likely to show current emotional lability or impulsivity with a high level of tension and little evidence of fatigue or inertia.

Not surprisingly, there was a correlation at the 0.001 level between the neurologic score and dyscontrol behavior as measured by the Monroe Scale (inasmuch as the Monroe Scale was one of the criterion variables in formulating the neurologic scale), but this seemed to be supported by institutional ratings of the custodial staff where there was also a correlation with institutional rule infractions.

Ratings by the institutional group therapist, who was totally naive regarding the research hypothesis, showed a correlation with a wide range of emotional responsiveness and verbal hostility toward the therapist.

On the psychometric tests the BIP-Bender indicated evidence for distractibility, and this as well as the Holtzman pattern suggested concrete thinking with a poor form response and a low capacity for abstraction—all suggesting the possibility of a minimal organic process. Other psychological variables that were found not significant and thus not reported in Table 5 were the Wechsler Adult Intelligence Test, the Minnesota Multiphasic Personality Inventory, the Memory for Design Test, the Porteus Mazes, Matching Familiar Figures, the Time Estimation Test, and the Slow Writing Test (see Table 3).

DISCUSSION

In a recent study by Davis et al. (2), it was noted that those schizophrenics receiving phenothiazine who also had cerebral dysrhythmias similar to those found in the above studies were more likely than others to have had birth trauma, head injuries, or high fever with delirium during childhood, and to demonstrate clumsiness, tantrums, phobias, and related behaviors. Also, a paper by Morrison and Minkoff (8) reports that individuals with childhood symptoms of hyperactivity as well as brain insult or epilepsy showed explosive dyscontrol behavior during adulthood. Considering these data and those presented on the correlations between neurologic scale and aggressive dyscontrol behavior—as well as the data previously reported on EEG abnormalities (7), which indicate that up to 88% of these recidivist aggressors show at least minimal EEG abnormalities, with 44% showing focal or transients suggesting organic CNS involvement or an epileptoid mechanism —it seems likely that central nervous system dysfunction plays a part in some aggressive antisocial action. The importance of these observations is highlighted by a recent Wolfgang study (10) regarding adolescent delinquency in an inner-city ghetto area. His finding that up to 35% of the adolescents will have a police record before they have reached adulthood is astounding, but even more so is that 52% of the offenses leading to the police record are committed by only 6.3% of this cohort. This suggests that there is a small group of recidivist offenders that is contributing mostly to these antisocial acts. The population that we are studying is probably this recidivist aggressor group. One must remember that on the average, subjects under investigation have had six or more convictions before the time of our study. Thus, if a significant group of offenders could be identified as having a neuropsychiatric disorder, and if such a disorder is treatable, as we believe it is, then the medical model for the control of considerable criminal behavior becomes important.

The most surprising finding and one that remains an enigma to the authors is that, despite other neurologic pathology, those dyscontrol recidivists with activated electroencephalographic abnormalities are more likely to be normal on sensory examinations and gross motor coordination than the rest of the Patuxent population.

Admittedly our findings leave many questions unanswered and demand further investigation. First, is our neurologic scale something that can be communicated to other neurologists, and would there be a high interrater reliability in using this scale? Such interrater reliability was tested for the psychiatric ratings but not for the neurologic evaluations. Second, we will have to ask how this neurological scale correlates with recidivism in an unselected group of convicted criminals, i.e., is the population of the Patuxent Institution that we have studied a highly unique group? Third, we will need prospective studies of the young delinquents to see how accurately this neurologic scale will predict recidivism.

Finally, the further analysis of our own data will be crucial with respect to the possibility of a limbic system ictal phenomenon as the underlying mechanism of this aggression, and its potential responsiveness to pharmacologic agents that raise seizural threshold. If this proves to be the case, as it has in mental hospital patients (5), then we already have an available, if at times inconsistent, medical regimen for controlling such delinquent behavior in those individuals who show these neurologic signs and symptoms.

ACKNOWLEDGMENT

This research is supported by NIMH grant MH 21035.

REFERENCES

1. Canter, A. (1968): The BIP-Bender Test for the detection of organic brain disorder: Modified scoring method and replication. *J. Consult. Clin. Psychol.*, 32:522–526.
2. Davis, R. K., Neil, J. F., and Himmelhoch, J. M. (1975): Cerebral dysrhythmias in schizophrenics receiving phenothiazines: clinical correlates. *Clin. Electroencephalogr.*, 6:103–115.

3. Endicott, J., and Spitzer, R. L. (1972): Current and Past Psychopathology Scales (CAPPS): Rationale, reliability and validity. *Arch. Gen. Psychiatry,* 27:678–687.
4. Hulfish, B. (1972): Psychophysiologic complaints and psychomatic illnesses: Section 1 – seizures. In: *Practice of Medicine, Vol. 10,* pp. 1–66. Harper & Row, New York.
5. Monroe, R. R. (1970): *Episodic Behavioral Disorders.* Harvard University Press, Cambridge.
6. Monroe, R. R. (1974): Maturational lag in central nervous system development as a partial explanation of episodic violent behavior. In: *Determinants and Origins of Aggressive Behavior,* edited by J. DeWit and W. W. Hartup, pp. 337–344. Mouton Publishers, The Hague, Netherlands.
7. Monroe, R. R., Balis, G. U., Rubin, J. S., Lion, J. R., Hulfish, B., McDonald, M., and Barcik, J. D. (1975): Limbic system seizures and impulsive antisocial behavior. Second International Symposium on Criminology, Sao Paulo, Brazil, August 4–8.
8. Morrison, J. R., and Minkoff, K. (1975): Explosive personality as a sequel to the hyperactive child syndrome. *Compr. Psychiatry,* 16:343–348.
9. Plutchik, R., Climent, C., and Ervin, F. (1974): Research strategies for the study of human violence. Presented at the 5th Annual Cerebral Function Symposium, Coronado, California, March.
10. Wolfgang, M. E. (1975): Delinquency and violence from the viewpoint of criminology. In: *Neural Bases of Violence and Aggression,* edited by W. S. Field and W. A. Sweet. Warren H. Green, St. Louis.

APPENDIX A. *Monroe Dyscontrol Scale*

Instructions

Here are statements that describe the way some people feel or act. Please read each statement carefully and place a check mark (✔) on the appropriate line to indicate how often you felt or acted that way.

	Never	Rarely	Sometimes	Often
1. I have acted on a whim or impulse.				
2. I have had sudden changes in my moods.				
3. I have had the experience of feeling confused even in a familiar place.				
4. I do not feel totally responsible for what I do.				
5. I have lost control of myself even though I did not want to.				
6. I have been surprised by my actions.				
7. I have lost control of myself and hurt other people.				
8. My speech has been slurred.				
9. I have had "blackouts."				
10. I have become wild and uncontrollable after one or two drinks.				
11. I have become so angry that I smashed things.				
12. I have frightened other people with my temper.				
13. I have "come to" without knowing where I was or how I got there.				
14. I have had indescribable frightening feelings.				
15. I have been so tense I would like to scream.				
16. I have had the impulse to kill myself.				
17. I have been angry enough to kill somebody.				
18. I have physically attacked and hurt another person.				

(Scorers code only: Never = 0; Rarely = 1; Sometimes = 2; Often = 3)

APPENDIX B. *Infraction ratings*

Rule infractions	Weight
Escape, break-out	10
Assault with weapon on officer	10
Assault on officer, no weapon	9
Assault with weapon on inmate	9
Possession of weapon	7
Possession of means of escape	7
Escape, walk-off	6
Assault on inmate with force, no weapon or perversion	4
Possession of contraband drug, alcohol, or under influence of same	3
Destruction of state property — very serious	3
Sexual perversion without force	3
Refusal to obey or insolence	2
Out of bounds	2
Possession of unauthorized items	2
Arguing with other inmates	2
Destruction of state property — minor	1
Other minor infractions of rules	1
Incident reports	
Argued with other inmates	2
Warning given	2
Uncooperative behavior	2
Refused to work	2
Reports of problems with other inmates	2
Cutting himself	1
Physical complaints	1
Griping	1
Unauthorized items	1
Refused medication	0
Sleeping reports	0

APPENDIX C. *Group therapist questionnaire (for events during the preceding month)*

1. Patient attends group regularly and on time	Always	1	2	3	4	5	6	Never
2. Participates meaningfully in sessions; active and verbal	Always	1	2	3	4	5	6	Never
3. Range of emotional responses	Flat	1	2	3	4	5	6	Volatile
4. Speech or action is impulsive	Thoughtful	1	2	3	4	5	6	Impulsive
5. A. Is verbally hostile to group members	Never	1	2	3	4	5	6	Extreme
B. Is verbally hostile to therapist	Never	1	2	3	4	5	6	Extreme
6. Physically hostile in group	Never	1	2	3	4	5	6	Usually
7. Motor activity in group	Quiet	1	2	3	4	5	6	Agitated
8. A. Thinking has been modified by group	Positively influenced	1	2	3	4	5	6	Negatively influenced
B. Behavior has been modified by group	Positively influenced	1	2	3	4	5	6	Negatively influenced
9. Acceptance by others in group	Liked	1	2	3	4	5	6	Disliked
10. Your feelings for patient	Like	1	2	3	4	5	6	Dislike
11. Your prognosis of group effect	Much benefit	1	2	3	4	5	6	None

Psychopathology
by C. Shagass, S. (
Raven Press, Nev

Evidence For A Neurologic Dis
Sociopath Syndrome: Aversive
And Recidivism

Eugene Ziskind, Karl Syndulko, and Ir

Gateways Hospital, Los Angeles, California; and University of California, Los Angeles, California 90026

In this chapter we present three different experiments in condition-ability in sociopaths and controls. For a long time we have been interested in the question of whether there are differences between sociopaths and controls. Currently we have three questions: (a) are there statistically significant differences in conditionability between sociopaths and controls; (b) are there differences in conditionability between acutely active sociopaths and those in a spontaneous remission; and (c) is there a correlation between recidivism in sociopaths and the defect in conditioning? For the first of these questions we have experiments that indicate statistically significant differences between sociopaths and controls.

We have been engaged in research on sociopaths since 1970 (15). Several of our reports appear in the literature (6,9,10,13–15,17–20), the earliest of which relate to the problem of the research definition to promote the selection of a homogeneous population and to increase communicability.

Because of the controversial literature related to psychophysiologic findings, particularly those reported by Hare (3), we drew up a set of hypotheses that included difficulties in establishing aversive conditioning and the failure of extinction in orienting responses (15). Among the experiments to establish our original hypotheses was the study by Schmauk (7) using the Lykken (5) mental maze, which we conducted in 1972. Avoid-ance conditioning here was never tested because the maze was too simple for our high IQ sociopaths and normal controls.[1]

In March 1975 I presented a heuristic paper (16) at the Western Federa-tion of Neurologic Sciences suggesting that the sociopath syndrome was a neurologic disorder. The argument was supported by a set of clinical findings and two speculations. The findings were an increased incidence of severity of enuresis, nailbiting, hyperkinesis, and specific learning disabilities in

---

[1] The maze can be made more complicated and the experiment completed.

ths as compared to matched controls (Table 1). The speculations

A. The stereotypy of the sociopath syndrome was characteristic of organic states and unlike syndromes produced by psychogenic and/or sociogenic stresses.
B. The interchangeability and concomitance of psychotic, manic, depressive, and delusional syndromes (currently recognized as organic disorders) were so commonly interlaced with the sociopath syndrome as to suggest that the latter was of the same biologic cloth. The conditions seemed to parallel the interlacing of syndromes seen in many organic psychotic disorders such as syphilitic general paresis.

When this presentation was completed, it was stated that I had no data, and that the considerations were primarily heuristic. They seemed logical and plausible. I therefore commented that the sociopath syndrome might some day take its place with the other psychotic disorders that were increasingly being accepted in the psychiatric profession as organic in origin. I mentioned, however, that the situation called for sound data.

It was therefore a great surprise when Robert Livingston, Head of the Department of Neurosciences at the University of California at San Diego, called attention to actual data and mentioned three items to support that statement. First, there were the experiments of de Wied (2) and his associates who had studied the effect of fragments of the synthetic ACTH on conditioning in rats. They found that aversive conditioning could be controlled by chemical fragments of the ACTH chain, one of which destroyed the capacity of the animal to undergo aversive conditioning, and by another chain that markedly enhanced the capacity for aversive conditioning by 100 to 1,000% (2). Second, the psychologist Robert Thompson (12) in Louisiana had found that aversive conditioning in the rat was not possible when he destroyed the posterior thalamus and the adjacent mesencephalon (2). Third, radioactive labeling of the fragments in the rats showed collection in the posterior thalamus (R. Livingston, *personal communication*). We were therefore quite excited to see whether or not conditioning in the

TABLE 1. *Frequency of childhood disorders in 60 sociopaths and 55 controls*

	Sociopaths		Controls	
Disorder	*No.*	*%*	*No.*	*%*
Hyperkinesis	12	20	2	4
Reading disabilities	16	26	1	1
Enuresis	16	29	4	7
Nailbiting	27	50	14	27

sociopath was impaired much as it is with omission of the critical peptide #7 of the chemical fragment ACTH 4–10 in the de Wied experiments. In other words, is the sociopath a human counterpart of the "de Wied rat with peptide #7 suppressed?" On this question, we report three experiments in a continuing investigation of conditioning in sociopathy.

EXPERIMENT 1

In Experiment 1 we recorded autonomic and central nervous system measures during differential conditioning procedures in 16 primary sociopaths and 16 normal controls matched for age, sex, and IQ. Recordings of EEG, skin conductance level (SCL), skin conductance response (SCR), and heart rate (HR) were taken. The positive conditioned stimulus (CS+) was the

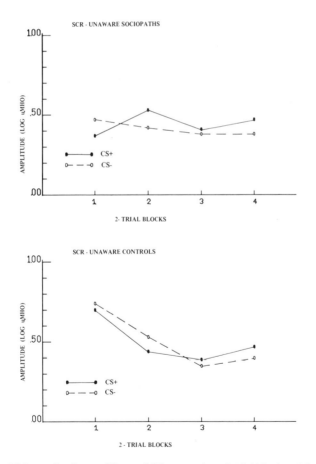

FIG. 1. Mean SCR amplitudes to CS+ and CS− over four 2-trial blocks of the acquisition series for unaware sociopaths and controls ($N = 8$/data point).

letter series 00000 (or NNNNN), whereas the unpaired conditioned stimulus (CS−) was the letter series NNNNN (or 00000). The unconditioned stimulus (UCS) was a 95-dB tone presented via biaural insert earphones. CS duration was 500 msec, and the CS-UCS onset-to-onset interval was 2.0 sec.

Initially the CS+ and the CS− were presented four times each in random order. Then 40 conditioning trials were presented, 20 trials each of the CS+ and CS−. The CS+ was followed by the UCS in 12 trials, whereas the remaining 8 CS+ trials served as test trials. The CS− was never followed by the UCS.

The subject's awareness of the CS-UCS contingency was assessed immediately after the last trial. Subjects were asked first if they could at any time predict when the tone would occur. Then they were asked to rate

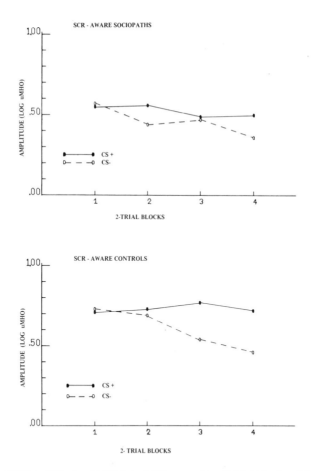

FIG. 2. Mean SCR amplitudes to CS+ and CS− over four 2-trial blocks of the acquisition series for aware sociopaths and controls ($N = 8$/data point).

the extent to which the UCS followed the CS+ and CS− using a 7-point scale. The results for the two questions were essentially the same, and on the basis of the combined score subjects were separated into aware and not aware subgroups.

Trace presentation of the CS and partial reinforcement of the CS+ resulted in verbal awareness of the CS-UCS contingency in approximately one-half of the sociopaths and controls. No significant differences in the number of aware subjects were found between sociopaths and controls, or between younger and older subjects.

Figure 1 shows the SCR data for unaware sociopaths and controls over the four 2-trial blocks. Each data point represents the averaged SCR data over eight subjects for the CS+ (*solid line*) and the CS− (*dotted line*).

As is evident from the curves, neither unaware sociopaths nor unaware controls showed differential SCR conditioning. Also there were no significant differences in overall SCR amplitude between the groups.

Figure 2 shows the corresponding averaged SCR data for eight aware sociopaths and eight aware controls. It is evident that a differential, conditioned SCR develops for controls over the trial blocks. The sociopaths, who were also able to verbalize the differential CS-UCS contingencies, did not show a significant differential electrodermal response. *Thus for the sociopaths there was a dissociation between verbal or cognitive learning of the stimulus-stimulus contingency and a physiological manifestation of that learning. In other words, the data indicate that sociopaths do have a deficiency in aversive conditioning, at least for electrodermal responses.*

EXPERIMENT 2

In Experiment 2 we attempted to assess aversive conditioning in sociopaths who have undergone various degrees of spontaneous remission of their sociopathic behavioral traits. It is well known that sociopaths tend to undergo spontaneous remission at midlife. In our series, this was true of approximately 50% of the subjects. It is our thinking that perhaps the percentage of remissions would have been higher if many sociopaths at this time in life had not so ruined themselves (by the use of drugs and alcohol and by excessive prison sentences, including solitary confinement) that remissions were not possible. Since recidivism is rather characteristic of sociopaths, the opportunity to examine individuals who have undergone spontaneous remission presents special experimental opportunities. We hypothesized that sociopaths in full remission of their symptoms would show no deficiency in aversive conditioning and would thus be comparable to normal subjects. Sociopaths who are currently manifesting all the requisite traits should, on the other hand, display deficient aversive conditioning similar to that reported previously.

As indicated in the first experiment, we found that awareness was a critical variable and that only aware sociopaths and controls yielded significant differences. Since only half of the subjects in the first study showed awareness of the relationship between CS+ and UCS, we decided to enhance the frequency of occurrence of awareness by modifying the conditioning procedure. The major modifications involved 100% reinforcement of the CS+ rather than 60% reinforcement, and separation of the habituation and acquisition phases. The CS+ was a visually presented square and the CS− was a triangle. Each was presented for 500 msec. The CS-UCS interval was 4 sec and the UCS was again a 95-dB tone presented via insert earphones. Habituation consisted of five presentations each of the CS+ and the CS−. Acquisition involved 20 presentations each, although in extinction there were 15 presentations of each CS. Skin resistance was recorded from the nondominant hand throughout the procedure. After the acquisition series, awareness of the CS-UCS contingencies was assessed by a brief questionnaire.

A total of 47 sociopaths were run who met our definition of sociopathy shown in Table 2. This group included all the sociopaths who were examined under the above procedure. They represent a mixed group of sociopaths: those in full activity and those showing varying degrees of improvement; compulsive gambler sociopaths and nongambler sociopaths [some of the compulsive gambler sociopaths were members of Gamblers Anonymous (G.A.) and others were not]; sociopaths who had had previous manic and depressive episodes of the manic-depressive type and those who were examined in these states; subjects who showed awareness of the experimental paradigm and those who did not. Few of the subjects were examined by two independent examiners. The majority were examined and rated on our diagnostic rating scale by either Eugene Ziskind, M.D., or Rodger K. Farr, M.D. Others were examined by Ruth Jens, M.D., or other psychiatrists. A group of 21 controls were also run in the experimental procedure and were found to be free of major clinical abnormalities using the same screening procedures as those employed for sociopaths. Both sociopath and control subjects were noninstitutionalized volunteers.

TABLE 2. *Definition of a sociopath*

Sociopathic traits	Sociopathic exclusions
1. Inability to profit from adverse experiences	1. Mental retardation
2. Superficiality of affect	2. Organic brain syndrome (or demonstrable brain damage)
3. Irresponsibility	3. Psychosis
4. Impairment of conscience	4. Neurosis
5. Implusiveness	5. Situational maladjustments

A sociopath is an individual whose behavior is asocial or antisocial, who manifests the above five traits and does not manifest the five exclusions.

Figure 3 shows averaged first-interval SCR data for the 47 sociopaths and the 21 controls. No significant differences were found between SCRs to the CS+ or CS− during the habituation (HABIT.) series for either group. During the conditioning series of trials, differential SCRs to the CS+ and CS− developed over the first 10 trial pairs in the two groups. Thus in this group of subjects, there were no significant differences in acquisition of a differentially conditioned electrodermal response among sociopaths and controls.

Significant differences between the sociopaths and controls, however, emerged with continued reinforcement of the CS+ during the latter 10 trial pairs of the conditioning series. Control subjects continued to show a signifi-

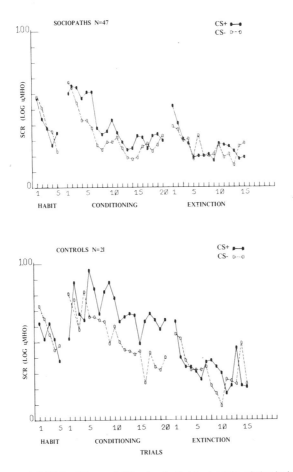

FIG. 3. First-interval SCR to CS+ and CS− for individual trials of the habituation, conditioning, and extinction phases in sociopaths and controls. The divergence between the curves for CS+ and CS− during the conditioning phase indicates differential conditioning of the SCR.

cant differential conditioned electrodermal response throughout the conditioning series. Sociopaths, on the other hand, showed rapid habituation of the conditioned response over the latter portions of the conditioning series, in spite of continued reinforcement of the CS+.

A repeated measures analysis of variance for the SCRs to the CS+ and CS— during the 20 trials of the conditioning series showed main effects for groups, trials, and stimuli and a significant groups × stimuli interaction. Further tests showed that controls had significantly larger SCR amplitudes overall than sociopaths; that there was a significant conditioning effect (SCRs for CS+ greater than SCRs for CS—) for both groups within the second 5-trial block (i.e., trials 6 to 10); that both sociopaths and controls showed a significant decrease in SCR amplitude over the 20 trials; and that only controls showed a significant conditioning effect over trials 11 to 20.

The groups did not differ in second-interval SCR amplitudes or in skin conductance level. More importantly, no significant differences were found among the two groups in SCRs to the UCS, nor in the rate of habituation of SCRs to the UCS. No significant differences were found among the groups during the extinction series.

We interpret these data as partial disconfirmation of our hypothesis of poorer conditioning in sociopaths since sociopaths did not show significant differences from controls in initial acquisition of a conditioned electrodermal response. Thus we failed to confirm the results of Experiment 1 in initial acquisition of a conditioned electrodermal response. We are currently exploring the possibility that poor acquisition of a conditioned electrodermal response in sociopaths may be related to the difficulty of the conditioning procedure. The procedure used in Experiment 1 was quite difficult and resulted in awareness of the CS-UCS contingency in only 50% of the subjects. The current procedure resulted in contingency awareness in over 78% of the subjects. Thus sociopaths may show poor acquisition of a conditioned response in a difficult conditioning procedure. It remains to be shown whether both poor conditioning in a difficult procedure and poor retention in a simple procedure can be demonstrated in the same group of sociopaths. If so, we may be tapping different manifestations of the same general conditioning deficit in sociopaths.

The experiment shows a statistically significant impairment in conditionability, namely, a failure to maintain the initial acquisition of the conditioning while the aversive stimuli are still being applied. This is a circumstance that fits in with our hypothesis that there is a deficit in conditionability. The deficit is manifested by a developing habituation of the conditioned response while the aversive UCS is still being applied. A change toward "normal" conditioning with ACTH 4–10 (or Org 2766) would establish a rational basis for a potentially adequate therapy.

That there is a difference in conditionability in sociopaths as compared to normals is demonstrated in our last experiments. Should the oral ACTH fragment Org 2766 still not be available, the rationale for such therapy would be enhanced if a correlation between the degree of recidivism and the deficiency in conditionability could be demonstrated.

Currently we have still not examined the number of compulsive gambler sociopaths with the best remissions (5 to 15 years of abstinence) to contrast with our gambling sociopaths. We hope to have the data at a later time.

Independent of the correlation of remission and recidivism, we have demonstrated a difference in conditionability between sociopaths and controls. This warrants a trial at therapy with Org 2766 whenever this drug becomes available to us.

EXPERIMENT 3

Experiment 3 employed a cognitive conditioning procedure conducted with 11 acute sociopaths and 11 normal controls matched for age, sex (male), and race (Caucasian). The procedure is a semantic conditioning paradigm used extensively in research on normal populations (8).

Briefly, the procedure involved random presentation of neutral, pleasant, and unpleasant words, each paired with a nonsense syllable. One nonsense syllable was consistently paired with pleasant words, whereas another was consistently paired with unpleasant words. Four other nonsense syllables were randomly paired with neutral words. Following presentations of a series of the word-nonsense syllable pairs, subjects were asked to rate the nonsense syllables on a 7-point scale of pleasantness-unpleasantness and then to explain why the ratings were made. Conditioning was defined as correctly rating the pleasantness of the nonsense syllable paired with pleasant words or rating the unpleasantness of the syllable paired with unpleasant words. Awareness was measured separately from conditioning by noting whether correct ratings were associated with appropriate verbalizations on why the ratings were made as they were. Subjects were categorized as showing conditioning or not, and as showing conditioning with or without awareness.

We found that sociopaths showed a lower incidence of conditioning (6/11) than controls (9/11), although this difference was not quite significant. When awareness was considered, sociopaths (4/11) showed a significantly ($p < 0.05$) lower incidence of conditioning with awareness than controls (9/11).

These results appear to indicate that some sociopaths showed conditioning and were not aware. This is suggested by the fact that the relative frequency of sociopaths showing conditioning is greater than the relative frequency of sociopaths reported to be aware. Therefore, some unaware sociopaths show conditioning. This finding is contrary to what the control subjects show and contrary to what the studies with college students show that attempt to determine whether their subjects are aware or not (1). A number of interpretations of this finding of conditioning in some unaware sociopaths are possible. Either the sociopaths were not being truthful and were denying that they were aware or they could not verbalize their awareness. The final possibility is that we have in fact found instances of cognitive conditioning in sociopaths in the absence of awareness.

CONCLUSION

We now have presented three experiments that showed differences in conditionability in sociopaths and matched controls. Additionally, studies are in progress to ascertain if active sociopaths and those who are in spontaneous remission show differences in conditionability. The present group contrasts acute compulsive gambler sociopaths with sociopaths in Gamblers Anonymous who have had 5 to 15 years of abstinence from gambling. On this same population we will ascertain if there is a correlation between the defect in conditionability and the degree of recidivism.

However, the time appears to be ripe for a therapeutic trial with the oral preparation of the ACTH fragment (Org 2766) to note its effect on sociopaths.

The evidence for central nervous system pathways mediating aversive and classic conditioning and their control by fragments of synthetic ACTH is so compelling that the claim that recidivist behavior of the sociopath must be explained on a chemical basis is the logical conclusion. Its actual demonstration in treatment with the appropriate chemicals represents the only proof. No amount of exhortation, no matter how loud, is a substitute — any more than all the "heuristic evidence" for the etiologic relationship of atrophy of the islet of Langerhans to diabetes was an adequate answer to that question. The logic was correct and it required only the experimental know-how of Banting and Best, the discoverers of insulin, to prove it. Does the same situation obtain for the chemical basis for sociopathy? It would seem that only the appropriate chemotherapeutic experiment should be necessary as proof. We hope the oral preparation Org 2766 will soon be available for a clinical trial.

ACKNOWLEDGMENTS

This research was supported in part by the generous support of the Andrew Norman Foundation.

REFERENCES

1. Brewer, W. F. (1974): There is no convincing evidence for operant or classical conditioning in adult humans. In: *Cognition and the Symbolic Processes,* edited by W. B. Weimer and D. S. Palermo, Lawrence Erlbaum Associates, New York.

2. de Wied, D. (1974): Pituitary-adrenal system hormones and behavior. In: *The Neuro-sciences – Third Study Program,* edited by F. O. Schmitt and F. G. Worden, pp. 653–666. MIT Press, Cambridge.
3. Hare, R. D. (1970): *Psychopathy: Theory and Research.* John Wiley and Sons, New York.
4. Hare, R. D., and Quinn, M. J. (1971): Psychopathy and autonomic conditioning. *J. Abnorm. Psychol.,* 77:223–235.
5. Lykken, D. T. (1957): A study of anxiety in sociopathic personality. *J. Abnorm. Psychol.,* 52:629–634.
6. Parker, D. A., Syndulko, K., Maltzman, I., Jens, R., and Ziskind, E. (1974): Orienting and habituation in sociopathic and normal subjects. *Psychophysiology,* 11:224.
7. Schmauk, F. J. (1969): A study of the relationship between kinds of punishment, autonomic arousal, subjective anxiety, and avoidance learning in the primary sociopath. Doctoral dissertation, Temple University, Philadelphia.
8. Staats, C. K., and Staats, A. W. (1957): Meaning established by classical conditioning. *J. Exp. Psychol.,* 54:74–80.
9. Syndulko, K., Parker, D. A., Jens, R., Maltzman, I., and Ziskind, E. (1975): Psychophysiology of sociopathy: Electrocortical measures. *Biol. Psychol.,* 3:185–200.
10. Syndulko, K., Parker, D., Maltzman, I., Jens, R., and Ziskind, E. (1974): The CNV and visual AEP in sociopathic and normal subjects. *Psychophysiology,* 11:237.
11. Syndulko, K., Parker, D., Maltzman, I., Jens, R., and Ziskind, E. (1976): Electrocortical studies in sociopaths. Paper presented at the 1st World Congress of Biological Psychiatry, Buenos Aires, September.
12. Thompson, R. (1963): Thalamic structures critical for retention of an avoidance conditioned response in rats. *J. Comp. Physiol. Psychol.,* 56:261–267.
13. Ziskind, E. (1970a): Do psychophysiological responses in the sociopath explain his difficulty in learning? Society of Psychophysiological Research Workshop, November 19.
14. Ziskind, E. (1970b): The maturational lag hypothesis for sociopaths – some research strategies. Paper presented at the Society of Biological Psychiatry, San Francisco, May.
15. Ziskind, E. (1972): The maturational lag hypothesis for sociopathy. Paper presented at the AAAS Meeting, Washington, D. C., December 26–31.
16. Ziskind, E. (1975): Is sociopathy a neurologic disorder? *Bull. Los Angeles Neurol. Soc.,* 40:124–128.
17. Ziskind, E., Jens, R., Maltzman, I., Parker, D., and Syndulko, K. (1974): Preventive and active treatment of the sociopath. Presented at 1st World Congress of Biological Psychiatry, Buenos Aires.
18. Ziskind, E., Jens, R., Maltzman, I., Parker, D., Slater, G., and Syndulko, K. (1971): Psychophysiological, chemical, and therapeutic research on sociopaths: A search for a homogeneous sociopath population. Excerpta Medica International Congress Series No. 274, 1058–1065, V World Congress of Psychiatry, Mexico City.
19. Ziskind, E., Parker, D., Syndulko, K., Maltzman, I., and Jens, R. (1974): Sociopaths: diagnosis and psychophysiology. Paper presented at American Psychiatry Association, Detroit, May 6–10.

Psychopathology and Brain Dysfunction, edited by C. Shagass, S. Gershon, and A. J. Friedhoff. Raven Press, New York © 1977.

Hereditary Chorea (Huntington's Chorea): A Paradigm of Brain Dysfunction with Psychopathology

John R. Whittier

State of New York Department of Mental Hygiene, Long Island Research Institute, Central Islip, New York 11722

Huntington's disease (HD) is chronic progressive hereditary chorea. It is outstanding by reason of the autosomal dominant mode of inheritance, without sex linkage, and by its occurrence in variant forms. The usual and customary form displays a middle-years onset of chorea with frequent antecedent psychopathology little characterized by dementia until after long course (10 to 15 years). The variants include (a) a first-decade early-onset or childhood variant, with mental retardation, rigidity, seizures, and short course (3 to 5 years); (b) an adult late-onset variant primarily with chorea, which may be minimal or dramatic in severity, and little dementia; and (c) a variant with rigidity and hypokinesia, little or no chorea, and often little psychopathology (Westphal variant).

Purposes of this article are three: (a) to focus on psychopathological characteristics of HD in its usual and variant forms, taking the heuristic position that the disease is without the remarkable neurologic motor feature of chorea, or those features of dysarthria, dysphagia, other pseudo-bulbar symptoms, ataxia, disturbances of ocular function, dysphasia, dyspraxia, epilepsy, and bulimia, any of which may appear in a formulary of symptoms in individuals affected; (b) to review brain dysfunction in HD; and (c) to attempt some correlations.

What would appear as psychopathological symptoms manifesting brain dysfunction in the usual and variant forms, and to what pathological changes might these be ascribed?

Some comments are in order concerning the title of this volume, *Psychopathology and Brain Dysfunction.* Semantics should forever be a proper concern for anyone interested in the neuraxis and behavior. From Crookshank (4) in the last supplement to Ogden and Richards' classic (pp. 337–355) on "The Meaning of Meaning," "In modern Medicine this tyranny of names is no less pernicious than in the modern form of scholastic realism." Thus, we should all realize that terms "psychopathology" and "brain dysfunction" bear different connotations for each of us and should be accepted

267

warily as concepts serving us for today and subject to revision, clarification, and specification more definitive and hence more generally useful in times to come. "Psychopathology" in this chapter, for example, relates to symptoms and signs, therefore, departures from usual and customary, manifested in behavior, feeling, and thinking. These departures arise from changes in brain tissue function, which can be accepted as "dysfunctional,"* but which by technical advances include not only changes traditionally those of gross and microscopic pathology, but now of ultrastructural and chemical pathology, which for many conditions are in urgent need of integration.

What do we know of the psychopathology in Huntington's disease? Huntington in his eponymic report (12) noted "three marked peculiarities in this disease: 1. Its hereditary nature. 2. A tendency to insanity and suicide. 3. Its manifesting itself as a grave disease only in adult life" (p. 320). Concerning the second "peculiarity," which touches on psychopathology, Huntington (who was 22 years old when he presented his report, subsequently published, before a medical society in Ohio) wrote:

> The tendency to insanity, and sometimes that form of insanity which leads to suicide, is marked. I know of several instances of suicide of people suffering from this form of chorea, or who belonged to families in which the disease existed. As the disease progresses the mind becomes more or less impaired, in many amounting to insanity, while in others mind and body both gradually fail until death relieves them of their sufferings. At present I know of two married men, whose wives are living, and who are constantly making love to some young lady, not seeming to be aware that there is any impropriety in it. They are suffering from chorea to such an extent that they can hardly walk, and would be thought by a stranger to be intoxicated. They are men of about 50 years of age, but never let an opportunity to flirt with a girl go past unimproved. The effect is ridiculous in the extreme.

And that was all Huntington had to say about psychopathology.

Before Huntington and after, psychopathology in HD has merited study, most of which has been limited either by the relatively low prevalence (6 per 100,000 general population) and slow evolution of the disease, and in its usual form, an annoying tendency by affected subjects to migrate away from or outlive interested investigators. Hughes (11) was among early students of the disease in the United States. Her delightful, detailed, and comprehensive survey of 218 Michigan cases showed 172 instances in which early temperamental traits were present in those who developed HD; in 42% of those "the signal characteristic was emotional instability in various degrees; the individuals were easily excited, restless, discontented." Seventy percent of Hughes' cases presented behavior problems after development of the

---

* "Dys-" has enjoyed preference in medicine rather than "mal-," as in dyskinesia, dysdiadochokinesis, and dysplasia, rather than "malkinesia," "maldiadochokinesis," or "malplasia," for reasons perhaps merely euphonious and esoteric. Conversely, why not "dyspractice insurance"?

disease, including such personality changes as aggressiveness, seclusiveness, suspiciousness, and excitability, and conduct disturbances including assaults, suicide and suicidal attempts, alcoholism, drug addiction, and stealing.

Parker (23) commented that "every variety of psychiatric syndrome has been observed in association with Huntington's chorea," and that the only constant feature was deterioration of intelligence in the advanced stages of the disease. He singled out alcoholism, suicide, crime, and unusual fecundity as symptoms worthy of special note.

Brothers (2) paid considerable attention to "mental symptoms" and "psychiatric syndromes" in his series of 312 cases recorded in Victoria, Australia. He stated that the earliest signs and symptoms were usually emotional rather than intellectual. He reported interviewing in detail the relatives of 133 choreics in an effort to determine the early mental signs and symptoms, noting that "lack of insight," akin to denial, was frequently encountered even in early stages of the illness, making patients poor sources of information. Since his report presents probably the largest body of observations on this matter, it is instructive to quote Brothers:

> Irritability, bad temper, "becoming increasingly more and more difficult to live with," violence, excitability and fault-finding were among the most often used descriptions given of early emotional symptoms.
>
> Subtle changes in character which made them "different from their brothers and sisters" were frequently noted by observers. These changes included irresponsibility, excessive alcoholism, erratic behaviour, sexual promiscuity, delinquent behaviour, wandering and purposeless travelling. In 3 families, our informants stressed over-fondness of gaiety and dancing as being characteristic of all females who later developed chorea in their family, whereas this did not apply in the case of the normal siblings.
>
> Early symptoms indicating possible mental deterioration included mental dullness, increasing inefficiency at work, untidiness, loss of interest in the home and family, deterioration of memory, moral blunting and defective judgment.

Heathfield (10) tabulated presenting symptoms in 80 patients, finding them with frequency to be psychiatric in 29 and neurologic in 25. In rank order, the psychiatric symptoms were "personality change, irritable and quarrelsome" (11), "depression" (8), "paranoid delusions" (5), and "anxiety" (4).

Oliver (20) tabulated earliest signs and symptoms of Huntington's disease in 100 patients by three "features" as neurological, social, and psychiatric, listing 60, 38, and 94, respectively. That psychiatric features were most numerous is of interest, and from Oliver's sublisting we can rank order these from "depressive symptoms" as most frequent, through "personality changes," "symptoms characteristic of dementia," "anxiety symptoms," and to "schizophreniform symptoms" as least frequent.

Dewhurst and Oliver (5) cited the prior study of Oliver and Dewhurst (20) in which 20% of 68 cases of HD were "ushered in with a personality disorder," and 15% were first admitted to mental hospitals with this diagnosis. Reviewing conflicting literature, they suggested from somewhat scanty data of their own that "adverse environment factors, rather than a deleterious gene, are more likely to cause a personality disorder."

Mattsson (18), studying 162 patients in Sweden for type of initial symptom, found psychiatric symptoms to be earliest in 78 patients (48%), neurologic in 35 patients (22%), and neurologic combined with psychiatric in 49 (30%). Patients presenting with psychiatric symptoms were thus almost half the total number, and in this 48% classes of presenting symptoms were personality disturbance in 20%, anxiety-depression in 16%, and schizophrenia-paranoia in 12% in Mattsson's series. In more than half the patients the diagnosis at first hospital admission was psychiatric, and in only one-third of the cases was the correct diagnosis established.

At Creedmoor Institute, from 131 charts reviewed for earliest symptoms following Oliver's categories came 101 cases with adequate details in anamnesis. In rank order, these were personality changes, depression, anxiety, and schizophreniform symptoms. Thus, from observations of five reports, arbitrarily categorized, rank order following Oliver's categories was personality change, depressive symptoms, anxiety symptoms, and schizophreniform symptoms.

Garron (9) discussed the suggested relationship between HD and schizophrenia. He reviewed literature and tended to the vexing matter of sequence and type of psychopathology in the two disorders, with reference to behavioral, psychotic without demented, and nonpsychotic and psychotic with demented manifestations:

> . . . There have been frequent descriptions of three kinds of behavioral disorders either coincident with or following the appearance of the chorea. . . . The first set consists of disordered behavior which is attributable to dementia, such as impaired memory, impaired concentration, and confusion. The second set consists of aberrant behavior which is often seen in other conditions involving a general deterioration of the brain, such as emotional lability, euphoria or depression, restlessness or apathy, irritability and self-neglect. The third set consists of behavior which is quite similar to that seen in schizophrenia, such as inappropriate sexual behavior, preoccupation with the imputed sexual misbehavior of others, delusional persecutory beliefs, delusions of grandiosity, and apparent hallucinations. These behaviors often lead to a primary diagnosis of mania, psychotic depression, paranoia, or schizophrenia. Even when the choreic movements are prominent, these accessory signs often lead to a diagnosis of catatonic schizophrenia.

There is a large body of observations and data in German literature, including reports by Panse (22) and Streletzki (28), detailing psychoses with depression or schizophrenia (usually paranoid) preceding onset of chorea.

Concerning suicide, Reed and Chandler (24) supplemented Huntington's observation that "suicide" was a "peculiarity" in hereditary progressive chorea, observing from distribution of suicides among individuals in sib-ships containing a Michigan choreic on April 1, 1940, that proportion of individuals committing suicide was 0.036 and 0.030 for male choreics and female choreics, respectively, contrasting with 0.012 and 0.006 for male and female nonchoreics, respectively.

Tamir et al. (29) from our unit, reporting on observations from 32 patients (19 female and 13 male), observed that there was a difference in certain psychopathologic symptoms between males and females. Males tended to show aggressive and homicidal activity, and females more depression. Although mean age for the two samples was similar, the females showed more severe evidence of the cerebral atrophy—despite the tendency of females in the general population to show greater longevity than males.

Although psychopathology of the early-onset childhood variant is usually retardation, in Markham's (17) series of nine cases of Huntington's disease in childhood (onset age 9 years or below), two were originally diagnosed as schizophrenic.

In the series of thirteen childhood or adolescent cases of HD studied by Dewhurst and Oliver (5) cases included subnormality (five cases), Fried-rich's ataxia (three cases), Sydenham's chorea (two cases), and abnormal personality (three cases). Other conditions they found confused with juve-nile forms included Wilson's disease, the juvenile form of Tay-Sachs' syndrome, postencephalitic parkinsonism, Ramsay-Hunt syndrome, epi-lepsy, behavior disorders, schizophrenia, tics, and habit spasms.

Brief reference should be made to other choreic disorders with brain dysfunction, including nonhereditary senile dementia with chorea, uni-lateral chorea (hemiballism) following lesions in contralateral subthalamic nuclei, experimentally reproducible in monkeys, [Whittier (33)] transient choreas with pregnancy, chorea with rheumatic disease (Syndenham), and hereditary nonprogressive chorea (1). Each of these lacks psychopathology or presents it depending on antecedent or concurrent brain abnormalities unrelated to the chorea.

It is apparent, especially from tabulation of the earliest symptoms and signs drawn from the series of five observers, that psychopathology in HD is almost as characteristic for the disease as is chorea.

Remarkable and perhaps significant for a principle we are approaching in this chapter is a notable absence of certain disease terms from the listing of symptoms or symptom-clusters most frequently cited by observers of early symptoms and signs. These include manic-depressive illness (unipolar or bipolar); neuroses of phobic, hysterical, or obsessive-compulsive type; and psychophysiologic disorders. This is not to say these do not occur, but they are apparently rare. To the extent dysfunctional neural systems in these illnesses differ from systems dysfunctional in HD by a lesser involve-ment of striatal inhibitory tissue, HD might be expected to generate symp-toms of "release" or dysinhibition in the nature of impulsive, erratic, vagabond, alcoholic, promiscuous, exhibitionist, criminal, assaultive, destructive, suicidal, and homicidal behavior.

These symptoms are not necessary in the patterns of psychopathology of HD, and they occur in a host of other disorders without presently demonstrable brain dysfunction. Occurring in HD, however, they suggest dyscontrol arising from progressive loss of inhibitory competence, by the same systems responsible for that progressive loss of inhibitory competence resulting in chorea. Interindividual differences in contributions from genetics, experience, and circumstance understandable from contingency theory of etiology [Whittier (32)] make possible the variants by age at onset of symptoms and ranges of severity for those observed.

Psychopathology in part determined by premorbid personality not necessarily because of the genetic error of HD has been the subject of reports by Werner and Folk (31) and Dewhurst and Oliver (5). Until we are provided with that hypothetical specific metabolic detector test for HD, before neurological signs appear, we must continue to work with the certainty that some at-risk and yet gene-free, hence disease-free direct-line family members are entitled to psychopathology peculiar to their experiences and circumstances. To date, no specific detector test has arisen from the efforts of psychologists using their traditional methods or from psychopharmacologists or neurochemists who, with the aid of a few courageous patients and families, have been manipulating neurotransmitters (such as L-DOPA) or sampling biopsied brain tissue for chemical profiles.

PATHOLOGY

What do we now know of the pathologic changes of brain in HD? Casting back to Huntington's report, we find him stating with candor and succinctness, "I know nothing of its pathology." We have advanced some distance from what was known by George in 1872, and we must review briefly what has been reported, viewed at the several levels of gross, microscopic, ultrastructural, and chemical changes in brain. Slater and Cowie (26) provide a melancholy review of the consistently negative, conflicting, or unresolved observations on chemical changes in any organ, tissue, or body fluid other than brain.

At the level of gross pathology, atrophy of the cerebrum is most striking. This is generalized but primarily the result of shrinking away by striatal tissue (caudate and putamen), and by cerebral cortical tissue in almost all areas except perhaps projections from certain sensory pathways, including acoustic and visual. The shrinkage in adult brains after 10 to 15 years of progression may be profound, and almost equally so in childhood cases with rapid evolution and onset-to-death durations of 5 to 7 years. In coronal section the lateral ventricles enlarge from appropriate clefts to gaping cavities, and thinning of the cerebral gyri open the sulci wide. The caudate-putamen complex practically vanishes.

At the level of microscopic pathology, there is a rather specific atrophy and ultimate disappearance of small-sized neurons or microneurons, 8 to 9 μm in diameter, also known as Golgi type II neurons without long projections, or internuncial neurons, which are normally abundant in striatum and cortex. Their disappearance is accompanied, however, by varying degrees of atrophy and death in larger cells in those structures and in pallidum.

As early as 1914 Kiesselbach (13) noted that small cells carried some special liability in HD. Recently, Dom, working with Baro and co-workers (6,7), has applied elegant cytometric methods to describe the specific anatomic sites and cell types by shape and volume undergoing that atrophy specific for Huntington's disease. His efforts show that microneuronal atrophy, although dramatic in striatum and cerebral cortex, extends to thalamic nuclei as well. In HD the macroneuron population distribution even in thalamus, for example, was quite comparable to the normal distribution, and there was only a slight decrease in cell diameter. The total numerical nerve cell density (amount of neurons per cubic millimeter tissue) in the normal ventral thalamus was 2,221. The numerical macroneuron density was 1,701 whereas the numerical microneuron density was 521. The mean total neuron density for all studied cases of HD was 1,949, and mean macroneuron density was 1,728, whereas the mean microneuron density was only 221. It is pertinent to mention that these microneurons are thought to generate gamma-aminobutyric acid (GABA) and to inhibit neighboring neuronal activity when activated.

Microscopically, several other features are notable. There is an accumulation of the normally occurring lipopigment, lipofuscin (LF), in astonishing amounts. Lipofuscin is not specific for HD, but the rate and amount of its accumulation may be 200% that in age- and sex-matched controls according to Siakotos, working with Zeman (*personal communication*). At Creedmoor we are observing the same phenomenon. LF is a remarkable compound, a polymer of polyunsaturated fatty acids, and perhaps arising from some perturbation of the lysosomes, intracellular ultrastructures filled with hydrolytic enzymes. The lipopigment (LF) accumulates in regions of high oxidative metabolism, eventually filling the cell, resulting in severe disruption of function by reason of its inert nature. Mann and Yates (16) recently came forth with evidence that LF accumulation in human brain was probably responsible for winding down vital RNA conversions. It takes stains for fat and exhibits blue-green autofluorescence under fluorescence microscopy.

Klintworth (15) has reviewed another histological characteristic of HD brain tissue—increased deposition of iron. This, like LF, is nonspecific but so intense as to mean something regarding etiology.

Histologically characteristic also is invasion by astrocytic glial cells, mainly astrocytes, in regions undergoing cell atrophy.

Ultrastructural characteristics noted by Roizin et al. (25), Tellez-Nagel et al. (30), and others include lipofuscinosis and abnormalities in membranes of intracellular organelles.

At the chemical level, interest has arisen in the decrease of amounts of inhibitory neurotransmitters such as GABA, although this is probably a reflection of the atrophy of the microneuron cell type so selectively stricken by the genetic and metabolic error responsible for the disease. Several relevant chapters appear in the book edited by Barbeau et al. (1). An almost unmanageable body of literature has been generated by the tempting contrasts between clinical aspects (hypokinesia, hyperkinesia) in the diseases of Parkinson (PD) and Huntington, and by the chemical observations relating to dysmetabolism of dopamine in PD and of GABA in HD. L-DOPA induced choreoid hyperkinesia in normal experimental animals, and, observed as a common adverse effect of overdosage in treatment of PD, this has induced hypotheses explaining both diseases and schizophrenia as well at the neurotransmitter level. Klawans et al. (14) recently cited pertinent literature and summarized their own views.

Neuronal atrophy responsible for HD appears to precede the dysmetabolic consequences in the several neurotransmitter systems. These latter may then explain, by nuances of difference in anatomic site and in individual differences in kind and dynamics of neurotransmitters, the great variation among patients respecting that psychopathology peculiar to childhood and adult variants of the disease. Enzymes have come under study, particularly the several lysosomal hydrolases, peroxidase, and others responsible for integrity of cellular membranes. In passing, relatively little attention has been paid to dysfunction in structures of the limbic system and of hypothalamus, which lack should be remedied.

Those wishing knowledge concerning pathology of Huntington's disease cannot do better than consult the article by Earle (8), which reviews the literature and offers observations from the Armed Forces Institute of Pathology cases. Earle cited the report by Stone and Falstein (27), which reviewed the world literature on pathology of hereditary chorea from 1841 to 1935, and reported their studies on pathologic changes of 159 cases. Earle tabulated the pathological abnormalities in the 159 cases, and 244 of the 694 abnormalities were attributed to "atrophy or degenerative changes in the neostriatum." Earle concluded that "subsequent studies have added very little to this review except for a better understanding of the rigid form of the disease in juveniles and an awareness that the lesions we see at autopsy are mostly the late effects of a slowly progressive hereditary metabolic defect at the cellular level that probably manifests itself clinically long before the neurons degenerate, disappear, or show any sign of anatomic damage by light microscopy."

Bruyn (3) reviewed pathologic changes in the rigid-hypokinetic (Westphal) and childhood variants and concluded, more or less with Jervis respecting the childhood cases, that these were not remarkably different from those of adult chorea, and that although lesions specific for adult chorea may be more pronounced, with occasional changes in the cerebellum, lateral thalamic nuclei, and dentatorubral tract, no lesions specific for these variants have emerged.

CORRELATIONS

Mettler and his collaborators have been among the most productive in drawing attention to a relation between basal ganglia dysfunction and neurologic or psychiatric disorders. It is pertinent to quote from his report, together with Crandell (19):

> Extrapyramidal and psychiatric dysfunctions may be causally related either to each other . . . or, alternatively, both to some common third factor.
>
> Dysfunction of the striatum results in an inability on the part of an organism to maintain adequate contact with its environment (probably the only entirely satisfactory, irreducible characteristic of a psychotic process, though not of this alone.)
>
> In Huntington's chorea, the striatum is more severely affected than the pallidum and mental deterioration also occurs, but obviously the cellular loss is not confined to the striatum. Still, we know of no neuropathologic state or case in which more than half the striatum of each side has been destroyed in which some mental impairment has not existed.
>
> . . . the process which is interfered with by striatal lesions is one which prepares the organism for somatomotor action, and for this process, akin to the ability which must lie behind the making of a choice, the term prohairesis is offered.
>
> If one includes prohairesis among the signs of extrapyramidal damage a high percentage of functional cases can be considered to display such a defect if indeed it is not a fundamental characteristic of the schizophrenic process.

These quotations, even taken out of the rich context of the particular report appearing midway in a series of publications beginning about 1940, show the relevance of the work of Mettler and his collaborators to the topic of this volume.

If the pathologic changes in HD are relatively site specific (striatal and cerebral cortical), and if they lead to a net reduction or disorganization in function of areas primarily inhibitory, one might expect all those consequences seen in the reported psychopathology typical of the disease reviewed in this chapter. Individual variations in involvement of sites or in onset times for symptoms of behavioral abnormality or of dementia could be expected and do indeed appear in the variants. Remember Freud's suggestion that thinking is trial movement; the progressive failure of inhibitory systems largely concentrated in the striatum would release symptoms controlling affective and intellectual aspects of behavior.

It may be seen that HD offers psychopathology at each end of the human age span, from that peculiar to the early-onset childhood variant with profound dementia, through usual adolescent and adult onset forms with antecedent behavioral and personality disorders, to terminal forms once more with dementia. Chorea is only a dramatic motor abnormality that may indeed be minimal in severity or even absent in childhood and rigid hypokinetic variants. The disease is a paradigm of brain dysfunction with psychopathology that should repay investigational efforts in ways not yet even foreseeable.

ACKNOWLEDGMENTS

The author thanks Charles Korenyi, M.D., Rita Arzt, R.N., and Roslyn Laiterman for assistance in preparing this chapter.

REFERENCES

1. Barbeau, A., Chase, T. N., and Paulson, G. W. (Eds.) (1973): *Advances in Neurology, Vol. 1: Huntington's Chorea 1872–1972*. Raven Press, New York.
2. Brothers, C. R. D. (1964): Huntington's chorea in Victoria and Tasmania. *J. Neurol. Sci.*, 1:405–420.
3. Bruyn, G. W. (1967): The Westphal variant and juvenile type of Huntington's chorea. In: *Progress in Neuro-Genetics, Vol. 1. Proceedings of the 2nd International Congress of Neuro-Genetics and Neuro-Ophthalmology, Montreal*. Excerpta Medica, Amsterdam.
4. Crookshank, F. G. (1938): The importance of a theory of signs and a critique of language in the study of medicine. In: *The Meaning of Meaning: A Study of the Influence of Language upon Thought and of the Science of Symbolism, 5th Ed.*, edited by C. K. Ogden and I. A. Richards. Harcourt, Brace, Jovanovich, New York.
5. Dewhurst, K., and Oliver, J. (1970): Huntington's disease of young people. *Eur. Neurol.*, 3:278–289.
6. Dom, R., Baro, F., and Brucher, J. M. (1973): A cytometric study of the putamen in different types of Huntington's chorea. In: *Advances in Neurology, Vol. 1: Huntington's Chorea, 1872–1972*, edited by A. Barbeau, T. N. Chase, and G. W. Paulson, pp. 369–385. Raven Press, New York.
7. Dom, R., Malfroid, M., and Baro, F. (1976): Neuropathology of Huntington's chorea. *Neurology (Minneap.)*, 26:64–68.
8. Earle, K. M. (1973): Pathology and experimental models of Huntington's chorea. In: *Advances in Neurology, Vol. 1: Huntington's Chorea 1872–1972*, edited by A. Barbeau, T. N. Chase, and G. W. Paulson, pp. 341–351. Raven Press, New York.
9. Garron, D. C. (1973): Huntington's chorea and schizophrenia. In: *Advances in Neurology, Vol. 1: Huntington's Chorea 1872–1972*, edited by A. Barbeau, T. N. Chase, and G. W. Paulson, pp. 729–734. Raven Press, New York.
10. Heathfield, K. W. G. (1967): Huntington's chorea: Investigation into the prevalence of this disease in the area covered by the North East Metropolitan Regional Hospital Board. *Brain*, 90(1):203–232.
11. Hughes, E. M. (1925): Social significance of Huntington's chorea. *Am. J. Psychiatry*, 4:537.
12. Huntington, G. (1872): On chorea. *The Medical and Surgical Reporter*, 26:317–321.
13. Kiesselbach, G. (1914): Anatomischer befund eines falles von Huntingtonscher chorea. *Monatsschr. Psych. Neur.*, 35:525–543.

14. Klawans, H. L., Goetz, C., and Westheimer, R. (1972): Pathophysiology of schizophrenia and the striatum. *Dis. Nerv. Syst.*, 33:711–719.
15. Klintworth, G. K. (1967): Cerebral iron deposition in Huntington's disease. In: *Progress in Neuro-Genetics, Vol. 1*. Proceedings the 2nd International Congress of Neuro-Genetics and Neuro-Ophthalmology of the World Federation of Neurology, Montreal. Excerpta Medica, Amsterdam.
16. Mann, D. M. A., and Yates, P. O. (1974): Lipoprotein pigments—their relationship to ageing in the human nervous system. *Brain*, 97:481–488.
17. Markham, C. H. (1967): Huntington's chorea in childhood. In: *Progress in Neuro-Genetics, Vol. 1*. Proceedings of the 2nd International Congress of Neuro-Genetics and Neuro-Ophthalmology of the World Federation of Neurology, Montreal. Excerpta Medica, Amsterdam.
18. Mattsson, B. (1974): Clinical, genetic and pharmacological studies in Huntington's chorea: Huntington's chorea in Sweden. II. Social and clinical data. *Umea Univ. Med. Dissertations*, 7:33–51.
19. Mettler, F. A., and Crandell, A. (1959): Relation between Parkinsonism and psychiatric disorder. *J. Nerv. Ment. Dis.*, 129:551–563.
20. Oliver, J. E. (1970): Huntington's chorea in Northamptonshire. *Br. J. Psychiatry*, 116:241–253.
21. Oliver, J. E., and Dewhurst, K. E. (1969): Six generations of ill-used children in a Huntington's pedigree. *Postgrad. Med. J.*, 45:757–760.
22. Panse, F. (1942): *Die Erbchorea*. G. Thieme, Leipzig.
23. Parker, N. (1958): Observations on Huntington's chorea based on a Queensland survey. *Med. J. Aust.*, 1:351–359.
24. Reed, T. E., and Chandler, J. H. (1958): Huntington's chorea in Michigan. I. Demography and genetics. *Am. J. Hum. Genet.*, 10(2):201–225.
25. Roizin, L., Nishikawa, K., Koizumi, J., and Kloseian, S. (1967): The fine structure of the multivesicular constituents of the central nervous system. *J. Neuropathol. Exp. Neurol.*, 26:223–249.
26. Slater, E., and Cowie, V. (Eds.) (1971): *The Genetics of Mental Disorders*. Oxford University Press, London.
27. Stone, T. T., and Falstein, E. I. (1938): Pathology of Huntington's chorea. *J. Nerv. Ment. Dis.*, 88:602–626.
28. Streletzki, F. (1961): Psychosen im verlauf der Huntingtonschen chorea unter besonderer berucksichtigung der wahnbildunger. *Arch. Psychiatr. Nervenkr.*, 202:202–214.
29. Tamir, A., Whittier, J., and Korenyi, C. (1969): Huntington's chorea: A sex difference in psychopathological symptoms. *Dis. Nerv. Syst.*, 30:103.
30. Tellez-Nagel, I., Johnson, A., and Terry, R. D. (1974): Studies on brain biopsies of patients with Huntington's chorea. *J. Neuropathol. Exp. Neurol.*, 33(2):308–332.
31. Werner, A., and Folk, J. J. (1969): Manifestations of neurotic conflict in Huntington's chorea. *Psychiatry Digest*, 86.
32. Whittier, J. R. (1961): Etiology: Theory and practice. *Psychosomatics*, 11(4).
33. Whittier, J. R., and Mettler, F. A. (1949): Studies on the subthalamus of the rhesus monkey. I. Anatomy and fiber connections of the subthalamic nucleus of Luys. II. Hyperkinesia and other physiologic effects of subthalamic lesions, with special reference to the subthalamic nucleus of Luys. *J. Comp. Neurol.*, 90:281–372.

Psychopathology and Brain Dysfunction, edited
by C. Shagass, S. Gershon, and A. J. Friedhoff.
Raven Press, New York © 1977.

A Genetic Study of Average Evoked Response Augmentation/Reduction in Affective Disorders

*E. S. Gershon and **M. S. Buchsbaum

*Department of Research, Jerusalem Mental Health Center, Ezrath Nashim,
Jerusalem, Israel; and **Adult Psychiatry Branch, National Institute of Mental
Health, Bethesda, Maryland 20014

INTRODUCTION

A role of heredity in primary affective disorder is supported by the excessively high rates of illness in persons with a genetic relationship to known patients and by twin studies as reviewed elsewhere (16,17). However, the clinically variable expression of the disorder and difficulties in identification of mildly affected relatives have made it very difficult to specify the mode of inheritance. A most important investigative strategy is identification of the "affective genotype" (or genotypes) on the basis of neurophysiological, biochemical, pharmacological, or other characteristics of persons and their relatives with the disorder. Such a biological indicator of a genetically determined vulnerability to affective illness would at least (a) distinguish persons with affective illness from normal controls, (b) be a heritable and stable individual characteristic, and (c) be demonstrable in the well state (thus capable of being evaluated in both remitted patients and asymptomatic relatives).

If, in addition, within families of patients with affective disorders, ill relatives share the biological indicator with the proband but well relatives do not, there is a strong suggestion that a single genetic diathesis is controlling both the illness and the biological indicator. This indicator thus identifies the genotype. However, if this is not so, then the genetic role of the indicator may be more complex, and many interpretations are possible.

A measure based on the visual average evoked response (AER) and its change with increasing intensity appears to meet the first three criteria. Several studies have now indicated that patients with affective disorders show greater rates of increase in AER amplitude (augmenting) for component P100–N140 than do matched normal controls (2,5,6), and unipolar patients may show lesser rates of increase or even amplitude decreases (reducing) (6). The slope of the AER amplitude/intensity function has been found to be a relatively stable individual trait (5,31,32). Amplitude/intensity slopes are partly set genetically (4), as has been found of AER waveform shape in animals (8) and in man (11,23,27,30,35). AER slope also appears to be relatively independent of the level of depression or mania (5). These findings suggest that the amplitude/intensity slope might serve as a marker for a genetically transmitted vulnerability to affective disorders.

METHODS

Population Studied

The Jerusalem Mental Health Center, Ezrath Nashim, admits patients from all levels of social class and ethnicity of the Jewish population of Jerusalem, as described elsewhere (14). During months when the unit is admitting, all patients admitted to the Jerusalem Mental Health Center are screened and offered admission to a research unit if they meet criteria for primary affective disorder. The diagnostic criteria for primary affective disorder followed those of Robins and Guze (28) and Feighner et al. (12) with minor modifications—patients with preexisting personality disorders who developed affective disorder were included.

Patients with a history of mania (12) or hypomania were diagnosed as bipolar; otherwise the diagnosis was unipolar.

All relatives of patients included in evoked response data were evaluated with systematic interviews for psychiatric diagnosis (19).

Psychiatric syndromes that are more frequent in relatives of persons with affective disorders than in relatives of controls are defined as "related disorders." In the current population these include neurotic depression, cyclothymic personality, and persons with a single episode of acute psychosis in their lifetimes to which a specific diagnosis could not be applied (19). These relatives were grouped with the unipolar and bipolar family members in genetic comparisons.

Controls were drawn from members of the hospital staff who were free of psychiatric illness and who did not have a known family history of psychiatric illness. Patients and ill relatives were examined at varying phases of illness or recovery while off all psychoactive or antihypertensive medication.

Evoked Response

Visual evoked responses were studied at three stimulus intensities. Stimuli were presented to subjects sitting with eyes closed in a darkened room using a Grass PS-2 photostimulator at intensity setting 16 at 1.2 m from their eyes. Intensity was controlled with neutral density filters of 0, 0.5, and 1.0 optical density, with the filters interposed in a randomized sequence of 15 flashes at 2-sec intervals. Sixty-five flashes at each intensity were presented. EEG was recorded between electrodes 3 cm posterior to vertex in the midline and right ear, amplified (0.3 and 100 Hz passband), and digitized at 500 Hz. AER was averaged separately on line for each intensity. Data were analyzed subsequently using a Geoscience Systems Med Lab-1 computer system. The amplitude between P100 (positive peak 50 to 125 msec) and N140 (negative peak 90 to 175 msec) was measured for each AER and the least-squares regression slope of the amplitude/intensity function calculated. Amplitude/intensity slopes are presented in arbitrary units [microvolts/(log optical density $\times$ 0.0576)].

Genetic Analysis

The offspring-mid-parent covariance was computed using the formula of Crow and Kimura (9). This was divided by the square root of the product of parent variance and offspring variance to get the offspring-mid-parent correlation, and by the parent variance to get the regression of offspring on mid-parents. All other correlations between relatives are intraclass correlation coefficients, calculated and tested for significance according to McNemar (26).

RESULTS

Comparison of Patients and Controls

Patients with primary affective disorders had greater increases in AER amplitude with increasing intensity (augmentation) than controls (Table 1).

TABLE 1. *AER amplitude/intensity slope in patients with primary affective disorder and controls*

	Male			Female		
	Mean	SE	N	Mean	SE	N
Patients	0.31	±0.07	17	0.30	±0.09	34
Controls	0.14	±0.07	23	0.08	⊥0.06	31

Analysis of variance:	Sum of squares	df	Mean square	F
Diagnosis	0.941	1	0.941	5.84[a]
Sex	0.031	1	0.031	0.19
Interaction	0.011	1	0.011	0.07
Within cells	16.261	101	0.161	

[a] $p < 0.05$.

TABLE 2. *AER amplitude/intensity slope in unipolar and bipolar patients*

	Male			Female		
	Mean	SE	N	Mean	SE	N
Bipolar	0.32	±0.06	14	0.31	±0.01	25
Unipolar	0.29	±0.23	3	0.26	±0.17	9
Analysis of variance:						
	Sum of squares	df		Mean square		F
Bipolar/unipolar	0.0121	1		0.012		0.06
Sex	0.0016	1		0.002		0.01
Interaction	0.0003	1		0.000		0.000
Within cells	9.97831	47		0.212		

All variance ratios are not significant.

Thus our AER measure meets the first criterion of distinguishing persons with affective illness from normal controls. No significant differences between men and women were observed; nor did we find a significant sex by diagnostic group interaction. Across the entire group, the correlation between AER slope and age was 0.097 (ns). Although bipolar patients did show slightly higher AER slopes than unipolar patients, which was consistent with earlier reports (6), these differences were not statistically significant (Table 2).

Correlation Between Relatives

Siblings tended to have similar AER amplitude-intensity slopes; intraclass correlations were 0.30 ($p < 0.05$) for offspring of patients and of controls and 0.29 for patients, controls, and their siblings (ns) (Table 3). The offspring-mid-parent correlation was −0.08, suggesting no observable additive genetic effects and possibly no epistatic effects. Heritability in the narrow sense (additive genic variance as a proportion of total phenotypic variance) may be approximated as twice the parent-offspring correlation—in this case negligible. However, heritability in the broad sense (including dominance and other factors) can be estimated from the sibling-sibling correlation. In the broad sense, AER slope thus appears heritable and fulfills our second criterion. A precise estimate of heritability cannot be made from these data because of the restricted range of AER slope values from which our data are drawn.

Assortative mating is suggested by the significant correlation ($r = 0.32$) between patients, controls, and their spouses. The correlation between parents was lower ($r = 0.18$) but was based on only 10 pairs.

TABLE 3. *Amplitude/intensity slope correlations between relatives*

1. Parents and offspring	
Covariance offspring-mid-parent	−0.02
Parent-offspring correlation	−0.08
Number of pairs	28
Number of offspring	54
2. Patients, controls, and their siblings	
Sibling-sibling correlation	0.29[a]
Number of siblings	23
Number of individuals	50
3. Patients, controls, and their spouses	
Correlation	0.32[b]
Number of families	32
Number of individuals	65
4. Offspring of patients and controls	
Offspring-offspring correlation	0.30[b]
Number of families	19
Number of individuals	50
5. Parents of patients and controls	
Parent-parent correlation	0.18
Number of parent pairs	10

[a] $p = 0.06$.
[b] $p = 0.05$.

Comparison of Well and Ill Members of Families of Patients

If the amplitude/intensity slope is by itself a genetic factor in affective illness, in any family, the persons with high amplitude/intensity slopes should be the persons with affective disorder. For these comparisons, relatives include parents, sibs, or offspring of probands. Within the probands' families, the well and ill relatives were not different (Table 4). Similar results were found for comparisons of all first-degree relatives in families in which two or more persons were observed in each category (ill and well) using a two-way analysis of variance (Table 5).

The fact that AER slope did not differ between well and ill relatives suggests that AER slope and affective disorders are not transmitted solely by a single genetic factor. That is, there appears to be independent assortment within families of the two characteristics, affective disorder and AER.

Even though AER slope and affective disorders do not appear to be transmitted by a single genetic factor, the AER may still be related to genetic vulnerability. This is suggested by the finding that the well relatives of probands with affective illness had significantly higher amplitude/intensity slopes (mean = 0.33) than normal controls (mean = 0.11, difference significant by t-test, $p < 0.005$). This was true both of well family members from families of bipolar probands (mean = 0.32) and of unipolar probands (mean = 0.40), and both comparisons were significantly different from normal ($p < 0.01$).

TABLE 4. *Assortment of evoked response amplitude/intensity slopes in families of patients with primary affective illness*

Family	Mean for well persons	N	Mean for ill persons	N	Proband diagnosis
2	0.522	5	0.375	2	BPI
3	0.430	2	0.790	1	UP
4	0.300	1	0.638	2	BPI
6	0.470	2	0.700	1	BPI
8	0.915	2	0.590	1	BPI
9	0.414	2	0.820	2	BPI
12	0.178	1	0.520	2	BPI
13	0.637	1	−0.130	1	UP
15	0.120	2	0.705	1	BPI
17	−0.073	1	0.655	2	UP
19	0.270	2	0.450	2	BPII
21	0.685	2	1.256	1	BPI
26	−0.350	2	0.040	1	BPI
27	−0.040	1	−0.080	1	BPI
28	0.574	3	0.685	2	UP
32	−0.110	1	−0.043	3	UP
34	−0.353	1	0.476	1	BPI
35	0.828	2	0.000	1	UP
39	1.380	1	0.660	1	BPI
41	0.030	1	−0.020	2	BPI
45	−0.005	2	0.117	1	BPI
48	0.122	2	0.135	2	BPI
49	−0.215	2	0.015	2	BPI
52	0.643	1	0.530	1	UP
53	0.336	1	0.357	1	BPI
54	0.785	2	0.360	1	BPI
56	1.029	3	−0.625	1	BPI
61	0.142	1	0.793	2	UP
65	0.136	1	0.470	3	BPI
67	−0.144	1	0.139	2	BPII
68	0.335	2	0.067	2	BPI
71	0.644	3	0.760	1	BPI
72	0.293	4	0.710	1	BPI
73	−0.145	2	−0.105	2	BPI
75	−0.039	1	0.420	1	BPI
77	−0.220	1	−0.150	2	BPI
81	0.280	1	−0.420	1	BPI
82	−0.150	1	0.430	2	BPI
86	−0.330	1	−0.130	1	UP
89	0.100	1	−0.005	2	BPI
91	0.120	1	−0.210	1	BPI
92	0.360	2	0.420	1	BPII
94	0.443	2	0.290	1	BPI
96	0.470	1	0.110	1	UP

Mean $\pm$ SEM: well persons, 0.269 ± 0.59; ill persons, 0.310 ± 0.058. Difference $= 0.0417 \pm 0.4736$; paired $t = 0.584$ (ns); df $= 43$.

TABLE 5. *Comparison of well and ill relatives — two-way analysis of variance*

Source of variance	df	Variance	F
Families	7	0.368	2.561
Diagnosis	1	0.042	0.294
Interaction	7	0.048	0.335
Within cells	20	0.144	

Families were included in this analysis if there were two or more persons observed in each of the two diagnostic categories, ill (unipolar, bipolar, or related disorders) and well (any other diagnosis).

DISCUSSION

The results of this study confirm earlier reports of (a) AER differences between patients with affective disorders and normal controls, and (b) the heritability of AER augmenting/reducing (amplitude/intensity slope differences). Thus, our first two criteria for selecting a biological measure as a marker of genetic vulnerability were met. However, the finding that both patients and "well" relatives of the patients had higher AER augmenting suggests that a single genetic diathesis cannot produce by itself both affective illness and AER augmenting, and more complex genetic relationships may be present. One possibility is that AER augmenting predisposes to affective illness only in conjunction with a second genetic or environmental factor. Alternatively, since the heritability of the AER slope does not appear large, the high AER slopes seen in the probands and their families may result from common familial environmental factors.

It has been previously found that there is a significant correlation in AER augmenting/reducing between monozygotic (MZ) twins and very low correlation between dizygotic (DZ) twins (4). Other investigators studying amplitude measures in the visual AER have reported similar results (23). In our own data, the correlations between siblings are slightly higher than the previously reported correlations between DZ twins. Osborne (27) also found very low (0.08 to 0.12) intraclass correlations in DZ twins for certain AER frequency parameters, together with much higher (0.30 to 0.60) correlations in MZ twins. Both EEG power spectra and evoked potential waveform are usually strikingly similar in MZ twins. Lykken, Tellegen, and Thorkelson (24) found intraclass correlations for EEG power spectra estimates of approximately 0.8 in MZ twins and nearly 0.0 in DZ twins. These findings suggest that the similarities between MZ twins are not primarily owing to additive genic or dominance effects, since such effects would create similarities between DZ twins also. A possible genetic mechanism that would produce similarities in MZ twins but not in other relationships is epistasis or dominance interactions involving several loci.

The probability of DZ twins having N loci identical by descent is $(1/2)^n$, whereas the probability for MZ twins is 1. Thus, for example, if the expression of phenotypes were dependent on a four-locus interaction, nearly all $(15/16)$ of DZ twins would be dissimilar. Disassortative mating is another mechanism that would make MZ twins alike and DZ twins heterogeneous, but our evidence suggests that assortative mating occurs instead.

Do such genetic effects appear in twin and family studies of affective illness? Two relatively recent studies (1,21) indicate concordance rates of 67 and 33% for MZ twins and 5 and 0% for DZ twins. A summary of twin studies by Gershon et al. (16) finds an overall concordance rate across six studies of 67% for MZ twins and only 13% for DZ twins. This MZ concordance is higher than expected for single-locus inheritance but is compatible with multifactorial inheritance (25) and with complex interactions involving several loci. Environmental factors may also act to increase the similarity of MZ twins for affective disorder or for AER variables, as discussed by Rosenthal (29).

In the current AER data, the additive genic variance of AER slope may be estimated from the offspring-mid-parent correlation, and is approximately zero. The correlation between siblings is higher. It appears that the genetic component in sibling-sibling correlation is attributable to factors such as dominance, interactive dominance between loci, and assortative mating. All these factors would increase the similarity between siblings without affecting the offspring-mid-parent correlation. The selection of subjects for sibling-sibling correlation largely from persons with affective disorders and their sibs may also have resulted in finding a greater correlation than is generally present, since the subjects in the correlation are selected from two ends of the range of AER slopes.

The presence of assortative mating for augmenting/reducing is of interest because of reports of assortative mating for affective disorders (18). It suggests that personality correlates of augmenting/reducing are expressed in the choice of a spouse. Zuckerman et al. (37) reported that AER augmenters scored high on the Disinhibition Subscale of the Sensation Seeking Scale. The positive items on this subscale are strikingly reminiscent of mania and hypomania including items such as "I like to gamble for money," "I like wild uninhibited parties," and "I often like to get high." Among college students, high scorers on the Sensation Seeking Scale also show high scores on the MMPI Hypomania (Ma) scale (36). AER augmenters received high neuroticism scores on the Eysenck Personality Inventory, and reducers scored significantly higher-than-normal pain threshold and tolerance levels in studies on depressed patients in Sweden (34). Studies in cats correlated behaviors of intrusiveness, curiosity, and increased activity with increased AER amplitude/intensity slopes (20). These factors may be related to behavior in the manic patient as well as to the personality style in the well state.

The lower amount of assortative mating in the parental than proband generation could reflect the great social and cultural changes experienced in Israel and their concurrent impact on spouse selection. The proband generation had more affectively ill individuals, however, and thus might use different criteria for spouse selection.

The absence of sex differences in this population may be of interest, as suggested elsewhere in this volume by J. Stevens. In our laboratory in Bethesda we have almost invariably found females to have higher amplitudes and amplitude/intensity slopes for visual stimuli (e.g., 6). In recent unpublished studies in which both visual and auditory stimuli were given in a randomly intermixed sequence, females showed significantly greater amplitude/intensity slopes for visual but not auditory stimuli for component P100, comparable to the P100–N140 component reported here.

The minimal AER differences found in this study between unipolar and bipolar patients parallel the findings using other biological variables in Jerusalem. The activity of erythrocyte catechol-O-methyl-transferase (COMT) distinguishes persons with mood disorders from controls in several studies (3,7,10,13), although the direction of abnormality in patients with affective disorder is not the same in all investigations. In the United States bipolar and unipolar women differed in their COMT activity (10), but in Israel there were no demonstrable unipolar-bipolar differences (13). Family studies in Israel showed higher prevalence of bipolar illness in the relatives of unipolar patients than had been reported elsewhere (19). Thus, family history, evoked potential, and erythrocyte COMT studies all suggest that unipolar and bipolar probands are more similar in this population than in other populations studied.

These similarities suggest that a single underlying diathesis might account for both disorders in this population, and that the differences in morbid risk in relatives and in pharmacologic response that are found between unipolar and bipolar patients may reflect quantitative differences in the single underlying diathesis, rather than qualitatively different disorders (15,16). Genetic models based on a single underlying liability to the affective disorders, where unipolar or bipolar disorders are manifestations of quantitatively different amounts of liability, can be successfully fitted to the family data on affective illness in Israel and in Switzerland (16). There are not enough currently available family data from the U.S. populations, on which previous observations of AER have been made, to determine if a single diathesis to all forms of affective illness can be supported in that population.

Subtle differences in diagnostic criteria also remain a problem for biological studies. A recent investigation of AER augmenting/reducing (33) also did not statistically confirm unipolar/bipolar AER differences. However, 70% of bipolar patients were augmenters whereas their nonbipolar patients were only 57% augmenters [a division probably more similar to the one used by Buchsbaum et al. (6)]. A significant difference was found, moreover, when patients were divided on a psychotic/nonpsychotic division — nonpsychotic were more augmenting. This parallels the reported comparison of bipolar and acute schizophrenic patients (22), as American workers may be more likely to classify psychotic patients as schizophrenic than affectively disturbed. Thus genetic and historical features as well as symptom patterns seem important in modifying the AER.

It is also possible that there are two or more forms of unipolar disorder, one of which is closely related to bipolar disorder, whereas the other is an independent entity. In Israel, where a relatively high proportion of all affective disorders are bipolar (14), a large proportion of unipolar patients would have bipolar-related illness. In populations where bipolar illness is relatively less common, the larger proportion of unipolar patients would have an independent entity, and unipolar-bipolar differences would be more pronounced.

ACKNOWLEDGMENTS

The authors wish to thank Deborah Benbenisty, Kirsten Ebbesen, Arlene Ammerman, and M. Belinda Whalen for technical assistance. This research was supported in part by USPHS Grant MH-20712-03, Israel Center for Psychobiology, The Wolfson Foundation, Paul Baerwald School of Social Work for The Hebrew University, Israel Ministry of Health.

REFERENCES

1. Allen, M. G., Cohen, S., Pollin, W., and Greenspan, S. I. (1974): Affective illness in veteran twins: A diagnostic review. *Am. J. Psychiatry*, 131:1234–1239.
2. Borge, G. F. (1973): Perceptual modulation and variability in psychiatric patients. *Arch. Gen. Psychiatry*, 29:760 763.
3. Briggs, M. H., and Briggs, M. (1973): Hormonal influences on erythrocyte catechol-O-methyl transferase activity in humans. *Experientia*, 29:278.
4. Buchsbaum, M. S. (1974): Average evoked response and stimulus intensity in identical and fraternal twins. *Physiol. Psychol.*, 2:365–370.
5. Buchsbaum, M. S., Goodwin, F. K., Murphy, D. L., and Borge, G. F. (1971): AER in affective disorders. *Am. J. Psychiatry*, 128:19–25.
6. Buchsbaum, M. S., Landau, S., Murphy, D. S., and Goodwin, F. K. (1973): Average evoked response in bipolar and unipolar affective disorders: Relationship to sex, age of onset, and monoamine oxidase. *Biol. Psychiatry*, 7:199–212.
7. Cohn, C. K., Dunner, D. L., and Axelrod, J. (1970): Reduced catechol-O-methyl transferase activity in red blood cells of women with primary affective disorder. *Science*, 170:1323–1324.
8. Creel, D. J., Dustman, R. E., and Beck, E. C. (1973): Visually evoked responses in the rat, guinea pig, cat, monkey and man. *Exp. Neurol.*, 40:351–356.
9. Crow, J. F., and Kimura, M. (1970): *An Introduction to Population Genetics Theory.* Harper & Row, New York.
10. Dunner, D. L., Cohn, C. K., Gershon, E. S., and Goodwin, F. K. (1971): Differential

catechol-O-methyl transferase activity in unipolar and bipolar affective illness. *Arch. Gen. Psychiatry*, 25:348–353.

11. Dustman, R. E., and Beck, E. (1965): The visually evoked potential in twins. *Electroencephalogr. Clin. Neurophysiol.*, 19:570–575.

12. Feighner, J. P., Robins, E., Guze, S. B., Woodruff, R. A., Jr., Winokur, G., and Munoz, R. (1972): Diagnostic criteria for use in psychiatric research. *Arch. Gen. Psychiatry*, 26: 57–63.

13. Gershon, E. S., and Jonas, W. Z. (1975): A clinical and genetic study of erythrocyte catechol-O-methyl transferase activity in primary affective disorders. *Arch. Gen. Psychiatry*, 32:1351–1356.

14. Gershon, E. S., and Liebowitz, J. H. (1975): Sociocultural and demographic correlates of affective disorders in Jerusalem. *J. Psychiatr. Res.*, 12:37–50.

15. Gershon, E. S., Baron, M., and Leckman, J. F. (1975): Genetic models of the transmission of affective disorders. *J. Psychiatr. Res.*, 12:301–317.

16. Gershon, E. S., Bunney, W. E., Leckman, J. F., Van Eerdewegh, M., and DeBauche, B. A. (1976): The inheritance of affective disorders: A review of the data and hypotheses. *Behav. Genet.* 6:3:227–261.

17. Gershon, E. S., Dunner, D. L., and Goodwin, F. K. (1971): Toward a biology of affective disorders. *Arch. Gen. Psychiatry*, 25:1–15.

18. Gershon, E. S., Dunner, D. L., and Goodwin, F. K. (1973): Assortative mating in the affective disorders. *Biol. Psychiatry*, 7:64–74.

19. Gershon, E. S., Mark, A., Cohen, N., Belizon, N., and Knobe, K. (1975): Transmitted factors in the morbid risk of affective illness. *J. Psychiatr. Res.*, 12:283–299.

20. Hall, R. A., Rappaport, M., Hopkins, H. K., Griffin, R., and Silverman, J. (1970): Evoked response and behavior in cats. *Science*, 170:998–1000.

21. Harvald, B., and Hauge, M. (1965): Heredity factors elucidated by twin studies. In: *Genetics and the Epidemiology of Chronic Diseases*, edited by J. V. Neel, pp. 61–76. U.S.P.H.S. Publication No. 1163, Government Printing Office, Washington, D.C.

22. Landau, S. G., Buchsbaum, M. S., Carpenter, W., Strauss, J., and Sacks, M. (1975): Schizophrenia and stimulus intensity control. *Arch. Gen. Psychiatry*, 32:1238–1245.

23. Lewis, E. G., Dustman, R. E., and Beck, E. C. (1972): Evoked response similarity in monozygotic, dizygotic, and unrelated individuals: A comparative study. *Electroencephalogr. Clin. Neurophysiol.*, 32:309–316.

24. Lykken, D. T., Tellegen, A., and Thorkelson, K. (1974): Genetic determination of EEG frequency spectra. *Biol. Psychol.*, 1:245–259.

25. Matthysse, S. (1976): Differences in incidence rates predicted by the single major locus and multifactional models. *Neurosci. Res. Prog. Bull.*, 14:69–71.

26. McNemar, Q. (1969): *Psychological Statistics*, p. 322. John Wiley & Sons, New York.

27. Osborne, R. T. (1970): Heritability estimates for the visual evoked response. *Life Sci.*, 9 (Part II):481–490.

28. Robins, E., and Guze, S. B. (1972): Classification of affective disorders: The primary-secondary, endogenous-reactive and neurotic-psychotic concepts. In: *Recent Advances in the Psychobiology of the Depressive Illnesses*, edited by T. A. Williams, M. M. Katz, and J. A. S. Shield, pp. 283–294. D.H.E.W. Publication No. (HSM) 70–9053, U.S. Government Printing Office, Washington, D.C.

29. Rosenthal, D. (1970): *Genetic Theory and Abnormal Behavior*, p. 44. McGraw-Hill, New York.

30. Rust, J. (1975): Genetic effects in the cortical auditory evoked potential: A twin study. *Electroencephalogr. Clin. Neurophysiol.*, 39:321–328.

31. Soskis, D., and Shagass, C. (1974): Evoked potential tests of augmenting-reducing. *Psychophysiology*, 11:175–190.

32. Stark, L. H., and Norton, J. C. (1974): The relative reliability of average evoked response parameters. *Psychophysiology*, 11:600–602.

33. Von Knorring, L. (1976): An experimental study of visual evoked responses and pain measures in patients with depressive disorders. *Biol. Psychol. (in press)*.

34. Von Knorring, L., Espvall, M., and Perris, C. (1974): Averaged evoked responses, pain measures and personality variables in patients with depressive disorders. *Acta Psychiatr. Scand. [Supp.]*, 255.

35. Young, J. P. R., Lader, M. W., and Fenton, G. W. (1972): A twin study of the genetic influences on the electroencephalogram. *J. Med. Genet.,* 9:13–16.
36. Zuckerman, M. (1974): The sensation seeking motive. *Prog. Exp. Pers. Res.,* 7:79–148.
37. Zuckerman, M., Murtaugh, T., and Siegel, J. (1974): Sensation seeking and cortical augmenting-reducing. *Psychophysiology,* 11:535–542.

Psychopathology and Brain Dysfunction, edited by C. Shagass, S. Gershon, and A. J. Friedhoff. Raven Press, New York © 1977.

Neurometrics Applied to the Quantitative Electrophysiological Measurement of Organic Brain Dysfunction in Children

E. R. John, B. Z. Karmel, L. S. Prichep, H. Ahn, and M. John

Brain Research Laboratories and Neurophysiology Clinic, Departments of Psychiatry and Physiology, New York Medical College, New York, New York 10029

In the half century that has passed since the discovery that the brain generates rhythmic electrical waves that can be recorded from electrodes placed on the scalp, innumerable articles in medical journals and books have described the features of this activity in normal individuals and documented changes from the normal pattern in different neurological diseases. It has become generally recognized that the electroencephalogram (EEG) provides an index of brain function that is sensitive to a wide variety of changes in state, whether caused by disease or by other influences. More recently, since the advent of special purpose computers of average transients and dedicated general purpose laboratory minicomputers, it has been established that the presentation of sensory stimuli causes a phase-locked oscillation to appear in the ongoing electrical activity recordable from many scalp regions. Careful study of the features of these oscillations, usually referred to as evoked responses, has demonstrated unequivocally that the waveshape of averaged evoked responses obtained under appropriate conditions can reflect sensory, perceptual, and cognitive functions of the brain, as well as provide additional sensitive indices of neuropathology. Thorough reviews of the extensive literature documenting these conclusions can be found in several recent volumes (5,7,8,15).

These discoveries have enormous practical implications. They open the possibility that techniques can be developed not only to improve the sensitivity of clinical electrophysiology in the traditional domain, diagnosis of brain disease, but to extend clinical electrophysiology into important new areas, the evaluation of sensory, perceptual, and cognitive processes. In spite of this invaluable potential, there has been little practical application of electrophysiological methods for such purposes. Several major reasons can be identified for the failure of these methods to enter routine practice. The apparatus required to provide appropriate stimulus conditions and to obtain average evoked response (AER) waveshapes has been costly, complex in design, and difficult to operate. Knowledge of the stimulus conditions under which AER waveshapes would optimally reflect particular

291

aspects of brain function has been limited to specialists in the field and has not been readily available to the practitioner. Probably most serious, inferences about brain function have depended on visual evaluation of features of the AER waveshape, a procedure that demands considerable experience and expertise and is subject to the same unreliability and lack of concordance as so many other subjective interpretations. In fact, even after half a century, the EEG itself is held in dubious regard by many practitioners who consider it only moderately sensitive at best and unreliable at worst because interpretation depends so completely on the skill and experience of the electroencephalographer, which varies enormously within the profession.

Nonetheless, a careful perusal of the abundant research literature together with extensive personal experience with AERs in experimental as well as clinical studies convinced us that electrophysiological methods could be brought to bear on a variety of enormously important practical problems in a routine and reliable manner, provided that five goals could be achieved. First, it was necessary to devise an integrated system of programmed stimulators and recording equipment that would be capable of automatically generating data uncontaminated by most artifacts, without depending on the skill of the operator. Second, standardized stimulus conditions would have to be constructed that would elicit brain activity reflecting sensory, perceptual, or cognitive processes. A variety of such individual tests of different aspects of brain function, selected on the basis of a careful and critical survey of the relevant literature, would have to be assembled into an automatically administered battery. Once such a standardized test battery became available, it would become possible for a practitioner to assess any one or more of a spectrum of brain functions without depending on personal familiarity with the research literature. Third, it would be necessary to develop quantitative indices that would extract from the electrical activity recorded under each of these test conditions those features that reflected the particular aspects of brain activity evaluated by that condition and would represent those critical features in a precise numerical fashion. Computer programs would have to be written to extract such objective measures automatically, thus removing the method from any reliance on subjective impressions. Fourth, normative data would be required to establish the reliability and stability of these numerical measures and to provide a baseline against which to assess the significance of deviations of possible clinical import. Fifth, mathematical methods would have to be developed to subject the large sets of numbers generated by these procedures to multivariate statistical analysis procedures so that the data could be evaluated automatically. Display methods would have to be devised that would permit presentation of the results of such evaluations in an intuitively comprehensible way. In view of the greatly enhanced sensitivity expected from this method, it seemed essential that these data analysis methods provide the capability for classification to be maximally determined by the structure of the data and minimally influenced by clinical preconceptions. Automatic analysis and classification programs of this sort would not only make these procedures independent of variations or limitations in the skill and experience of the individual practitioner but would relieve the practitioner of limitations on his understanding that might arise as a result of errors in preclassification or restrictions on diagnostic categories reflecting the limitations of other methods previously available for such purposes.

Some years ago we undertook a research program with the intent of achieving all of these goals. The purpose of this chapter is to report that in our opinion the program has been successful, to provide a brief overview of the means by which each of the goals has been attained, and to present preliminary results illustrating the potency of these new methods when applied to one type of disorder in cognitive processes — learning disabilities in children. More detailed information is being published elsewhere (8,10). We refer to this new technology as "neurometrics." The theoretical need to quantify neurological observations, including electrophysiological measurements, was pointed out by Denckla (2) who coined this term.

NEUROMETRIC TECHNOLOGY

Automatic Data Acquisition and Analysis System

An automatic digital electrophysiological data acquisition and analysis system (DEDAAS) has been constructed, based on a PDP 11/45 minicomputer, a computer-controlled multisensory stimulator, and specially constructed amplifiers. DEDAAS is programmed to do the following: (a) present sequences of stimuli constructed so as to constitute test items in the Neurometric Test Battery described below; (b) digitize up to 20 channels of electrophysiological signals; (c) monitor the quality of data in every channel, rejecting data contaminated by eye blinks, eye movements, or other artifacts; (d) encode acceptable data in an automatically retrievable format including a complete stimulation protocol; and (e) store data thus encoded onto standard digital magnetic tapes or "floppy" disks. These functions are performed "on-line" as the subject is being tested. A portable field acquisition unit has also been built, in which all of the above functions have been implemented in a PDP 11/10.

Neurometric Test Battery

A quantitative electrophysiological test battery, referred to as the neurometric test battery or NB, has been constructed. The NB consists of EEG and AER measurements obtained under a variety of standardized "conditions." Each of these conditions is based on results previously described in the literature and is intended to probe a particular aspect of the sensory, perceptual, or cognitive functions of the brain. These conditions were selected on the basis of findings reported in the experimental or clinical literature and will undoubtedly be supplemented and to some extent replaced by better measures as experience with this new technology is accumulated. Each such condition is considered as a test item and yields several different kinds of scores that quantify separate features of the electrical activity. Differences between the responses of the brain in two different NB conditions constitute an additional source of information about aspects of brain function. These composite conditions, in which information obtained under one condition is evaluated *relative* to information obtained under another condition, are referred to as "challenges." The NB includes a total of 92 challenges and conditions, which are fully described elsewhere (8). Administration of the full NB requires approximately 53 min of data acquisition time. Actual running time may be longer because of "time-outs" caused by the presence of artifacts. NB test items can be administered separately in any desired order. A functional description of the major items of the NB is shown in Table 1.

Quantitative Indices

Data analysis is carried out "off-line" after the desired items of the NB have been administered. The initial steps of data analysis are performed in the PDP 11/45 using programs that detect the protocols encoded onto the digital data file and automatically process the data in the manner defined as appropriate for the protocol of each different NB test item. Some of the subsequent steps in data reduction involving lengthy multivariate analysis are carried out in the PDP 11/45, whereas others are currently being implemented in larger, faster computers such as the CDC 6600 or IBM 370 using available statistical software packages, for instance, SPSS (14).

The first step in data analysis is to construct all desired bipolar or multipolar derivations by computation. Bipolar derivations computed conventionally include the 19 derivations representing the difference between adjacent electrodes located in the same *sagittal* plane and the 19 derivations combining adjacent electrodes in the same *coronal* plane. These 38 bipolar derivations, plus the 19 electrodes of the International 10/20 System recorded monopolar referenced to linked earlobes, yield a sample of the simultaneous activity in 57 derivations for routine evaluation. In addition, multipolar leads can be defined which represent summations or other desired combinations of activity in a set of leads. Thus, one can construct a left-hemisphere, right-hemisphere, or whole-head lead, or a left-minus-right hemisphere lead, for example. The EEG and AER waveshapes observed in each of the defined derivations is computed, together with the variance of the AER.

TABLE 1. *Conditions and challenges contained in the neurometric test battery*

1. EEG conditions and challenges	
Eyes open, spontaneous EEG	Baseline measures
Eyes closed, resting EEG	Yields age-dependent EEG frequency spectrum
Eyes open minus eyes closed	Shows effect of removal of visual input
Photic driving at 2.5, 5, 10, 18 Hz	Yields reactivity in delta, theta, alpha, and beta ranges when compared with base-line measures
2. AER conditions and challenges	
a. Sensory acuity	
65 lines/inch, 50% transmission	Perceived as a blank flash
27 lines/inch, 50% transmission	Seen as a grid pattern if visual acuity is approximately 20/20
7 lines/inch, 50% transmission	Seen as a grid pattern unless visual acuity is worse than 20/200
45-dB click	Elicits auditory AER unless hearing loss is sufficiently severe to interfere with language acquisition
b. Pattern perception of forms	
Large square	Provides estimates of perception of differences
Small square	in geometric forms and preservation of shape
Large diamond	or size invariance
Small diamond	
c. Pattern perception of reading-related forms	
b	Provides estimates of central discrimination
d	between shapes of letters, the meaning of
p	which depends on orientation and spatial
q	form discrimination, which are commonly reversed by dysfunctional readers
d. Prediction of temporal order	
Random versus regular flash	Change in AER waveshape reflects diminished
Random versus regular click	response to predictable stimuli, indicates
Random versus regular tap	recognition of repeated temporal sequence
Phasic habituation 1	Reveals rate and amount of suppression of information input about a meaningless monotonous event, reflects attention and short-term memory
Dishabituation	Indicates if suppressed input is nonetheless continuously monitored to permit detection of possible change
Rehabituation	When compared with initial phasic habituation, reveals if suppression of meaningless input is facilitated by memory of previous experience
e. Sensory-sensory interactions	
Passive interactions among visual, auditory, and somatosensory systems	Reveals increase or decrease in response of brain as a result of simultaneous presentation of simple stimuli in different sensory modalities
Flash followed by click 250 msec later	Measures recovery cycle after visual input
Click followed by flash 250 msec later	Measures recovery cycle after auditory input
f. Figure-ground relations	
Interaction between meaningful visual input ("figure," consisting of scenes on a video screen) and meaningless visual, auditory, or somatosensory input ("ground")	Reflects dynamic structuring of figure-ground relationships that require discrimination between relevant "signal" and irrelevant "noise," which may be either ipsimodal (video-visual) or cross-modal (video-auditory or video-somatosensory)

Interaction between meaningful auditory input ("figure," consisting of a tape recording of a musical selection or story) and meaningless visual, auditory, or somatosensory input ("ground")	Reflects dynamic structuring of figure-ground relationships requiring discrimination between relevant auditory "signal" and irrelevant "noise," which may be either ipsimodal (music-auditory) or cross-modal (music-visual or music-somatosensory)
g. Conditioned response evaluation	
Visual stimulus, before conditioning	Baseline control measures
Auditory stimulus, before conditioning	
Somatosensory stimulus, before conditioning	
After sensory-sensory conditioning with visual CS and auditory US:	
Visual stimulus	Reflects effects of conditioning as specific changes in response to CS
Auditory stimulus	Controls for "sensitization," revealed as generalized change to US as well as CS
Somatosensory stimulus	Controls for "pseudo-conditioning," revealed as generalized change to any stimulus
After sensory-sensory conditioning with auditory CS and visual US:	
Visual stimulus	Controls for sensitization
Auditory stimulus	Yields estimate of specific conditioning effect
Somatosensory stimulus	Controls for pseudo-conditioning
3. EEG conditions and challenges	
Eyes open, spontaneous EEG	
Eyes closed, resting EEG	Replicates initial measures
Eyes open minus eyes closed	
Eyes open, beginning, minus eyes open, end	Yields estimate of effects owing to state, such as anxiety about test or fatigue because of testing, vs. characteristics of individual
Eyes closed, beginning, minus eyes closed, end	

A variety of quantitative indices is then extracted from the EEG, AER, and variance of the AER for each NB condition and challenge for which data are available. These indices are briefly described in Table 2, and precise definitions are provided elsewhere (8). As is evident from this table, for each spontaneous EEG condition in the Neurometric Test Battery, a total of more than 1,000 numerical indices are extracted from the full set of derivations, and for each AER condition in the Neurometric Test Battery, well over 2,000 numerical indices are extracted from the full set of derivations. Further, for every challenge, defined as the difference between AERs obtained under two different conditions, the change in each of the measures shown in Table 2 is computed and its statistical significance is assessed.

TABLE 2. *Quantitative indices extracted from neurometric test battery*

QUANTITATIVE MEASURES

The conditions of the Neurometric Test Battery provide samples of both the ongoing EEG and AER elicited by different sensory stimuli. For each separate electrode derivation, these two different types of brain electrical activity are described by two different sets of numerical indices, as follows:

EEG Indices

Absolute power (microvolts squared) in seven frequency bands, i.e., low delta (0.5–1.5 Hz), high delta (1.5–3.5 Hz), theta (3.5–7 Hz), alpha (7–13 Hz), low beta (13–19 Hz), high beta (19–25 Hz), and wide band (0.5–25 Hz).

Relative power (% of total power) in the low delta, high delta, theta, alpha, low beta, and high beta frequency bands.

Age-dependent quotient (ADQ). A metric reflecting maturational development is obtained for major cortical regions by calculating the ratio between the delta and theta energy usually observed in that head region in a normal person the same age as the patient and the amount of delta and theta energy actually measured in the patient. If the ratio

$$ADQ = \frac{\text{normal energy in frequency band}}{\text{patient energy in frequency band}}$$

is approximately 1.0, the amount of slow activity in the recording is appropriate for a healthy person of that age. Many brain diseases, as well as maturational lags, are reflected by an excess of slow activity and ADQ values significantly less than 1.0. Progress of an abnormal brain state, such as might ensue from head trauma, space-occupying lesion, cerebrovascular accident, or maturational lag, can be followed quantitatively by comparing values of ADQ obtained sequentially after appropriate time intervals. Effects of medication or other treatment can be similarly measured.

Coherence between homologous pairs of derivations (phase-locked correlation) in the low delta, high delta, theta, alpha, low beta, and high beta bands.

Amplitude symmetry between homologous derivations in the low delta, high delta, theta, alpha, low beta, and high beta bands.

Overall waveshape symmetry between homologous pairs as assessed by the cross-correlation coefficient for the wide-band EEG signal.

AER Indices

The following indices are extracted from the AER waveshape and the variance of the AER, which constitute the initial level of computation.

Signal strength. The energy represented by the variance of the AER in the 4 latency intervals: For instance, 40–99 ms, 100–199 ms, 200–500 ms, and 500–999 ms.

Noise. The variance of the AER in the same 4 latency intervals.

Signal/noise ratio. The value of the average signal strength across each of the 4 latency intervals divided by the average value of the noise during the corresponding interval.

Pairwise energy asymmetry. The difference in AER signal strength between homologous pairs of electrode derivations, computed for each of the 4 latency intervals.

Pairwise waveshape asymmetry. The difference in AER waveshape between homologous pairs of electrodes, as represented by the Pearson correlation coefficient, computed for each of the 4 latency intervals.

Latency of the peak of every component in the AER for up to 7 components.

Amplitude of the peak of every component in the AER for up to 7 components.

Amplitude excursions between the peaks of up to 7 successive negative and positive components in the AER.

Latency differences between corresponding peaks in homologous electrode pairs.

Amplitude differences between corresponding peaks in homologous electrode pairs.

t-Test for statistical significance of differences between AER waveshapes recorded simultaneously from bilaterally symmetrical derivations. The *t*-test is obtained by computing the amplitude difference between the two waves at each point in time along the analysis epoch and dividing that difference by the square root of the sums of the variances of the two waves at the corresponding latency. Thus, the significance of differences is tested at all points throughout the analysis epoch.

TABLE 3. *Normative data available for neurometrics (July, 1976)*

| | Available average data | | | | | | | | | | | |
| | EEG | | | | Sensory acuity | | | | Perception of patterns | | | |
Groups for which average data now exist[a]	Eyes open	Eyes closed	Open minus closed	Photic driving (4 frequencies)	65 lines/inch	27 lines/inch	7 lines/inch	45 dB clicks	Large square	Small square	Large diamond	Small diamond
0–21 years at yearly intervals $N = 1000$		X										
Young adult $N = 144$		X		X								
Neurological patients: tumor, stroke, epilepsy $N = 221$		X		X								
Normal children 7–11 years old $N = 110$	X	X	X	X	X	X	X	X	X	X	X	X
Learning disabled children 7–18 years old $N = 700$	X	X	X	X	X	X	X	X	X	X	X	X
Learning disabled children 5 years old $N = 35$	X	X	X		X	X	X					
Normal elderly 60–80 years old $N = 90$		X			X			X				
Senile elderly 60–80 years old $N = 50$		X			X			X				
Normal newborn $N = 25$		X			X			X				
"At risk" newborn $N = 25$		X			X			X				

[a] Sample size varies from index to index, minimum 20.

Data from Matoŭsek and Petersén (1973): *Automation of Clinical Electroencephalography*, pp. 75–102; Harmony Otero et al. (1973): *EEG*, 35:237–240; Harmony, Ricardo et al. (1973): *Brain Res.*, 61:133–140; Otero et al. (1975): *Activities Nerv.*, 17: (Suppl) 120–126, 127–130; John, Ahn, Brown, Easton, Karmel, Avitable (1975): Unpublished observations; John, Prichep, Toro, Brown, Karmel, Pavel (1976): Unpublished observations; Ahn, John, Brown (1975): Unpublished observations; John, Gerson, Bartlett, Koenig, Brown (1975): Unpublished observations; Kaye, Karmel, John, McDonald, Pavel (1975): Unpublished observations.

Normative Data

Normative data have been gathered from reasonably large samples in different age ranges. For some age ranges norms are presently available for only a small subset of the NB conditions, although for other age ranges norms are available for the full set of 92 conditions and challenges. Some of these normative data have been provided by other laboratories and some by us. Table 3 shows the age ranges and NB conditions for which normative

b	d	p	q	Predictability		Sensory-sensory interaction		Figure-ground relationships						Conditioning	
				Random vs. regular	Habituation Dishabituation Rehabituation	Visual-auditory-somatosensory interaction	Recovery cycles visual-auditory auditory-visual	Video figure visual ground	Video figure auditory ground	Video figure somatosensory ground	Music figure visual ground	Music figure auditory ground	Music figure somatosensory ground	Visual CS auditory US somatosensory control	Auditory CS visual US somatosensory control
X	X	X	X	X	X	X	X	X	X	X	X	X	X	X	X
X	X	X	X	X	X	X	X	X	X	X	X	X	X	X	X
X	X			X		X		X	X	X					
						X			X			X		X	X
						X			X			X		X	X

data are now available and indicates the sources of those data. Detailed norms will be published in a volume currently being prepared (9).

Data Reduction, Display, and Classification by Numerical Taxonomy

The full standard NB provides over 285,000 numerical measures of brain function. In addition, this huge volume of data can be augmented by over 5,000 (92 conditions × 57 derivations) AER waveshapes, each with 100 numerical values at 10-ms intervals along the analysis epoch. These waveshapes can be represented as multivariate vectors. Quantitative analysis of these waveshape vectors can then be accomplished by techniques such as principal components factor analysis, analysis of variance and covariance, and other readily available multivariate analytic procedures.

First, means and standard derivations are calculated for each of the measures available for individuals in a specified age range. Next, variables displaying non-gaussian distributions are submitted to a logarithmic transform. Then the values of each individual measure obtained from every individual are subjected to Fisher's Z-transformation, so that each value is represented in terms of the probability that it constitutes a significant deviation from the normal population value for that index.

Once these transformations have been accomplished, intuitively comprehensible displays of the large volume of data available for any individual can be easily constructed. For every individual variable, or for selected combinations of variables, the value of the Z-transformed index is encoded as the density of a mark made at the position on a diagram of a head corresponding to the anatomical location of the derivation from which those data were obtained. The more deviant the value, the denser the entry on the head. If the values are significantly above the mean, the entries are comprised of plus signs; if below the mean, of minus signs. Derivations for which data are found to be within normal limits are indicated by a pair of spots. Using an electrostatic matrix plotter, one can plot head diagrams for all variables for which that individual displayed abnormal values anyplace on the head. If no abnormal values are found for a particular index, the whole corresponding head diagram is suppressed. These head diagrams, displaying density-encoded Z-transforms of abnormal findings, constitute a sort of "electrophysiological brain scan." This scan gives a clear anatomical picture of significant deviations from normal structure and usual patterns of spontaneous EEG activity, as well as activity reflecting sensory, perceptual, and cognitive processes. Figure 1 illustrates prototypic examples of topographical displays of Z-transformed neurometric indices. Detailed explanations of these examples can be found in the legend. For any subject, the DEDAAS system will produce a series of such topographical displays, one for every neurometric index for which any significantly aberrant value is found in the measures obtained from the full 10/20 system for that individual. The statistical criteria for "significantly aberrant" can be altered by the operator of the system, and plots of all nonsignificant, or "normal," values are suppressed. The full set of Z-deviant displays thus obtained provides a catalogue of abnormal features of the electrophysiological brain scan in that patient.

Once the Z-transformations used to compress the initial body of data into the individual profile of significant deviations from normative values have been computed, a Z-deviate vector is constructed that represents each individual as a point in a multivariate deviation space. The Z-deviate vector for a totally normal individual, whose NB indices do not deviate significantly from expected values in any instance, will not be significantly distant from

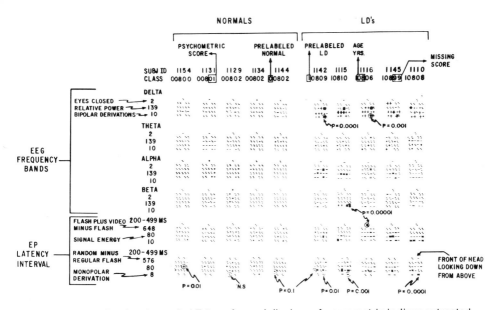

FIG. 1. Illustrative density-coded Z-transformed displays of neurometric indices extracted from various EEG and AER conditions of the NB. Each column of displays represents data obtained from 1 subject, whereas each row represents 1 univariate or multivariate index. Each display represents an array of entries: each entry corresponds to the value of the index measured at that point on the subject's head, whereas the position of the entries in the array corresponds to the electrode locations of the 10/20 system. For each index the entry at any location has been density coded to reflect the Z-transformation of the measure obtained from that subject referred to the mean of the whole population. If the Z-transformed value was such that the *p*-level of obtaining that value by chance was not less than 0.1, two small spots (•.) were entered to convey that the measure was assessed and found within the normal range. If the value of Z was such that *p* was between 0.1 and 0.01, a small + was entered to show that the index was unusually large, and a small − was entered if the index was unusually small; if *p* was between 0.01 and 0.001, a large + was entered if the value was abnormally high and a large − if it was abnormally low; if *p* was between 0.001 and 0.0001, ++ or = was entered; between 0.0001 and 0.00001, +++ or ≡ was entered; *p*-levels below 0.00001 were indicated by large solid shapes in the form of + or − signs.

The prototypic data illustrated show 5 normal and 5 learning disabled (LD) children selected from a much larger sample and are to be considered as illustrative examples rather than as invariable findings.

Top 4 rows of displays represent the distribution of relative power in the spontaneous EEG, recorded from bipolar derivations with eyes closed, from top down in the delta, theta, alpha, and beta bands, respectively. Note the typical excess of slow delta activity predominantly in posterior head regions of the LD subjects, usually coupled with a deficiency of alpha and sometimes of beta activity. **5th row:** LD subjects show significantly less change in the signal energy of the bipolar EP in the latency region between 200 and 500 msec when a flash delivered randomly while the subject is watching a TV cartoon is compared with a flash delivered randomly while the subject looks at the defocused TV screen. **6th row:** LD subjects display significantly less change in the signal energy of the monopolar EP in the latency region between 200 and 500 msec when a random is compared with a regular flash. Although the particular head region displaying this less-than-expected difference when the two conditions are compared varies from subject to subject, such findings show that LD children tend to display less suppression of P300 to an irrelevant stimulus ("ground") in the presence of meaningful environmental input ("figure"), and, analogously, display less of a tendency to distinguish between predictable and unpredictable events in the environment, reflected in the similarity of late positive components in EPs elicited by these two different kinds of events.

the origin of this space. The more deviant an individual's NB indices, the further into this space the corresponding Z-deviate vector will project. The direction in which the Z-deviate vector points in the multivariate space corresponds to the diagnostic definition of abnormal electrophysiological activity in the brain of that patient. The greater the overall length of the Z-deviate vector, the more severe the quantitative abnormality.

A number of statistical pattern recognition methods are available for the objective classification of point swarms representing sets of such vectors in multivariate space. The general field of these pattern recognition and cluster analysis classification methods is referred to as "numerical taxonomy" (17). A common starting point shared by many of these methods is the computation of a distance matrix defining the distance from each point to every other point in the swarm. A useful strategy is then to compute the average distance between points in the data space and to select some minimum distance as the definition of points that lie significantly closer than random to one another. Various schemes have been devised to use such definitions of proximity to construct clusters that reflect the natural groupings which emerge from such an examination of the data.

Since the constituent tests comprising the NB have been carefully selected from the literature documenting that these electrophysiological measures not only reflect anatomical and functional integrity but are sensitive to sensory, perceptual, and cognitive processes, application of these available powerful multivariate analysis techniques to the actual data waveshapes as well as the quantitative features extracted from NB measures should provide a great increase in the descriptive capability and diagnostic sensitivity of electrophysiological information.

At present, our working hypothesis is that many of the groupings revealed by such numerical taxonomic methods will correspond to diagnostic entities with meaningful functional or etiological implications. We expect that in many instances existing functional indices such as psychometric or neurological evaluations will be insufficiently sensitive to reveal the functional correlates of membership in certain clusters. Obviously, a great deal of careful study will be necessary before we will be able to distinguish definitively between those clusters that have significant practical implications and those that do not. For the moment, our contention is that if NB measures are demonstrated to be statistically reliable in the sense of test-retest reliability, and if appreciable numbers of individuals are found to belong to a cluster that shares a common profile of statistically significant deviations from normative values on a specific subset of NB indices, then that cluster is a neurophysiologically real cluster. Whether or not the functional implications of membership in such a cluster can be discerned with present psychometric, behavioral, and neurological measures, such a neurometrically based cluster is nonetheless real and represents features of function hitherto not detected.

The demonstration of homogeneous subgroups or clusters within a population of individuals who share a demonstrable functional disorder, such as senile deterioration of memory or learning disability, is of special interest. It raises the possibility that the same overt functional incapacity may be manifested in different individuals as a consequence of dysfunction in qualitatively different neurophysiological processes. Even the most superficial consideration of the many mechanisms involved in learning or memory makes it obvious that a wide variety of different neurophysiological or neurochemical malfunctions might produce the same functional deficit. The existence of neurophysiologically homogeneous subgroups within a presumably heterogeneous population, such as "the learning disabled," implies that different therapeutic procedures might perhaps be differentially beneficial to members of different clusters. The neurometric technology greatly improves the resolution with which such subgroups can be identified. It remains to be seen whether the improved resolving power for discerning abnormal brain function leads to an improved capability for individualized prescriptive therapies.

AN ILLUSTRATIVE EXAMPLE—"LEARNING DISABILITY"

As an illustration of the results of applying the neurometric approach to a difficult and important clinical problem when conventional electrophysiological methods have not been conspicuously useful, we have elected to present some partial results of our extensive study on normal and learning handicapped children. Although previously published literature on the electrophysiological features of learning handicapped children reveals a general consensus that such children display a higher incidence of abnormalities such as excessive posterior slow waves or unusual latencies or amplitudes of particular components of the AER (for reviews of this literature see refs. 4 and 8), as yet no quantitative criteria have been provided for the accurate separation of learning disordered children with an organic basis for their difficulty from children with primarily emotional disturbances or from normal children, let alone for the objective classification of learning disabled children with brain dysfunction into distinct subgroups. The difficulty of this differential diagnosis can readily be ascertained by examining any of the recent volumes of this topic (e.g., refs. 19 and 20) or by examining current procedures for evaluation and treatment of such children. The importance of proper diagnostic capability for this disorder can be appreciated if one realizes that current estimates of its incidence in the U.S. population range between 5 and 15% (20, reviewed in ref. 8). Whatever the exact figure, it seems probable that recent advances in medical technology leading to the survival of many children who previously might have succumbed to perinatal trauma or diseases of early childhood may have resulted in an increase in numbers of children with subtle forms of brain damage. It will be shown below that neurometric methods not only provide a rapid, efficient, and highly accurate separation between normal and learning disabled children, but they also permit objective classification of children categorized as learning disabled into many subgroups with distinctly different features.

Methods

SUBJECTS

The neurometric test battery and a psychometric battery composed of a variety of standardized tests usually presumed to measure organic aspects of learning dysfunction were administered to a sample of 172 children. Of these children, 110 were tentatively preclassified as "normal" and 62 as "learning disabled" on the basis of school performance and opinions of the referral sources. This total population included 101 black and 71 while male children ranging between 7.7 and 11.5 years of age, with 97% falling between 7.8 and 10.4 years. The population was restricted to males in view of reports of sex-linked effects related to learning handicaps in this age range. "Normal" children were paid volunteers recruited from local schools by informing parents that this project was in progress and offering a $25 fee plus transportation and lunch costs for participation of children with no record of academic problems. "Learning disabled" children were recruited by referral from psychologists affiliated with local schools. Testing usually occupied a full day. Psychometric testing was divided into segments, intermingled with occasional rest periods and/or lunch. The neurometric battery was usually administered in a continuous manner, bracketed by rest periods and/or lunch.

PSYCHOMETRIC TESTS

Psychometric indices were extracted from the following test instruments: Wechsler Intelligence Scale for Children (WISC); Wide Range Achievement Tests (WRAT) for spelling, arithmetic, and word comprehension; Peabody Picture Vocabulary Inventory scales for vocabulary IQ, picture recognition, and expression; McCarthy Scales subscores for Picture Memory, Tapping Sequence, and Verbal Memory I and II; Illinois Tests for Perceptual Abilities, subscores for Visual Association and Auditory Association; and Bender Gestalt (Koppitz) scoring method.

A number of other psychometric tests or subscales were included in the battery. These tests were either found to be ineffectual for separating the subgroups in our sample according to the prelabeled classification or were not obtained on sufficient numbers of children in our sample to warrant inclusion at this time.

A "composite organicity score," the 3M score (Table 4), was constructed

TABLE 4. *Three-M scale for brain dysfunction*

Points	0	1	2
Bender Gestalt scores[a]	0–2	3 +1 for 1 or 2 signs	4 and up +2 points for more than 2 signs
WRAT Spelling and Reading	OK in both areas	Low in 1[b]	Low in 2[b]
Block Design Scaled scores	8 or above	7	6 or below
Object Assembly Scaled scores	8 or above	7	6 or below
Coding	8 or above	7	6 or below
Digit Span	8 or above	7	6 or below (D.B. 3 or more) +1 for large discrepancy
McCarthy[c]	5,5,14,8	Low in 1 area	Low in 2 areas
Expressive PPVT			
Perfect 27	(1–4)	5 or 6 more	7 or more
Scores	18–22	17–16 or below	Below 16
ITPA		Low[b]	
Auditory association		2 years below	
Visual association		normal grade	

[a] On Bender, in addition to points given on the basis of the score, additional points are added if signs specifically correlated with brain dysfunction are found.

[b] Low means 1.6 years below grade level.

[c] On McCarthy, scores refer to Pictorial Memory, Tapping Sequence, Verbal Memory I and Verbal Memory II in this order. Perfect scores would be 6, 9, 15, and 11.

If only a subset of these tests was available for any one subject, the 3M score was estimated at the minimum possible value. Estimates were taken from the existing incomplete data and knowledge of the correlations among the obtained and missing scale. A more exact regression equation could have been constructed but the coarseness of the scale was felt sufficiently gross that any finer gradation would be misleading.

by combining a weighted sum of scores from various subscales of these instruments, which are commonly presumed or reported in the literature to reflect organic brain dysfunction in children. Finally, the full set of psychometric scores was factor analyzed, and scores for each factor were calculated for each individual and included in the final set of psychometric variables.

Results

COMPARISON BETWEEN NEUROMETRIC AND PSYCHOMETRIC SEPARATION OF NORMAL FROM LEARNING DISABLED CHILDREN

In order to provide the reader with an estimate of the relative effectiveness of neurometric and conventional psychometric methods for the identification of children with learning disabilities owing to organic brain dysfunction, we compare in this section the discriminating accuracy of a small subset of NB conditions with the accuracy of the full psychometric test battery.

Only two conditions of the neurometric test battery (1 min of eyes closed EEG and 1 min of eyes open EEG) were selected for this comparison for two reasons: (a) these measures can be obtained from almost every subject since there is no requirement for behavioral reaction or more than absolutely minimal cooperation, and they require no special equipment to provide standardized stimulus parameters; and (b) numerous workers have reported a high incidence of abnormal features in the spontaneous EEG recorded from children with learning disabilities compared with age-matched normal controls (4,16,20).

The following subset of neurometric indices were extracted from the EEG data obtained under these two conditions: absolute and relative power in the low delta, high delta, theta, alpha, low beta, and high beta frequency bands for the full 10/20 electrode system, and amplitude ratios and coherence within each of these bands between the eight homologous electrode pairs of the standard 19-lead monopolar montage. These measures were computed separately for the "eyes open" and "eyes closed" conditions. The same measures were computed for the "challenge" defined as the alterations in the EEG brought about by the change from open to closed eyes. This challenge reflects the effect of visual input on overall reactivity. In addition, factor analyses were carried out on the combined set of indices from the eyes open and closed conditions. For each of the factors yielded by this analysis, individual factor scores were computed for each subject and included in the total measure set.

For full appreciation of the implications of this comparison, it should be kept in mind that although this set of neurometric variables was quite extensive, it represents only a small portion of the total possible univariate measures calculable from the full NB if evoked potential (EP) conditions are included and does not even include all of the measures that can be extracted from these two conditions; for example, the numerous indices of the cross-spectral coherence matrix were not used. The neurometric measures used in this computation were gathered semi-automatically with the aid of a moderately skilled technician, from 2 min of artifact-free data, which could almost invariably be recorded in less than 5 min of real time. By contrast, the psychometric measures represented the majority of the behavioral information gathered in several hours of testing requiring a great deal of cooperation and effort on the part of both the subject and a trained examiner, who spent substantial additional time scoring the results.

In order to make this evaluation of the two types of metrics as comparable as possible, as well as to ensure that any obtained effects be robustly related to brain dysfunction and minimally confounded by variables indirectly related to organic differences and deficits, we made an effort to select only those indices that were not significantly correlated with such variables as socioeconomic status (low versus middle), culture, or chronological age. For this purpose we used the regression analysis of variance (ANOVA) procedures available in the standard SPSS statistical computer program library. In this procedure variance because of confounding covariates was controlled while the residual variance because of the correlation of each variable to the prediagnosis was evaluated and its statistical significance tested.

Unfortunately, only one psychometric scale in the test battery (the performance scale of the WISC) could pass these stringent controls. Thus, it was necessary to include all psychometric measures, found by simple univariate ANOVA procedures to discriminate between the prediagnosed normal and learning disabled subgroups, in the set of "psychometric variables" from which a multiple discriminant function was to be computed, regardless of the presence of confounding variance not directly related to organic dysfunction.

The neurometric measure set contained a much larger number of variables. As a result, sufficient variables were available so that it was possible to use only those univariate indices whose correlation with the prediagnosis increased when the contribution of the confounding variables mentioned above was regressed out of the total variance. Of the 1,193 univariate neurometric variables thus evaluated, 421 (35%) were significantly correlated with the prediagnosis. Approximately half of these, or 16% of the total, showed increased correlation with prediagnosis after the confounding variance was removed. The details of these findings are presented in Appendix A, Table 1.

Factor Structure of the Psychometric Measure Set

Both the neurometric and psychometric measure sets were augmented by composite scores reflecting their corresponding factor structure, as mentioned above. Principal component factor analysis with a Varimax rotation was used to obtain the factor structure. The psychometric set was expanded to include four multivariate factor scores, whereas 24 factor scores were added to the neurometric set. The four orthogonal factors that spanned the psychometric space (Appendix B, Table 1) were interpreted to represent successively: (a) a verbal intelligence factor; (b) a disability factor loading most on measures usually considered to reflect psychometric manifestations of organic brain damage; (c) an achievement factor loading on indices of performance or achievement relative to the population as a whole; and (d) a visual and auditory association factor possibly related to sensory-sensory interactions. The extent to which this factor structure can be considered representative of the dimensionality of this psychometric battery for the population as a whole is difficult to estimate, but the structure corresponds to ideas about the major processes reflected in the identification of "minimal brain dysfunction" currently expressed by many workers in this area of endeavor.

Factor Structure of the Neurometric Measure Set

The factor structure of the neurometric measure set (Appendix B, Tables 2, 3, and 4) was ascertained for the 10/20 electrode system separately for indices related to absolute power in slow frequencies, absolute power in fast frequencies (7 to 25 Hz), relative power (percentage) in slow frequencies, and relative power in fast frequencies. Each of these four separate analyses yielded six statistically significant factors that accounted for approximately 82% of the communality. Careful examination of the four sets of factor loadings revealed that essentially the same factor structure described the four sets of indices. Furthermore, the loadings of each of the six factors found in every analysis on the 19 electrode locations showed an invariant anatomical pattern. Examination of this pattern clearly establishes the existence of three topographical patterns of covariance across the electrode locations of the 10/20 system with respect to certain sets of EEG indices. Since these indices display one set of values when the eyes are open and a different set when eyes are closed, each topographical pattern is manifested in two different states. The six factors therefore represent three anatomical patterns of covariance times two states per pattern. These "spatiostate" patterns are illustrated in Fig. 2.

The results of the factor analysis of the neurometric EEG indices support two conclusions. First, most of the information about the distribution of power in different anatomical regions of the International 10/20 system and the different frequency bands of the spontaneous EEG recorded with eyes open and eyes closed can be reduced to six basic factors. Thus, there is a great deal of redundancy in the six frequency bands conventionally analyzed for the 19 electrodes of the 10/20 system. Second, three basic anatomical domains can be identified that display a high degree of covariance with respect to certain sets of EEG indices. These domains—which can be categorized as (a) a posterior, centro/parieto/occipital sector in dynamic opposition to a midline section, (b) a temporo/frontal domain, and (c) a frontal/pole/frontal/central domain—presumably reflect three underlying systems of corticocorticothalamic organization. Further study will be necessary to establish whether differential dysfunction in these three neuroanatomical systems is correlated with particular types of behavioral disability.

Obviously, the neurometric EEG variables provide a far greater pool of potentially independent dimensions than the psychometric variables, whether as univariate indices or as multivariate factor scores, along which to describe subjects. However, the EEG variables represent only approxi-

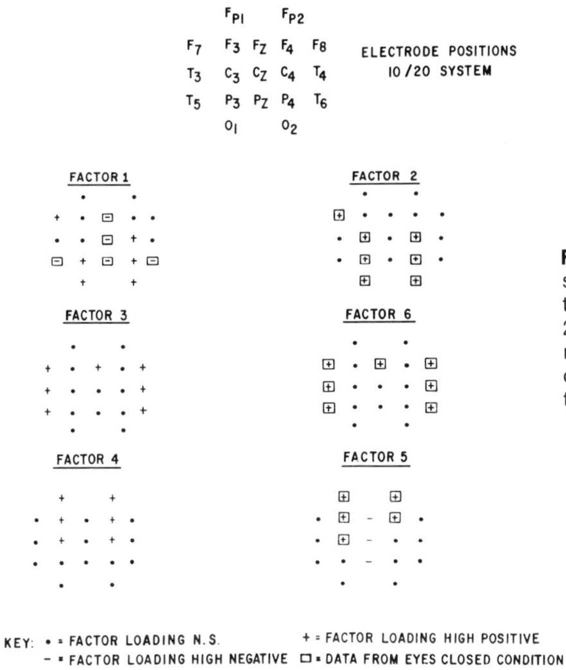

F_{P1} F_{P2}

F_7 F_3 F_Z F_4 F_8 ELECTRODE POSITIONS

T_3 C_3 C_Z C_4 T_4 10 /20 SYSTEM

T_5 P_3 P_Z P_4 T_6

O_1 O_2

FACTOR 1

FACTOR 2

FIG. 2. Topography of factor structure in the EEG. For details, see Appendix B: Tables 2, 3, and 4. Each set of patterns refers to positions of electrodes on the head, as illustrated at the top of the figure.

FACTOR 3

FACTOR 6

FACTOR 4

FACTOR 5

KEY: • = FACTOR LOADING N.S.   + = FACTOR LOADING HIGH POSITIVE
      − = FACTOR LOADING HIGH NEGATIVE   ⊡ = DATA FROM EYES CLOSED CONDITION

mately 5% of the neurometric information generated by a complete evaluation by the NB system. The EP conditions representing the remaining 95% are potentially far more informative in that they assess sensory, perceptual, and cognitive processes under more controlled behavioral conditions requiring dynamic information processing, in contrast to the passive EEG conditions here being analyzed.

Discriminant Analyses Using the Psychometric and Neurometric EEG Measure Set

Discriminant functions were computed separately for each of the psychometric and neurometric variable sets. Since there were far more measures in the neurometric set than the number of subjects, proper calculation of a discriminant function entailed extraction of the most effective univariate discriminating variables from the neurometric set and subsequent combination of those variables into a more inclusive multiple discriminant function. For this purpose, we used the stepwise discriminant procedures available in the SPSS package (14). This stepwise procedure permitted selection of a subset of the univariate variables that best discriminated between the normal and learning disabled subgroups in our sample. A similar procedure was followed for the psychometric variables.

These two discriminant procedures yielded a single composite score for each metric consisting of a weighting of the best nonredundant variables in the total set. Thus, each composite score represents the numerical pattern of differences that best separated the two subgroups of children within our sample, using either psychometric or neurometric variables alone. The statistical significance of each discriminant function was tested by computing the F-test difference between the two subgroups, classified according to prelabeling, based on that single, derived discriminant score. The "performance" of the discriminant function was further tested in two ways: first, by comparing the scores with respect to proportion of variance accounted for after confounding variables were removed from the analysis [using regression analysis of covariance procedures); and second, by classifying children independently when their scores were not included in the construction of the discriminant function (using "leave-one-out" replication (11).] The bottom part of Table 5 presents the results of a regression analysis of covariance on the psychometric discriminant score, whereas the top part presents the same data for the neurometric EEG discriminant score. The subgroups in our sample that had been preclassified as normal or learning disabled could be significantly separated by either

TABLE 5. *Regression analysis of covariance in two types of discriminant scores: EEG based or psychometric based*

Source of variation	Sum of squares	df	F	% of total variance
EEG discriminant score				
Main effects				
Prediagnosis	132.36	1	60.54[a]	23.0
Culture	4.10	1	1.88	—
SES	0.02	1	0.01	—
Covariates				
Age	4.98	1	2.28	0.9
WISC-IQ	4.07	1	1.86	0.7
Psychometric	0.44	1	0.20	—
Residual	310.43	142		
Total	574.36[b]	148		
Psychometric discriminant score				
Main effects				
Prediagnosis	13.99	1	8.84[c]	5.0
Culture	0.66	1	0.42	—
SES	0.10	1	0.06	—
Covariates				
Age	2.70	1	1.70	0.6
WISC-IQ	4.93	1	3.12	1.1
EEG Discriminant	0.32	1	0.20	—
Residual	224.62	142		
Total	277.35[b]	148		

[a] $F = 0.001$.
[b] The total sources of squares is greater than the sum of the regression terms because of correlation among the sources of variations.
[c] $F = 0.01$.

the psychometric or the neurometric discriminant score. However, the neurometric discriminant score, when corrected for correlation with socioeconomic status (SES), culture, age, and full-scale WISC-IQ, accounted for 4.6 times more independent variance related to the original classifications than did the psychometric score (23 versus 5%).

Certain portions of the results in Table 5 seem paradoxical and merit more detailed discussion. First, can we discern plausible reasons for the lack of significant covariation between the neurometric and psychometric discriminant scores? This lack of covariation may reflect a critical feature of the way these analyses were carried out. All of the neurometric variables were selected on the basis of their demonstrated lack of covariation with cultural variables, representing the most discriminating variables listed in column 3 of Appendix A, Table 1. Since we failed to identify any psychometric variables other than the composite performance score of the WISC-IQ, which did not display covariation with cultural variables, it was impossible to construct a similarly unconfounded subset of psychometric measures. The observed absence of relationship between the neurometric and psychometric measures, independently confirmed by the absence of significant correlation between the two kinds of discriminant scores, the failure to find any significant canonical correlations between the two sets of measures or significant covariation between the two individual discriminant scores, may be because each measure used to construct the neurometric discriminant was unconfounded with respect to culture, SES, and IQ, whereas each measure used in the psychometric discriminant was confounded by one or more of these variables.

If we accept this explanation, we are confronted with a second paradoxical finding. If the individual psychometric discriminants are confounded with culture, why was no significant covariance found between culture and the discriminant score yielded by the multivariate psychometric set? For the multivariate neurometric set, the absence of significant covariation with culture poses no problem. The individual variables were selected precisely so as to exclude such covariance. But how can the multivariate psychometric set fail to show covariance with culture even though each of the univariate measures in that set displays such covariance?

In order to understand this apparent statistical contradiction, it is necessary to examine in further detail the steps in the statistical analyses that yielded the end results presented in Table 5. The influences contributing to the single-discriminant analyses can be decomposed into a variety of sources of variance: main effects, statistical covariates, and residual variance. The residual variance used to test for the significance of main effects and covariates can be considered as the sum of all the contributions to the error variance which might arise from each subordinate variable in the multivariate set. Since each psychometric subordinate scale that entered into the superordinate discriminant analysis was confounded with cultural factors, contributions to the error variance must exist from these sources. If correlated or confounding effects owing to culture are embedded within the error or residual variance terms, it becomes analytically impossible to rule out cultural bias from the main effects.

A statistical model for this situation represented below in Eq. 1 specifies the possible sources of variance for both sets of metrics:

$$\sigma_{(T)}^2 = \sigma_{(A)}^2 + \sigma_{(B)}^2 + \sigma_{(AB)}^2 + \sigma_{e(A)}^2 + \sigma_{e(B)}^2 + \sigma_{e(AB)}^2 + \sigma_{e(R)}^2 \qquad \text{Eq. 1}$$

where $\sigma_{(T)}^2$ = total variance

$\sigma_{(A)}^2$ = main effect owing to preclassification (A)

$\sigma_{(B)}^2$ = confounding effect (e.g., SES, culture, etc.) (B)

$\sigma_{(AB)}^2$ = interaction between (A) and (B)

$\sigma_{e(A)}^2$ = sampling error associated with (A)

$\sigma_{e(B)}^2$ = sampling error associated with (B)

$\sigma_{e(AB)}^2$ = sampling error associated with the interaction between (A) and (B)

$\sigma_{e(R)}^2$ = residual variation

The residual variance, $\sigma_{e(R)}^2$, is a critical determinant of the statistical significance of the main effect represented by $\sigma_{(A)}^2$. In the psychometric case, the confounding effects of culture $[\sigma_{(B)}^2$ and $\sigma_{e(B)}^2]$ and the interaction of preclassification and culture $[\sigma_{(AB)}^2 + \sigma_{e(AB)}^2]$ were not removed from the error term $[\sigma_{e(R)}^2]$ at the univariate level and were therefore included in the analysis. This necessarily occurs whenever psychometric (or any other) measures are used without explicitly partialling out such effects. Since the neurometric set excluded variables related to confounds, $\sigma_{(B)}^2$ and $\sigma_{(AB)}^2$ are expected to be zero, and the sampling error associated with each term $[\sigma_{e(B)}^2$ and $\sigma_{e(AB)}^2]$ is eliminated from the error term used to test for significance. The statistical model for the neurometric analysis, therefore, can be reduced to Eq. 2 below:

$$\sigma_{(T)}^2 = \sigma_{(A)}^2 + \sigma_{e(A)}^2 + \sigma_{e(R)}^2 \qquad \text{Eq. 2}$$

If confounding effects and interactions such as $\sigma_{(B)}^2$ and $\sigma_{(AB)}^2$ are not properly regressed out of the multivariate set before analysis for main effects by removal at the univariate level absolutely as done for neurometrics and not statistically as required for psychometrics, such effects may remain within the residual term used to test the significance of the main effects. Failure to recognize the need for this procedure or inability, as in the case for psychometrics, to do this may lead to type 1 errors in conclusions.

The hypothesis formulated above could be tested by constructing a new neurometric discriminant using those variables that are confounded with culture (see Appendix A, Table 1, column 4) since both measure sets would then be culturally bound. We would expect to find: (a) significant canonical correlations between the two sets of measures; (b) significant covariance between the discriminants; and (c) a significant correlation between the discriminant scores in multivariate space. We are presently in the process of testing this hypothesis.

It is conceivable that these findings might reflect sampling or other factors peculiar to our study. However, the absence of even a low correlation between these two scores in this analysis raises doubts that the two types of measurements are mutually sensitive to common aspects of brain dysfunction related to learning disabilities. The neurometric measures discriminate between normal and learning disabled children in a fashion that yields higher concordance with prelabeling than do the psychometric measures, and they also measure electrophysiological processes directly and intimately related to brain function. Not only do the psychometric measures account for far less of the independent variance related to the distinction between normal and learning disabled children, but the relationship between the psychometric measures and brain function is far more inferential and indirect than is the case with the neurometric measures. Thus, these findings cast doubts on whether the psychometric measures in our test battery, which included most of the instruments commonly used to assess organicity in learning disability, possess any significant specific sensitivity to brain dysfunction. In view of the results of the regression analyses of covariance, it seems far more likely that the relationship between these psychometric measures and brain dysfunction is of secondary rather than direct origin.

Performance on the psychometric instruments is strongly influenced by the extent to which a child has mastered many of the skills necessary for adequate performance in school. Failure to perform well on psychometric tasks might thus be expected to correlate with learning difficulties, since learning difficulties or handicaps impede acquisition of those skills. However, it seems gratuitous to assume that these psychometric measures provide any direct information about brain dysfunction, rather than merely reflecting the unspecific failure to acquire essential skills as a result of brain dysfunction.

In view of these considerations, we suggest that it might be useful to separate learning handicapped children into two distinct categories of dysfunction, for which we propose the labels "learning disorders" and "learning disabilities." By learning disorders, we refer to interference with learning because of factors of primarily environmental, cultural, or motivational origin. By learning disabilities we refer to interference with learning because of factors primarily related to organic brain dysfunction. Such organic factors might: be responsible for inadequate levels of excitation or inhibition of neuroanatomical systems, prevent the sustained focus of attention and inhibition of irrelevant input required to structure figure-ground relationships, produce inability to control movement or impulsive behavior, produce hyperirritability and inappropriate affect, impede sensory-sensory interactions or cross-modal integration, or result in inadequate encoding, transmission, storage, or retrieval of information in the brain. Dysfunctions of these types would seriously and directly disrupt the sensory, perceptual, and cognitive processes involved in learning and skilled performance.

Psychometric measures may be particularly sensitive to factors related to learning disorders, whereas neurometric measures may be primarily sensitive to factors related to learning disabilities. Children who display learning difficulties can be learning disordered, learning disabled, or both. The primary causes for learning disorders and learning disabilities seem to be essentially, if not completely, independent under the conditions of selection, testing of children, and analyses used in our study. Thus, although both categories of factors result in inadequate learning, it appears erroneous to presume that standard psychometric tests by themselves constitute a sufficient basis for the assessment of organic brain dysfunction, or that neurometric measures confined to features of the EEG can predict performance on psychometric tests.

We must emphasize that these conclusions are limited at the present time only to features of the EEG. Continuing analyses of the far more extensive neurometric measures represented by the AER conditions in the NB, which reflect information processing and dynamic interactions with the information sources in the environment and may therefore be more behaviorally relevant than the spontaneous rhythms observed in the passive EEG conditions, may reveal organic correlates of psychometric performance in future studies. However, thus far our analysis of EEG variables has provided no insight into any brain functions that might be reflected in psychometric testing performed in this study.

Accuracy of the Discriminant Functions

The neurometric discriminant score, based on the combined, weighted values of those neurometric EEG indices that individually correlated best with prediagnosis, accurately classified 93.5% of the sample of children in this study. The comparable psychometric discriminant score, based on the combined psychometric indices that were individually most discriminating, accurately classified 75.6% of the sample. The discriminant functions yielding these results were then subjected to "leave-one-out" replication. In this procedure a discriminant function based on all but one subject is first calculated and is then used to classify the subject who was "left out." That subject is then returned to the population, a second subject taken out, and the discriminant function again computed. This new discriminant function is now used to classify the second subject. Successive independent discriminant functions are computed in this recursive fashion until every subject has been classified by a discriminant function computed using a sample from which the subject was excluded. Although computation is costly, this method provides an evaluation of the accuracy of a discriminant function without an experimentally costly, independently drawn second sample (11). If the initial accuracy of the discriminant function reflects merely chance influences, then the classification of the left-out subjects in leave-one-out replication should be at no better than the chance level.

The accuracy of the neurometric EEG discriminant score as assessed by leave-one-out replication was 76%. The accuracy of the psychometric discriminant score assessed the same way was 71%. These results are presented in Table 6.

In order to examine the relationships between the neurometric and psychometric discriminant scores, we plotted the values of these two indices for every subject on a plane defined by a neurometric and a psychometric axis. A surface was then constructed the height of which was proportional to the number of subjects whose values were located in each local region on that plane.

Figure 3 displays the results of this graphic construction. Each of the eight contours represents a view of this "neurometric-psychometric discriminant score density surface" from a different perspective. Examination of these different views of the density surface reflects the greater discriminability between the two subgroups afforded by the neurometric discriminant; separate peaks in the distribution are more clearly evident when the surface is viewed orthogonally to the neurometric axis than to the psychometric axis.

A concordance analysis of accurate and inaccurate diagnosis among the three available descriptors of learning handicap (prediagnosis, neurometric discriminant score, and psychometric discriminant score) was possible for 153 children (103 prelabeled normal and 50 prelabeled learning handicapped) and yielded interesting results. Whereas no child prediagnosed as

TABLE 6. *Concordance performance of leave-one-out replication of psychometric and neurometric discriminant*

	Predicted "normal"	Predicted "learning handicapped" (LH)	Total
	Psychometric discriminant		
Prediagnosed "normal"	101 (61%)	9 (5%)	110
Prediagnosed "LH"	39 (23%)	17 (10%)	56
Total	140	26	166
	Neurometric discriminant		
Prediagnosed "normal"	91 (58%)	11 (7%)	102
Prediagnosed "LH"	25 (16%)	29 (19%)	54
Total	116	40	156

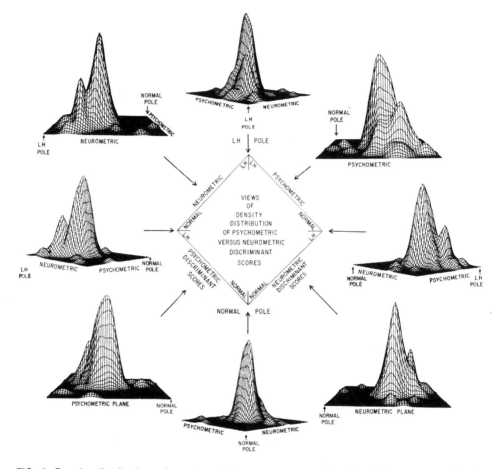

FIG. 3. Density distribution of psychometric versus neurometric discriminant scores. The 2 scores for each subject have been plotted with respect to a psychometric and neurometric axis. Surfaces illustrated represent the number or density of subjects whose scores fell at the corresponding points. These surfaces are presented as if viewed from different vantage points to permit visualization of the distributions.

normal was classified as dysfunctional by both neurometric and psychometric criteria, almost all (87% or 20 out of 23) of the children prelabeled as learning handicapped who were considered normal by neurometrics were also classed as normal by psychometric scores.

Apparently about one-third of the children prelabeled as learning handicapped display neither neurometric nor psychometric dysfunctions. One might speculate that these children display learning difficulties because of situational stresses and inadequacies more related to motivational or social factors than to fundamental inability to learn. Approximately the same proportion of children initially classified as normal was classified as dysfunctional by either neurometrics or psychometrics alone. Presumably, these children represent "overachievers" who have successfully compensated for dysfunctions that might otherwise have impeded learning. Whereas only a small proportion of children prediagnosed as learning handicapped were considered dysfunctional by neurometric but not by psychometric criteria (3 children), a much larger number were considered dysfunctional by psychometric but not by neurometric criteria (15 children). These discrepancies reinforce the conclusions above that the two types of measures as defined in this study reflect different aspects of dysfunction, learning disorder and learning disability. Finally, 24% ($N = 12$) of the children prelabeled as learning handicapped were found to be dysfunctional by both neurometric and psychometric criteria, i.e., were both learning disordered and learning disabled. This value may be lower than the actual value because of the poor discriminating power of the psychometric instruments in our battery.

Summary

The comparison of classifications of normal and learning handicapped children obtained using discriminant scores derived from neurometric EEG indices, psychometric indices, and prelabeling supports several tentative conclusions. First, using neurometric measures derived from 2 min of automatically recorded spontaneous EEG subjected to analysis by numerical taxonomic methods, it is possible to discriminate between normal and learning handicapped children as well as or better than with psychometric measures derived from 4 hr of tests administered and scored by skilled examiners. Second, a substantial proportion (17%, $N = 18$) of children prediagnosed as *normal* display significant neurometric and/or psychometric dysfunction, and presumably reflect overachievers who have successfully compensated for potentially significant dysfunctions. Third, a substantial proportion (40%, $N = 20$) of children prediagnosed as learning handicapped display neither neurometric nor psychometric dysfunction and presumably reflect classification errors made by clinicians and educators who referred these children to our study, or in the EEG as evaluated here. Fourth, although 24% ($N = 12$) of children preclassified as learning handicapped display both neurometric and psychometric dysfunction, presumably reflecting that they suffer from learning disabilities as well as learning disorders, a substantial proportion (46%, $N = 20$) showed only one or the other type of dysfunction. These findings reinforce the conclusion that the neurometric and psychometric indices evaluated in this part of our study are sensitive to independent, separable types of dysfunction. Finally, in 83% ($N = 15$) of cases of children prelabeled as learning handicapped in which neurometric and psychometric classifications contradicted each other, the child was classified as normal by neurometric criteria. This suggests that many children now placed in special schools or classes for brain-injured children may have been misdiagnosed and may be receiving inappropriate or unnecessary remedial treatment.

APPLICATION OF NUMERICAL TAXONOMIC METHODS TO NEUROMETRIC DATA

Although discriminant scores based on neurometric indices extracted from EEG features provide a powerful and procedurally efficient way to discriminate between normal and learning disabled children, the result is essentially to dichotomize the population into two groups, normal and disabled. Such a dichotomy has obvious utility since it permits accurate, rapid, and economical screening by personnel with no neurological or psychological training. At the same time, the attempt to develop individualized prescriptive therapies requires more than this screening dichotomy. It is essential to provide as detailed as possible a profile of the differential aspects of brain function, adequate as well as impaired, in each individual considered at risk for learning disability or other brain dysfunctions. In the remainder of this chapter, we shall present ways to achieve such differential categorization of subgroups within the learning disabled population by use of numerical taxonomic and related methods.

Functional Interpretation of the "Electrophysiological Brain Scan"

In an earlier section of this chapter ("Data Reduction, Display, and Classification by Numerical Taxonomy"), we described the methods used to construct a topographical display of Z-transformed values of any neurometric index or multivariate combinations of such indices. By plotting all of the displays that correspond to NB indices which show significantly deviant value anywhere on the head, and suppressing those which do not, it is possible to obtain a catalog of all electrophysiological features, related to spontaneous activity or reflecting sensory, perceptual, or cognitive processes, that indicate brain dysfunction in a particular individual. We refer to this catalog as an electrophysiological brain scan. In the section "Neurometric Test Battery," the conditions and challenges of the NB were itemized together with the aspects of brain function which they were devised to evaluate. Certain neurometric indices extracted from these EEG and EP measures were defined in the section "Quantitative Indices." Thus, the dimensionality of the measure space available for construction of a full electrophysiological brain scan is represented by that set of neurometric indices for all NB conditions and challenges.

At this point, it becomes essential to consider that the electrophysiological brain scan provides this abundance of information about every location in the International 10/20 system of electrode placement. Obviously, in order to interpret the possible functional implications of a significantly deviant Z-transformed value of any neurometric index, it is essential to take into account not only the NB condition or challenge from which the deviant index was extracted but also the region of the head where the dysfunction was manifested. Since the brain shows a significant amount of functional specialization, the consequences of a specified neurometric abnormality in one region can be expected to be quite different from the consequences of the same level of abnormality in another region. We have cautioned elsewhere (6) on the dangers of too rigid an assumption of functional localization.

Thus, we might expect a significant and perhaps often decisive interaction between type of neurometric dysfunction and the anatomical locus of the dysfunction. In order to obtain a general indication of the possible functional implications of a neurometric abnormality localized to a particular electrode location, we have divided the placements of the 10/20 system into five gross regions: frontal (FP_1/FP_2, F_3/F_4, F_7/F_8, F_z), central (C_3/C_4, C_z), temporal (T_3/T_4, T_5/T_6), parietal (P_3/P_4, P_z), and occipital ($0_1/0_2$). Following Luria, Thatcher (*unpublished data*) has constructed a table showing the major functions believed to be mediated by these five gross cortical domains. Luria (13) based his description of the differential mediation of specific functional processes by different cortical regions on detailed neuropsychological evaluations of the results of localized destruction of different regions by penetrating wounds suffered by large numbers of Soviet soldiers during World War II. In our opinion, this is the most complete study of this type currently available, although Teuber's (18) work in this area has also been substantial.

With the aid of Table 7, together with the list of processes assumed to be assessed by the test items of the NB as shown previously, we have the initial basis for inferring the probable behavioral functional consequences of neurometric dysfunctions found in an electrophysiological brain scan. At present, these inferences can be considered only as "best guesses." These best guesses are constructed as follows: Some NB test items are unspecific in that they provide a measure of brain state or integrity without challenging any specific system or function. The spontaneous EEG is an example of an unspecific challenge. Certain aspects of unspecific test items may have different specific functional implications. For example, generalized excessive delta activity in the EEG indicates a maturational lag with generalized learning difficulties, whereas generalized excessive theta activity indicates a short attention span. Other NB test items are more specific in that they are intended to measure a specific function. For example, comparison of large and small versions of the same geometric form (i.e., large versus small square) is intended to evaluate size constancy and visual abstraction. When unspecific test items reveal a localized dysfunction, a class of behavioral functions can be considered at risk. As specific test items challenge

TABLE 7. *Summary of probable behavioral functional deficits*

Occipital-parietal	Frontal
General	General
Visual acuity	Voluntary attention control
Vision of simple forms	General plan of motor acts
Complex pattern perception	Temporal sequencing of complex
Left	entities (e.g., expression of
Letter and word perception	compound sentences)
Representation of abstract	Mediation of general cortical
verbal forms	tonus or arousal
Perception of complex	Left
relationships	Syntactical representations
Right	Regulation of acts formulated
Perception of spatial	by speech
relationships	Attention regulation – inhibition
Representation of geometric	of old habits (switching)
forms	Direction and control of
Temporal	behavior through speech
General	Series operations (e.g., counting
Auditory sequencing	backward by 7s or 13s)
Short-term verbal memory	Right
Left	Attention regulation –
Audio-verbal representations	inhibition of old habits
Object naming	Medial and basal zones
Word recall	General inhibition
Representation of visual	Affective processing
images evoked by auditory	Regulation of cortical tonus and
input	sleep-wakefulness
Right	Concept organization
Orientation in space	Maturational lag (delta)
Wholistic perceptions	Parieto-occipital
Central	Temporal
General	Central
Control over skilled movement	Attention (theta)
Integration of motor impulses	Parieto-occipital
in time	Temporal
Mispronunciation of poly-	Central
syllabic words	Locus of control (alpha)
Short-term memory	Internal (excessive alpha)
Left	Parieto-occipital
Writing	Temporal
Articulation of speech	Central
Perseveration of speech sounds	Complex information processing (beta)
and written words	Parieto-occipital
Right	Temporal
Somatic spatial relations	Central

Unpublished table from Thatcher, derived in part from ref. 13.

the mediation of those functions by the brain, three possibilities arise: the specific test item will reveal dysfunction in the region considered primarily responsible for the particular behavioral capability, it will reveal dysfunction in a region not considered to be involved in a primary way, or it will reveal no dysfunction. In the first case marked behavioral disability is expected in tasks involving that function. In the second case moderate or slight behavioral disability is expected. In the third case functional compensation for dysfunction revealed by nonspecific measures seems to have been achieved, at least for the modest span of difficulty represented by items in the present version of the NB. Checks for internal consistency and reliability on these inferences are provided by the redundant nature of sets of test items in the NB.

In current work we are attempting to construct detailed inventories of functional capabilities based on brief behavioral tests. Canonical correlations between neurometric dysfunctions and behavior impairments will be carried out. The result should provide a more reliable and meaningful understanding of the differential functional implications of different profiles of neurometric abnormality as revealed by the "electrophysiological brain scan," hopefully with significant covariations between AER conditions and psychometric performance.

Differential Profiles Revealed by Neurometric Indices Extracted from AER Test Items of the NB

As described briefly earlier in this chapter and in full detail elsewhere (8), the AER conditions and challenges of the NB provide test items evaluating a wide spectrum of sensory, perceptual, and cognitive processes. These portions of the NB were envisaged to provide estimates of five types of functions:
1. Sensory activity in visual, auditory, and somatosensory modalities
2. Distinctions between three types of visual stimuli
    a. Spatial grids
    b. Geometric forms of different sizes and shapes
    c. Letters of the alphabet
3. Ability to recognize and predict orderly relations between aspects of the environment in different modalities
    a. Distinctions between predictable and unpredictable events
    b. Suppression of responses to predictable, irrelevant input
4. Sensory-sensory interactions
    a. Simultaneous versus sequential multimodal stimuli
    b. Recovery cycles
    c. Ipsi- and cross-modal focus of attention on relevant "figure" with suppression of irrelevant "ground"
5. Establishment of conditioned responses

To the extent that the AER conditions and challenges devised in the present version of the NB actually test these different classes of sensory, perceptual, and cognitive processes, the electrophysiological brain scan offers the ability to construct a differential quantitative profile characterizing the detailed capabilities of a particular individual. In order to ascertain the practical utility of the NB and numerical taxonomy for such differential profiles, logically we must perform two steps. First, we must establish that the test items in the five functional categories of the NB actually measure different processes in the brain. Second, we must establish that application of numerical taxonomic methods to such neurometric data actually reveals the existence of homogeneous subgroups sharing similar profiles and contained within the heterogeneous group of children classified as learning disabled. The remainder of this chapter presents evidence related to these two steps.

Use of Multivariate ANOVA to Establish that Different Functional Categories of NB Items Measure Different Processes

In order to establish that the test items comprising the different functional categories of the NB actually measure different functional processes in the brain, we adopted the following strategy. We reasoned that such different functions as sensation, perception, and cognition could logically be expected to require different amounts of time in the brain. Since the stimulus durations in the NB are very brief with respect to the analysis epoch of the AER (1,000 ms), and since latency reflects time after stimulus presentation, the crucial and distinctive features of the differential processing of information involved in these different functions could reasonably be expected to occur at different *latencies* along the epoch. Therefore, we carried out a series of multivariate analyses of variance (MANOVA), a substantial number of AER conditions of the NB. In each analysis, data were collapsed across the full 19-lead electrode set of the 10/20 system with the average voltage at each latency considered as a dependent variable. F ratios between the normal and learning handicapped subgroups were computed at each of 100 successive latency points, located at 10-ms intervals from 0 to 1,000 ms after stimulus onset. This multivariate analysis (12) is similar in concept to *t*-test differences between any two evoked potentials. The *t*-test is the limiting case of the more general F test, where the number of levels of a factor is reduced to two. If leads are considered to be independent factors in a multivariate neurometric space, then the difference between the two subgroups can be expressed as a series of univariate F statistics, as a function of the dependent variable time, or latency in seconds from stimulus onset. Differences between subgroups can then be represented as the degree to which any single latency point, or sequence of latency points, significantly separates them. A significant F value is interpreted to reflect that the mean voltage value, averaged across all electrode locations, was significantly different between the two subgroups at each latency where such F values were found. Averaging across all derivations serves to collapse differences between scalp locations into a value integrated across the whole head.

The consistent finding of high F values with this treatment may reflect the fact that dysfunction, although perhaps most strongly expressed in a particular region, is likely to be displayed across a fairly extensive cortical domain. Step-down discriminant functions were computed to assess the independence of F values at successive latency points. The 0.01 level was selected as the value at which processes at different latencies would be considered to reflect differences between groups independently. All peaks of F values reported below were independent by this criterion.

The results showed that highly significant differences between the normal and learning handicapped subgroups could be demonstrated for *every* AER condition and challenge of the NB thus far analyzed (through function 3b on page 321). More important for the purposes of the present discussion, these significant differences were found at different latencies, depending on the particular function types or challenges. These results are illustrated, for a portion of the data, in Fig. 4.

Figure 4 presents the results of the MANOVA computation for three groups of NB test items from the first type of function: spatial grids of different spatial frequency equated for percentage transmission of light, different sizes and shapes of geometric forms, and different letters of the alphabet. Examination of Fig. 4 reveals that highly significant F ratios

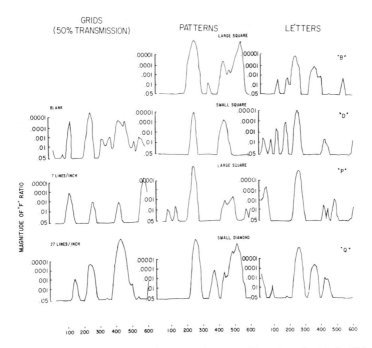

FIG. 4. Graphs describing the F ratio between normal and learning disabled children as a function of latency for 11 EP conditions of the NB. For further details, see text.

were found at approximately comparable latencies within each group of AER conditions, but that these latencies differed from group to group. Thus, the latencies showing major effects for spatial grids were approximately 130, 240, and 430 msec. The major differences between the two subgroups in responses to geometric forms were approximately 240 and 450 msec with no significant effect at 130 msec. The major differences in responses to different letters were about 240, 360, and 450 msec.

Comparison of these results with the literature evaluating AER features of learning handicapped children by conventional univariate methods reveals that the multivariate neurometric approach has uncovered possible powerful AER component differences between normal and learning handicapped children which have hitherto been masked by univariate approaches to "component identification" by use of limited sets of electrodes and by reliance on conditions. Analysis of these results component by component or condition by condition would tend to obscure the existence of different critical time domains and the possibility of differential profiles of dysfunction. No reliable reports of significant differences in AER between normal and learning handicapped children at latencies beyond P300 have appeared in the literature, yet our data show clear strong effects beyond 600 msec. Examination of the full set of data clearly indicates that neurometric methods provide a detailed, multivariate description of dysfunction, that the different groups of AER conditions of the NB provide estimates of brain processes occurring at substantially different latencies and therefore presumably reflecting functionally distinct events, and that substantial reliability and consistency exists within items belonging to the same NB function type. The detailed analyses on which this conclusion is based will be reported elsewhere. In view of these conclusions, we contend that neurometric evaluation of the multiple AER conditions and challenges of the NB provides an estimate of a multidimensional functional space, and that the latency characteristics of the F ratios found in different test items support the belief that the test items within a functional group in the NB constitute different independent estimates of closely similar processes.

Use of Cluster Analysis Methods for Numerical Taxonomic Classification of Subgroups of Learning Disabled Children

The findings described above provide support for the belief that a vector reflecting significant Z-deviations from population norms on this set of test items does in fact constitute a very detailed (albeit still rudimentary) profile of the sensory, perceptual, and cognitive capabilities of an individual. Application of numerical taxonomic methods to such vectors should provide the basis for an objective, unbiased classification of characteristic profiles of neurometric dysfunction shared by distinct clusters of learning handicapped and/or normal children. Should such clusters in fact be found, that finding would indicate that certain multivariate patterns of dysfunction were shared by substantial fractions of the population of children displaying learning difficulties. Such a finding would raise the possibility of identifying different etiologies responsible for the different patterns of dysfunction and would provide an indispensable basis for the search for prescriptive therapies optimized for the remediation of individuals belonging to a particular cluster.

A cluster analysis method was specifically devised for this purpose in our laboratory by Daniel Brown after evaluation of a variety of previously existing methods. This method, briefly, is as follows: The first step is to represent each individual as a point in a neurometric space, in which each neurometric index corresponds to a different dimension. The distance matrix between each individual and every other individual in the neurometric space is next computed. Using prelabeling or other criteria, the investigator defines tentative initial clusters. As will be seen from what follows, these initial clusters could, in fact, be selected arbitrarily, since the same final outcome would ensue but after additional computation. Using the distance matrix, the average distance between the individuals comprising each such initial cluster is computed. Next, an average distance is computed between every individual and all of the members of each initial cluster. An F ratio can now be constructed, relating the average distance between members of the same cluster to the average distance between any individual and all of the members of that cluster. The initial clusters are now "purified" in view of the results of the F ratio computation; that is, individuals who fail to meet a minimum F ratio criterion are removed from the corresponding cluster. Further, individuals who lie so nearly equidistant between two cluster centers that the corresponding F ratios are closer together than some "guard band" defined by ΔF (difference between the F ratios) are categorized as "unclassified." This procedure is repeated until the initial cluster membership stabilizes at some residual set of members. At this point, that unclassified subject who has the largest number of unclassified nearest neighbors is selected as the center around which a new cluster is to be grown. This individual and those nearest neighbors are defined as a new cluster. The purification procedure is then iterated on this new constellation of clusters. The process continues until no new clusters can be grown which satisfy the criteria selected (1). The method was initially applied for the successful separation of a population of senile subjects into homogeneous subgroups, using data from a subset of NB conditions (3). In our studies of learning disability, the method has thus far been applied to data from only three EP conditions of the NB, drawn from the first functional type listed on page 321, illustrated in Fig. 5.

Using data from 50 children preclassified as learning handicapped, we identified five clusters. The average AER waveshapes for two electrode placements, P_4 and C_3, for the five different clusters are shown in Fig. 5.

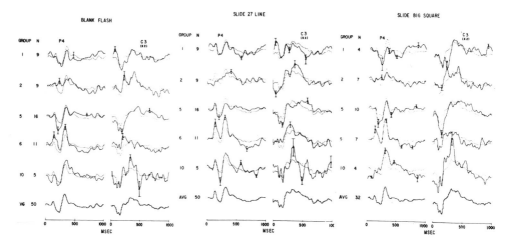

FIG. 5. Average evoked potentials characteristic of leads P_4 and C_3 in 5 clusters of learning disabled children under three different EP conditions of the NB. Each row depicts the average response of a different cluster. Bottom row of waveshapes represents the average response of the whole population, also depicted as the light waveshapes over which the individual cluster averages are superimposed. Bracket in the AER curves indicates the mean $\pm$ 2 SEs at each time point where the cluster average deviates significantly (< 0.05) from the population average. Note the relatively minor differences between the "population average" waveshapes obtained in the 3 different conditions. This illustrates how combining heterogenous subgroups into an ostensibly homogeneous pool can obscure important features that characterize salient aspects of the AER waveshape displayed by any particular cluster across the 3 different conditions (for example, the large positive-negative wave between 350 and 500 ms shown in electrode C_3 by cluster 5).

Inspection of the figure reveals characteristic similarities between the waveshapes of the EP displayed by members of each cluster across the three different test conditions. Thus the neurometric method, in combination with numerical taxonomic procedures, does in fact achieve the separation of a sample of learning handicapped children into clusters with features internally consistent across a variety of NB conditions. Similar results have been obtained for neurometric indices reflecting the absolute spectral power in the EEG for infants. Cluster groupings in this case appear to be somewhat correlated with gestational age. Since the likelihood of dysfunction in later childhood is correlated to gestation age at birth, use of the neurometric cluster analytic methodology may be able to predict developmental trajectories for dysfunctional characteristics.

The extension of these methods to multivariate vectors representing significant Z-deviations at latency points revealed as sensitive by the MANOVA method is currently in progress and is expected to result in further differentiation of the learning handicapped population. Data have been gathered on 500 additional learning handicapped children for this purpose. One advantage of this technology is the ability to construct a cumulative data bank, merging subjects from different experiments conducted at different times into one single, more inclusive analysis that better approximates true population parameters, with less bias by sample size than has previously been possible. This feature is a great advantage, yielding improved accuracy of representation of normal function and dysfunction.

DISCUSSION

These data support a number of conclusions:

First, a new clinical and research tool has been developed that permits mass screening of children at risk for brain dysfunction related to learning handicaps. This tool is rapid, economical, and accurate and requires no specialized neurological or psychological training for its use. Methods for reducing and displaying this massive volume of neurometric indices have been devised. First approximations of the functional implications of deviant values on this electrophysiological information have been obtained by reference to studies of the behavioral consequences of localized brain damage.

Second, with neurometric indices derived from 2 min of EEG recording, it is possible to discriminate between normal and learning handicapped children as well as or better than with psychometric measures derived from several hours of tests administered and interpreted by experienced personnel with the added advantage of being potentially more culture-fair.

Third, neurometric EEG measures and psychometric measures used in this study may be almost completely unrelated. In view of this finding, we suggest that learning handicapped children can be divided into two distinct dysfunctional categories, "disordered" and "disabled." Psychometric measures appear to be sensitive to factors related to learning disorders, perhaps of environmental or cultural origin. Neurometric measures appear to be sensitive to factors related to learning disabilities, presumably more directly reflecting organic brain dysfunction. Although children can be both "disordered" and "disabled," the primary causes for these two categories of dysfunction may be independent. It would appear that the presumption that psychometric tests alone can reflect organic brain dysfunction is erroneous or that the type of brain dysfunction correlated with psychometric performance is not reflected in the spontaneous EEG as measured and analyzed thus far in our studies.

Fourth, evaluation of the differences between normal and learning handicapped children with respect to AER waveshapes elicited by the various conditions and challenges of the NB using MANOVA reveals that significant F ratios occur at particular latencies characteristic of the members of each subset of NB test items, and that different subsets of items display different discriminating latencies. These results indicate that the spectrum of AER conditions and challenges in the NB assess a wide variety of brain functions and reveal considerable internal consistency within each subset of measures devised to assess a particular function.

Fifth, application of cluster analysis methods reveals the existence of at least five distinct clusters within the heterogeneous learning handicapped population. These clusters display comparable and consistent features across several AER conditions. Extension of these methods to the full set of neurometric indices obtained from a larger population is expected to provide a typology of learning disability across the life span.

Sixth, it is expected that further studies will reveal distinct etiologies for at least some of these different classes of brain dysfunction. Studies of the differential effectiveness of various types of remediation applied to members of particular clusters should eventually lead to the development of optimal individualized prescriptive therapies and remedial curricula. Such studies are in progress or under design.

Finally, the application of this method to the problem of differential diagnosis of learning handicaps is considered as merely one example of the potential utility of neurometric methods, in conjunction with numerical taxonomic classification, for the differential diagnosis, prevention, and treatment of a wide variety of brain disorders hitherto beyond the domains of competence of neurology, psychology, and psychiatry.

ACKNOWLEDGMENTS

These studies were supported by a grant from the NSF-Research Applied to National Needs Program ERP72–03494 and by Grant GI-34946. The authors wish to express their sincere appreciation to D. Brown, B. Corning, J. Davis, and R. Pector for their assistance with various aspects of this study. We wish especially to thank G. Chaikin along with the computer staff of the Courant Institute for Applied Mathematics, New York University, and the University of Connecticut Computer Center for assistance with computer analyses and computer graphics displays. Finally, we wish to thank M. Lobell and I. Wehr for their long hours spent typing this manuscript for publication. E. Roy John was supported by Career Scientist Award I-375 from the Health Research Council of the City of New York. B. Z. Karmel was supported by a sabbatical leave from the University of Connecticut and a special postdoctoral fellowship from the NINCDS NS-5235. We also wish to thank P. Easton, H. Kaye, and R. Siegel.

REFERENCES

1. Brown, D. (1977): (Unpublished PDP 11/45 program).
2. Denckla, M. B. (1973): Research needs in learning disabilities: A neurologist's point of view. *J. Learn. Disabil.*, 6:43–52.
3. Gerson, I. M., John, E. R., Koenig, V., and Bartlett, F. (1976): Average evoked response (AER) in the electroencephalographic diagnosis in the normally aging brain: A practical application. *Clin. Electroencephalogr.*, 7:77–91.

4. Hughes, J. R. (1968): Electroencephalography and learning. In: *Progress in Learning Disabilities, Vol. 1,* edited by H. R. Myklebust. Grune & Stratton, New York.
5. John, E. R. (1976): Neurometrics: The use of numerical taxonomy to evaluate brain functions. *Science (in press).*
6. John, E. R. (1967): *Mechanisms of Memory.* Academic Press, New York.
7. John, E. R., and Prichep, L. S. (1977): Neurometrics: Quantitative electrophysiological analysis for diagnosis of learning disabilities and other brain dysfunctions. *Proceedings of the 4th International Conference on Event Related Potentials (in press).*
8. John, E. R., and Thatcher, R. W. (1977): *Functional Neuroscience.* Lawrence Erlbaum Associates, Hillsdale, N.J.
9. John, E. R., Karmel, B. Z., and Prichep, L. S. (1977): *Functional Neuroscience, Vol. 3.* Lawrence Erlbaum Associates, Hillsdale, N.J. *(in preparation).*
10. John, E. R., Karmel, B. Z., Prichep, L. S., Ahn, H., and Brown, D. (1976): *(in preparation).*
11. Lachenbruch, P., and Mickey, M. R. (1968): Estimation of error rates in discriminant analysis. *Technometrics,* 10:1–11.
12. Lieb, J., and Karmel, B. Z. (1974): The processing of edge information in visual areas of the cortex as evidenced by evoked potentials. *Brain Res.,* 76:503–519.
13. Luria, A. R. (1973): *The Working Brain.* Penguin Press, Middlesex, England.
14. Nie, N. H., Hull, C. H., Jenkins, J. G., Steinbrenner, K., and Bent, D. H. (1975): *Statistical Package for the Social Sciences, 2nd Ed.* McGraw-Hill, New York.
15. Regan, D. (1972): *Evoked Potentials in Psychology, Sensory Physiology and Clinical Medicine.* Wiley-Interscience, New York.
16. Satterfield, J. H., Cantwell, D. P., Lesser, L. I., and Podosin, R. L. (1972): Physiological studies of the hyperkinetic child. *Am. J. Psychiatry,* 128:1418–1424.
17. Sneath, P. H. A., and Sokol, R. R. (1973): *Numerical Taxonomy; the Principles and Practices of Numerical Classification.* W. H. Freeman, San Francisco.
18. Teuber, H.-L. (1975): Alterations of perception after brain injury. In: *Brain and Conscious Experience,* edited by J. C. Eccles. Springer-Verlag, New York.
19. Walzer, S., and Wolff, P. H. (Eds.) (1973): *Minimal Cerebral Dysfunction in Children.* Grune & Stratton, New York.
20. Wender, P. H. (1971): *Minimal Brain Dysfunction in Children.* Wiley-Interscience, New York.

APPENDIX A: TABLE 1. *Summary of number of variables from eyes open and eyes closed EEG used in neurometric discriminant function*

Measure set		Total possible variables in set	No. variables significant	No. variables improved	No. variables worsened
EEG	Absolute power, eyes open	133[a]	27	13	14
EEG	Absolute power, eyes closed	133	43	8	35
EEG	Relative power, eyes open	114[b]	24	18	6
EEG	Relative power, eyes closed	114	39	13	26
EEG	Real pair correl. coef., eyes open	56[c]	0	—	—
EEG	Real pair correl. coef., eyes closed	56	26	9	17
EEG	Imag. pair correl. coef., eyes open	56	20	16	4
EEG	Imag. pair correl. coef., eyes closed	[56]	Not included		
EEG	Absolute power (eyes closed–eyes open)	133	110	50	60
EEG	Relative power (eyes closed–eyes open)	114	75	40	35
EEG	Real pair correl. coef. (eyes closed–eyes open)	56	0	—	—
EEG	Imag. pair correl. coef. (eyes closed–eyes open)	[56]	Not included		
EEG	Absolute power slow frequencies $(D_1 + D_2 + \Theta)$ (eyes open + eyes closed)	38[d]	11	3	8
EEG	Relative power slow frequencies $(D_1 + D_2 + \Theta)$ (eyes open + eyes closed)	38	11	4	7
EEG	Absolute power fast frequencies $(\alpha + B_1 + B_2)$ (eyes open + eyes closed)	38	10	3	7
EEG	Relative power fast frequencies $(\alpha + B_1 + B_2)$ (eyes open + eyes closed)	38	14	7	7
EEG	Ratio slow/fast frequencies (absolute power) (eyes open + eyes closed)	38	4	4	0
EEG	Ratio slow/fast frequencies (relative power) (eyes open + eyes closed)	38	7	5	2
		1,193 (100%)	421 (35%)	193 (16%)	228 (19%)

[a] 133 variables represent the values of the *absolute power* in each of the 6 frequency bands as well as the total power values for the 19 leads in the 10/20 system ($7 \times 19 = 133$).

[b] 114 variables represent the *relative power* calculated for each of 6 frequency bands for the 19 leads ($6 \times 19 = 114$).

[c] 56 variables represent the information for each of 6 frequency bands and the total band for the 8 pairs of homologous bilateral pairs in this 19 lead derivation set (e.g., $0_1 = 0_2$ pair, etc.; $8 \times 7 = 56$).

[d] 38 variables represent the values for each of the 19 leads for two conditions, eyes open and eyes closed ($19 \times 2 = 38$).

APPENDIX B: TABLE 1. *Loading coefficients of factors on discriminating psychometric tests*

Test[a]	Factor 1	Factor 2	Factor 3	Factor 4
WISC				
IQV	0.86	0.32	0.37	0.15
IQP	0.41	0.80	0.03	0.20
IQFS	0.72	0.63	0.23	0.20
INFO	0.71	0.24	0.24	0.25
COMP	0.72	0.18	0.05	0.17
ARITH	0.45	0.47	0.35	0.12
SIM	0.68	0.18	0.26	0.13
VOCAB	0.81	0.09	0.13	0.26
DIG	0.25	0.32	0.60	−0.04
COD	0.07	0.54	0.11	−0.01
DIGBACK	0.10	0.26	0.54	−0.08
PICOM	0.42	0.43	0.07	0.24
WRAT				
SP	0.25	0.06	0.73	0.28
ARITH	0.10	0.36	0.51	0.23
WORD	0.35	0.06	0.73	0.36
McCarthy				
TAP	−0.08	0.27	0.33	0.23
VMEM I	0.16	−0.05	0.35	0.25
VMEM II	0.26	−0.05	0.13	0.22
PPVT				
EXPVOC	0.37	0.10	0.19	0.52
RECVOC	0.42	0.15	0.11	0.62
ITPA				
AUDASS	0.46	0.31	0.16	0.63
VISASS	0.09	0.29	0.12	0.49
Bender Gestalt	−0.11	−0.52	−0.26	−0.24
Composite 3M	−0.33	−0.59	−0.35	−0.38

[a] Abbreviations are defined as follows: WISC, Wechsler Intelligence Scale for Children; IQV, verbal IQ; IQP, performance IQ; IQFS, full-scale IQ; INFO, information; COMP, verbal comprehension; ARITH, arithmetic; SIM, similarities; VOCAB, vocabulary; DIG, digit span; COD, coding; DIGBACK, backward digit span; PICOM, picture comprehension. WRAT, Wide Range Achievement Test; SP, spelling; ARITH, arithmetic; WORD, word comprehension. McCarthy, The McCarthy Scales of Children's abilities; TAP, tapping sequences; VMEM I, verbal memory scale, part I; VMEM II, verbal memory scale, part II. PPVT, Peabody Picture Vocabulary Test; EXPVOC, expressive vocabulary; RECVOC, recognition vocabulary. ITPA, Illinois Test for Perceptual Abilities; AUDASS, auditory association; VISASS, visual association. Bender Gestalt, Bender Gestalt (Koppitz scoring method). Composite 3M, organic dysfunction scale (see Table 4, text).

Coefficients underlined relate to derivations that receive the major contributions from that factor.

APPENDIX B: TABLE 2. Loading coefficients: EEG factors 1 and 2

| | Factor 1 | | | | Factor 2 | | | |
| | Slow | | Fast | | Slow | | Fast | |
Analysis: Derivation	Absolute	Relative	Absolute	Relative	Absolute	Relative	Absolute	Relative
Eyes open								
F_{p1}	0.12	0.10	0.10	0.13	−0.47	−0.39	−0.36	−0.34
F_{p3}	0.17	0.11	0.12	0.18	−0.37	−0.28	−0.27	−0.26
F_3	0.19	0.20	0.17	0.23	−0.21	−0.14	−0.11	−0.09
F_4	0.24	0.29	0.22	0.34	−0.06	−0.00	0.05	0.04
C_3	0.33	0.41	0.34	0.43	0.07	0.10	0.16	0.17
C_4	0.49	0.56	0.53	0.55	0.15	0.16	0.19	0.25
P_3	0.64	0.69	0.66	0.68	0.21	0.24	0.22	0.25
P_4	0.75	0.80	0.78	0.75	0.22	0.18	0.20	0.21
O_1	0.80	0.80	0.79	0.77	0.22	0.17	0.23	0.13
O_2	0.75	0.76	0.75	0.65	0.19	0.18	0.23	0.09
F_7	0.63	0.61	0.62	0.51	0.17	0.12	0.19	0.09
F_8	0.44	0.44	0.45	0.33	0.16	0.14	0.19	0.15
T_3	0.27	0.27	0.30	0.15	0.16	0.21	0.17	0.20
T_4	0.15	0.13	0.19	0.02	0.23	0.26	0.21	0.27
T_5	0.02	−0.01	0.06	−0.09	0.28	0.34	0.26	0.27
T_6	−0.10	−0.10	−0.07	−0.16	0.33	0.35	0.28	0.27
F_z	−0.20	−0.17	−0.16	−0.23	0.33	0.29	0.26	0.20
C_z	−0.23	−0.16	−0.15	−0.24	0.27	0.21	0.18	0.09
P_z	−0.21	−0.15	−0.16	−0.21	0.17	0.05	0.06	−0.05
Eyes closed								
F_{p1}	0.45	0.38	0.38	0.38	−0.03	−0.01	0.07	0.03
F_{p2}	0.40	0.32	0.32	0.32	0.07	0.14	0.21	0.13
F_3	0.29	0.24	0.22	0.23	0.18	0.30	0.33	0.32
F_4	0.15	0.17	0.11	0.16	0.33	0.45	0.47	0.51
C_3	0.11	0.14	0.12	0.14	0.52	0.62	0.64	0.72
C_4	0.14	0.12	0.14	0.18	0.67	0.76	0.74	0.82
P_3	0.16	0.13	0.16	0.19	0.77	0.84	0.80	0.81

P_4	0.19	0.21	0.20	0.19	0.82	0.85	0.82	0.74
O_1	0.19	0.20	0.22	0.16	0.84	0.79	0.82	0.63
O_2	0.19	0.19	0.23	0.10	0.75	0.66	0.72	0.46
F_7	0.12	0.11	0.16	−0.00	0.61	0.48	0.55	0.29
F_8	0.00	−0.03	0.05	−0.18	0.44	0.29	0.37	0.16
T_3	−0.13	−0.18	−0.09	−0.33	0.26	0.14	0.15	0.06
T_4	−0.27	−0.36	−0.21	−0.53	0.12	0.05	0.06	−0.05
T_5	−0.41	−0.55	−0.36	−0.66	0.06	0.01	0.00	−0.07
T_6	−0.57	−0.66	−0.51	−0.77	0.02	−0.02	−0.04	−0.05
F_z	−0.72	−0.76	−0.67	−0.82	−0.00	−0.03	−0.04	−0.07
C_z	−0.76	−0.76	−0.71	−0.76	−0.05	−0.09	−0.10	−0.09
P_z	−0.72	−0.67	−0.65	−0.65	−0.10	−0.13	−0.16	−0.12

Factor loading coefficients obtained from 4 separate factor analyses for each of the 6 different factors accounting for the power in the EEG spectrum. Note the extremely high concordance between the coefficients yielded by the 4 different factor analyses. Each factor analysis used 38 variables, obtained from the 19 monopolar electrodes of the 10/20 system recorded relative to linked earlobes under eyes open and eyes closed conditions. The 4 separate factor analyses evaluated 4 different sets of data: (a) absolute slow power (low delta plus high delta plus theta); (b) relative slow power (% low delta plus % high delta plus % theta); (c) absolute fast power (alpha plus low beta plus high beta); (d) relative fast power (% alpha plus % low beta plus % high beta).

Coefficients underlined with a solid line (XY) related to those derivations that receive the major contributions from that factor; coefficients underlined with a dotted line (XY) represent derivations expected to receive major contributions based on the overall pattern of results but which failed to meet that expectation; coefficients underlined with an interrupted bar (X Y) represent derivations receiving major contributions but not belonging to a clearly discernible pattern.

There are 152 loading coefficients for each factor. For Factor 1, 42 of the 152 are quite high (0.50) and fall in a clear pattern. Two coefficients expected to correspond to that pattern fail to do so, although one large coefficient belongs to no discernible pattern. For factor 2, 24 of the coefficients are high and fit a clear pattern. Three other coefficients are high but fail to fit a pattern. For factor 3, 28 high coefficients fit a clear pattern whereas one other seems aberrant. For factor 4, 23 high coefficients fit a clear pattern, 1 coefficient in the pattern is unexpectedly low, and 2 high coefficients belong to no pattern. For factor 5, 26 high coefficients fit a clear pattern, but 2 coefficients belonging to that pattern are slightly lower than expected. For factor 6, 21 high coefficients fit a clear pattern, although 3 coefficients in the pattern are slightly lower than expected. Two high coefficients seem to belong to no pattern.

Selection of 0.50 as the size of a loading coefficient reflecting a "major" contribution is of course quite arbitrary and has no valid statistical basis. It does serve, however, as a crude criterion drawing attention to salient features of the pattern of factor loadings and further provides a crude index of concordance between the results of the various analyses. Thus, of a total of 912 factor loadings in the four factor analyses, 164 coefficients were greater than 0.50 and fell into clear and consistent patterns. Eight coefficients expected to be high on the basis of those patterns were lower than expected. Nine coefficients that were high failed to fit into any discernible patterns.

APPENDIX B: TABLE 3. Loading coefficients: EEG factors 3 and 4

	Factor 3				Factor 4			
	Slow		Fast		Slow		Fast	
Analysis: Derivation	Absolute	Relative	Absolute	Relative	Absolute	Relative	Absolute	Relative
Eyes open								
F_{p1}	−0.30	−0.21	−0.23	−0.23	0.54	0.54	0.63	0.41
F_{p2}	−0.21	−0.14	−0.14	−0.16	0.68	0.65	0.74	0.56
F_3	−0.13	−0.09	−0.08	−0.09	0.78	0.72	0.79	0.67
F_4	−0.10	−0.09	−0.07	−0.08	0.76	0.71	0.78	0.67
C_3	−0.04	−0.03	−0.02	−0.04	0.72	0.69	0.74	0.62
C_4	0.02	0.04	0.04	0.03	0.63	0.64	0.61	0.59
P_3	0.06	0.05	0.09	0.05	0.50	0.51	0.48	0.48
P_4	0.11	0.17	0.15	0.14	0.38	0.38	0.36	0.40
O_1	0.21	0.29	0.22	0.29	0.24	0.26	0.25	0.22
O_2	0.36	0.41	0.36	(0.49)	0.10	0.09	0.14	0.07
F_7	0.54	0.59	0.54	0.66	−0.00	0.03	0.06	−0.01
F_8	0.73	0.76	0.71	0.81	−0.07	−0.04	0.00	−0.07
T_3	0.84	0.84	0.82	0.87	−0.12	−0.03	−0.05	−0.09
T_4	0.83	0.86	0.83	0.83	−0.11	−0.06	−0.09	−0.06
T_5	0.81	0.81	0.81	0.77	−0.09	−0.06	−0.09	−0.01
T_6	0.73	0.71	0.72	0.66	−0.09	−0.12	−0.13	0.00
F_z	0.63	0.57	0.61	0.52	−0.16	−0.20	−0.19	−0.01
C_z	0.50	0.40	0.46	0.38	−0.23	−0.23	−0.22	−0.11
P_z	0.31	0.23	0.27	0.25	−0.39	−0.36	−0.39	−0.19

Eyes
closed

F_{p1}	-0.28	-0.18	-0.21	-0.17	0.25	0.21	0.27	0.28
F_{p2}	-0.13	-0.02	-0.05	-0.03	0.23	0.17	0.25	0.23
F_3	0.06	0.13	0.11	0.14	0.25	0.19	0.27	0.20
F_4	0.19	0.21	0.21	0.24	0.21	0.17	0.28	0.14
C_3	0.28	0.29	0.27	0.29	0.20	0.17	0.26	0.07
C_4	0.28	0.31	0.28	0.25	0.13	0.15	0.17	0.05
P_3	0.29	0.26	0.29	0.24	0.05	0.07	0.06	0.04
P_4	0.25	0.22	0.23	0.19	-0.05	-0.09	-0.08	-0.00
O_1	0.20	0.18	0.15	0.18	-0.16	-0.16	-0.19	-0.10
O_2	0.20	0.17	0.13	0.24	-0.28	-0.23	-0.29	-0.15
F_7	0.21	0.19	0.15	0.26	-0.42	-0.33	-0.42	-0.20
F_8	0.25	0.22	0.20	0.29	-0.45	-0.33	-0.39	-0.28
T_3	0.27	0.28	0.26	0.30	-0.47	-0.31	-0.41	-0.28
T_4	0.26	0.31	0.27	0.26	-0.37	-0.27	-0.32	-0.25
T_5	0.24	0.29	0.25	0.24	-0.29	-0.20	-0.25	-0.17
T_6	0.21	0.22	0.22	0.13	-0.18	-0.10	-0.13	-0.12
F_z	0.14	0.11	0.11	0.05	-0.10	-0.07	-0.06	-0.02
C_z	0.00	-0.03	-0.01	-0.12	-0.09	-0.03	-0.00	-0.06
P_z	-0.12	-0.23	-0.13	-0.26	-0.12	-0.04	-0.04	-0.10

See footnote to Appendix B: Table 2.

APPENDIX B: TABLE 4. Loading coefficients: EEG factors 5 and 6

	Factor 5				Factor 6			
	Slow		Fast		Slow		Fast	
Analysis: Derivation	Absolute	Relative	Absolute	Relative	Absolute	Relative	Absolute	Relative
F_{p1}	0.33	0.45	0.41	0.40	-0.06	-0.27	-0.09	-0.36
F_{p2}	0.34	0.44	0.40	0.41	-0.06	-0.31	-0.13	-0.35
F_3	0.32	0.41	0.31	0.40	-0.17	-0.32	-0.22	-0.39
F_4	0.30	0.39	0.26	0.34	-0.29	-0.34	-0.31	-0.38
C_3	0.23	0.27	0.16	0.25	-0.35	-0.33	-0.34	-0.37
C_4	0.15	0.16	0.10	0.16	-0.26	-0.24	-0.29	-0.27
P_3	0.13	0.11	0.11	0.12	-0.17	-0.14	-0.22	-0.10
P_4	0.07	0.05	0.05	0.10	-0.06	-0.07	-0.16	0.05
O_1	0.12	0.11	0.12	0.15	0.05	0.03	-0.04	0.16
O_2	0.20	0.20	0.20	0.20	0.09	0.13	0.03	0.24
F_7	0.22	0.20	0.21	0.22	0.07	0.22	0.11	0.23
F_8	0.19	0.15	0.14	0.11	0.06	0.24	0.14	0.16
T_3	0.09	0.06	0.02	-0.00	0.13	0.22	0.12	0.16
T_4	-0.01	-0.06	-0.06	-0.15	0.22	0.18	0.15	0.20
T_5	-0.12	-0.22	-0.14	-0.30	0.20	0.18	0.24	0.26
T_6	-0.27	-0.39	-0.30	-0.44	0.17	0.14	0.19	0.31
F_z	-0.43	-0.58	-0.49	-0.57	0.17	0.12	0.18	0.34
C_z	-0.58	-0.68	-0.66	-0.65	0.13	0.15	0.15	0.35
P_z	-0.64	-0.70	-0.68	-0.64	0.11	0.15	0.14	0.36

Eyes open

Eyes
closed

F_{p1}	0.60	0.69	0.65	0.66	−0.07	−0.16	−0.14	−0.01
F_{p2}	0.74	0.79	0.75	0.77	−0.02	−0.11	−0.10	0.01
F_3	0.78	0.80	0.74	0.76	−0.07	−0.10	−0.13	−0.04
F_4	0.72	0.73	0.61	0.65	−0.20	−0.13	−0.19	−0.08
C_3	0.61	0.56	0.44	0.48	−0.23	−0.08	−0.15	−0.11
C_4	0.44	0.38	0.31	0.27	−0.20	−0.03	−0.11	0.04
P_3	0.27	0.19	0.19	0.06	−0.07	0.02	−0.04	0.24
P_4	0.12	0.01	0.06	−0.07	0.05	0.14	0.07	0.44
O_1	−0.01	−0.11	−0.09	−0.13	0.16	0.34	0.19	0.58
O_2	−0.09	−0.17	−0.14	−0.16	0.31	⟨0.51⟩	0.36	0.69
F_7	−0.13	−0.18	−0.16	−0.14	0.40	0.62	0.47	0.76
F_8	−0.13	−0.16	−0.14	−0.13	0.52	0.74	0.51	0.76
T_3	−0.13	−0.17	−0.16	−0.09	0.60	0.77	0.66	0.74
T_4	−0.13	−0.18	−0.16	−0.07	0.70	0.73	0.74	0.64
T_5	−0.12	−0.16	−0.12	−0.13	0.74	0.63	0.77	0.51
T_6	−0.17	−0.19	−0.19	−0.19	0.63	0.55	0.67	0.38
F_z	−0.23	−0.31	−0.29	−0.26	0.46	0.34	0.51	0.25
C_z	−0.32	−0.41	−0.41	−0.34	0.25	0.18	0.33	0.13
P_z	−0.38	−0.46	−0.45	−0.36	0.12	0.07	0.21	0.03

See footnote to Appendix B: Table 2.

Psychopathology and Brain Dysfunction, edited
by C. Shagass, S. Gershon, and A. J. Friedhoff.
Raven Press, New York © 1977.

Event-Related Slow Potentials
in Psychiatry

M. Dongier, B. Dubrovsky, and F. Engelsmann

*Department of Psychiatry, Allan Memorial Institute, McGill University,
Montreal, Quebec, Canada*

Event-related slow potentials (ERSPs) explore cerebral functioning at the
symbolic level and reflect processing of information and preparation for
action. The potential usefulness of ERSPs as a diagnostic and prognostic
tool in psychiatry is examined. Contingent negative variation amplitude,
duration of the postimperative negative variation (PINV), and their major
behavioral correlations are discussed. The neurophysiological origins and
nature of these slow potentials are probably different. Several psychophysiological explanations of the PINV phenomenon are offered.

The search for objective tools (either biochemical or neurophysiological)
of daily applicability in clinical psychiatry has not been successful yet.
ERSPs may be one of the avenues we are looking for: their major advantage is that they are related to volition and movement, which underlie
all behavior or active mental involvement, and that they explore the brain
functioning at the *symbolic* level, i.e.; (a) processing meaningful stimuli;
(b) making decisions; (c) carrying out actions, after an imperative stimulation
or spontaneously; and (d) reacting to feedback about its actions.

These explorations have been made possible by technological developments (averagers, computers, long time constants, nonpolarizable electrodes). The most familiar of these slow potential shifts is the contingent
negative variation (CNV), described initially under the term of expectancy
wave by Walter et al. (32) who paved the way for these studies.

Unfortunately, only a few laboratories (less than a dozen in the whole
world to our knowledge) investigate the ERSP in psychiatric patients, and
their findings are somewhat controversial (4,19,26,27,30). This is probably
because of technical difficulties related to the elimination of artifacts (eye
movements and galvanic skin responses among others), as well as to variations in laboratory procedures. These latter factors emphasize the need to
establish universal standard references for ERSP recording, as has been
done for clinical EEG. However, in our own experience, more than one-
third of recordings in psychiatric patients and some 15% in normal controls

have to be dismissed, but once this selection has been carried out on the basis of appropriate criteria, the data are reliable and duplicable (8,10).

THE CNV, ITS COMPONENTS AND AMPLITUDE

The CNV (Fig. 1) was initially viewed as an electrical manifestation of conditioning, which occurs during the interval between a warning stimulus (S_1) and a subsequent imperative stimulus (S_2) that requires a mental or motor response (e.g., pushing a button to stop a tone or a series of flashes). Its amplitude, obtained by summation of 10 sequences, is maximum at the vertex and ranges between 10 and 25 μV.

Nobody questions anymore the existence of the CNV as a genuine cerebral phenomenon, but a consensus tends to develop that it involves several independent psychophysiological components. Recently, by prolonging the duration of the interstimulus interval to more than 4 sec, Weerts and Lang (33) and Loveless and Sanford (16) were able to demonstrate clearly an early negativity, which they associate with the orienting response, and a late negative component in the CNV, which they think relates to the anticipation of the imperative stimulus.

Although in agreement with the existence of two components, Rohrbaugh et al. (24) noted that the early negativity grows in amplitude over repeated trials, a finding not easy to reconcile with the orienting response hypotheses. Further, these authors believe that the late CNV wave is primarily a readi-

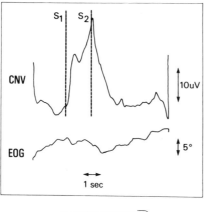

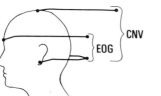

FIG. 1. Normal CNV. Supraorbital electrode recording for EOG is referred like the vertex electrode to both earlobes.

ness potential as described by Kornhuber and Deecke (15) and Vaughan et al. (31). These various components are at least in part responsible for the shape of the CNV (Fig. 2). This shape is usually a stable feature and enables one to recognize a subject within a group most of the time.

In addition to the CNV and the readiness potential (RP), a whole family of slow potentials has now been described, preceding or following external stimulation or spontaneous mental or motor activity; hence the name "event-related slow potential" shifts. These ERSPs are of interest not only to psychophysiologists but also to clinical psychiatrists. For instance, different patterns of RPs have been described by Timsit (28) in normal and psychiatric populations. However, we will not deal here with the clinical relationships of RPs or of other slow potentials following nonimperative stimuli, but we will concentrate on (a) CNV amplitude and (b) the phenomena following the imperative stimulation (6), which we have called "postimperative negative variations" (PINVs). We will show their independence and different clinical significance.

The amplitude of the CNV has been shown repeatedly to fluctuate easily and to be sensitive to a number of psychological variables, especially level of attention and of motivation (20).

It has been shown also that CNV amplitude is related to psychopathology. For instance, CNVs of low amplitude (less than 5 μV for a summation of 10 sequences) are frequently observed in psychotic patients (18). Timsit-Berthier (29) found low-amplitude CNVs in 24% of her psychotic patients.

Among neurotics, low-amplitude CNV is relatively frequent in hysterical neurosis (14%) and is almost never observed in obsessional neurosis.

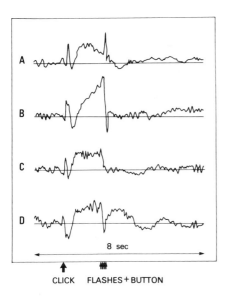

FIG. 2. Four types of normal CNVs. **A:** Fast-rising negativity followed by decline. **B:** Slow-rising negativity followed by decline. **C:** Plateau-shape. **D:** PINV within normal limits (less than 2 sec duration).

TABLE 1. *CNV amplitude (in μV) in antisocial personalities*

Source	Subjects (N)	Average ampl.	Controls (N)	Average ampl.
McCallum 1973	18	9 ± 5.2	20	16 ± 5.6
Allan Memorial Institute 1975	40	15.9 ± 4.8	30	19.1 ± 7

McCallum (17) found in his sample of antisocial personalities a low average CNV amplitude and interpreted these findings as related to the limited conditionability of this type of individual, but this finding has been contradicted (12). Table 1 compares the data of McCallum with those of Engelsmann et al.

The amplitude of CNV has also been found statistically higher in psychosomatic patients (7).

Finally, the amplitude of the CNV can be experimentally manipulated in patients suffering from specific phobias; if the imperative stimulus (S_2) is a slide picturing the feared object, the CNV amplitude usually increases (1).

But in general one can say that the relationships between CNV amplitude and psychopathology are labile, rather weak statistically, and rarely of help in any single case. Thus practical application of the CNV studies does not seem to have much future in clinical psychiatry.

DURATION OF THE POSTIMPERATIVE NEGATIVITY

Delayed return to the base line has been observed after the imperative stimulus in several laboratories, and especially in psychiatric populations. However, the existence of this postimperative negative variation is much more controversial than the CNV itself. For instance, Picton and Low (22) recorded 12 patients from psychiatric wards and could show no significant differences "between measured data from psychiatric patients including the schizophrenics and the asymptomatic volunteers." They considered the recordings "unreliable because of artefact contamination."

A typical PINV may be observed either in a CNV paradigm (Fig. 3) or independently of any warning stimulation (Fig. 4). The two PINVs in Fig. 4 were both obtained in medical students. The bottom record shows a markedly abnormal PINV lasting approximately 4 sec; this subject developed an active paranoid episode a few months later. This of course is only an isolated example of the predictive value of the PINV in psychopathology, but we have reported statistically significant results concerning behavior prediction in psychiatric residents and marriage counselors (9).

Like the CNV, the PINV probably encompasses several different phenomena, possibly originating from various cerebral structures; its early part may be related to anxiety in the performance situation. This could account

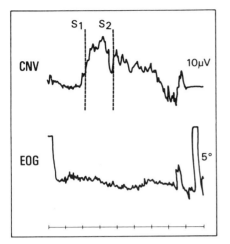

FIG. 3. Postimperative negative variation (3 sec after S_2).

for the different resolution modes of the PINV in normal and psychiatric populations, well described by Timsit-Berthier (29): a certain shape of PINV (Fig. 5) seems to be more normal than others (although there is no difference in total duration when maximum amplitude is observed immediately after S_2 and declines henceforth. It may be hypothesized that the early part of PINV is related to a continued orienting reaction, whereas the middle part (prominent in dome shape) is a prolonged post-motor negativity.

Like the CNV, the PINV may be manipulated experimentally in the following ways: (a) in phobic patients by using the fear-inducing stimulus as S_2 (slide picturing the feared object) (Fig. 6), as shown by Barbas et al. (1); (b) by making the task more complicated (e.g., requiring multiple choice questions to be answered by pushing one of four buttons); (c) by suspending

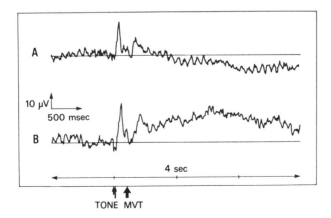

FIG. 4. PINV without preceding CNV. Subject **A:** Negative shift subsides 500 msec after the motor response. Subject **B:** PINV lasting more than 3 sec.

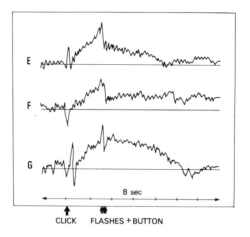

FIG. 5. Three types of abnormal PINVs. **E:** Negativity declines immediately after S_2. **F:** Plateau shape. **G:** Dome shape. (According to M. Timsit-Berthier, type E is more frequently found in normal controls and type G in psychotic subjects.)

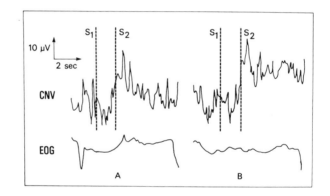

FIG. 6. When a phobogenic (fear-provoking) stimulus is substituted as S_2 **(B)** to a nondisturbing (innocuous) stimulus **(A)**, a PINV develops.

feedback so that the subject after acting on S_2 sees no effect (for instance, via a disconnection of the button); this type of PINV is more like a second CNV, where expectancy is prolonged, in vain, and is probably different in nature from the ones observed in most psychotic patients.

MAJOR CLINICAL CORRELATIONS OF THE PINV

The clinical relationships of the PINV are more stable and more meaningful than those of the CNV (9).

The essential correlation concerns severity of psychopathology, as shown

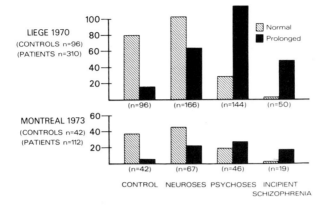

FIG. 7. PINV and severity of illness.

in Fig. 7. As can be seen from this figure, the findings obtained in our laboratory in Belgium (28) have been duplicated in Montreal: the proportion of abnormally prolonged PINV is higher in the group of neurotic patients than in the control population, and still much higher in the psychotic group where it reaches 75% (3,8).

The higher proportion of abnormalities is in early schizophrenia (94%), whereas the percentage may fall as low as 39% in a group of residual schizophrenics.

Personality disorders usually show a proportion of abnormalities lying in between those of the normal controls and the neurotic group.

It is noteworthy that the PINV is an unspecific phenomenon that does not discriminate, for instance, among mania, psychotic depression, schizophrenia, or severe obsessional neurosis.

However, we found in our sample of 103 psychiatric patients positive and significant correlations of the PINV with several psychopathological indices: both the total pathology score on the Brief Psychiatric Rating Scale (BPRS) as well as the score on the Clinical Global Impression scale yielded $r = 0.32$ with the PINV duration ($p < 0.01$). Correlations with the BPRS thinking disturbance and withdrawal-retardation cluster scores reached the 5% level of statistical significance. And $r = 0.28$ indicates a significant relationship at the 5% level between the PINV duration and the poorer prognosis of the examined patients. On the other hand, some negative correlations are also of interest (2); schizophrenics with normal PINV show on the BPRS more symptoms of depression, anxiety, and guilt feelings than those with abnormal PINVs: in other words, a schizoaffective, depressive component in a schizophrenic patient, possibly with better prognosis, is statistically related to a normal PINV.

In blood relatives of psychotic patients, preliminary results of studies

TABLE 2. *PINV classification and sex of patient*

	M	F	Total
Normal PINV	9	4	13(27.1%)
Abnormal PINV	14	17	31(64.6%)
Uninterpretable	1	3	4(8.3%)
Total	24	24	48

$x_2^2 = 3.21$; $p = 0.20$.

TABLE 3. *PINV classification and age of patient*

	Normal PINV		Abnormal PINV		Uninterpretable	
	M	F	M	F	M	F
Mean age	43.2	39.5	41.2	42.1	41.0	46.0
SD	10.1	7.9	8.6	9.5	–	2.7
Number	9	4	14	17	1	3

still underway show a proportion of abnormal PINV higher than that in normal controls, in whom it is observed in up to 15% of cases.

Like the CNV, the PINV does not seem to be influenced by gender or age (3) (Tables 2 and 3). In this respect, these slow-potential shifts behave in different ways in comparison with the somatosensory evoked potentials (25).

NEUROPHYSIOLOGICAL ORIGIN AND NATURE OF THE ERSP

The cerebral condition during CNV on one hand and PINV on the other is probably different as shown by the differential effect of probe stimulation: if during the CNV a visual or auditory test stimulus without special meaning is delivered, it induces an additional evoked potential of shorter latency and heightened amplitude, whereas the contrary—prolonged latency and decreased amplitude—occurs if a test stimulus is applied during the PINV. This implies a condition of cerebral inhibition during the PINV versus a state of arousal during the CNV. Another neurophysiological difference between PINV and CNV has been put forward by Dubrovsky et al. (11) by measuring the influence of metabolic changes in patients with PINVs: whereas hyperventilation had no effect on CNV amplitude (Fig. 8), the duration of the PINV was markedly reduced (Fig. 9). Inhalation of 5% CO_2 had an opposite effect on PINV duration. Table 4 summarizes the data obtained by Dubrovsky et al. (11) in this study of the effect of CO_2 changes on slow potentials.

On the basis of these experimental data, Dubrovsky et al. have suggested that the brain generators of the PINV are more sensitive to metabolic

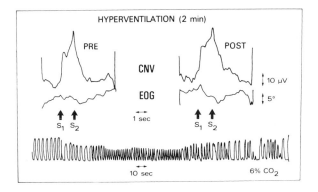

FIG. 8. Hyperventilation has no effect on CNV.

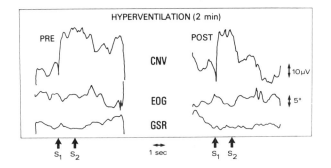

FIG. 9. Hyperventilation markedly reduces PINV amplitude and duration.

TABLE 4. *Hyperventilation effects*

	Control CNV		CNV with hyperventilation	
	Mean amplitude	Mean duration	Mean amplitude	Mean duration
Patients $N = 12$	16.8 μV	3.9 sec	13.6 μV $p = $ ns	1.6 sec $p \leq 0.001$
Controls $N = 10$	18.3 μV	1.1 sec	15.7 μV $p = $ ns	0.5 sec $p = $ ns

Effect of hyperventilation on the duration and amplitude of CNV in a group of psychiatric patients and in a normal control population.

changes than the generators of the CNV, and that the PINV may be a cortical after-event highly sensitive to biochemical changes in the tissue environment.

From which cerebral structures do the CNV and PINV arise? Many studies in animals as well as man show that the origin of the CNV is both cortical and subcortical, but investigators disagree about which structure comes first: contradictory findings have been published on compared latencies, for instance, of CNV recorded in mesencephalic versus prefrontal regions (13,21,23). Among the subcortical areas are the mesencephalic reticular formation and the thalamic median nucleus, while positivity develops in the caudate nucleus, preoptical areas, angular gyrus, and amygdala.

As to its basic neurophysiological nature, the CNV may be a combination of excitatory postsynaptic potentials (EPSPs) of superficial, axodendritic origin and of inhibitory postsynaptic potentials of deep, axosomatic origin.

PSYCHOPHYSIOLOGICAL SIGNIFICANCE OF THE PINV

As to the general understanding of the PINV, three interpretations may be offered.

First, Weinberg (34) designed an experiment in which resolution of the CNV was delayed by giving delayed feedback to the subject about the correctness of his response. He has hypothetized that the rapidity with which the negative shift returns to base line after S_2 is related to the action "resolving" the situation, i.e., terminating the processing of information relative to the task to be performed. In this case the PINV would be a state of prolonged expectancy because of an abnormality of feedback. In this perspective, it would be interesting to compare the reactivity of the brain during two types of PINVs: the one that is an obvious continuation of expectancy in a normal or anxious subject and the PINV of a psychotic patient. Probe stimuli and hyperventilation might yield different results.

Second, the PINV may be a peculiar response to an imperative stimulation, independent of the task carried out (29).

Third, it may reflect a post-motor neurophysiological dysfunction, totally different in nature from the CNV. Whereas a high CNV amplitude would be a witness of arousal, a prolonged PINV would witness a condition of cortical inhibition, a disturbance of cerebral electrogenesis related to voluntary activity, correlated with the psychotic process. The CNV would be governed from bilaterally activated structures in the brainstem and hypothalamus, whereas the PINV would be a sign of cortical inhibitory condition. Of interest in this context, as mentioned by Dubrovsky, are the observations of Hubbard et al. (14) on the powerful influence of beta-adrenergic catecholamines in the generation of steady potential shifts. This may be a possible fruitful line for exploration of the possible links between brain catecholamines, slow brain potentials, and the effect of antipsychotic drugs (which all have side effects on the regulation of motor activity).

DISCUSSION

Hundreds of biological correlates of schizophrenia and manic-depressive psychosis have been described over the years. They have been accumulated, some have been confirmed, others not, and many are either forgotten or vaguely remembered as supporting one of the dozens of conflicting heuristic theories.

What we need for a breakthrough are biological correlates that will be significant enough (and, we should add, easy enough to be used in practice, and not only in a small cohort of research patients) to be used by the psychiatrist as a much needed addition in his assessment of diagnosis and prognosis.

ERSPs in their present state obviously represent a very gross approach: a single electrode at the vertex picks up a collection of phenomena that originate in many parts of the brain and are related to a variety of psychological and psychophysiological variables. Let us, however, collect a few illustrations of how, even in their present primitive condition, they could contribute to diagnosis and prognosis.

(a) Differential diagnosis between schizoid personality and early schizophrenia: if over two or three consecutive recordings the PINV is consistently normal, the diagnosis of early schizophrenia may be almost certainly eliminated. As mentioned earlier, approximately 96% of early schizophrenics show an abnormal pattern.

(b) Differential diagnosis between a schizoaffective condition, with a manic component, and a schizophrenic process: If ERSP recordings show consistently abnormal PINVs, even if the clinical picture shows clinical improvement, the neurophysiological data may be suggestive of a schizophrenic process rather than affective psychosis. Psychopharmacological and psychosocial management of the case can be influenced by this prediction.

(c) Differential diagnosis between characterological depression and endogenous depression: The failure to respond to antidepressant drugs for 1 month is not convincingly in favor of either diagnosis. The finding on two consecutive recordings of abnormally prolonged PINVs with dome shape incites the consultant to advise EST (as a normal CNV is the most usual finding in a personality disorder).

The above examples suggest that a longitudinal study of the ERSP is probably the best way leading to clinical usefulness. Parallel clinical and neurophysiological improvement is observed in a majority of cases (32 out of 41 longitudinal studies at relatively short term so far). Psychotropic drugs do not seem to have any direct influence on PINV morphology and duration (5).

The prognostic value of ERSPs as compared with clinically judged prognosis remains to be tested by long-term longitudinal studies. Nevertheless, some patients in their evolution toward chronicity do show a normalization of ERSPs. (It was mentioned above that the percentage of normal recordings in personality disorders, of whatever severity, is 78%, and in residual schizophrenia, 61%.) One may speculate that patients with personality disorders, chronic characterological depressions, or stabilized residual schizophrenias have developed homeostatic adjustments to the stresses and/or genetic factors that originated the cerebral dysfunction and clinical syndrome so that often no electrical sign of the cerebral dysfunction remains apparent.

One final unanswered crucial question is, How frequent will the false-positive and the false-negative data be after refinement of the technique? That makes the whole difference between usable and unusable data as far as clinical applicability is concerned.

We feel that in some problems of differential diagnosis concerning schizophrenia or types of depression, ERSP measurements can help determine clinical decisions. We know that the predictive ability of the clinician in psychiatry is poor, and the predictive ability of our neurophysiological methods is not better established. Can the combination of clinical judgment and neurophysiological data be shown to be superior to clinical prediction alone? We need a few years to test this hypothesis, but we have the tools to do so.

ACKNOWLEDGMENTS

The technical contributions of H. Barbas, L. Armour, S. Schwartz, and J. Tepper are gratefully acknowledged. Supported by Grant No. MA-5319 of the Medical Research Council of Canada.

REFERENCES

1. Barbas, H., Solyom, L., Dubrovsky, B., and Stevenson, I. (1975): Characteristics of the CNV of subjects with specific phobias. Society of Biological Psychiatry Annual Meeting, New York. (Also presented at the IVth International Congress on ERSP, Hendersonville, N.C. 1976, and to be published in proceedings of the above.)
2. Chouinard, G., Annable, L., and Dongier, M. (1977): Differences in psychopathology of schizophrenic patients with normal and abnormal post imperative negative variations (PINV). Compr. Psychiatry, 18:83–87.
3. Chouinard, G., Annable, L., Dubrovsky, B., and Dongier, M. (1975): Post-imperative negative variation in ambulatory schizophrenic patients. Compr. Psychiatry, 16:457–460.
4. Dargent, J., and Dongier, M. (Eds.) (1969): Variations Contingentes Négatives. Universite de Liège, Liège, Belgium.
5. Dongier, M. (1973): Clinical applications of the CNV. Event-related slow potentials of the brain: their relations to behavior. Electroencephalogr. Clin. Neurophysiol. Suppl. 33:309–315.
6. Dongier, M., and Bostem, F. (1967): Essais d'application en psychiatrie de la variation contingente négative. (Trial application of the contingent negative variation in psychiatry.) Acta Neurol. Belg., 67:640–645.
7. Dongier, M., and Koninckx, N. (1970): Present-day neurophysiological models of mind-body interaction. Psychother. Psychosom., 18:123–129.
8. Dongier, M., Dubrovsky, B., and Garcia-Rill, E. (1974): Les potentiels cérébraux lents en psychiatrie. Can. Psychiatr. Assoc. J., 19:177–183.
9. Dongier, M., Timsit-Berthier, M. Koninckx, N., and Delaunoy, J. (1973): Compared clinical significance of CNV and other slow potential changes in psychiatry. Event-related slow potentials of the brain: Their relations to behavior. Electroencephalogr. Clin. Neurophysiol., Suppl. 33:321–326.

10. Dubrovsky, B., Garcia-Rill, E., Tepper, E., and Vanagas, J. (1973): Some aspects of the methodology of recording slow potential changes. In: *Biological Diagnosis of Brain Disorders. The Future of Brain Sciences*, edited by Samuel Bogoch, pp. 300–309. S. P. Books Division of Spectrum Publications, Flushing, N.Y.
11. Dubrovsky, B. O., Garcia-Rill, E., Simkus, R., and Dongier, M. (1976): Effects of changes in carbon dioxide tension in abnormally prolonged contingent negative variation. *Biol. Psychiatry,* 11(5):535–541.
12. Engelsmann, F., Reid, J., Dubrovsky, B., and Dongier, M. (1975): The CNV in antisocial personalities. Paper presented to the Canadian Psychiatric Association Annual Meeting (*to be published*).
13. Groll-Knapp, E., Ganglberger, J. A., and Haider, M. (1974): Voluntary movement related slow potentials in cortex and thalamus in man. Paper presented at the International Symposium on Cerebral Evoked Potentials in Man, Brussels.
14. Hubbard, J. H., Corrie, W. S., Thompson, H. K., and Marshall, W. H. (1971): Beta-adrenergic mechanisms influencing brain steady potentials in cats and rhesus monkeys. *Int. J. Neurosci.,* 2:57.
15. Kornhuber, H. H., and Deecke, L. (1964): Hirnpotentialänderungen beim Menschen vor und nach Willkürbewegungen, dargestellt mit Magnetbandspeicherung und Rückwärtsanalyse. (Changes in the human brain potential before and after voluntary movement, stored on magnetic tape and analyzed backwards.) *Pflüegers Arch.,* 281:52.
16. Loveless, N. F., and Sanford, A. J. (1975): The impact of warning signal intensity on reaction time and components of the contingent negative variation. *Biol. Psychol.,* 2:217–226.
17. McCallum, W. C. (1973): The CNV and conditionability in psychopaths. Event-related slow potentials of the brain: Their relations to behavior. *Electroencephalogr. Clin. Neurophysiol.,* Suppl. 33:337–343.
18. McCallum, W. C., and Abraham, P. (1973): The contingent negative variation in psychosis. Event-related slow potentials of the brain: Their relations to behavior. *Electroencephalogr. Clin. Neurophysiol.,* Suppl. 33:329–335.
19. McCallum, W. C., and Knott, J. R. (Eds.) (1973): Event-related slow potentials of the brain: Their relations to behavior. *Electroencephalogr. Clin. Neurophysiol.,* Suppl. 33.
20. McCallum, W. C., and Walter, W. G. (1968): The effects of attention and distraction of the contingent negative variation in normal and neurotic subjects. *Electroencephalogr. Clin. Neurophysiol.,* 25:319.
21. McCallum, W. C., Papakostopoulos, D., Grombi, I., Winter, A. L., Cooper, R., and Griffith, H. B. (1973): Event related slow potential changes in human brain stem. *Nature,* 242:465–467.
22. Picton, T. W., and Low, M. D. (1971): The CNV and semantic contents of stimuli in the experimental paradigm. Effects of feedback. *Electroencephalogr. Clin. Neurophysiol.,* 31:451–456.
23. Rebert, C. S. (1974): Intracerebral slow potentials associated with learning and anticipation. Paper presented at the International Symposium on Cerebral Evoked Potentials in Man, Brussels.
24. Rohrbaugh, J. W., Syndulko, K., and Lindsley, D. B. (1976): Brain wave components of the contingent negative variation in humans. *Science,* 191:1055–1057.
25. Shagass, C. (1972): *Evoked Brain Potentials in Psychiatry,* p. 273. Plenum Press, New York.
26. Small, J. G., and Small, I. F. (1971): CNV correlates with psychiatric diagnosis. *Arch. Gen. Psychiatry,* 25:550.
27. Straumanis, J. J., Jr., Shagass, C., and Overton, D. A. (1969): Problems associated with application of the contingent negative variation to psychiatric research. *J. Nerv. Ment. Dis.,* 148:170–179.
28. Timsit, M. (1970): The Kornhuber and Deecke phenomenon in schizophrenics and borderline cases. *Electroencephalogr. Clin. Neurophysiol.,* 29:535.
29. Timsit-Berthier, M. (1973): La variation contingente négative et les maladies mentales. Thesis, Doctorate in Biomedical Sciences. Université de Liège, Belgium.
30. Timsit, M., Koninckx, N., Dargent, J., Fontaine, O., and Dongier, M. (1970): Variations contingentes négatives en psychiatrie. (Contingent negative variation in psychiatry.) *Electroencephalogr. Clin. Neurophysiol.,* 28:41–47.

31. Vaughan, H. G., Jr., Costa, L. D., and Ritter, W. (1968): Topography of the human motor potential. *Electroencephalogr. Clin. Neurophysiol.,* 25:1–100.
32. Walter, W. G., Cooper, R., Aldridge, V. J., McCallum, W. C., and Winter, A. L. (1964): Contingent negative variation: an electrical sign of sensorimotor association and expectancy in the human brain. *Nature,* 203:380–384.
33. Weerts, T. C., and Lang, P. J. (1973): The effect of eye fixation and stimulus and response location on the contingent negative variation (CNV). *Biol. Psychol.,* 1:1–19.
34. Weinberg, H. (1973): The contingent negative variation: Its relation to feedback and expectant attention. Related slow potentials of the brain: Their relations to behavior. *Electroencephalogr. Clin. Neurophysiol.,* Suppl. 33:219–228.

Psychopathology and Brain Dysfunction, edited
by C. Shagass, S. Gershon, and A. J. Friedhoff.
Raven Press, New York © 1977.

Twisted Thoughts, Twisted Brain Waves?

Charles Shagass

*Temple University Medical Center, and Eastern Pennsylvania Psychiatric Institute,
Philadelphia, Pennsylvania 19129*

My task is to provide an overview of clinical neurophysiological research
in psychiatry. I propose to discuss some general issues and trends in this
field and to present a summary of the main research findings. The title of
this chapter expresses a core fantasy that continues to guide much research
in psychiatric electrophysiology. Can the assertion by Linus Pauling and
Ralph Gerard about twisted thoughts and twisted molecules be para-
phrased to say that behind every twisted thought lies a twisted brain wave?
I hope to show that, given a little bit of scientifically based qualification, the
fantasy may not be entirely quixotic.

GENERAL ISSUES

Statistical Nature of Surface Brain Potentials

The raw data of clinical neurophysiology are the brain potentials that
can be recorded by means of electrodes placed on the scalp. There are two
major types: "spontaneous" rhythms of the electroencephalogram (EEG)
and event-related potentials (ERPs) (96). Whereas the EEG can be recorded
directly after amplification, an averaging procedure is usually required to
reveal ERPs. The main kinds of ERPs include: (a) sensory evoked potentials (EPs); (b) potentials associated with movement; (c) long latency
potentials associated with psychological rather than with physical attributes
of stimuli; and (d) slow potentials, of which the contingent negative variation (CNV) is a prime example.

Psychiatric studies involving brain potentials can employ any of several
approaches. These include: (a) cross-sectional comparisons of populations,
defined clinically by diagnosis or symptoms; (b) longitudinal studies of the
same patient in different clinical phases, occurring either in response to
therapy or spontaneously; and (c) attempts to relate short-term variations
in brain potentials to concurrent fluctuations in behavior. Although literal
interpretation of the "twisted thoughts" question would require the third
approach, most studies have relied on cross-sectional comparisons. Im-
plicitly, investigators have sought brain potential indicators of the same

duration as the illness, rather than correlates of short-lasting episodic events, such as delusional thoughts. Instead of investigating twisted thoughts, they have studied the statistical predisposition toward generating them, as implied in a psychiatric diagnosis.

Unfortunately for psychiatry, distinctive brain wave patterns have not been discovered for any of the major "functional" psychiatric disorders. The absence of diagnostic "signature" waveforms has led investigators to search for quantitative rather than qualitative deviations from normal in the brain potentials of psychiatric patients. This implies that, if found, the "twists" in brain waves will be relatively abstract and expressed as quantitative abnormalities and deviant patterns of measurements. However, adequate quantification of brain potentials is a difficult task. The difficulty arises not only from the overwhelming amount of information involved, but also from the need to express, in some understandable form, data involving at least three dimensions: time, voltage, and space. Thus, even though there were many earlier quantitative EEG studies, they could at best provide only partial analyses until the development of computer technology. Even now, techniques for reducing and expressing three-dimensional EEG data in quantitative form are not well developed. Consequently, the number of psychiatric studies containing adequately quantified EEG data is small.

With the necessary emphasis on quantification and dependence on computer analysis, it is imperative for the psychiatric electrophysiologist to be aware that his raw data are statistical in nature at every step. The electrical signals recorded from the head represent the resultants of electrical signs originating in relatively large aggregates of nerve cells. Methods such as averaging and Fourier analysis introduce further statistical transformation; the data resulting from such procedures must then be reduced even further to make them understandable. In the usual clinical study, when one compares two populations defined by psychopathological criteria, one is performing statistics on several series of previous statistics. These procedures can be justified only if one assumes that the final statistical abstraction may reflect clinically relevant attributes of the myriad phenomena taking place in the neuronal populations contributing to the initial recording.

Those investigators who have been able to record directly from electrodes placed on or into the brains of psychiatric patients have obtained evidence suggesting that abnormal discharges may occur frequently, particularly during states of behavioral disturbance (26,65). Many of these electrical events take place in subcortical structures and are not readily apparent in surface recordings. However, it may be that subtle reflections of subcortical phenomena are present in scalp EEGs and that these could be detected by special techniques (92). Other kinds of neuronal events, such as single-unit potentials, do not seem accessible to scalp recording, but one can hope that neurophysiological research in animals on relationships between

potentials at the unit and surface levels may ultimately permit some interpretation of surface potentials in terms of unit phenomena (46). However,
for now, the clinical investigator has no direct way of relating the scalp
potential correlates of psychopathology to fundamental mechanisms.

The statistical nature of surface brain potentials makes it highly improbable that they can reflect the detailed patterns of neuronal electrical
activities that should be associated with specific mental events. It may be
that surface potentials can reflect variations in neuronal activity associated with grossly differing categories of mental phenomena, but they are
not likely to correlate with fine gradations within the same category. Even
though the depth recording of Sem-Jacobsen et al. (65) showed that focal
slow discharges, not seen at the surface, were associated with hallucinosis
and agitation, the discharges were not related to specific thought content.
The implication for psychiatric studies is that the psychopathological
phenomena (twisted thoughts) to be correlated with brain waves must be
placed into appropriate categories. Brain potentials may reflect presence
or absence of auditory hallucinations but not what the voices are saying.

Role of Electrophysiology in Psychiatric Research

Considering the statistical nature of electrophysiological data, the need
for complicated and expensive computer equipment to achieve adequate
quantification, and the uncertainty about basic mechanisms underlying the
electrical phenomena, it seems appropriate to present reasons for believing
that electrophysiology has a significant role to play in psychiatric research.

The first reason is the practical one that electrophysiological methods can
be totally noninvasive; this is an extremely important attribute because we
still lack convincing animal models of major mental illness, and demonstration of clinical relevance depends on direct study of patients. Non-
invasiveness has become even more important in this era of high concern for
the welfare of human subjects. The second reason is that electrophysiological phenomena occupy a strategic position at the interface, by which I mean
an intermediate level of observation, between behavior and events in nerve
cells. Brain potentials can be modified by psychological stimuli and changes
in behavioral state, and they must also reflect the activity of underlying
neural structures. Third, if strong correlations between brain potentials
and behavioral events are established, the potentials can provide objective
indicators of a class of behavioral phenomena; sleep is an outstanding
example. Fourth, I believe that successful psychiatric electrophysiological
research offers the main hope for bringing the advances and investigative
resources of basic neuroscience research to bear on the problems of mental
illness. This is because human brain potential phenomena can be replicated
in animal studies that permit experimental manipulations to elucidate

mechanisms. In essence, to demonstrate brain potential correlates of an illness offers the possibility of developing an animal experimental model based on intermediary neural events.

I consider the fourth reason to be the most important. Given a strong clinical correlate of an electrical deviation, one can determine the ways in which the change can be brought about experimentally in animals — whether by drugs, stimulation, lesions, alterations of electrolyte balance, etc. Unfortunately, there are usually several ways of generating an abnormal shift in a single kind of measurement. For example, we have found that the amplitude of early somatosensory evoked potential events is increased in chronic schizophrenia (82); this one finding can be brought about by several conditions, such as natural sleep, anesthesia, or electrical stimulation at slow rate in subcortical areas (63,64,75). On the other hand, if one could demonstrate several EP correlates of a given psychiatric condition, in essence forming a pattern, or a "neurophysiological syndrome," this would increase the probability that any experimental maneuver that can bring about the entire syndrome is influencing a pertinent mechanism. For this reason I consider it important, even if a single variable should have high clinical discriminative ability, to seek patterns of electrical correlates of psychopathology.

Electrophysiology's interface position and noninvasive character are potentially of great importance for biochemical research in psychiatry. The exciting advances of neurochemical research are limited in their direct applicability to man by the obvious prohibition against sampling human brain tissue for investigative purposes. Accessible body fluids may not reflect the state of brain chemistry and cannot usually be sampled continuously as can brain potential events. Animal models based on brain potential indicators of psychopathology could be used to test neurochemical hypotheses, thus providing a bridge between neurochemical observations and behavioral phenomena.

Although I have emphasized the importance of electrophysiological research for generating useful animal models, there are some more obvious possible benefits of establishing electrophysiological correlates of behavior. Such correlates could provide the basis for objective diagnostic tests, for which there is certainly a great need in psychiatry. However, the main applications of electrophysiological correlates have so far been in research utilizing the fact that brain potential characteristics clearly change concomitantly with major alterations in level of consciousness. Sleep research is, of course, highly dependent on the EEG. Other psychophysiological research aims at establishing correlations between brain potentials and gradations of behavioral state that are more subtle than crude levels of consciousness. It is hoped that such objective brain potential indicators can then be used to define psychological states more reliably and also to investigate underlying mechanisms.

State Versus Trait

The distinction between transitory (state) phenomena and enduring (trait) characteristics is a fundamental problem in biological psychiatric research. Cross-sectional differences between clinical populations can arise either because of basic traits associated with particular illnesses, or because illness increases the probability that certain kinds of transitory reactions will occur while observations are made. Obviously, state and trait differences do not have the same significance. The fact that brain potentials can change rapidly in response to psychological stimuli, e.g., those of an alerting nature, would suggest that they reflect state rather than trait phenomena. However, this is not wholly the case, as indicated by findings that given relatively uniform recording conditions, both EEG and ERP measures are quite stable over time (34,35,69). Furthermore, studies involving comparisons of similarity between monozygotic and dizygotic twins have indicated important genetic determination of both EEG and evoked-response characteristics (1,14,40,58). The relative stability and the evidence of heritability indicate that trait factors contribute a considerable portion of the variance of brain potential characteristics.

Because as much as half of the variance in EEG and EP characteristics may be genetically determined, the outcome to be expected when clinical populations are compared depends on the relationships between the illness and the genetic factors determining electrophysiological characteristics. Assuming reasonably uniform conditions and control of such state variables as gross level of consciousness, the variance in electrophysiological measurements can be partitioned into three main compartments. Compartment 1 would reflect traits, which may be both genetically and nongenetically determined; it appears to contain perhaps half of the variance. This leaves half or less of the remaining variance to be partitioned into two other compartments: compartment 2, which reflects state, possibly including the illness under study; and compartment 3, which contains uncontrolled "noise." If that portion of the variance related to the state of illness is only in compartment 2, the comparison of healthy and sick populations would be expected to show considerable overlapping because the trait and noise compartments would be equally represented in both; differences between groups would then be small. There are two other possibilities. One is that there is a linkage between the illness and the genetically determined portion of the electrophysiological variance; in this case, compartment 1 would contribute group differences. The second possibility is that the state of illness could override the genetically determined expression of electrophysiological variance, thus reducing compartment 1 and increasing compartment 2. Given either of these two possibilities, the electrophysiological differences between healthy and sick populations would be considerably greater than those to be expected when the illness factors are independent of, and do not influence, the genetic and trait factors. Awareness of these various possibilities is relevant both to realistic expectations from research in this area and as a guide to research strategy. Longitudinal studies of the same patients in various degrees of remission can give an indication of the extent to which measurements are related to trait or state. Studies of monozygotic twins, concordant and discordant for the illness, can define the role of genetic factors.

Psychophysiology and Pathophysiology

I have elsewhere formulated two basic orientations in electrophysiological research, the psychophysiological and the pathophysiological (74). These orientations are related to the state-trait problem. The psychophysiological orientation is essentially toward state; the investigator seeks covariation between events at the psychological and physiological levels. His ideal is a one-to-one relationship, so that he may infer events at one level from observations at the other. For psychiatry, the utility of such psychophysiological findings is that objective physiological measurements could be used instead of less-reliable psychological observations; again, sleep research provides an excellent example. The pathophysiological approach differs from the psychophysiological in that the physiological event is assumed to be primary rather than a time-linked concomitant of the behavior. Also, the pathophysiological orientation does not require a one-to-one correlation between events at the behavioral and physiological levels. Emergence of behavioral resultants of altered physiology can be allowed by assuming the possibility that physiological changes must pass a certain threshold before being reflected in behavior; an example could be the behavioral consequences of increasing or decreasing blood sugar. While the psychophysiological orientation must emphasize state, the pathophysiological approach is compatible with any combination of state and trait. I consider both orientations to be useful and valid, but it is important to recognize explicitly that they differ.

Methodological Problems

Electrophysiology shares the methodological problems common to all research in biological psychiatry, and I shall comment on only a few points. In essence, the problems are of two major kinds: (a) adequacy of clinical criterion variables, and (b) control over factors that may contaminate the predictor variables. On the clinical side, increasing attention is being given to subtyping patients within major diagnostic categories, such as the schizophrenias and affective psychoses. As Garmezy (19) has indicated, different subgroups of schizophrenics may deviate from normal in opposite directions, so that fallacious negative conclusions can be reached from absence of difference between controls and an entire schizophrenic group.

In addition to subtyping within a major diagnostic category, it is desirable to include more than one such category of patients in the populations studied, in order to have some basis for evaluating diagnostic specificity of biological differences.

It is well recognized that electrophysiological measurements can vary with age and sex, and that control for these factors is necessary. However, it has also become apparent that age and sex differences occur in psychiatric patient groups when they are minimal or absent in nonpatients (81,82). Appropriate statistical designs are required to demonstrate such interactions among age, sex, and illness.

Psychoactive drugs create the most difficult methodological problem in psychiatric electroencephalography. Relatively few patients have not had some previous therapy, and even though they are not receiving drugs when tested, residual drug effects may be having some influence. Longitudinal studies of the same patients with and without drugs can help to clarify the extent and nature of possible drug influences.

ELECTROPHYSIOLOGICAL FINDINGS IN THE MAJOR PSYCHOSES

I have recently reviewed EEG and ERP studies of schizophrenic and affective psychoses (72–74). An outline of the main results of these studies will be given here as a means of indicating the current status of knowledge in the field.

EEG Findings in Schizophrenia

Much of the EEG literature in psychiatry, particularly from earlier years, is derived from statistical compilations of findings obtained in the conventional clinical EEG examination performed on a "resting" awake subject with eyes closed. The trained electroencephalographer's visual evaluation of the principal waveforms contained in the record is occasionally supplemented by measurements of amplitude and frequency performed on small portions of the record. The effects of routine activation procedures, such as opening and closing the eyes, hyperventilation, intermittent photic stimulation, and sleep may be included in the clinical evaluation or, in some reports, provide the focus of investigation. Several reports deal with specially developed activation methods including: combined intermittent photic stimulation and pentylenetetrazol (Metrazol®) injection (photo-pentylenetetrazol threshold); intravenous thiopental (Pentothal®) injection to bring out particular rhythms (22); and intravenous amobarbital injection to measure sedation threshold (66). Automatic quantification methods were introduced relatively early (25) but have only recently received wider use; the most common analyses are power spectrum, period analysis, and time series analysis (variations in amplitude and frequency over time). Whereas most of the clinical EEG studies have involved recordings from electrodes placed over the entire head, few quantitative studies have dealt with more than one or two lead derivations.

Table 1 lists the main EEG findings in schizophrenia. Although many workers have reported a high incidence of abnormal waveforms in schizophrenic populations, there is reason to doubt that clinical EEG abnormalities occur with greater frequency in schizophrenics than in the general population. This is because the reported incidence of abnormalities has ranged from 5 to 80% in different samples, and the lowest incidence was obtained in the largest and most representative schizophrenic population (9,88). One must suspect that those series containing frequent abnormalities were biased by overrepresentation of patients referred for EEG because they manifested signs suggestive of brain disease, such as convulsive disorder. One finding, consistent in many studies, distinguishes between chronic (process) and acute (reactive) cases of schizophrenia. Extremely regular resting EEG tracings have been found more frequently in chronic than in acute patients (28). These very regular EEG tracings have been described as "hyperstable" or "hypernormal."

Findings with activation techniques, when positive, have generally involved discriminations between subgroups of schizophrenics. Thus, low photopentylenetetrazol thresholds have been found in catatonics (42). B-

TABLE 1. *EEG findings in schizophrenia*

1. Clinical EEG abnormalities—incidence 5 to 80% in different samples. Sample selection?
2. Hyperstable, hypernormal records in "process" cases
3. Lower photo-pentylenetetrazol threshold in catatonics (42)
4. Greater thiopental response (22)
5. Sleep "activation"
   a. More B-mittens (21)
   b. B-mittens mainly in "reactive" cases (93)
   c. 14 and 6 positive spikes in suicidal, assaultive cases (94)
6. Sedation threshold low in acute, high in chronic (67)
7. All-night sleep (38)
   a. Less REM time and activity in acute and latent
   b. REM rebound absent
   c. Shorter REM latency in schizoaffective
8. Power spectrum and period analysis
   a. Greater alpha frequency spread (37)
   b. Lower alpha frequency (20,33,56,85)
   c. Less alpha activity (33,56)
   d. More nonalpha activity (33,37,97)
   e. "Poor" organization across leads (37)
9. Amplitude analysis (time series)
   a. Low temporal variability (CV) (23,44,45,48)
   b. Less drowsiness than normals (33,44) but CV of beta also less (45)
   c. Greater amplitude in females (85)
   d. Deviant interhemispheric asymmetry (20,24)

mittens during sleep activation occur mainly in reactive cases (93), and 14 and 6/sec positive spikes (sleep activation) are more frequent in suicidal and assaultive cases (94). Goldman (22) found that intravenous thiopental elicited paroxysmal rhythms more often in schizophrenics than in patients with other psychiatric disorders, but the attempt by Sila et al. (87) to replicate Goldman's results produced equivocal findings. Positive findings in my own sedation threshold studies of schizophrenia were also related to subtype, the thresholds being approximately the same as normal in acute schizophrenics but higher in chronic patients (67).

All-night sleep studies have begun to reveal in the sleep of schizophrenics alterations related to phase and subtype of illness (38). Reduction of rapid eye movement (REM) sleep time and REM activity were found in acute schizophrenics and during acute exacerbations of chronic schizophrenia; furthermore, the normal compensation for REM sleep loss was absent in these patients. Comparisons of borderline and acute schizophrenic patients with normals showed less REM time and REM activity in the patients, with greater reductions in the acute group. Schizoaffective patients had much lower REM latency (time to first REM period) than acute and borderline schizophrenics. Ratings of symptoms reflecting "cognitive disorganization," such as hallucinations, were inversely correlated with amount of REM activity.

Quantitative EEG studies in schizophrenia have revealed a number of deviations from normal. In general, power spectra of schizophrenic patients have tended to contain more energy outside of the alpha frequency band and less energy in the alpha band than those of normals. When more than one lead has been quantitatively analyzed, the evidence suggests some differences from normal in organization across the leads (37) or in the relations between the hemispheres (20,24). Time series analysis has revealed relatively consistent evidence that amplitude does not vary as much in time in chronic schizophrenics as in normals (23,44,45,48). This reduced temporal variability may be related to a greater tendency for the normal controls to become drowsy during the EEG examination (33,44). However, the data of Lifshitz and Gradijan (45) indicated that in chronic schizophrenics reduced amplitude variability occurred also in the 18 to 32-cps band and provided the most effective discrimination from controls of any EEG frequency band.

If one considers the quantitative EEG findings from the standpoint of consistency across studies and probable influence by artifactual factors, it appears that lower central frequency of chronic patients is the most consistent EEG difference from normal in schizophrenia (20,33,56,85). The lower mean frequency (approximately 1 cps) agrees with the observation that chronic patients of process type often have hyperstable, hypernormal EEGs. The frequent finding of more EEG activity that is slower or faster than alpha in schizophrenic patients is not as consistent as the reports of reduced central frequency. For example, Volavka et al. (97) did not find excessive fast activity. Also, as Gibbs and Gibbs (21) have indicated, fast activity can be owing to muscle tension, and this form of artifactual contamination is often difficult to discern.

The lower central frequency in chronic patients is probably not caused by drugs or drug washout, as the patients studied by Rodin et al. (56) had been drug-free for a long time. Since it has not been shown in other kinds of patients, it may be fairly specific. Also, one would expect excessive muscle artifact to increase rather than decrease EEG frequency.

Evoked Potential Findings in Schizophrenia

Evoked potential studies have involved a variety of techniques and indicators. The commonly measured potentials have been generated by: (a) simple sensory stimuli, such as electrical pulses applied to the skin over a peripheral nerve (somatosensory, SEP), brief tones or clicks (auditory, AEP), and brief flashes of light (visual, VEP); (b) psychological manipulation of expectations about the stimulus, resulting in positive waves at 300 to 500 msec latency (P3, P300 wave); (c) task instructions involving contingency, as in a reaction time situation, in which the initial (alerting) signal indicates whether or not a second stimulus will require a motor response; this generates a slow negative potential, the contingent negative variation (CNV) between the two signals; and (d) requirements for motor acts, resulting in a "readiness" potential preceding the act and a sequence of "motor" potentials. More complicated sensory evoked potential studies have involved measurements of recovery cycles, in which pairs of stimuli are applied, the interstimulus interval being varied. By varying stimulus strength systematically, curves relating response amplitude or latency to stimulus intensity have been generated. In addition to amplitude and latency measurements, the consistency in time of EP waveshape has been estimated by means of a method introduced by Callaway et al. (7).

Table 2 lists the main evoked potential findings in schizophrenia. It can be seen that differences from normal have been reported with respect to most kinds of measurement, but that some differences tend to occur, particularly in certain subtypes of schizophrenia. Thus, in our own studies of SEP, we found greater-than-normal amplitudes in the early portion of the response (before 100 msec) in chronic but not in latent or acute schizophrenics (70,82). Within the heterogeneous group of schizophrenic patients, those with relatively predominant depressive symptoms had amplitudes like those of normals, whereas those with more overt schizophrenic symptoms (unusual thoughts, hallucinations, etc.) had greater-than-normal amplitudes (83). These SEP findings paralleled the schizodepressive contrast function of Overall and Klett (52). Although we did not find significant differences in amplitude of the later SEP (more than 100 msec latency) in our previous

TABLE 2. *Evoked potential findings in schizophrenia*

1. SEP amplitude
   a. Higher in chronic than in acute or latent (82)
   b. Higher in nondepressed, floridly psychotic (83)
2. AEP
   a. Amplitude lower than normal (8,36,60)
   b. Latency faster than normal (60)
3. VEP
   a. Amplitude varies
   b. Latency faster (79)
   c. Less afterrhythm (79)
   d. "Reactives" tend to be "reducers" (39, 82)
4. Waveshape variability
   a. Less in chronics before 100 msec (SEP) (84)
   b. Greater in chronics after 100 msec (all) (7,8,43,83)
5. Reduced SEP, AEP, and VEP amplitude recovery (VEP recovery less, particularly in hallucinated patients) (8,16,31,78,91)
6. Faster SEP latency recovery (82)
7. Reduced P3, less effect of uncertainty (41,57)
8. CNV
   a. Lower amplitude (12,50,89)
   b. Prolonged negativity (12,95)
9. Prolonged negativity and less "readiness" potential with motor responses (12,95)

work, this was probably because of limitations of technique (analysis time of 250 msec and bipolar lead derivations). Preliminary analysis of SEP data currently being collected without such technical limitations indicates that the amplitude of later activity is reduced in schizophrenic patients.

Consistently lower-than-normal AEP amplitudes have been found in schizophrenics (8,36,60). Also, AEP latency may be shorter than normal (60). VEP amplitude findings have not been constant, but faster latencies and less late rhythmic activity have been reported (79). Amplitude-stimulus intensity curves of both VEP and SEP suggest less amplitude increase ("reducing" tendency) among acute or reactive than among chronic or process schizophrenic patients (39,82).

Variability of waveshape has been consistently greater than normal in schizophrenics for all sensory modalities tested (7,8,43,83). However, this applies only to the activity after 100 msec. In chronic patients, SEP activity before 100 msec was less variable than normal (82,83). The contrasting findings for early and late variability parallel the differences between early and late amplitude findings. However, even though amplitude and variability are inversely correlated, covariance analysis revealed independently reduced early SEP variability in chronic patients (71).

Recovery functions can be measured with respect to both amplitude and latency. Reduced amplitude recovery in schizophrenia has been found for potentials evoked by stimuli of three sensory modalities (8,16,31,78,91). In contrast, SEP latency recovery was more rapid than normal in schizophrenics (68,82).

Studies of the P300 wave, involving both passive and active attention, have shown the amplitude of this wave to be reduced in schizophrenic patients (41,57). The CNV is also of lower amplitude in schizophrenics (12,50,89). Deviant slow potentials associated with movement have been found in schizophrenics. The amplitude of readiness potentials preceding the movement was lower in patients, and they showed abnormally prolonged negativity following the movement. Unusually prolonged negativity after movement has been found in schizophrenics not only in the contingent reaction time situation, but also when no contingency was present and when movements were self-paced (13,95).

Distinctive Features of the Chronic Schizophrenic Subgroup

Although many evoked potential measurements have been reported to differ from normal in schizophrenics, not many deviations are specific for schizophrenia. Thus, the changes in recovery cycles and in potentials associated with movement are found in other psychiatric disorders. However, within the broad schizophrenic group itself, there appear to be some consistent differences between chronic process patients and other subtypes. Table 3 lists the differences between chronic schizophrenics and normals found in both EEG and ERP studies. The evoked potential findings show shorter AEP and VEP latencies, higher SEP amplitude and lower variability before 100 msec, and lower amplitude and greater variability after 100 msec in EPs of all modalities. There is some evidence that reduced P3 amplitude may be relatively specific for schizophrenia, as it was not demonstrated in depressions (41).

Investigators have been inclined to interpret the consistently reduced amplitude and greater variability of later EP and slow potential events as electrical signs reflecting schizophrenic impairments in functions such as attention, information processing, or ability to maintain perceptual constancy. Such interpretations are consistent with some of the known corre-

TABLE 3. *Distinctive EEG and EP differences from normal in chronic schizophrenics*

EEG
    Lower frequency
    Hyperstability
EP
    Faster latency (AEP, VEP)
    Higher amplitude before 100 msec (SEP)
    Lower amplitude after 100 msec (AEP, VEP)
    Lower variability before 100 msec (SEP)
    Greater variability after 100 msec (SEP, AEP, VEP)
    Lower P3

lates of these potentials; for example, CNV amplitude increases with attention and decreases with distraction (51). The deviations in schizophrenia would thus be psychophysiological correlates of altered attentive functioning, etc. I believe it possible, however, that the changes in the later events are secondary to the deviations found in early EP characteristics, namely, increased amplitude and reduced variability (74). I have suggested that these early EP deviations reflect impaired functioning of a filtering mechanism regulating sensory input. Poor functioning of this regulatory mechanism would lead to input overloads and dysfunction of information processing mechanisms.

There are several possible candidates for the postulated impaired input filtering mechanisms in chronic schizophrenics. I have pointed out that reduced activity of septum and mesencephalic reticular formation leads to alterations in cortical evoked potentials like those observed in chronic schizophrenics (75). The reduced EEG frequency and hyperstability of the EEG are consistent with the hypothesis that such subcortical regulatory mechanisms are underactivated in chronic schizophrenia, as are also the similarities between the directional shifts in EP characteristics associated with sleep and the deviations from normal found in chronic schizophrenics (69). Recent findings of altered distribution of regional cerebral blood flow in chronic schizophrenics are in accord with the EP findings (30). Although total cerebral blood flow to a hemisphere is the same in normals and patients, the posterior areas receive more blood and the anterior areas less blood in chronic schizophrenics. Assuming blood flow to reflect degree of activity, this suggests that in chronic schizophrenics there is relatively increased sensory activity and relatively reduced interpretive activity, since the function of the posterior areas is more predominantly sensory, and the anterior areas mainly subserve interpretive functions.

Unfortunately, my hypothesis rests heavily on data from studies of early EP events in psychiatric patients, which have been investigated mainly in our laboratory. Although Ikuta (29) has also found increased SEP amplitudes in schizophrenics, the results pertaining to early events require additional confirmation; the findings for later events and slow potentials seem to be reliable and reproducible.

EEG Findings in Affective Psychoses

Table 4 lists the main results obtained in EEG studies of affective psychoses. Most workers have concluded that there are no specific clinical EEG abnormalities in these disorders, and studies reporting a high incidence of nonspecific abnormalities have not usually been controlled adequately for age (47). There appear to be some quantitative differences between patients prone to mania and those prone to depression. Alpha frequency was faster in patients with predominantly manic phases of manic-depressive disease

TABLE 4. *EEG findings in affective psychoses*

---

1. Abnormalities—nonspecific and probably related to age
2. Alpha frequency faster in mania than in depression (27)
3. Prolonged alpha blocking to flash in depression (11,100)
4. More photic driving (27)
5. Higher frequency photic driving in manics than in depressives (27)
6. Sleep activation
   a. B-mittens higher than normal, less than in schizophrenics (21)
   b. Small sharp spikes more common—correlated with sex and family history (90)
7. All-night sleep in depression
   a. Frequent wakening, less slow-wave sleep (49)
   b. Shorter REM latency in severe depression (38)
8. Lower sedation threshold in psychotic than in neurotic depressives (76)
9. Power spectrum—more fast activity (27)

---

than in those with predominantly depressed phases; this difference was present regardless of the clinical phase at the time of the test (27). Longer duration blocking of alpha rhythm to flashes of light has been reported in depressives than in normals or schizophrenics (11,100). Manic-depressives have also shown more photic driving than normals (27), with manic patients displaying more harmonics and flicker following in the beta range than the depressives. EEG power spectra in manic-depressive patients contained more low-voltage fast activity than those of normals (27).

With sleep activation, patients with affective psychoses have shown more B-mittens than normal but less than are shown by schizophrenics (21). Recently, Small et al. (90) have reported that another EEG variant observed during drowsiness, namely, small sharp spikes in temporal and anterior areas, occurred in 43% of manic-depressive patients and in only 12% of normals. The small sharp spike variant was related to family history of mental illness. Women with spikes had mentally ill relatives on the maternal side, whereas absence of variants in female patients was associated with mental illness on the paternal side; small sharp spikes in male patients did not relate to parental psychopathology, but half of the sisters of these men were mentally ill. Small et al. proposed the possibility that the small sharp spike characteristic might be inherited and related in some way to familial transmission of manic-depressive disease; they suggested that it could be a genetic marker. Sedation threshold studies of depression have distinguished between neurotic and psychotic types of depression, the threshold being low in the psychotic and high in the neurotic groups (53,76).

All-night sleep studies of psychotic depressives have generally revealed frequent wakening and less slow-wave sleep (49). Shortened REM latency appears to be a distinctive feature of severe depression, both of psychotic and unipolar nonpsychotic types (38). In terms of REM sleep alterations, there is considerable resemblance between psychotic depressives and schizophrenics of schizoaffective type.

Evoked Potential Findings in Affective Psychoses

Table 5 summarizes the positive EP results obtained in studies of patients with affective psychosis. The VEP test for augmenting-reducing, introduced by Buchsbaum and Silverman (2), discriminated between bipolar and unipolar depressive patients (3); the bipolars were augmenters whereas unipolars were reducers. Further studies of Buchsbaum et al. (4) showed the reducing tendency in unipolar depressives to occur primarily in male but not female patients. They also found that VEP latencies were shorter than normal in their depressive patients, and that latency deviation was greatest in the unipolar patients.

Perris and his co-workers (54,55) have compared the VEPs to flash recorded from right and left hemispheres and found relatively lower amplitude of the left-hemisphere VEP in psychotic depressives but not in neurotic depressives and schizophrenics.

TABLE 5. *Evoked potential findings in affective psychoses*

Depressives
1. Bipolar are VEP "augmenters," male unipolar are "reducers" (3,4)
2. Shorter VEP latencies, more in unipolar (4)
3. Right VEP > left VEP before treatment (54)
4. Reduced SEP amplitude recovery (77,80)
5. Faster SEP latency recovery (68,82)
6. Less AEP recovery with positive family history (62)
7. Low CNV (89)
8. Prolonged slow potential negativity (13)

Manics
1. Greater-than-normal SEP variability before 100 msec (72)
2. Low CNV (89)
3. Prolonged slow potential negativity (13)

SEP amplitude recovery was consistently reduced in psychotic depressions (68,77,80). In contrast, SEP latency recovery was faster (68,82). A study of AEP recovery showed a wide range of recovery values (62); when the extremes were compared, it was found that the patients with reduced AEP recovery had positive family histories of affective psychoses. CNV amplitude appears to be reduced in both mania and depression (89).

There have been relatively few studies of manic patients. One recent finding indicates that their early SEP variability is greater than normal (72). In common with schizophrenics, both manic and depressive patients exhibit prolonged slow potential negativity associated with movement (13).

Comparisons Between Schizophrenic and Affective Psychoses

Table 6 was compiled to bear on the question of electrophysiological differences between the two groups of major psychoses; it summarizes the

TABLE 6. *Probable EEG and ERP differences between schizo-*
phrenic and affective psychoses

EEG
  1. More low-voltage, "choppy" records in schizophrenics
  2. Longer alpha blocking to flash in depressives
  3. More B-mittens in schizophrenics
  4. Quantitative differences (frequency, amplitude, variability) from matched normals more prevalent in schizophrenics
  5. More small sharp spikes in depressives

EP
  1. AEP in schizophrenics
     a. Lower amplitude
     b. Shorter latency
  2. VEP
     a. Less afterrhythm in schizophrenics
     b. Schizophrenics are "reducers," bipolar depressives are "augmenters"
  3. Waveshape variability
     a. Before 100 msec—less than normal in schizophrenics, greater in manics
     b. After 100 msec—greater in schizophrenics
  4. Reduced P3 in schizophrenics

---

probable EEG and ERP differences between them. Unfortunately, relatively few direct comparisons have been made between these groups because they tend to differ in age and sex, so comparisons depend mainly on relative differences in deviations from control groups (72).

The EEG differences between the two groups of disorders are few in number and not striking in magnitude. Schizophrenics have been found to differ to a much greater extent from normal in quantitative EEG characteristics than have patients with affective psychoses. In particular, the lower-than-normal mean frequency in chronic schizophrenics was not found in psychotic depressives of the same age (85). The more prolonged blocking of alpha rhythm to flash in depressives is a finding of considerable interest; this appears to be a state variable since it normalizes with effective treatment (11). The high incidence of small sharp spikes in affective psychoses may be a genetically determined trait variable that deserves further investigation.

Many ERP deviations from normal are common to both schizophrenic and affective psychoses, including reduced CNV, prolonged slow potential negativity, faster latency recovery, and shorter VEP latency. The AEP appears to be of lower amplitude and shorter latency in schizophrenic than in affective psychosis patients. There is less VEP afterrhythm in schizophrenics, and acute schizophrenics tend to be reducers in contrast to the augmenting tendency of bipolar depressives. Manics differ from schizophrenics in SEP waveshape variability before 100 msec, and depressives show less variability after 100 msec than schizophrenics. P300 wave amplitude is also reduced in schizophrenics compared to depressives. Thus, although the two groups of psychoses share a number of ERP deviations from normal, differences between them suggest that some of the later phenomena, related to "information processing," may be less disturbed in affective than in schizophrenic psychoses. The predominant impression to be gained from the comparative data is that it may be less appropriate to seek overall differences between the major psychoses than to investigate differences between clinically defined subgroups within each category. Furthermore, there is some suggestion that the relevant clinical correlates may often transcend diagnostic categories; for example, severe depression is associated with reduced REM latency in both affective psychoses and schizoaffective schizophrenia (38).

EEG-SEP Relationships

Although many kinds of brain potential phenomena can be measured, most of the studies reviewed have involved either single measurements or combinations of several measurements made on the same type of potential. In other words, individual investigations have been limited to one or very few dimensions of brain potential activity, and the relationships between measurements along different dimensions have not been treated as variables in themselves. Since psychiatric diagnosis is usually based on patterns rather than single dimensions of behavior, one might expect clinical variables to be better correlated with patterns of electrophysiological events than with measurements in any single dimension. For example, the relationships between two classes of electrophysiological phenomena, such as EEG and ERP, might provide pattern variables correlating better with clinical criteria than either EEG or ERP measurements by themselves. Recognizing this possibility, we have recently conducted and reported the first study in which psychiatric correlates of the patterns of relationship between EEG and SEP variables were investigated (86).

The SEP data were obtained by means of the modified recovery function procedure (82). This procedure yields a number of measurements reflecting amplitude, amplitude recovery, and stimulus intensity-amplitude relationships. The EEG measures were mean amplitude, mean frequency, and indices of amplitude and frequency variability rendered independent of mean level by adjustment for covariance. The analytic strategy employed was to test the significance of differences in correlations between EEG and SEP measurements in different clinical groups. Psychiatric patients were compared with age- and sex-matched controls. The results suggested a specific pattern of EEG-SEP relationship differences from normal for each of four major patient groups: chronic schizophrenics; neurotics; those with personality disorders; and depressed manic-depressives. Figure 1 summarizes the median correlations between EEG and SEP variables in those

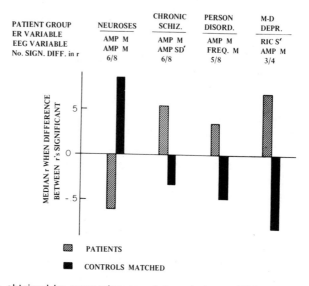

FIG. 1. Results obtained by comparing correlations between EEG and somatosensory evoked potential (ER) measurements in 4 patient groups and nonpatient controls of same age and sex. Only those groups of correlations yielding 50% significant differences are shown; number of possible correlation differences is shown as denominator (No. SIGN. DIFF. in r). Bars indicate medians of significantly different correlations. Note that the EEG-ER combinations are different for each patient group.

instances where at least half of the possible correlations differed significantly between the patient group and matched controls.

For the neuroses, the main differences from normal occurred in correlations between mean SEP amplitude and mean EEG amplitude; correlations were negative in the patients and positive in the controls. Figure 2 shows the scattergram for one of these correlation differences between neuroses and matched controls. For chronic schizophrenics, Fig. 1 indicates that the main differences from normal occurred in correlations between mean SEP amplitude and the level-independent measure of EEG amplitude variability in time (SD'). Whereas greater SEP amplitudes were associated with greater EEG variability in the patients, the reverse trend was found in the normals. For personality disorders, the main correlation differences occurred between mean SEP amplitude and mean EEG frequency, correlations tending to be positive in the patients and negative in the controls. For manic-depressive, depressed patients, the main differences in correlation were obtained between the slope of the intensity-amplitude curve adjusted for mean level (RIC S') and mean EEG amplitude. As illustrated in Fig. 3, greater slopes, indicative of augmenting tendency, were associated with greater EEG amplitude in the depressive patients, whereas the reverse was true in the matched normals.

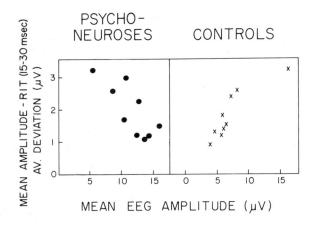

FIG. 2. Scattergrams depicting relationships between mean EEG amplitude and mean SEP amplitude for the epoch 15 to 30 msec after stimulus. Correlation was negative in psychoneurotic patients and positive in controls of same age and sex.

The most interesting aspect of these results is that different combinations of EEG and SEP variables deviated from normal for each patient group. The findings require confirmation, but they suggest that combinations of EEG and ERP variables may give results unobtainable with either kind of variable alone, and that the combinations may deviate from normal in diagnostically specific patterns. Also, since only one lead derivation was used for the EEG and SEP recordings, it seems possible that greater specificity may emerge when both kinds of variables are recorded from a number of areas.

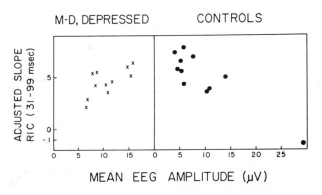

FIG. 3. Scattergrams for correlations between mean EEG amplitude and the slope of the curve relating SEP amplitude (31 to 99 msec epoch) to stimulus intensity; slope (RIC S' in Fig. 1) is adjusted to be independent of mean SEP amplitude. Correlation was positive in manic-depressive depressed patients and negative in nonpatient controls of same age and sex.

OVERVIEW

Two contrasting impressions are gained from surveying the literature on electrophysiological studies in psychiatry. On the one hand, it is difficult not to be disappointed by the relatively small yield of truly important results after more than 40 years of EEG research and 15 years of ERP investigation. On the other hand, the positive findings that have emerged, particularly in recent years, do support an optimistic outlook for the future. It seems reasonably clear that the field's increasing yield of encouraging results has depended on continuing technical and methodological improvements. Computer technology has provided the means for quantifying and reducing large amounts of data, for examining the relationships between many kinds of variables, and for testing with relative ease concepts about the mathematical properties of brain potentials. More and more factors requiring experimental controls have been identified, thus leading to improved methodology. Also, concurrent advances in classification and quantification of psychopathological variables have improved clinical criteria. Thus, although electrophysiological methods have been available for quite a long time, the specific techniques now in use have advanced greatly from those employed in the past and will undoubtedly become much more sophisticated in the future. In essence, psychiatric electrophysiology has really just begun to harness its technology. From this perspective, there should be little discouragement about the paucity of its important contributions to psychiatric research and considerable optimism about its future productivity.

One of the functions of an overview is to attempt to forecast future developments. Several predictions can be made with reasonable confidence.

A. Cross-sectional clinical comparison will remain the most commonly employed research strategy for some time to come. However, cross-sectional studies can be expected to yield more definitive results by using improved methods of clinical classification, better controls over contaminating variables related to both the subject and the experimental situation, a broader range of electrophysiological recordings, and more sophisticated analytic techniques.

B. Biochemical measures will more often be obtained in conjunction with brain potential studies of clinical populations. The relationships between brain potentials and measurement of electrolytes, enzymes, endocrines, and neurotransmitter substances in body fluids can be expected to help clarify the significance of clinical correlates at both levels of observation.

C. Increasing attention will be given to topography, the dimension of brain potential phenomena which has been largely neglected in clinical psychiatric studies. I consider the investigation of specific functioning of the two brain hemispheres to be a special aspect of topographic study. Interest in hemispheric functional specialization has already led to demonstrations that EEG and evoked potential changes reflect lateralized cognitive processes (17,18). A technique for measuring the degree of coupling between potentials from different cortical areas has been developed (5) and has been applied clinically to demonstrate altered coupling in dyslexic subjects (6). We are planning to apply similar analytic methods to topographic studies of psychiatric patients. The coupling measure is one approach to the more general problem of quantifying the spatial relationships between brain potentials recorded from different locations.

D. More investigations will focus on the pattern of relationships between different types of brain potentials. These studies will require development of improved methods to express such relationships quantitatively. The method used in our EEG-SEP study (86) was rather primitive, and we are attempting to apply factor analytic and canonical correlation techniques to this problem.

E. More longitudinal studies of patients in different phases of illness will be conducted as the number of clinical correlates established in cross-sectional investigations increases. These will often be linked to investigations of psychoactive drug effects. EEG and ERP studies have already given encouraging results in predicting the clinical effects of drugs (15,32) and response to therapy (59,61). Also, some of the SEP changes produced by drugs such as lithium and amitriptyline have suggested possible relationships between events at the neurochemical and electrophysiological levels (84).

F. There will be more genetically oriented studies, using twin comparisons and other methods, to explore the possible role of EEG and ERP indicators as genetic markers.

G. As clinical correlates of brain potentials are established, more investigations will be conducted to determine whether these reflect state or trait relationships. Psychophysiologists using brain potential techniques have already been dealing with these problems. For example, the prolonged slow negative potential, which is an abnormal accompaniment of CNV, and of frequent occurrence in psychosis, has been produced experimentally in normal subjects by manipulating conditions of feedback after the motor response (10,99). Another example is provided by the results of Wasman and Gluck (98), who observed that SEP amplitude recovery differences between slow learners and college students were like those found between patients and controls in our studies (68). Since effective therapy normalizes reduced amplitude recovery (77), it is probably an illness-related state variable. However, Wasman and Gluck's findings also suggest that the key psychological correlate of reduced amplitude recovery may be the temporary intellectual impairment often accompanying psychotic states. Such demonstrations not only help to assess whether a brain potential deviation in mental illness is of state or trait nature, they also provide important clues about the kind of psychological dysfunction associated with altered electrical signals.

H. Animal models, based on clinical electrophysiological findings, will serve to test hypotheses about neurochemical, neuroendocrine, and neuro-physiological mechanisms underlying psychopathology.

Summary

This chapter provided an overview of clinical neurophysiological research in psychiatry. Several general issues were discussed, including: the statistical nature of surface brain potentials and the psychopathological criteria with which correlations are sought; the role of electrophysiology in psychiatric research; and problems of distinguishing between state and trait factors. The main EEG and evoked potential findings obtained in studies of schizophrenic and affective psychoses were outlined. The author's hypothesis concerning impaired sensory input "filtering" mechanisms in chronic schizophrenia was presented. Encouraging positive results obtained in a first investigation of EEG-evoked potential relationships in several categories of psychiatric disorders were described; these suggest that EEG-EP variables may be patterned in a diagnostically specific way. The review of progress to date suggested an optimistic outlook for the future of the field, and several predictions were made about the lines along which future developments will occur.

ACKNOWLEDGMENTS

Research of the author supported in part by Grant MH12507 from the USPHS. Professional collaborators include Drs. M. Amadeo, D. A. Overton, R. A. Roemer, and J. J. Straumanis, Jr.

REFERENCES

1. Buchsbaum, M. S. (1974): Average evoked response and stimulus intensity in identical and fraternal twins. *Physiol. Psychol.,* 2:365–370.
2. Buchsbaum, M., and Silverman, J. (1968): Stimulus intensity control and the cortical evoked response. *Psychosom. Med.,* 30:12–22.
3. Buchsbaum, M., Goodwin, F., Murphy, D., and Borge, G. (1971): AER in affective disorders. *Am. J. Psychiatry,* 128:51–57.
4. Buchsbaum, M., Landau, S., Murphy, D., and Goodwin, F. (1973): Average evoked response in bipolar and unipolar affective disorders: Relationship to sex, age of onset, and monoamine oxidase. *Biol. Psychiatry,* 7:199–212.
5. Callaway, E., and Harris, P. R. (1974): Coupling between cortical potentials from different areas. *Science,* 183:873–875.
6. Callaway, E., Bali, L., and Gevins, A. (1975): Applications of a new measure of cortical coupling. Presented at Annual Meeting of the American EEG Society, Mexico City.
7. Callaway, E., Jones, R. T., and Layne, R. S. (1965): Evoked responses and segmental set of schizophrenia. *Arch. Gen. Psychiatry,* 12:83–89.
8. Cohen, R. (1973): The influence of task-irrelevant stimulus variations on the reliability of auditory evoked responses in schizophrenia. In: *Human Neurophysiology, Psychology, Psychiatry. Average Evoked Responses and Their Conditioning in Normal Subjects and Psychiatric Patients,* edited by A. Fessard and G. Lelord, pp. 373–388. Inserm, Paris.

9. Colony, H. S., and Willis, S. E. (1956): Electroencephalographic studies of 1,000 schizophrenic patients. *Am. J. Psychiatry,* 113:163–169.
10. Delaunoy, J., Timsit-Berthier, M., Rousseau, M. C., and Gerono, A. (1975): Modification expérimentale de la phase terminale de la VCN. *Rev. Electroencephalogr. Neurophysiol. Clin.,* 5:10–14.
11. d'Elia, G., Laurell, B., and Perris, C. (1974): EEG photically elicited alpha blocking responses in depressive patients before and after convulsive therapy. *Acta Psychiatr. Scand. [Suppl.],* 255:159–172.
12. Dongier, M. (1973): Event related slow potential changes in psychiatry. In: *Biological Diagnosis of Brain Disorders,* edited by S. Bogoch, pp. 47–59. Spectrum, New York.
13. Dongier, M., Dubrovsky, B., and Garcia-Rill, E. (1974): Slow cerebral potentials in psychiatry. *Can. Psychiatr. Assoc. J.,* 19:177–183.
14. Dustman, R. E., and Beck, E. C. (1965): The visually evoked potential in twins. *Electroencephalogr. Clin. Neurophysiol.,* 19:570–575.
15. Fink, M. (1974): EEG profiles and bioavailability measures of psychoactive drugs. In: *Psychotropic Drugs and the Human EEG. Modern Problems in Pharmacopsychiatry, Vol. 8,* edited by T. M. Itil, pp. 76–98. Karger, Basel.
16. Floris, V., Morocutti, C., Amabile, G., Bernardi, G., and Rizzo, P. A. (1968): Recovery cycle of visual evoked potentials in normal, schizophrenic and neurotic patients. In: *Computers and Electronic Devices in Psychiatry,* edited by N. S. Kline and E. Laska, pp. 194–205. Grune & Stratton, New York.
17. Galin, D., and Ellis, R. R. (1975): Asymmetry in evoked potentials as an index of lateralized cognitive processes. Relation to EEG alpha asymmetry. *Neuropsychologia,* 13:45–50.
18. Galin, D., and Ornstein, R. (1972): Lateral specialization of cognitive mode. An EEG study. *Psychophysiology,* 9:412–418.
19. Garmezy, N. (1970): Process and reactive schizophrenia. Some conceptions and issues. *Schizophrenia Bull.,* 2:30–74.
20. Giannitrapani, D., and Kayton, L. (1974): Schizophrenia and EEG spectral analysis. *Electroencephalogr. Clin. Neurophysiol.,* 36:377–386.
21. Gibbs, F. A., and Gibbs, E. L. (1963): The mitten pattern. An electroencephalographic abnormality correlating with psychosis. *J. Neuropsychiatry,* 5:6–13.
22. Goldman, D. (1959): Specific electroencephalographic changes with pentothal activation in psychotic states. *Electroencephalogr. Clin. Neurophysiol.,* 11:657–667.
23. Goldstein, L., Murphree, H. B., Sugerman, A. A., Pfeiffer, C. C., and Jenney, E. H. (1963): Quantitative electroencephalographic analysis of naturally occurring (schizophrenic) and drug-induced psychotic states in human males. *Clin. Pharmacol. Ther.,* 4:10–21.
24. Goldstein, L., Sugerman, A. A., Marjerrison, G., and Stoltzfus, N. (1973): Interhemispheric EEG relationships in mental patients and in normal subjects under modified behavioral states. Presented at Annual Meeting of Society of Biological Psychiatry, Montreal.
25. Grass, A. M., and Gibbs, F. A. (1938): Fourier transform and the electroencephalogram. *J. Neurophysiol.,* 1:521–526.
26. Heath, R. G. (1966): Schizophrenia. Biochemical and physiologic aberrations. *Int. J. Neuropsychiatry,* 2:597–610.
27. Hurst, L. A., Mundy-Castle, A. C., and Beerstecher, D. M. (1954): The electroencephalogram in manic-depressive psychosis. *J. Ment. Sci.,* 100:220–240.
28. Igert, C., and Lairy, G. C. (1962): Prognostic value of the EEG in the course of the development of schizophrenics. *Electroencephalogr. Clin. Neurophysiol.,* 14:183–190.
29. Ikuta, T. (1974): Somatosensory evoked potentials (SEP) in normal subjects, schizophrenics and epileptics. *Fukuoka Acta Med.,* 65:1010–1019.
30. Ingvar, D. H., and Franzén, G. (1974): Distribution of cerebral activity in chronic schizophrenia. *Lancet,* 2:1484.
31. Ishikawa, K. (1968): Studies on the visual evoked responses to paired light flashes in schizophrenics. *Kurume Med. J.,* 15:153–167.
32. Itil, T. M. (1974): Quantitative pharmaco-electroencephalography. In: *Psychotropic Drugs and the Human EEG. Modern Problems of Pharmacopsychiatry, Vol. 8,* edited by T. M. Itil, pp. 43–75. Karger, Basel.

33. Itil, T. M., Saletu, B., and Davis, S. (1972): EEG findings in chronic schizophrenics based on digital computer period analysis and analog power spectra. *Biol. Psychiatry,* 5:1–13.
34. Itil, T. M., Saletu, B., Davis, S., and Allen, M. (1974): Stability studies in schizophrenics and normals using computer-analyzed EEG. *Biol. Psychiatry,* 3:321–335.
35. Johnson, L. C., and Ulett, G. A. (1959): Stability of EEG activity and manifest anxiety. *J. Comp. Physiol. Psychol.,* 52:284–288.
36. Jones, R. T., and Callaway, E. (1970): Auditory evoked responses in schizophrenia. A reassessment. *Biol. Psychiatry,* 2:291–298.
37. Kennard, M. A., and Schwartzman, A. E. (1957): A longitudinal study of electroencephalographic frequency patterns in mental hospital patients and normal controls. *Electroencephalogr. Clin. Neurophysiol.,* 9:263–274.
38. Kupfer, D. J., and Foster, F. G. (1975): The sleep of psychotic patients. Does it all look alike? In: *Biology of the Major Psychoses. A Comparative Analysis,* edited by D. S. Freedman, pp. 143–159. Raven Press, New York.
39. Landau, S. G., Buchsbaum, M. S., Carpenter, W., Strauss, J., and Sacks, M. (1975): Schizophrenia and stimulus intensity control. *Arch. Gen. Psychiatry,* 32:1239–1245.
40. Lennox, W. G., Gibbs, F. A., and Gibbs, E. L. (1942): Twins, brain waves and epilepsy. *Arch. Neurol. Psychiatry,* 47:702–706.
41. Levit, A. L., Sutton, S., and Zubin, J. (1973): Evoked potential correlates of information processing in psychiatric patients. *Psychol. Med.,* 3:487–494.
42. Lieberman, D. M., Hoenig, J., and Hacker, M. (1954): The metrazol-flicker threshold in neuropsychiatric patients. *Electroencephalogr. Clin. Neurophysiol.,* 5:9–18.
43. Lifshitz, K. (1969): An examination of evoked potentials as indicators of information processing in normal and schizophrenic subjects. In: *Average Evoked Potentials. Methods, Results and Evaluation,* edited by E. Donchin and D. B. Lindsley, pp. 318–319 and 357–362. National Aeronautics and Space Administration, Washington, D.C.
44. Lifshitz, K., and Gradijan, J. (1972): Relationships between measures of the coefficient of variation of the mean absolute EEG voltage and spectral intensities in schizophrenic and control subjects. *Biol. Psychiatry,* 5:149–163.
45. Lifshitz, K., and Gradijan, J. (1974): Spectral evaluation of the electroencephalogram. Power and variability in chronic schizophrenics and control subjects. *Psychophysiology,* 11:479–490.
46. MacKay, D. M. (Ed.) (1969): Evoked brain potentials as indicators of sensory information processing. *Neurosciences Res. Prog. Bull.,* 7.
47. Maggs, R., and Turton, E. C. (1956): Some EEG findings in old age and their relationship to affective disorder. *J. Ment. Sci.,* 102:812–818.
48. Marjerrison, G., Krause, A. E., and Keogh, R. P. (1968): Variability of the EEG in schizophrenia. Quantitative analysis with a modulus voltage integrator. *Electroencephalogr. Clin. Neurophysiol.,* 24:35–41.
49. Mendels, J., and Hawkins, D. R. (1967): Sleep and depression. A controlled EEG study. *Arch. Gen. Psychiatry,* 16:344–354.
50. McCallum, W. C. (1973): Some psychological, psychiatric and neurologic aspects of the CNV. In: *Human Neurophysiology, Psychology, Psychiatry. Average Evoked Responses and Their Conditioning in Normal Subjects and Psychiatric Patients,* edited by A. Fessard and G. Lelord, pp. 295–324. Inserm, Paris.
51. McCallum, W. C., and Walter, W. G. (1968): The effects of attention and distraction on the contingent negative variation in normal and neurotic subjects. *Electroencephalogr. Clin. Neurophysiol.,* 25:319–329.
52. Overall, J. E., and Klett, C. J. (1972): *Applied Multivariate Analysis.* McGraw-Hill, New York.
53. Perez-Reyes, M. (1972): Differences in sedative susceptibility between types of depression. Clinical and neurophysiological significance. In: *Recent Advances in the Psychobiology of the Depressive Illnesses,* edited by T. A. Williams, M. M. Katz, and J. A. Shields, pp. 119–130. U.S. Government Printing Office, Washington, D.C.
54. Perris, C. (1974): Averaged evoked responses (AER) in patients with affective disorders. A pilot study of possible hemispheric differences in depressed patients. *Acta Psychiatr. Scand. [Suppl.],* 255:89–98.

55. Perris, C., and d'Elia, G. (1974): Electroencephalographic hemispheric differences and affective disorders. Proceedings of the First World Congress of Biological Psychiatry, Buenos Aires.
56. Rodin, E., Grisell, J., and Gottlieb, J. (1968): Some electrographic differences between chronic schizophrenic patients and normal subjects. In: *Recent Advances in Biological Psychiatry, Vol. 10*, edited by J. Wortis, pp. 194–204. Plenum Press, New York.
57. Roth, W. T., and Cannon, E. H. (1972): Some features of the auditory evoked response in schizophrenics. *Arch. Gen. Psychiatry*, 27:466–471.
58. Rust, J. (1975): Genetic effects in the cortical auditory evoked potentials. A twin study. *Electroencephalogr. Clin. Neurophysiol.*, 39:321–327.
59. Saletu, B. (1974): Classification of psychotropic drugs based on human evoked potentials. In: *Psychotropic Drugs and the Human EEG. Modern Problems of Pharmacopsychiatry, Vol. 8*, edited by T. M. Itil, pp. 258–285. Karger, Basel.
60. Saletu, B., Itil, T. M., and Saletu, M. (1971): Auditory evoked response, EEG, and thought process in schizophrenics. *Am. J. Psychiatry*, 128:336–344.
61. Saletu, B., Saletu, M., and Itil, T. M. (1973): The relationships between psychopathology and evoked responses before, during and after psychotropic drug treatment. *Biol. Psychiatry*, 6:45–74.
62. Satterfield, J. H. (1972): Auditory evoked cortical response studies in depressed patients and normal control subjects. In: *Recent Advances in the Psychobiology of the Depressive Illnesses*, edited by T. A. Williams, M. M. Katz, and J. A. Shields, pp. 87–98. U.S. Government Printing Office, Washington, D.C.
63. Schwartz, M., and Shagass, C. (1962): Effect of different states of alertness on somatosensory and auditory recovery cycles. *Electroencephalogr. Clin. Neurophysiol.*, 14:11–20.
64. Schwartz, M., and Shagass, C. (1963): Reticular modification of somatosensory cortical recovery function. *Electroencephalogr. Clin. Neurophysiol.*, 15:265–271.
65. Sem-Jacobsen, C. W., Peterson, M. C., Lazarte, J. A., Dodge, H. W., and Holman, C. B. (1955): Intracerebral electrographic recordings from psychotic patients during hallucinations and agitation. *Am. J. Psychiatry*, 112:278–288.
66. Shagass, C. (1954): The sedation threshold. A method for estimating tension in psychiatric patients. *Electroencephalogr. Clin. Neurophysiol.*, 6:221–233.
67. Shagass, C. (1959): A neurophysiological study of schizophrenia. *Report of Second International Congress for Psychiatry, Vol. 2*, pp. 248–254. Swiss Organizing Committee, Zurich.
68. Shagass, C. (1968): Averaged somatosensory evoked responses in various psychiatric disorders. In: *Recent Advances in Biological Psychiatry, Vol. X*, pp. 205–219. Plenum Press, New York.
69. Shagass, C. (1972): *Evoked Brain Potentials in Psychiatry*. Plenum Press, New York.
70. Shagass, C. (1973a): Evoked response studies of central excitability in psychiatric disorders. In: *Human Neurophysiology, Psychology, Psychiatry. Average Evoked Responses and Their Conditioning in Normal Subjects and Psychiatric Patients*, edited by A. Fessard and G. Lelord, pp. 223–252. Inserm, Paris.
71. Shagass, C. (1973b): Evoked potential studies of the dynamic range of cerebral responsiveness in psychiatric patients. In: *Psychiatry (Part I)*, edited by R. de la Fuente and N. Maxwell, pp. 771–781. Excerpta Medica, Amsterdam.
72. Shagass, C. (1975a): EEG and evoked potentials in the psychoses. In: *Biology of the Major Psychoses. A Comparative Analysis*, edited by D. X. Freedman, pp. 101–127. Raven Press, New York.
73. Shagass, C. (1975b): Psychobiological measurement of change. Neurophysiological aspects. Proceedings of IX Congress of the Collegium Internationale Neuropsychopharmacologicum. *Neuropsychopharmacology*, pp. 176–185. Excerpta Medica, Amsterdam.
74. Shagass, C. (1976): An electrophysiological view of schizophrenia. *Biol. Psychiatry*, 11:3–30.
75. Shagass, C., and Ando, K. (1970): Septal and reticular influences on cortical evoked response recovery functions. *Biol. Psychiatry*, 2:3–18.
76. Shagass, C., and Jones, A. L. (1958): A neurophysiological test for psychiatric diagnosis. Results in 750 patients. *Am. J. Psychiatry*, 114:1002–1009.
77. Shagass, C., and Schwartz, M. (1962): Cerebral cortical reactivity in psychotic depressions. *Arch. Gen. Psychiatry*, 6:235–242.

78. Shagass, C., and Schwartz, M. (1963): Psychiatric correlates of evoked cerebral cortical potentials. *Am. J. Psychiatry,* 119:1055–1061.
79. Shagass, C., and Schwartz, M. (1965): Visual cerebral evoked response characteristics in a psychiatric population. *Am. J. Psychiatry,* 121:979–987.
80. Shagass, C., and Schwartz, M. (1966): Somatosensory cerebral evoked responses in psychotic depression. *Br. J. Psychiatry,* 112:799–807.
81. Shagass, C., Overton, D. A., and Straumanis, J. J. (1972): Sex differences in somatosensory evoked responses related to psychiatric illness. *Biol. Psychiatry,* 5:295–309.
82. Shagass, C., Overton, D. A., and Straumanis, J. J. (1974): Evoked potential studies in schizophrenia. In: *Biological Mechanisms of Schizophrenia and Schizophrenia-like Psychoses,* edited by H. Mitsuda and T. Fukuda, pp. 214–234. Igaku-Shoin Co., Ltd., Tokyo.
83. Shagass, C., Soskis, D. A., Straumanis, J. J., and Overton, D. A. (1974): Symptom patterns related to somatosensory evoked response differences within a schizophrenic population. *Biol. Psychiatry,* 9:25–43.
84. Shagass, C., Straumanis, J. J., and Overton, D. A. (1973): Effects of lithium and amitriptyline therapy on somatosensory evoked response "excitability" measurements. *Psychopharmacologia,* 29:185–196.
85. Shagass, C., Straumanis, J. J., and Overton, D. A. (1974): Psychiatric correlates of some quantitative EEG variables. *Proceedings of First World Congress of Biological Psychiatry, Buenos Aires (in press).*
86. Shagass, C., Straumanis, J. J., and Overton, D. A. (1975): Psychiatric diagnosis and EEG-evoked response relationships. *Neuropsychobiology,* 1:1–15.
87. Sila, B., Mowrer, M., Ulett, G., and Johnson, M. (1962): The differentiation of psychiatric patients by EEG changes after sodium pentothal. In: *Recent Advances in Biological Psychiatry, Vol. IV,* edited by J. Wortis, pp. 191–203. Plenum Press, New York.
88. Small, J. G., and Small, I. F. (1965): Re-evaluation of clinical EEG findings in schizophrenia. *Dis. Nerv. Syst.,* 26:345–349.
89. Small, J. G., and Small, I. F. (1971): Contingent negative variation (CNV) correlations with psychiatric diagnosis. *Arch. Gen. Psychiatry,* 25:550–554.
90. Small, J. G., Small, I. F., Milstein, V., and Moore, D. F. (1975): Familial associations with EEG variants in manic-depressive disease. *Arch. Gen. Psychiatry,* 32:43–48.
91. Speck, L. B., Dim, B., and Mercer, M. (1966): Visual evoked responses of psychiatric patients. *Arch. Gen. Psychiatry,* 15:59–63.
92. Stevens, J. R., Lonsbury, B., and Goel, S. (1972): Electroencephalographic spectra and reaction time in disorders of higher nervous function. *Science,* 176:1346–1349.
93. Struve, F. A., Becka, D. R., and Klein, D. F. (1972): B-mitten EEG pattern and process and reactive schizophrenia. *Arch. Gen. Psychiatry,* 26:189–192.
94. Struve, F. A., Klein, D. F., and Saraf, K. R. (1972): Electroencephalographic correlates of suicide ideation and attempts. *Arch. Gen. Psychiatry,* 27:363–365.
95. Timsit-Berthier, M. (1973): CNV, slow potentials and motor potential studies in normal subjects and psychiatric patients. In: *Human Neurophysiology, Psychology, Psychiatry. Average Evoked Responses and Their Conditioning in Normal Subjects and Psychiatric Patients,* edited by A. Fessard and G. Lelord, pp. 327–366. Inserm, Paris.
96. Vaughan, H. G. (1969): The relationship of brain activity to scalp recordings of event-related potentials. In: *Average Evoked Potentials. Methods, Results and Evaluations,* edited by E. Donchin and D. B. Lindsley, pp. 45–75. National Aeronautics and Space Administration, Washington, D. C.
97. Volavka, J., Matousek, M., and Roubicek, J. (1966): EEG frequency analysis in schizophrenia. *Acta Psychiatr. Scand.,* 42:237–245.
98. Wasman, M., and Gluck, H. (1975): Recovery functions of somatosensory evoked responses in slow learners. *Psychophysiology,* 12:371–376.
99. Weinberg, H. (1972): The contingent negative variation. Its relation to feedback and expectant attention. *Neuropsychologia,* 10:229–306.
100. Wilson, W. P., and Wilson, N. J. (1961): Observations on the duration of the photically elicited arousal responses in depressive psychoses. *J. Nerv. Ment. Dis.,* 133:438–440.

Subject Index